Microsoft® Office 2013
Illustrated Projects™

Microsoft® Office 2013
Illustrated Projects™

©Hluboki Dzianis/Shutterstock

Carol M. Cram

CENGAGE
Learning·

Australia • Brazil • Mexico • Singapore • United Kingdom • United States

CENGAGE
Learning®

Microsoft Office 2013 Illustrated Projects
Carol M. Cram

General Manager: Dawn Gerrain

Senior Product Manager: Marjorie Hunt

Senior Content Developer: Natalie Pashoukos

Developmental Editor: Pamela Conrad

Senior Content Project Manager: Cathie DiMassa

Art Director: GEX Publishing Services

Cover photo: GEX Publishing Services

For product information and technology assistance, contact us at
Cengage Learning Customer & Sales Support, 1-800-354-9706

For permission to use material from this text or product,
submit all requests online at **cengage.com/permissions**
Further permissions questions can be emailed to
permissionrequest@cengage.com

Library of Congress Control Number: 2013954497

ISBN-13: 978-1-285-17032-9

ISBN-10: 1-285-17032-6

Cengage Learning
200 First Stamford Place, 4th Floor
Stamford, CT 06902
USA

Cengage Learning is a leading provider of customized learning solutions with office locations around the globe, including Singapore, the United Kingdom, Australia, Mexico, Brazil, and Japan. Locate your local office at: **www.cengage.com/global**

Cengage Learning products are represented in Canada by Nelson Education, Ltd.

For your course and learning solutions, visit **www.cengage.com**

Purchase any of our products at your local college store or at our preferred online store **www.cengagebrain.com**

Microsoft and the Office logo are either registered trademarks or trademarks of Microsoft Corporation in the United States and/or other countries. Cengage Learning is an independent entity from the Microsoft Corporation, and not affiliated with Microsoft in any manner. Microsoft product screen shots reprinted with permission from Microsoft Corporation.

Printed in the United States of America
1 2 3 4 5 6 7 16 15 14 13

A Note from the Author

As instructors, I believe our goal is to teach our students to become independent learners who have the confidence to tackle and solve problems. My greatest satisfaction in the classroom comes when my students learn the information, skills, and techniques they need to function effectively in the workplace and to accomplish tasks related to their own needs and interests. Students need to learn what to do with a software application. They need to "see the forest" and not just the trees.

To address this need, I developed a philosophy of teaching software applications that has evolved into the Illustrated Projects series. Each project in this series provides students with step-by-step instructions to create documents or perform tasks appropriate to the software package they are learning. As students complete the projects, they learn how a variety of functions combine together to produce a tangible product.

But the Illustrated Projects approach to teaching software doesn't stop with the projects. The significant learning occurs when students are given the opportunity to create their own version of a project document. That's when you'll feel a kind of magic creeping into your classroom. Students take the structure offered by a project and then, in the Independent Challenges, adapt this structure to explore practical business applications and express their own interests. Suddenly, students are willing to take risks, to solve problems, and to experiment with new features as they work toward the creation of a document that belongs to them. Pride of ownership inspires learning!

Most of the projects in Office 2013 Illustrated Projects are brand new and take advantage of many of the new features of Office 2013. Also new in this edition are team projects. Students work in teams of three to complete a series of guided tasks that require both independent and team input. Grading rubrics are provided to help you identify the skills that students practice.

This book owes everything to the talent and dedication of the Cengage Learning Illustrated team. I particularly wish to thank Pam Conrad, the Developmental Editor of this book, for her encouragement, patience, and unflagging support along with her amazing attention to detail. This book is dedicated to all the wonderful students I have taught during my years at Capilano University.

Carol M. Cram
Carol M. Cram, December 2013

Contents

Preface

Welcome to *Microsoft Office 2013—Illustrated Projects*. This highly visual book offers a wide array of interesting and challenging projects designed to apply the skills learned in any Office 2013 book. The Illustrated Projects book is for people who want more opportunities to practice important software skills.

Organization and Coverage

This text contains a total of nine units. Six units contain projects for the individual programs: Word (two units), Excel (two units), Access (one unit), and PowerPoint (one unit). Three other units contain projects that take advantage of the powerful integration capabilities of the Office suite. Each unit contains three projects followed by three Independent Challenges, a Team Project, and a Visual Workshop.

About this Approach

What makes the Illustrated Projects approach so effective at reinforcing software skills? It's quite simple. Each activity in a project is presented on two facing pages, with the step-by-step instructions on the left page and large screen illustrations on the right. Students can focus on a single activity without having to turn the page. This unique design makes information extremely accessible and easy to absorb. Students can complete the projects on their own, and because of the modular structure of the book, can also cover the units in any order.

The two-page layout for each activity contains some or all of the elements shown below.

Road map—It is always clear which project and activity you are working on.

Introduction—Concise text that introduces the activity and summarizes new procedures. Steps are easier to complete when they fit into a meaningful framework.

Numbered steps—Clear step-by-step directions explain how to complete the specific activity. These steps get less specific as students progress to the third project in a unit.

Troubles and Hints—Troubleshooting advice to fix common problems that might occur and tips for using Microsoft Office 2013 more effectively. These appear right next to the step where students need help.

More Practice—Provides information on which end-of-unit exercises allow students to practice the same set of skills.

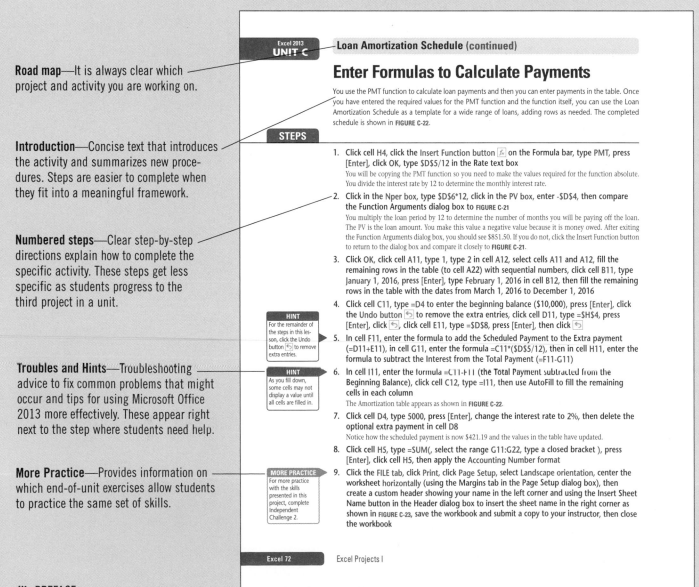

Excel 2013
UNIT C

Loan Amortization Schedule (continued)

Enter Formulas to Calculate Payments

You use the PMT function to calculate loan payments and then you can enter payments in the table. Once you have entered the required values for the PMT function and the function itself, you can use the Loan Amortization Schedule as a template for a wide range of loans, adding rows as needed. The completed schedule is shown in **FIGURE C-22**.

STEPS

1. Click cell H4, click the Insert Function button ƒₓ on the Formula bar, type PMT, press [Enter], click OK, type $D$5/12 in the Rate text box
   You will be copying the PMT function so you need to make the values required for the function absolute. You divide the interest rate by 12 to determine the monthly interest rate.

2. Click in the Nper box, type $D$6*12, click in the PV box, enter -$D$4, then compare the Function Arguments dialog box to **FIGURE C-21**
   You multiply the loan period by 12 to determine the number of months you will be paying off the loan. The PV is the loan amount. You make this value a negative value because it is money owed. After exiting the Function Arguments dialog box, you should see $851.50. If you do not, click the Insert Function button to return to the dialog box and compare it closely to **FIGURE C-21**.

3. Click OK, click cell A11, type 1, type 2 in cell A12, select cells A11 and A12, fill the remaining rows in the table (to cell A22) with sequential numbers, click cell B11, type January 1, 2016, press [Enter], type February 1, 2016 in cell B12, then fill the remaining rows in the table with the dates from March 1, 2016 to December 1, 2016

4. Click cell C11, type =D4 to enter the beginning balance ($10,000), press [Enter], click the Undo button ↺ to remove the extra entries, click cell D11, type =$H$4, press [Enter], click ↺, click cell E11, type =$D$8, press [Enter], then click ↺

   HINT
   For the remainder of the steps in this lesson, click the Undo button ↺ to remove extra entries.

5. In cell F11, enter the formula to add the Scheduled Payment to the Extra payment (=D11+E11), in cell G11, enter the formula =C11*($D$5/12), then in cell H11, enter the formula to subtract the Interest from the Total Payment (=F11-G11)

   HINT
   As you fill down, some cells may not display a value until all cells are filled in.

6. In cell I11, enter the formula =C11-H11 (the Total Payment subtracted from the Beginning Balance), click cell C12, type =I11, then use AutoFill to fill the remaining cells in each column
   The Amortization table appears as shown in **FIGURE C-22**.

7. Click cell D4, type 5000, press [Enter], change the interest rate to 2%, then delete the optional extra payment in cell D8
   Notice how the scheduled payment is now $421.19 and the values in the table have updated.

8. Click cell H5, type =SUM(, select the range G11:G22, type a closed bracket), press [Enter], click cell H5, then apply the Accounting Number format

   MORE PRACTICE
   For more practice with the skills presented in this project, complete Independent Challenge 2.

9. Click the FILE tab, click Print, click Page Setup, select Landscape orientation, center the worksheet horizontally (using the Margins tab in the Page Setup dialog box), then create a custom header showing your name in the left corner and using the Insert Sheet Name button in the Header dialog box to insert the sheet name in the right corner as shown in **FIGURE C-23**, save the workbook and submit a copy to your instructor, then close the workbook

Excel 72   Excel Projects I

The Projects

The two-page activity format featured in this book provides students with a powerful learning experience. Additionally, this book contains the following features:

► **Meaningful Examples**—This book features projects that students will be excited to create including a program brochure, a research paper in MLA style, a budget, an integrated report, and a sales presentation. By producing relevant documents that will enhance their own lives, students will more readily master skills.

► **Start from Scratch**—To truly test if a student understands the software and can use it to reach specific goals, the student should start from the beginning. In this book, students create projects from scratch, just like they would in the real world. In selected cases, supplemental data files are provided.

► **Outstanding Assessment and Reinforcement**—Each unit concludes with three independent challenges, a challenging team project (in every unit except Unit F), and a Visual Workshop. Independent Challenges 1 to 3 relate directly to Projects 1 to 3 and provide students with instructions to create their own version of the project document. In the Team Project, a group of three students is provided with guidelines to create three documents related to the software applications and documents covered in the unit. Projects require both independent and team input. In the Visual Workshop, students see a completed document, worksheet, database, or presentation, and must recreate it on their own.

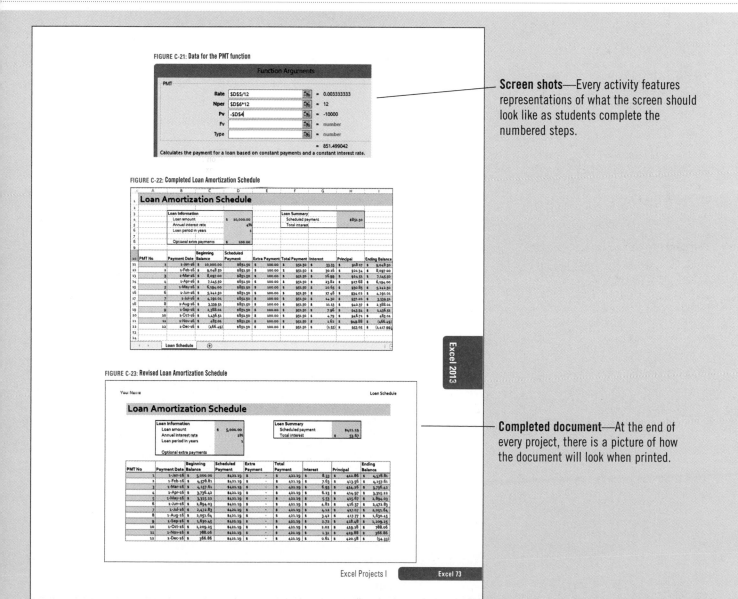

Screen shots—Every activity features representations of what the screen should look like as students complete the numbered steps.

Completed document—At the end of every project, there is a picture of how the document will look when printed.

Instructor Companion Site

The Instructor Companion Site is Cengage Learning's way of putting the resources and information needed to teach and learn effectively into your hands. With an integrated array of teaching and learning tools that offer you and your students a broad range of technology-based instructional options, we believe this site represents the highest quality and most cutting edge resources available to instructors today. The resources available with this book are:

Instructor's Manual

Available as an electronic file, the Instructor's Manual includes detailed lecture topics with teaching tips for each unit.

Sample Syllabus

Prepare and customize your course easily using this sample course outline.

Figure Files

The figures in the text are provided on the Instructor Companion Site to help you illustrate key topics or concepts. You can create traditional overhead transparencies by printing the figure files, or you can create electronic slide shows by using the figures in a presentation program such as PowerPoint.

Solutions to Exercises

Solutions to Exercises contain every file students are asked to create or modify in the lessons and end-of-unit material.

Data Files for Students

Data Files contain every file students need to create the projects and end-of-unit material. You can post the Data Files on a file server for students to copy.

Students' Frequently Asked Questions

What are Data Files?

A Data File is a partially completed file that is used to complete the steps in the units and exercises to create the final document that is submited to your instructor.

Where are the Data Files?

Your instructor will provide the Data Files a location on a network drive from which they can be downloaded.

What software was used to write and test this book?

This book was written and tested using a typical installation of Microsoft Office 2013 installed on a computer with a typical installation of Microsoft Windows 8. The browser used for any steps that require a browser is Internet Explorer 10.

Do I need to be connected to the Internet to complete the steps and exercises in this book?

Some of the exercises in this book assume that your computer is connected to the Internet. If you are not connected to the Internet, see your instructor for information on how to complete the exercises.

What do I do if my screen is different from the figures shown in this book?

This book was written and tested on computers with monitors set at a resolution of 1366 × 1024. If your screen shows more or less information than the figures in the book, your monitor is probably set at a higher or lower resolution. If you don't see something on your screen, you might have to scroll down or up to see the object identified in the figures.

The Ribbon (the white area at the top of the screen) in Microsoft Office 2013 adapts to different resolutions. If your monitor is set at a lower resolution than 1366 × 1024, you might not see all of the buttons shown in the figures. The groups of buttons will always appear, but the entire group might be condensed into a single button that you need to click to access the buttons described in the instructions.

Word Projects I

Projects

In this unit you will create the following:

Event Program
Change page orientation • Create columns • Set custom margins • Insert text from a file • Apply themes • Apply styles • Format tabs • Add text effects • Use Format Painter • Sort paragraphs • Cut and paste text • Modify pictures (*Skills also practiced in Independent Challenge 1*)

Feedback Form
Customize themes • Apply style sets • Create, edit, and format tables • Insert symbols • Modify a clip art picture (*Skills also practiced in Independent Challenge 2*)

Research Paper in MLA Style
Insert headers • Create a new source • Insert and edit citations • Generate a Works Cited list (*Skills also practiced in Independent Challenge 3*)

Team Project

Files You Will Need

PR A-01.docx	PR A-04.docx
PR A-02.docx	PR A-05.docx
PR A-03.docx	PR A-06.docx

Event Program for Author Readings

A group of writers living on Marcus Island near Seattle, WA, have put together an evening of readings for the local community. You have volunteered to create a program for the event that will be distributed to audience members. You will **Set Up Columns**, **Format Text**, and **Modify Graphics**. The completed program appears in **FIGURE A-6** on page 7.

Set Up Columns

First, you set up the document on two pages in landscape format with two columns per page so that the completed program can be printed on two sides of an 8½ × 11" paper and folded in half to make a simple booklet. This format results in four panels, which are organized as shown in **FIGURE A-1**.

STEPS

1. Open a new blank document in Word, click the Show/Hide button ¶ in the Paragraph group to show the paragraph marks if they are not already displayed, click the PAGE LAYOUT tab, click the Orientation button in the Page Setup group, then click Landscape

2. Click Margins in the Page Setup group, click Custom Margins, set the Left and Right margins at .6, click OK, then save the document as PR A-Event Program for Author Readings to the location where you save your files for this book

3. Click the Columns button in the Page Setup group, click More Columns, click Two, select the contents of the Spacing text box, type 1, press [Tab], compare the Columns dialog box to FIGURE A-2, click OK, press [Enter] once, click Breaks in the Page Setup group, then click Page

   Page 1 of the program includes the front cover (panel 1) and the back cover (panel 4) and page 2 of the program contains information about the program (panels 2 and 3).

   > **HINT**
   > The blank first page will become panels 4 and 1 of your two-sided program.

4. Click the INSERT tab, click the Object list arrow in the Text group, then click Text from File

   Most of the text that you need for the program is included in a Data File.

5. Navigate to the location where you store your Data Files, then double-click PR A-01.docx

6. Click the DESIGN tab, click Themes, select the Frame theme, click the HOME tab, scroll up and select the heading Marcus Island Writers, click the Heading 1 style in the Styles gallery, then click the Center button ≣ in the Paragraph group.

7. Select the text from "Mary Royce" to "Short Story: *Blue Moon*," click the launcher ⌐ in the paragraph group, then click Tabs

8. Type 4.25, click the Right option button, click the 2 option button, then click OK

9. Center Master of Ceremonies: Jerry Walter, center Intermission, then save the document.

   The list of readers on panel 2 is formatted as shown in FIGURE A-3.

FIGURE A-1: Diagram of the Program

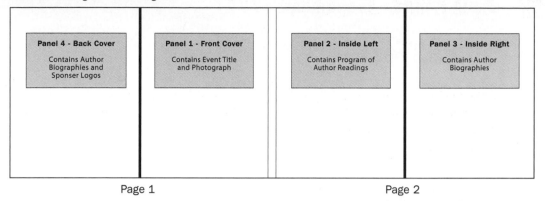

Panel 4 - Back Cover	Panel 1 - Front Cover	Panel 2 - Inside Left	Panel 3 - Inside Right
Contains Author Biographies and Sponser Logos	Contains Event Title and Photograph	Contains Program of Author Readings	Contains Author Biographies

Page 1   Page 2

FIGURE A-2: Columns dialog box

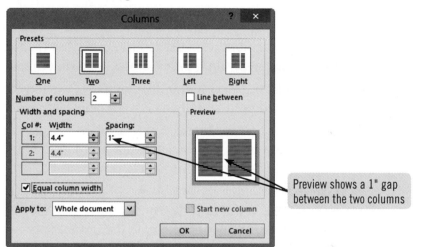

Preview shows a 1" gap between the two columns

FIGURE A-3: Panels 2 and 3

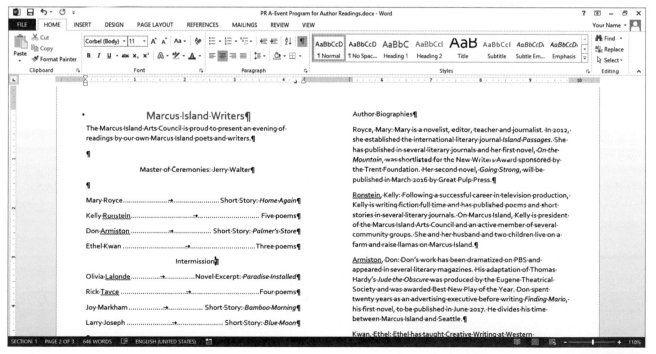

Format Text

You need to add text to the front cover (panel 1) of the program. You use Text Effects to enhance the text on the front cover. You also need to format the author biographies that appear on panels 3 and 4 of the program. In addition, you sort the author biographies in alphabetical order by last name.

STEPS

1. **Press [Ctrl][Home], click the PAGE LAYOUT tab, click Breaks, then click Column**
   The insertion point is positioned at the top of the second column on page 1, which is panel 1 (the front cover) of the program.

2. **Enter text for the front panel as shown in FIGURE A-4**

3. **Select Marcus Island Writers at the top of the panel, click the HOME tab, click the Text Effects and Typography button in the Font group, select Fill - Turquoise, Accent 1, Shadow (second option in the top row), increase the font size to 28 pt, click the Font Color list arrow 𝐀 ▾ in the Font group, then click the Orange, Accent 4 color box**

4. **Scroll to page 2, select Author Biographies at the top of the second column (panel 3 in the completed program), then click Heading 2 in the Styles gallery**

5. **Select the text from "Royce, Mary" to "Marcus Island" at the end of the entry for Larry Joseph on the next page, click the Sort button ↓ in the Paragraph group, verify that Paragraphs is selected, then click OK**
   The author biographies are sorted in alphabetical order by the last name of the author.

6. **Scroll up, select Armiston, Don under the Author Biographies heading, apply Bold and Italic, double-click Format Painter in the Clipboard group, apply the formatting to each of the author names in the Author Biographies section, then click Format Painter to turn off the Format Painter**

7. **Click the VIEW tab, click Multiple Pages in the Zoom group, click to the left of Markham, Joy at the bottom of the second column on page 2 (panel 3), then select text from Markham, Joy to the end of the document**

8. **Click the HOME tab, click the Cut button in the Clipboard group, click at the top of column 1 on page 1 (panel 4) to the left of the Column Break, then click the Paste button**
   The two pages and four panels of the document appear as shown in FIGURE A-5.

9. **Save the document**

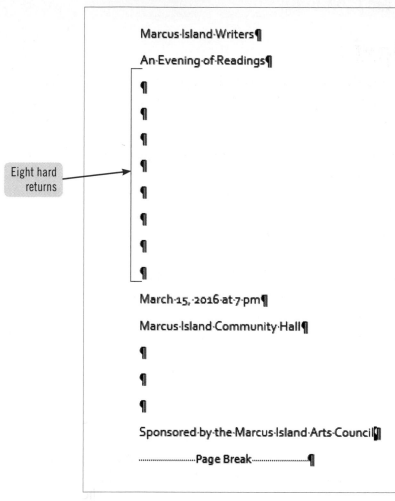

FIGURE A-5: Document in Two Page view

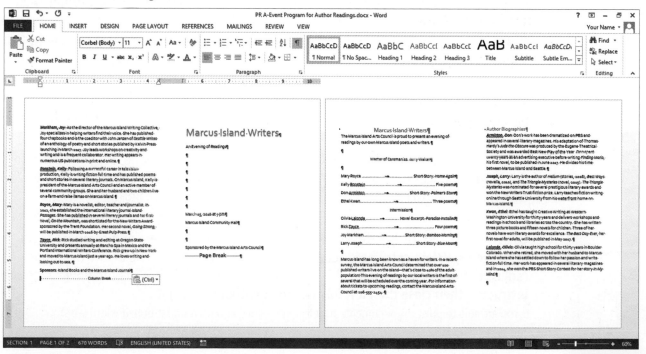

Word 2013

Add Graphics

You enhance the completed program with a picture on the front cover (panel 1) and insert logos for the two sponsors on the back cover (panel 4). The completed program is shown in **FIGURE A-6**.

STEPS

1. **Click to the left of** Marcus Island Writers **at the top of the front cover (panel 1 on page 1), press** [Enter] **two times, increase the zoom to** 70% **or until only the two panels on page 1 appear in the document window, click the first paragraph mark at the top of the second column, click the** FILE **tab, click** Open**, navigate to the location where you store your Data Files, then double-click** PR A-02.docx

   This document contains the pictures you need to complete the program.

2. **Click the** island picture, **click the** Copy button **in the Clipboard group, switch to the** PR A-Event Program for Author Readings **document, then click the** Paste button **in the Clipboard group**

3. **Double-click the picture to show the PICTURE TOOLS FORMAT tab, click the** Wrap Text button **in the Arrange group, then click** Behind Text

4. **Click the** launcher **in the Size group, click the** Lock Aspect Ratio check box **to deselect it, set the Height at** 7" **and the Width at** 4.5"**, then click** OK

5. **Click the** Color button **in the Adjust group, click** Turquoise, Accent color 1 Light, **(2nd column, 3rd row in the Recolor section), click the** Corrections button **in the Adjust group, click** Brightness: +40% Contrast: 0% (Normal) **(5th column, 3rd row in the Brightness/Contrast section), select all the lines of text on the front cover, then apply** bold **and** center **the text**

6. **On panel 4 (the back cover), click after Journal on the last line, press** [Enter]**, increase the Zoom to** 130%**, click the** INSERT **tab, click** Table**, drag to create a table that is two columns and 1 row, click the** Table Move Handle ⊞**, click the** Borders list arrow**, then click** No Border

   You insert a table form to contain the two logos. Tables are an excellent tool to use when you want to align elements on a page.

7. **Switch to the PR A-02 data file, copy the "Island Books" logo, return to the program document, click in the first cell in the table, click the** HOME **tab, click the** Paste button**, double-click the** logo image**, then in the Size group on the PICTURE TOOLS FORMAT tab, change the height of the logo to** .6"

8. **Switch to the PR A-02 data file, click the** Marcus Island Journal logo**, copy it, return to the Program document, paste the logo in the second table cell, reduce its width to** 2"**, click the** TABLE TOOLS LAYOUT **tab, then click the** Align Center button ≡ **in the Alignment group**

MORE PRACTICE
For more practice with the skills presented in this project, complete Independent Challenge 1.

9. **Click the** FILE **tab, click** Print**, view pages 1 and 2 of the program and compare them to** FIGURE A-6**, delete extra hard returns if necessary, add your name below the logos (adjust the bottom margin to** .8"**), save the document, submit a copy to your instructor, then close the PR A-02 document without saving it**

   If you are able to print the document, print it double-sided and then fold it in half width-wise.

Markham, Joy: As the director of the Marcus Island Writing Collective, Joy specializes in helping writers find their voice. She has published four chapbooks and is the coeditor with John Janzen of *Seattle Writes* of an anthology of poetry and short stories published by Kelvin Press launching in March 2015. Joy leads workshops on creativity and writing and is a frequent collaborator. Her writing appears in numerous US publications in print and online.

Ronstein, Kelly: Following a successful career in television production, Kelly is writing fiction full time and has published poems and short stories in several literary journals. On Marcus Island, Kelly is president of the Marcus Island Arts Council and an active member of several community groups. She and her husband and two children live on a farm and raise llamas on Marcus Island.

Royce, Mary: Mary is a novelist, editor, teacher and journalist. In 2012, she established the international literary journal *Island Passages*. She has published in several literary journals and her first novel, *On the Mountain*, was shortlisted for the New Writers Award sponsored by the Trent Foundation. Her second novel, *Going Strong*, will be published in March 2016 by Great Pulp Press.

Tayce, Rick: Rick studied writing and editing at Oregon State University and presents annually at Rancho Spa in Mexico and the Portland International Writers Conference. Rick grew up in New York and moved to Marcus Island just a year ago. He loves writing and looking out to sea.

Sponsors: Island Books and the Marcus Island Journal

Island Books   Marcus Island Journal

Your Name

Marcus Island Writers

An Evening of Readings

March 15, 2016 at 7 pm

Marcus Island Community Hall

Sponsored by the Marcus Island Arts Council

Marcus Island Writers

The Marcus Island Arts Council is proud to present an evening of readings by our own Marcus Island poets and writers.

Master of Ceremonies: Jerry Walter

Mary Royce...Short Story: *Home Again*

Kelly Ronstein..Five poems

Don Armiston...Short Story: *Palmer's Store*

Ethel Kwan...Three poems

Intermission

Olivia Lalonde...............................Novel Excerpt: *Paradise Installed*

Rick Tayce ....Four poems

Joy Markham...Short Story: *Bamboo Morning*

Larry Joseph..Short Story: *Blue Moon*

Marcus Island has long been known as a haven for writers. In a recent survey, the Marcus Island Arts Council determined that over 100 published writers live on the island—that's close to 10% of the adult population! This evening of readings by our local writers is the first of several that will be scheduled over the coming year. For information about tickets to upcoming readings, contact the Marcus Island Arts Council at 206-555-2454.

Author Biographies

Armiston, Don: Don's work has been dramatized on PBS and appeared in several literary magazines. His adaptation of Thomas Hardy's *Jude the Obscure* was produced by the Eugene Theatrical Society and was awarded Best New Play of the Year. Don spent twenty years as an advertising executive before writing *Finding Mario*, his first novel, to be published in June 2017. He divides his time between Marcus Island and Seattle.

Joseph, Larry: Larry is the author of *Helium* (stories, 2008), *Best Ways* (novella, 2010), and *The Triangle Mysteries* (novel, 2015). *The Triangle Mysteries* was nominated for several prestigious literary awards and won the New Writers Trust fiction prize. Larry teaches fiction writing online through Seattle University from his waterfront home on Marcus Island.

Kwan, Ethel: Ethel has taught Creative Writing at Western Washington University for thirty years and delivers workshops and readings in schools and libraries across the country. She has written three picture books and fifteen novels for children. Three of her novels have won literary awards for excellence. *The Best Day Ever*, her first novel for adults, will be published in May 2017.

Lalonde, Olivia: Olivia taught high school for thirty years in Boulder Colorado. When she retired, she moved with her husband to Marcus Island where she has settled down to follow her passion and write fiction full time. Her work has appeared in several literary magazines and in 2014, she won the PBS Short Story Contest for her story *In My Mind*.

Feedback Form for Summer Day Camp

You've taken a summer job as an intern at a local college that is offering summer camps for children. One of your duties is to put together a feedback form for parents to complete following a summer camp experience. You use Word's table feature to create a simple one-page printed form that will be handed out to parents. To complete the form, you need to **Set Up the Document**, **Build the Table Form**, and **Modify a Clip Art Picture**. The completed form appears in **FIGURE A-12** on page 13.

Set Up the Document

First, you open a document containing some of the text and a graphic required for the completed form, save the document, apply a theme and Style Set, then create a table to contain the form.

STEPS

HINT

Click ¶ in the Paragraph group on the HOME tab to turn on paragraph marks.

1. Start Word, open the file PR A-03.docx from the location where you store your Data Files, save it as PR A-Summer Day Camp Feedback Form, then display paragraph marks

2. Select Evergreen College Summer Day Camps, click Title in the Styles gallery, select Feedback Form, then click Heading 1 in the Styles gallery

3. Click the DESIGN tab, click Themes, then click Depth

4. Click the More button ⤓ in the Document Formatting group to show the Style Set gallery, then click Lines (Simple) as shown in FIGURE A-7

5. Click the Colors button in the Document Formatting group, then click Green

6. Click the Colors button, click Customize Colors, click the Hyperlink list arrow, click Dark Green, Hyperlink, Darker 50%, then click Save

   You can experiment with different combinations of themes, Style Sets, colors, and customized colors to format a document precisely the way you want it. You can also customize fonts, paragraph spacing, and effects.

7. Click to the left of the paragraph mark below the first paragraph (ends with "camp instructor."), click the INSERT tab, click Table, then click Insert Table

8. Enter 2 for the number of columns and 14 for the number of rows, then click OK

9. Enter text into the table form as shown in FIGURE A-8, then save the document

FIGURE A-7: Style Set gallery

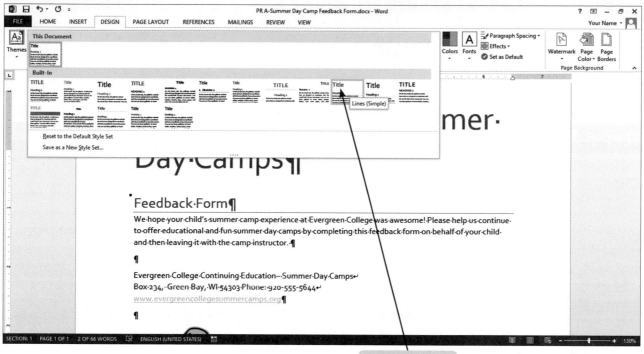

Lines (Simple) Style
Set selected

FIGURE A-8: Table text

Camp·Name¤	¤
Camp·Instructor¤	¤
Camp·Date¤	¤
Please·check·the·box·that·best·represents·your· opinion·of·each·item.·¤	¤
Evaluation¤	¤
Overall·assessment·of·the·summer·day·camp¤	¤
Overall·effectiveness·of·the·instructor¤	¤
Design·and·pacing·of·the·day·camp¤	¤
Your·child's·overall·assessment¤	¤
Day·camp·registration·and·administration¤	¤
Comments¤	¤
The·best·part·of·the·day·camp·for·my·child·was¤	¤
The·day·camp·could·be·improved·by¤	¤
Additional·comments¤	¤

¶

Build the Table

You use a table to contain all the information needed for the feedback form. In the completed feedback form, some cells are merged to create larger cells and some cells are split to create a series of smaller cells. You need to merge selected cells, split other cells, then add the ranking information and check boxes.

STEPS

1. Click to the left of row 1 (contains "Camp Name"), drag to select only the first three rows of the table (to "Camp Date"), then drag the column divider to the left to 1.5" on the ruler

2. Click to the left of row 4 to select it, click the TABLE TOOLS LAYOUT tab, then click Merge Cells

3. Select from row 5 ("Evaluation") to row 10 ("Day camp registration and administration"), then drag the column divider just to the left of 3" (approximately 2.8") on the ruler

4. Select the six cells shown in FIGURE A-9, click the Split Cells button in the Merge group, type 5 for the number of columns, click OK, then separately merge each of the last four rows into one row each

5. Select the row containing "Evaluation," click the Insert Below button in the Rows & Columns group, select the cell containing "Evaluation" and the blank cell below, then merge the two cells into one cell

   You can use the Merge Cells and Split Cells commands, as well as the insert and remove rows and cells commands to create an unlimited variety of table forms.

TROUBLE
Be sure to enter the text and the numbers in the row under the text.

6. Click the cell to the right of "Evaluation," type Excellent, then enter the remaining text as shown in FIGURE A-10

7. Click the cell below "5" to the right of the Overall Assessment row, click the INSERT tab, click Symbol in the Symbols group, click More Symbols, click the Font list arrow, select Wingdings, select the contents of the Character code text box, type 168, click Insert, then click Close

TROUBLE
Select the cells and click ☰ if the check boxes are not centered.

8. Select the cell containing the check box, increase the font size to 14 pt, click the Center button ☰ in the Paragraph group, click the Copy button in the Clipboard group, select the remaining four cells in the row, then click the Paste button

9. Select the remaining four rows under the rankings that require check boxes, click the Paste button, center the boxes if necessary, compare the form to FIGURE A-11, then save the document

FIGURE A-9: Table rows selected

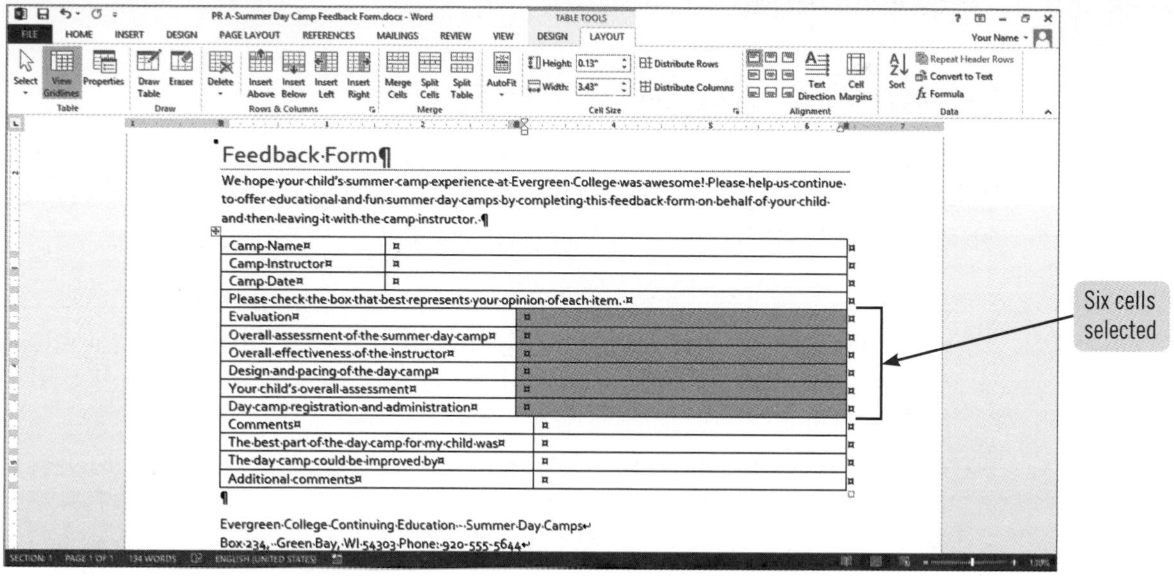

Six cells selected

FIGURE A-10: Ranking text entered

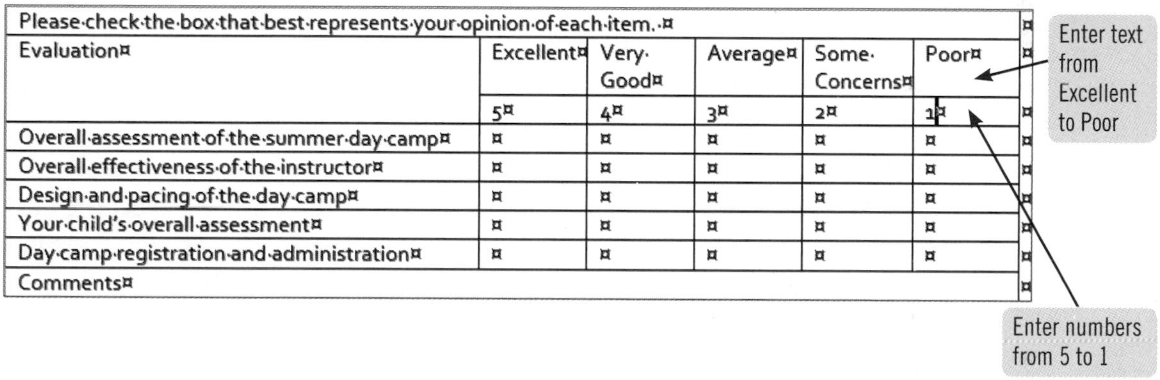

Please-check-the-box-that-best-represents-your-opinion-of-each-item.·¤					
Evaluation¤	Excellent¤	Very·Good¤	Average¤	Some·Concerns¤	Poor¤
	5¤	4¤	3¤	2¤	1¤
Overall·assessment·of·the·summer·day·camp¤	¤	¤	¤	¤	¤
Overall·effectiveness·of·the·instructor¤	¤	¤	¤	¤	¤
Design·and·pacing·of·the·day·camp¤	¤	¤	¤	¤	¤
Your·child's·overall·assessment¤	¤	¤	¤	¤	¤
Day·camp·registration·and·administration¤	¤	¤	¤	¤	¤
Comments¤					

Enter text from Excellent to Poor

Enter numbers from 5 to 1

Word 2013

FIGURE A-11: Form with check boxes entered and formatted

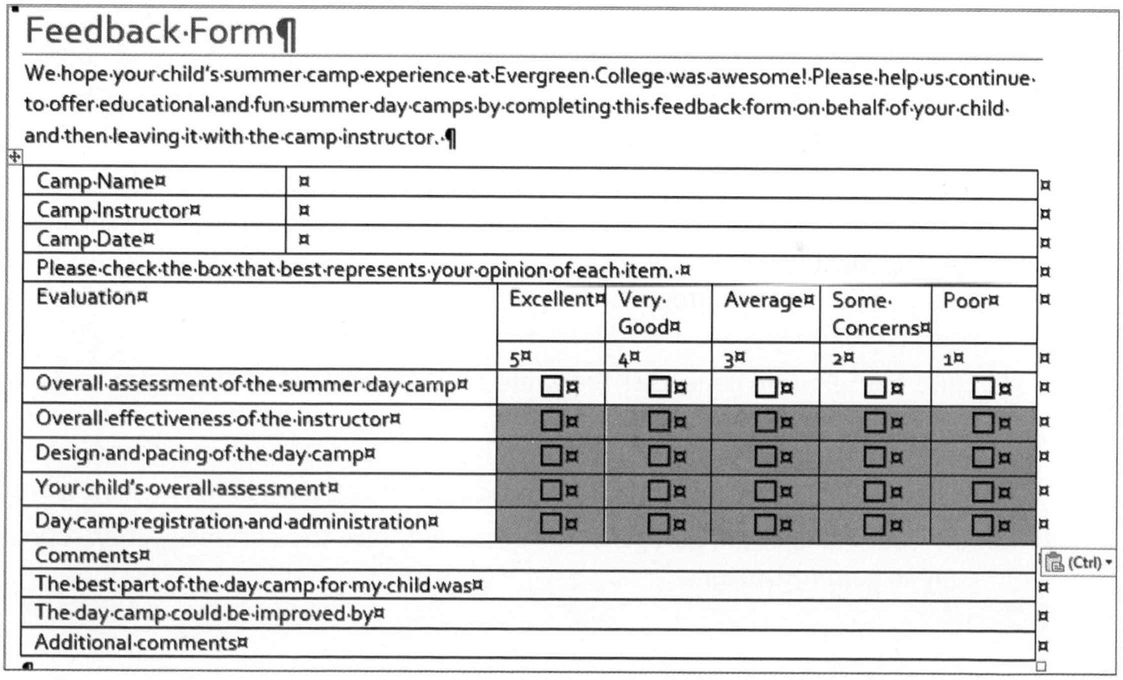

Feedback·Form¶

We·hope·your·child's·summer·camp·experience·at·Evergreen·College·was·awesome!·Please·help·us·continue· to·offer·educational·and·fun·summer·day·camps·by·completing·this·feedback·form·on·behalf·of·your·child· and·then·leaving·it·with·the·camp·instructor.·¶

Camp·Name¤	¤					
Camp·Instructor¤	¤					
Camp·Date¤	¤					
Please·check·the·box·that·best·represents·your·opinion·of·each·item.·¤						
Evaluation¤		Excellent¤	Very·Good¤	Average¤	Some·Concerns¤	Poor¤
		5¤	4¤	3¤	2¤	1¤
Overall·assessment·of·the·summer·day·camp¤		☐¤	☐¤	☐¤	☐¤	☐¤
Overall·effectiveness·of·the·instructor¤		☐¤	☐¤	☐¤	☐¤	☐¤
Design·and·pacing·of·the·day·camp¤		☐¤	☐¤	☐¤	☐¤	☐¤
Your·child's·overall·assessment¤		☐¤	☐¤	☐¤	☐¤	☐¤
Day·camp·registration·and·administration¤		☐¤	☐¤	☐¤	☐¤	☐¤
Comments¤						
The·best·part·of·the·day·camp·for·my·child·was¤						
The·day·camp·could·be·improved·by¤						
Additional·comments¤						

Modify a Clip Art Picture

You enhance the completed table form with a table style and format select text, then edit the clip art picture of the camp counselor. When you edit the picture, you can remove, modify or add individual objects. The completed document is shown in **FIGURE A-12**.

STEPS

TROUBLE
To see the Table Move Handle, move the pointer over the top left corner of the table.

1. **Click the** Table Move Handle ⊞, **click the** TABLE TOOLS DESIGN tab, **click the** More button **in the Table Styles group, then select** Grid Table 4 - Accent 2
   You can adjust table style options to get exactly the look you want.

2. **Click the** Header Row check box **in the Table Style Options group to deselect it, then click the** First Column check box **to deselect it**

3. **Refer to the completed document in** FIGURE A-12, **select rows 1 to 3, click the** TABLE TOOLS LAYOUT TAB, **type** .3 **in the Height text box in the Cell Size group, click the** Align Top Right button 🔲, **apply bold and align text as shown in** FIGURE A-12, **then add three hard returns in each of the last three table rows**

4. **Scroll to the next page, click the** camp counselor picture, **click the** Cut button **in the Clipboard group, press** [Backspace] **once, press** [Ctrl][Home], **click the** Paste button, **right-click the** camp counselor picture, **then click** Edit Picture
   The picture appears in the top left corner of the document.

HINT
You can modify individual components in a clip art picture because a clip art picture is composed of drawn objects.

5. **Click anywhere in the** white area **to the left of the girl's face to select the drawing canvas, click the** DRAWING TOOLS FORMAT tab, **then click** Selection Pane **in the Arrange group**
   Thirty Freeform objects are listed in the Selection pane. You can click an item in the Selection pane and view which object in the picture is selected.

6. **Click** Freeform 26 **in the list, notice that the green tent on the girl's shirt is selected, then press** [Delete] **to delete the black outline**
   You can also click and delete or format items directly in the picture.

HINT
A square appears to indicate the entire shape that makes up the shirt is selected and Freeform 6 is selected in the Selection pane.

7. **Increase the zoom to** 170%, **scroll to view the entire picture in the screen, click and delete the remaining two objects that make up the green tent, click the girl's** yellow shirt, **click the** Shape Fill list arrow **in the Shape Styles group, then click the** Dark Teal, Accent 4, Darker 25% color box

8. **Click the** HOME tab, **click** Select **in the Editing group, click** Select All **(all the objects that make up the clip art picture are selected), click the** DRAWING TOOLS FORMAT tab, **click** Group **in the Arrange group, then click** Group
   Notice that Group 29 appears above the list of Freeform items in the Selection pane

9. **Close the Selection pane, click the** white area **to the left of the girl's face in the clip art picture, verify that one box appears around the picture, click** Position **in the Arrange group, click the** Position in Top Right with Square Text Wrapping option **(top row, third column), then verify that the picture is positioned as shown in the** FIGURE A-12

MORE PRACTICE
For more practice with the skills presented in this project, complete Independent Challenge 2.

10. **Add your name at the bottom of the document, save the document, then submit a copy to your instructor**

Word Projects I

Evergreen College Summer Day Camps

Feedback Form

We hope your child's summer camp experience at Evergreen College was awesome! Please help us continue to offer educational and fun summer day camps by completing this feedback form on behalf of your child and then leaving it with the camp instructor.

Camp Name	
Camp Instructor	
Camp Date	

Please check the box that best represents your opinion of each item.

Evaluation	Excellent	Very Good	Average	Some Concerns	Poor
	5	4	3	2	1
Overall assessment of the summer day camp	☐	☐	☐	☐	☐
Overall effectiveness of the instructor	☐	☐	☐	☐	☐
Design and pacing of the day camp	☐	☐	☐	☐	☐
Your child's overall assessment	☐	☐	☐	☐	☐
Day camp registration and administration	☐	☐	☐	☐	☐

Comments

The best part of the day camp for my child was

The day camp could be improved by

Additional comments

Evergreen College Continuing Education - Summer Day Camps
Box 234, Green Bay, WI 54303 Phone: 920-555-5644
www.evergreencollegesummercamps.org

Your Name

Research Paper in MLA Style

Most research papers are formatted according to one of the three common academic styles: MLA, APA, and Chicago, depending on the requirements of the course and the discipline. You will practice formatting and adding references in the MLA style to a research paper on the Jane Austen novel *Pride and Prejudice*. TABLE A-1 lists the general requirements for formatting a paper in MLA style. You need to **Format the Text in MLA Style**, **Add and Format References**, and **Add a Works Cited List**. Selected pages from the formatted research paper appear in FIGURE A-18 on page 19.

Format the Text in MLA Style

You open a document and format it according to the MLA style.

STEPS

1. **Start Word, open the file** PR A-04.docx **from the location where you store your Data Files, save it as** PR A-Jane Austen Research Paper, **click the** PAGE LAYOUT **tab, click the** Margins button **in the Page Setup group, then click** Normal

   All four margins are set to 1", which is the setting required by the MLA format.

2. **Click the** HOME **tab, click** Select **in the Editing group, click** Select All, **click the** Line and Paragraph Spacing button ‡≡ ▾ **in the Paragraph group, then click** 2.0

3. **Verify that all the text is still selected, click the** Font list arrow, **type** ti **to move quickly to Times New Roman, click** Times New Roman, **click the** Font Size list arrow, **then click** 12

4. **Click at the beginning of the paper, press** [Tab] **once to indent the first line, then increase the zoom to** 140%

   The remaining paragraphs in the paper are already indented.

5. **Click the** INSERT **tab, click** Header **in the Header & Footer group, click** Edit Header, **then verify that the** Different First Page check box **in the Options group is not checked**

   The text you enter into the header on the first page will appear on every page in the research paper.

6. **Press** [Tab] **two times to move to the right margin, type your last name, press** [Spacebar], **click the** Page Number button **in the Header & Footer group, point to** Current Position, **select the** Plain Number **style as shown in** FIGURE A-13, **then click the** Close Header and Footer button **in the Close group**

7. **Press** [◄] **once, press** [Enter], **press** [▲] **to position the insertion point at the left margin, type your full name, press** [Enter], **type the name of your instructor or professor, press** [Enter], **type** English 402, **then press** [Enter]

8. **Click the** INSERT **tab, click** Date & Time **in the Text group, verify that the** Update automatically check box **is not selected, click the date format corresponding to** 20 April 2016, **then click** OK

HINT
Be sure to apply italic to *Pride and Prejudice* in the title.

9. **Press** [Enter], **click the** HOME **tab, click the** Center button ≡ **in the Paragraph group, type** Social Values in Jane Austen's *Pride and Prejudice*, **return the zoom to** 100%, **compare your screen to** FIGURE A-14, **then save the document**

FIGURE A-13: Inserting a page number at the current position

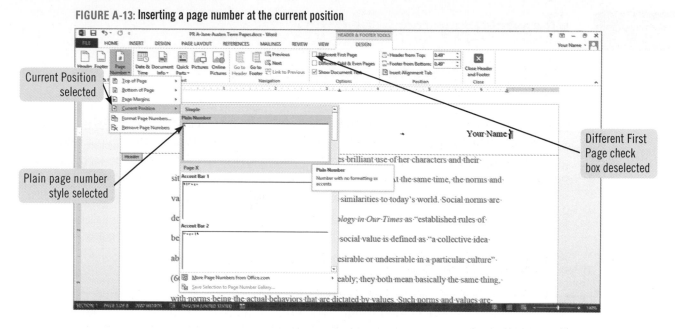

Current Position selected

Plain page number style selected

Different First Page check box deselected

FIGURE A-14: Research paper header, course information, and title

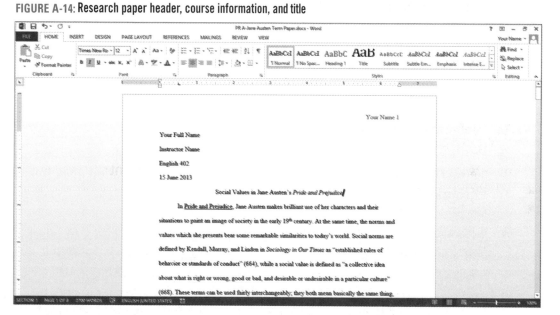

TABLE A-1: Summary of general MLA guidelines for formatting a research paper*

guideline	description
Paper and margins	Print the research paper on standard, white, 8.5" × 11" paper and set all four margins to 1".
Spacing	Double-space all content including quotations and the bibliography or works cited list.
Font and font size	Use a legible font and font size such as, Times New Roman and 12 pt.
Sentence spacing	Leave only one space after a period and before the start of the next sentence.
Paragraphs	Use the [Tab] key to indent the first line of each paragraph one-half inch from the left margin.
Header	Include a header with your last name and a page number in the upper-right corner of each page.
First page	Include each of the following on its own line in the upper-left corner of page 1 of the paper: your name, the professor's name, the course name and number, and the current date written in day, month, year format. On a new line after the course information, center the title of the essay; italicize book titles such as *Pride and Prejudice*, but do not underline or otherwise change the formatting.

* Find more detailed information and the most current requirements in the *MLA Handbook for Writers of Research Papers*.

Add and Format References

A paper formatted in the MLA style includes source information in the body of the research paper at the location where the source is cited. In the MLA style, source information is included in parenthesis and follows the format author page. For example, a quotation from page 202 of a work by Gillian Watts would be cited as (Watts 202). Some exceptions occur. If you provide the name of the author in the sentence preceding the citation, you include only the page number in the parenthesis. If the citation references a quotation from the literary work that is the subject of the paper (for example, *Pride and Prejudice*), then only the page number is included. The title of any book included in the text of a research paper is italicized. You use the Find and Replace function to find every instance of <u>Pride and Prejudice</u> and replace it with *Pride and Prejudice*, and then you insert a citation to a new source and a citation to an existing source.

STEPS

1. **Click** Replace **in the Editing group, type** Pride and Prejudice **in the Find what text box, click** More **if necessary to expand the dialog box, click** Format, **click** Font, **click the** Underline style list arrow, **click the** single underlining style, **then click** OK

    Word will use these settings to find every instance of <u>Pride and Prejudice</u> formatted with underlining.

2. **Click in the** Replace with text box, **type** Pride and Prejudice, **click** Format, **click** Font, **click** Italic **in the Font style list, click the** Underline style list arrow, **click** (none), **compare the Find and Replace dialog box with** FIGURE A-15, **then click** OK

3. **Click** Replace All, **click** OK, **then click** Close

    All underlined instances of <u>Pride and Prejudice</u> are replaced with italicized instances of *Pride and Prejudice*.

4. **Click** Find **in the Editing group to open the Navigation pane, type** history and geography **in the Navigation pane, click in the document after the quotation mark following "geography" and before the period**

    You need to ensure that the current citation style is set to MLA.

5. **Click the** REFERENCES **tab, click the** Style list arrow, **then click** MLA **to select it if it is not already selected**

HINT
MLA style specifies that the page number where the quotation is located in the source document should appear in a citation.

6. **Click** Insert Citation **in the Citations & Bibliography group, click** Add New Source, **click the** Type of Source list arrow, **click** Book, **enter the information for the source as shown in** FIGURE A-16, **then click** OK

    The name of the author (Faye) appears in parenthesis.

7. **Click the citation, click the** Citation Options list arrow, **click** Edit Citation, **type** 87–88 **in the Pages text box, click** OK, **then click away from the citation to deselect it**

    The author's name and quotation page numbers are entered as a citation.

8. **Search for** deportment, **click after the ending quotation mark and before the period, click** Insert Citation, **click** Faye, Diedre Le, **then edit the citation and enter the page number** 90

9. **Search for** late teens, **insert a citation to** Diedre Le Faye's book, **then save the document**

    In the next section, you modify the (Faye) citation by adding a page number, and then edit the source to change the way the author's name is displayed.

FIGURE A-15: Find and Replace options specified

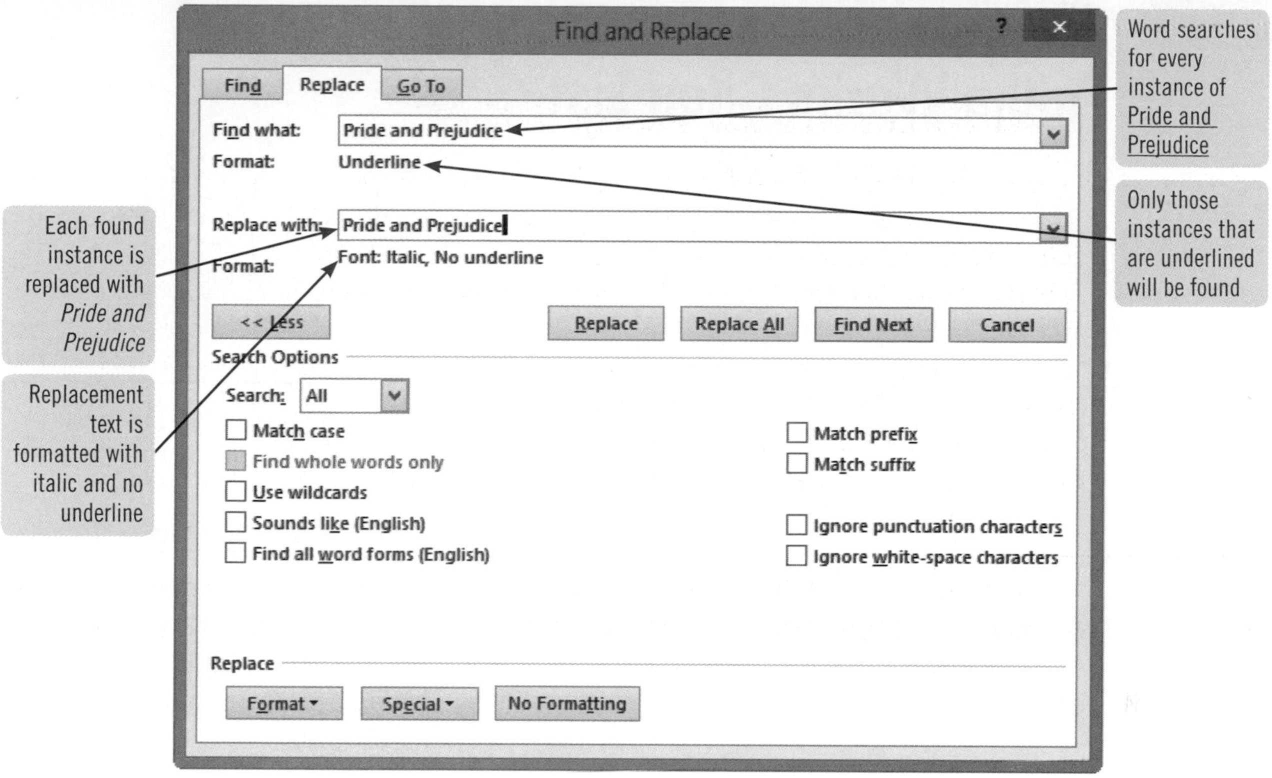

Word searches for every instance of Pride and Prejudice

Only those instances that are underlined will be found

Each found instance is replaced with *Pride and Prejudice*

Replacement text is formatted with italic and no underline

Find and Replace

Find | Replace | Go To

Find what: Pride and Prejudice
Format: Underline

Replace with: Pride and Prejudice
Format: Font: Italic, No underline

<< Less | Replace | Replace All | Find Next | Cancel

Search Options

Search: All

☐ Match case
☐ Find whole words only
☐ Use wildcards
☐ Sounds like (English)
☐ Find all word forms (English)

☐ Match prefix
☐ Match suffix

☐ Ignore punctuation characters
☐ Ignore white-space characters

Replace

Format ▾ | Special ▾ | No Formatting

FIGURE A-16: Source information

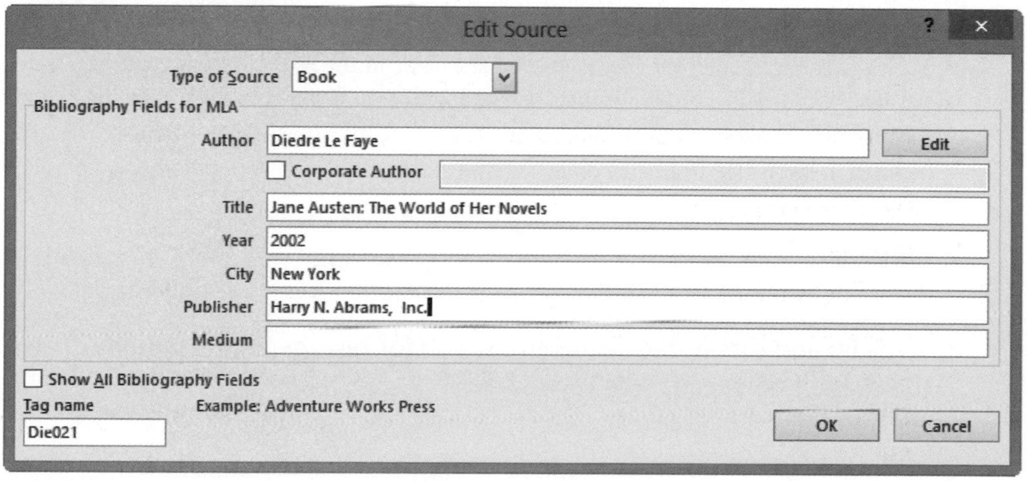

Edit Source

Type of Source: Book

Bibliography Fields for MLA

Author: Diedre Le Faye | Edit
☐ Corporate Author
Title: Jane Austen: The World of Her Novels
Year: 2002
City: New York
Publisher: Harry N. Abrams, Inc.
Medium:

☐ Show All Bibliography Fields

Tag name: Die021
Example: Adventure Works Press

OK | Cancel

Add a Works Cited List

On a new page following the last page of your research paper, you can insert a bibliography or a works cited list. A bibliography lists all the sources you consulted when writing the research paper, even if you did not quote them in the paper. A works cited list includes only the sources you quoted. You edit some citations, view the citations in the Manage Sources dialog box so you can edit the sources, and then you generate and update a works cited list.

1. **Click (Faye), click the** Citation Options list arrow, **click** Edit Citation, **enter** 113 **in the** Pages text box, **click** all three check boxes **in the Suppress area as shown in** FIGURE A-17 **to select them, then click** OK

   Only the page number appears. You do not need to include the name of the author because the author name appears at the beginning of the sentence that includes the citation.

2. **Press** [Ctrl][End] **to move to the end of the paper, then press** [Ctrl][Enter] **to insert a page break**

3. **Click the** Bibliography list arrow **in the Citations & Bibliography group, click** Works Cited, **then scroll up to view the list of works cited**

   The list of works cited in the research paper appears. Two of the entries are incorrect. The entry for "Faye" should be listed as "Le Faye" and "Jane Austen" should be listed as "Austen, Jane."

4. **Click** Manage Sources **in the Citations & Bibliography group, note the list of citations on the right side of the Source Manager dialog box, click the entry for** Faye, **then click** Edit

5. **Select the contents of the** Author text box, **type** Le Faye, Diedre, **click** OK, **then click** Yes

   Because "Le" is part of the author's last name, you need to enter the name exactly as you want it to appear in the Works Cited list.

You need to carefully check the MLA Guidelines and your entries to ensure your citations follow standard MLA citation formatting; you should not rely solely on the software for correct formatting.

6. **Click the** Jane Austen entry, **click** Edit, **change Jane Austen to** Austen, Jane, **click** OK, **then click** Yes **if prompted**

   Normally, you can enter the first name and last name in the Author text box in the Create Source dialog box and Word will insert the source in the last name, first name format in the Works Cited list or Bibliography. In a source that includes more than one author, however, the name of the first author should be listed in last name, first name order, and the names of the other authors should be listed in first name, last name order.

7. **Click** Close, **click** Works Cited, **then click** Update Citations and Bibliography

   The entries for Diedre Le Faye and Jane Austen are now correct.

8. **Scroll up and click in the document, search for** history and geography, **then verify that the citation now reads "(Le Faye 87–88)"**

   The Works Cited list should be double-spaced.

For more practice with the skills presented in this project, complete Independent Challenge 3.

9. **Close the Navigation pane, scroll to the Works Cited list, select the text in the Works Cited list from "Works Cited" to the end of the source for James Thompson, right-click the selected text, click** Paragraph, **click the** Line spacing list arrow, **click** Double, **then click** OK

10. **Save the document, submit a copy to your instructor, then close the document**

    Four pages from the research paper appear as shown in FIGURE A-18.

FIGURE A-17: Edit Citation dialog box

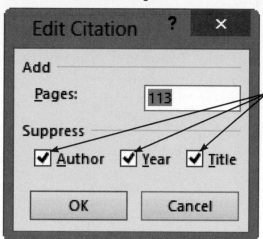

Select all three check boxes to suppress the associated information from being included in the citation

FIGURE A-18: Pages 1, 4, 6, and 9 of the completed research paper

Your Full Name

Instructor Name

English 402

15 June 2013

Social Values in Jane Austen's *Pride and Prejudice*

In *Pride and Prejudice*, Jane Austen makes brilliant use of her characters and their situations to paint an image of society in the early 19th century. At the same time, the norms and values which she presents bear some remarkable similarities to today's world. Social norms are defined by Kendall, Murray, and Linden in *Sociology in Our Times* as "established rules of behavior or standards of conduct" (664), while a social value is defined as "a collective idea about what is right or wrong, good or bad, and desirable or undesirable in a particular culture" (668). These terms can be used fairly interchangeably; they both mean basically the same thing, with norms being the actual behaviors that are dictated by values. Such norms and values are shown in a multitude of ways throughout *Pride and Prejudice*. There are norms associated with most every aspect of society, including the norms for class, money, gender, and marriage most commonly explored in Austen's novels. Austen shows society's values both through satire and through presenting what she considers to be the better alternative. The society of Austen's time no doubt differs from today in closely examined, it becomes

Money and class had a 19th century. The higher one's in society. Darcy, with his £10 the Bennets, who make only £

gentleman is a harsh shock, and he realizes that he must change his behavior. Later in the book, Darcy's true nature as a gentleman is revealed when Elizabeth goes to Pemberley. His housekeeper, Mrs. Reynolds, describes him as "the best landlord, and the best master" (213), and she has nothing but praise for him. When Darcy arrives at Pemberley, he proves himself to be courteous and well-mannered, and Elizabeth is amazed at "his behavior, so strikingly altered" (216).

In Austen's world, merely being born an aristocrat does not make someone a lady or a gentleman. Lady Catherine de Bourgh is a prime example of the ill-breeding that can be found in people of high class and wealth. She is a very rich, upper-class widow who owns a great deal of land and who has a great deal of power over her tenants. Her behavior, however, is not at all befitting of a lady. She is rude and inconsiderate, as she proves when Elizabeth visits her and later when she tries to force Elizabeth not to marry Darcy. When Elizabeth visits Rosings, Lady Catherine talks constantly and "in so decisive a manner as proved that she was not used to having her judgment controverted" (145). She exerts firm control over her tenants, and she spends a great deal of time telling them how to run their households, as can be seen when she "enquired into Charlotte's domestic concerns familiarly and minutely, and gave her a great deal of advice, as to the management of them all" (145). Austen satirizes Lady Catherine by

pleasantness in a near-comical manner. Mr. Collins, too, is certainly not a he attempts to act in a courteous manner, he evidently has very little grasp on society, as can be seen when he introduces himself to Mr. Darcy and is ridiculed the rest of the party. He is a figure of constant mockery, and the other characters down upon h when he prov

reads a passage from the book in volume 1, chapter 14. Here, again, we see conflicting values. As the Longman Cultural Edition of *Pride and Prejudice* states, "[the sermons'] lessons are pointedly and disastrously ignored by the one character who needs to listen" (385). This person is, of course, Lydia Bennet, who could in fact do with a few lessons in propriety. On the other hand, as the book continues to state, "Austen, like many writers of her day, was clearly skeptical about the authoritativeness of conduct-book stands of femininity" (385). Education for young women at the time was usually minimal. They were taught "needlework, both for necessity and for pleasure; simple arithmetic; fine hand writing, which was considered a very elegant accomplishment; enough music to be able to sing and play...; a little drawing...; and some very scrappy ideas of history and geography" (Le Faye 87-88). For women educated at private seminaries, "the prime object was to instill Decorum, Manners, and Deportment" (Le Faye 90). The emphasis on proper manners in *Pride and Prejudice* is evident, and can be seen at the Netherfield Ball when Elizabeth is embarrassed by her mother's and younger sisters' improper behavior: "To Elizabeth it appeared, that had her family made an agreement to expose themselves as much as they could during the evening, it would have been impossible for them to play their parts with more spirit, or finer success" (95). Certainly, Lydia's disgraceful behavior shows the norms and values of the time. In running off with a dishonorable man such as Wickham, she brings shame to her entire family. Sexual relations out of wedlock were taboo at the time; Fordyce, in his *Sermons*, speaks of the suffering parents feel "when a daughter...turns out unruly, foolish, wanton; when she disobeys her parents...; when she throws herself away on a man unworthy of her...". Mr. Collins' reaction, as stated earlier, would not have been uncommon at the time, especially among clergymen.

Works Cited

Austen, Jane, Claudia L. Johnson, Susan J. Wolfson. *Pride and Prejudice, A Longman Cultural Edition*. New York: Longman, 2003.

Kendall, Diane, Jane Lothian Murray, Rick Linden. *Sociology in Our Times*. Scarborough, Ontario: Thomson Canada Limited, 2004.

Le Faye, Diedre. *Jane Austen: The World of Her Novels*. New York: Harry N. Abrams, Inc., 2002.

Litz, A. Walton. "Into the Nineteenth Century: Pride and Prejudice." *Interpretations of Pride and Prejudice*. Ed. Rubinstein. E. Englewood Cliffs: Prentice-Hall, Inc., 1969. 59-69.

Thompson, James. *Between Self and World: The Novels of Jane Austen*. University Park and London: The Pennsylvania State University Press, 1988.

Independent Challenge 1

Use columns to set up a document in landscape format to contain a program for an event of your choice. For example, you could create a program for a play produced by a local community theater group, a concert of music by a school choir, or another event of your choice. To help you determine the information required for your event program, follow the directions provided.

1. Determine the type of event for your program (concert, play, presentation, etc.), then enter a short description of the event in the box below. For example, you could describe a concert as "Musical Tribute: A Concert to Raise Funds for Tornado Victims."

    Event Description: _____
    _____
    _____

2. Determine the details related to the event presented in the program, then list them in the box below.

    Event Date: _____ Event Time: _____

    Event Location: _____

    Event Participants: _____

3. On a blank piece of paper, sketch the four panels (two panels on each side of the paper) that will make up the program and then determine what content appears on each panel. Remember that the cover of the program is panel 1 which appears in column 2 of page 1. Use the diagram in **FIGURE A-1** on page 3 as your guide. In the box below, briefly describe the contents of each of the four panels. Include information about any graphics such as pictures or logos that you plan to include.

    Panel 1 (front cover) _____

    Panel 2 (inside left) _____

    Panel 3 (inside right) _____

    Panel 4 (back cover) _____

4. Open a new blank document, set up your document so that it prints in landscape orientation, apply the theme of your choice, add a page, then create two columns on each page. Note that you can modify the page margins and the column margins as needed.

5. Save the document as **PR A-My Event Program** to the location where you save the files for this book.

6. On the front cover, enter the title, time, date, and location of the event and any other information you want to include. Apply the text effect of your choice to the event title, then format the text so that it is spaced attractively on the cover. Insert a picture, change the text wrapping of the picture to Behind Text, then modify the picture so that the text is easy to read.

7. On page 2 of the program (the inside two panels), enter information about the event. Panel 2 generally lists the program events (for example, the list of pieces performed in a concert or the cast of a play) and panel 3 can carry on from panel 2 or contain additional information about the event. For the program events, set a tab with the leader option of your choice.

8. On the back cover of the program, enter additional text as needed. This text may be a continuation of the text on panel 3 or new text, depending on the nature of the event.

9. View the two pages of the program event in Multiple Pages view, then make adjustments to the spacing so the program prints correctly.

10. Print a copy of the program, double-sided if possible, and check that the spacing is correct. Make adjustments as needed until you are satisfied with the appearance of the program.

11. Enter your name at the bottom of the back cover of the program, check the spelling and grammar, save the program and submit it to your instructor, then close it.

Independent Challenge 2

Use the Table feature to create a form to evaluate a course, program, or other event of your choice. For example, you could create a form to evaluate a workshop you've presented to your classmates, or you could create a form that a small hotel could distribute to guests to evaluate their experience. To help you determine the information required for your form, follow the directions provided below.

1. Determine the purpose of your form and enter it in the box below. For example, the purpose of a workshop evaluation form could be "to evaluate workshop content, materials, and facilitator performance."

Form Purpose: _____
_____
_____

2. Determine the user information you want to collect. For example, do you want to leave space for the person's name and personal information, or should the form be completed anonymously? The user information can also include the name of the workshop, hotel, restaurant, etc., being evaluated, and the date. Enter up to three fields for user information in the box below.

User Information: _____
_____
_____

3. Develop up to five questions or elements that you want users to evaluate and enter them in the box.

Question 1 : _____

Question 2: _____

Question 3: _____

Question 4: _____

Question 5: _____

4. Open a new document, then save it as **PR A-My Feedback Form** to the location where you save the files for this book.
5. Enter a title and subtitle (for example "Feedback Form") for your form. Format the title with the Title style and the subtitle with the Heading 1 style.
6. Apply the theme of your choice, select a new Style Set, then change the color scheme.
7. Write a paragraph describing the purpose of the feedback form. This paragraph is addressed to the people who will be completing the form.
8. Insert a table consisting of two columns and ten rows. This grid is your starting point for creating the feedback form. Enter text, merge and split cells as needed to develop the form so that it is clear and easy for users to complete. Include the user information in up to three rows at the beginning of the form, enter questions or elements for users to rate, and include a ranking scale and check boxes. Refer to the feedback form you completed for Project 2 for ideas.
9. Insert a clip art picture from the Online Clip Art gallery. (*Hint*: Click the INSERT tab, click Online Pictures, enter a keyword in the text box to the right of Office.com Clip Art, then select a clip art picture but *not* a photograph. You will know that you have selected a clip art picture that you can modify when you right-click the picture and see Edit Picture. If the picture is not separated into its component objects, then delete the picture and insert a different picture.)
10. Edit the clip art picture by removing some of the objects that make up the picture and recoloring some objects. Regroup all the objects into one picture, then adjust its position on the page.
11. Enter your name at the bottom of the document, check the spelling and grammar, save the document and submit it to your instructor, then close it.

Independent Challenge 3

Format a research paper in the APA style (American Psychological Association) according to the guidelines provided below. You are provided with the text of the research paper and information about what citations and sources to include. The APA style is most commonly used to format papers and cite sources in disciplines within the social sciences, such as psychology and sociology.

1. Start Word, open the file PR A-05.docx from the drive and folder where you store your Data Files, save it as **PR A-Sociology Research Paper** to the location where you save the files for this book, then format the paper according to the guidelines included in **TABLE A-2**.

TABLE A-2: Summary of general APA guidelines for formatting a research paper

guideline	description
Margins	Set all four page margins to 1".
Spacing	Double-space all content, including the list of references after it is generated.
Title page	Format the title page as shown in **FIGURE A-19**, including the text and page number in the first page header; start the title about 10 lines from the top margin (press [Enter] five times).
Header on subsequent pages	On page 2, create a header that is different from page 1 and that includes only the title of the paper in uppercase at the left margin of the page header (without the text "Running Head:") and the page number (starting at page 2) at the right margin of the page header.
Abstract	Center "Abstract" on page 2 of the research paper, and indent the second paragraph of the abstract. The indent should be one-half inch.
Research Paper Text	On the first page of the research paper following the abstract page, type the title of the paper using title case (the first letter of each word is capitalized except words such as "in" and "of") above the first paragraph, and then center it.

2. Use the Search function to find the text "participation in the wider society", then create a new source for a book as follows:
   Author: Denis McQuail
   Title: Audience Analysis
   Year: 1997
   City: Thousand Oaks, CA
   Publisher: Sage Publications

3. Insert a citation for Denis McQuail so that it immediately follows the closing quotation mark. (*Note:* In the APA style, a citation uses the author, date format, and includes the page number preceded by "p." unless the author's name appears in the preceding sentence. Edit the citation so only the page number (p. 99) appears. You do not need to type the "p." as it is added automatically.)

Independent Challenge 3 (continued)

4. Find "offline social skills" insert the citation for Zweerink (the source is included in the list of available sources associated with the paper), then edit the citation so it shows only "p. 12".

5. In the Source Manager, create a new source for a book as follows:

   Author: Matt Hills
   Title: Fan Cultures
   Year: 2002
   City: London
   Publisher: Routledge

6. Search for "cultural creativity" and insert citations based on the Matt Hills book after the closing quotation marks that include only page numbers (p. 90 for the first citation after "creativity or 'play'" and p. 106 after "between 'fantasy' and 'reality'").

7. Find the text "ideals into practice" and edit the citation so that only the page number appears.

8. Add a new page at the end of the paper and generate a list of references. Center the "References" title, then double-space the list of references.

9. Save the document, submit a copy to your instructor, then close the document.

FIGURE A-19

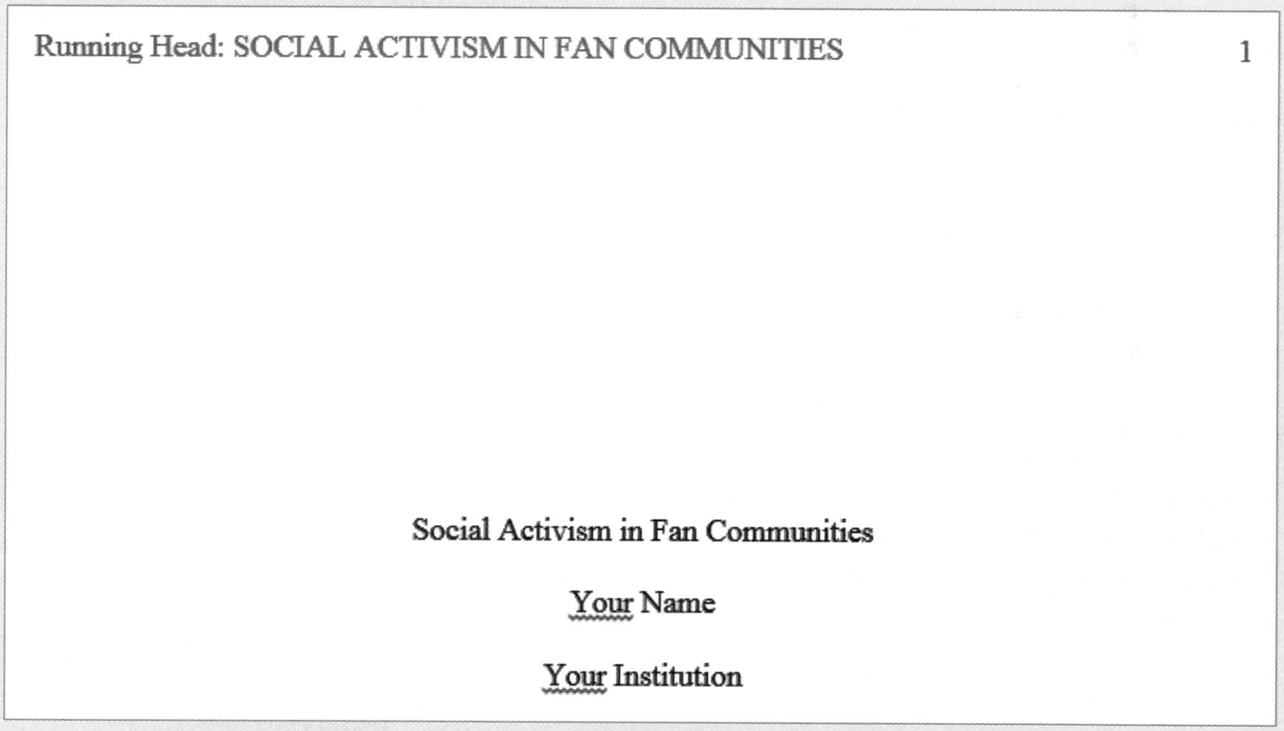

Running Head: SOCIAL ACTIVISM IN FAN COMMUNITIES   1

Social Activism in Fan Communities

Your Name

Your Institution

Independent Challenge 4 - Team Project

To further explore how you can develop a wide range of documents with Word 2013, you will work with two other people to complete a team project. The subject of the team project is the planning of a special event of your choice, such as a class party, a lecture, or a concert. The special event should be limited to a single afternoon or evening. Follow the guidelines provided below to create the three documents required for the team project. When you have completed the project, the team will submit a document containing information about the project, as well as three files related to the project: an event description, an event schedule, and an event feedback form.

 Project Setup

1. As a team, work together to complete the following tasks.
   - Share e-mail addresses among all three team members.
   - Set up a time (either via e-mail, an online chat session, Internet Messaging, or face to face) when you will get together to choose your topic and assign roles.
   - At your meeting, complete the table below with information about your team and the event you are creating documents for.

Team Name (last names of the team members or another name that describes the project; for example, "Jones-Cho-Knorr" or "Concert Fundraiser").
Team Members 1. 2. 3.
Event type (for example, party, lecture, concert, etc.)
Event purpose (for example, fundraiser for a specific cause, celebrate the completion of a research paper, feature a special guest, etc.)
Event location, date, and time
Team Roles: Indicate who is responsible for each of the following three files (one file per team member). Event Description: Event Program: Event Feedback Form:
Document Formatting: Select a theme, Style Set, and color scheme that will be used to format all of the documents created for the Team Project. Theme: Style Set: Color Scheme:

Independent Challenge 4 - Team Project (continued)

▶ Document Development

Individually, complete the tasks listed below for the file you are responsible for. You need to develop appropriate content, and format the file attractively. Be sure team members use the same theme, style set, and color scheme when creating the documents as detailed in the table above. Include the team name on all documents.

Event Description

This document contains a description of your special event and includes a table listing responsibilities and a time line. Create the document as follows:

1. Create a new Word document and save it as **PR A-Team Project_Event Description** to the location where you save files for this book, then apply the document theme, Style Set, and color scheme selected by your team.
2. Include a title with the name of your project and a subtitle with the names of your team members. Format the title with the Title style and the subtitle with the Subtitle style.
3. Write a paragraph describing the special event—its topics, purpose, the people involved, etc. You can paraphrase some of the information your team discussed in your meeting.
4. Create a table similar to the table shown below and then complete it with the required information. Include up to ten rows. A task could be "Contact the caterers" or "Pick up the speaker." Visualize the sequence of tasks required to put on the event.

Task	Person Responsible	Deadline

5. Format the table using the table style of your choice. If the table extends to two pages, click in the header row, then click the TABLE TOOLS LAYOUT tab, then click Repeat Header Rows in the Data group.
6. Below the table, enter the heading **Resources** and format it with the Heading 1 style.
7. From the REFERENCES tab, click the Manage Sources dialog box in the Citations & Bibliography group, then click New and create a source for information about your special event. For example, you could create a source for a Web site you or a team member used to find information related to the event, or a book, an interview, or another source. Refer to the list of source types provided for ideas.
8. Create two more sources for a total of three sources.
9. Following the "Resources" heading, generate a bibliography that lists the three sources you created. (*Hint*: Click "Insert Bibliography" to insert a list of sources that does not include the Bibliography or Works Cited heading.)
10. Add a header to the document that includes your team name at the left margin and the page number at the right margin.
11. Save the document and submit it to your instructor along with the other documents created by your team members.

Independent Challenge 4 - Team Project (continued)

Event Program

This document contains a program that lists the specific activities and the people involved in your special event. The finished program should fit over four panels (columns) of an 8 1/2 × 11" piece of paper in landscape orientation folded in half and printed double-sided. Create the event program as follows:

1. Create a new Word document and save it as **PR A-Team Project_Event Program** to the location where you save files for this book, then apply the document theme, Style Set, and color scheme selected by your team.
2. Set up the document so that it prints in landscape orientation, add a page, then create two columns on each page. Note that you can modify the page margins and the column margins as needed.
3. On the front cover, enter the title, time, date, and location of the event and any other information you want to include. Be sure the cover also includes the name of the team.
   Apply a text effect to the event title, then format and space the text attractively. Insert a picture, change the text wrapping of the picture to Behind Text, then modify the picture so that the text is easy to read. You can include a collage of pictures if you wish. Be creative and experiment with the many ways in which you can use pictures to create a compelling cover for the event program.
4. On page 2 of the program (the inside two panels), enter information about the event. For the program events, set a tab with the leader option of your choice.
5. On the back cover of the program, enter additional text as needed. This text may be a continuation of the text on panel 3 or new text, depending on the nature of the event. If possible, include one or two logos for event sponsors. You can insert these logos into a separate table.
6. View the two pages of the program event in Multiple Pages view, then make adjustments to the spacing so the program prints correctly.
7. Print a copy of the program, double-sided if possible, check that the spacing is correct when the program is folded, then make adjustments as needed.
8. Include your name and the team name on the document, then save the document and submit it to your instructor along with the other documents created by your team members.

Independent Challenge 4 - Team Project (continued)

Event Feedback Form

This document contains the questions or elements you want participants in your special event to evaluate. Note that the event feedback form will be distributed to event participants in paper form following the event. The purpose of the form is to provide users with a way to voice their opinion about the various event components (for example, activities, catering, entertainment, etc.).

1. Create a new Word document and save it as **PR A-Team Project_Event Feedback** to the location where you save files for this book, then apply the document theme, Style Set, and color scheme selected by your team.

2. Enter a title and subtitle (for example "Event Feedback Form") for the form. Format the title with the Title style and the subtitle with the Heading 1 style.

3. Write a paragraph describing the purpose of the event feedback form. This paragraph is addressed to the people who will be completing the form.

4. Insert a table consisting of two columns and ten rows. This grid is your starting point for creating the feedback form. Enter text, merge and split cells as needed to develop the form so that it is clear and easy for users to complete. Make sure the form includes at least five items that participants will rank. For ideas about how to set up the form and the kinds of questions to ask, view one of the many survey services available on the Web. Most of these services allow you to view sample surveys. Note that any Web sites you consult can be included in the Event Description document created by one of your team mates.

5. Insert a clip art picture from the Online Clip Art gallery. (*Hint*: Click the INSERT tab, click Online Pictures, enter a keyword in the text box to the right of Office.com Clip Art, then select a clip art picture but *not* a photograph. You will know that you have selected a clip art picture that you can modify when you right-click the picture and see Edit Picture. If the picture is not separated into its component objects, then delete the picture and insert a different picture.)

6. Edit the picture by removing some of the objects that make up the picture and recoloring some objects. Regroup all the objects into one picture, then adjust its position on the page.

7. Include your name and the team name on the document save the document, then submit it to your instructor along with the other documents created by your team mates.

▶ Project Summary

As a team, complete the project summary as follows.

1. Open PR A-06.docx from the location where you save your Data Files, then save it as **PR A-Team Project Summary** to the location where you save files for this book.

2. Read the directions in the document, then ensure that each team member enters his or her name in one of the tables along with a short description of the skills used and the challenges faced by each member while creating the Word document.

3. Save the document, then submit all four documents to your instructor.

Visual Workshop

Create the letterhead shown in **FIGURE A-20** in a new document. Save the document as **PR A-On Safari Adventures Letterhead** to the location where you save the files for this book. Select the Vapor theme with the Red Orange color scheme, then apply the Gradient Fill – Gold, Accent 1, Reflection text effect, bold, and 24 pt font size. Find the clip art picture by searching the Office.com Clip Art using the keyword **elephant**. You will need to scroll to find the elephant (the background is red). Edit the picture by changing the two objects that make up the background to Gold, Accent 2, Darker 25% and Gold, Accent 2, Darker 50%, group the object, then rotate the picture so that it faces the direction shown in the figure (select Flip Horizontal from the menu of Rotate options in the Arrange group). Select the Clip Art picture by clicking a white area and verifying that only one box appears around the picture and the Layout Options button appears, drag sizing handles to modify the size of the picture, then click the Position button to set the position of the Clip Art picture at the top right as shown in **FIGURE A-20** along with the address text.

FIGURE A-20

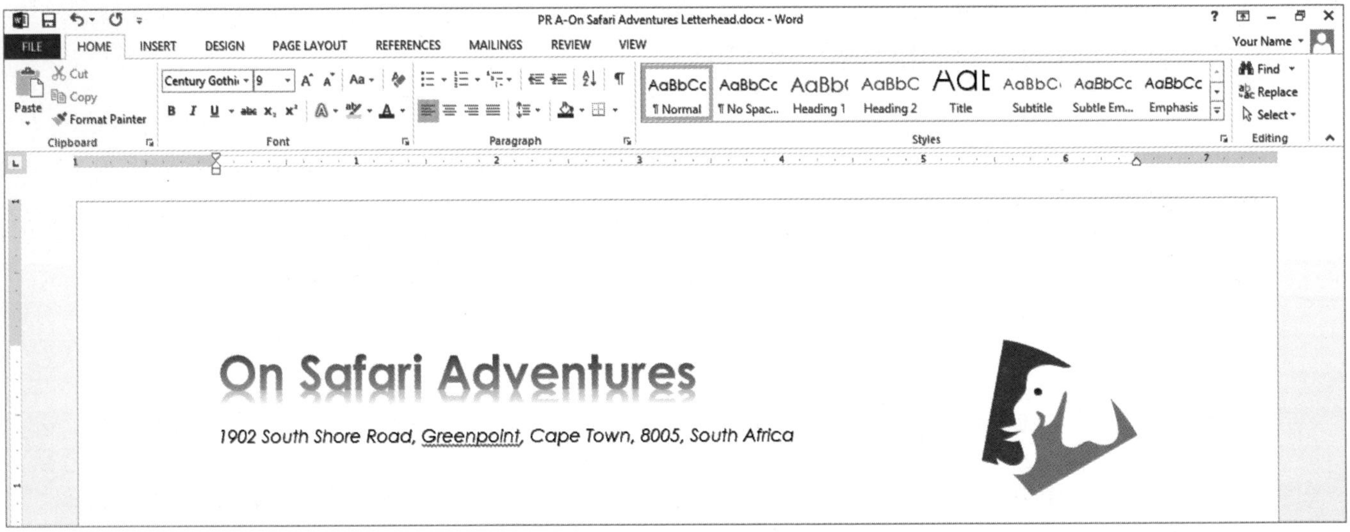

Word
Projects II

Projects

In this unit you will create the following:

Multipage Proposal

Work in Outline view • Modify and update styles • Change case • Convert tabbed text to a table • Sort table rows • Insert and modify pictures • Add captions • Use the Navigation pane • Customize bullets • Insert a SmartArt graphic • Create sections • Add page numbers • Modify page numbering • Insert a table of contents • Add a cover page (*Skills also practiced in Independent Challenge 1*)

Brochure

Create shapes (lines) • Change page orientation • Modify styles • Insert and modify clip art in footers • Use a table grid for brochure columns • Apply artistic effects, color, and corrections to a photograph • Change text direction in a table • Crop a picture to a shape (*Skills also practiced in Independent Challenge 2*)

Résumé

Select a Style set • Modify styles • Modify table properties • Set up a résumé in a table form (*Skills also practiced in Independent Challenge 3*)

Team Project

Files You Will Need

PR B-01.docx	PR B-07.docx
PR B-02.jpg	PR B-08.jpg
PR B-03.jpg	PR B-09.jpg
PR B-04.jpg	PR B-10.docx
PR B-05.jpg	PR B-11.jpg
PR B-06.jpg	

Multipage Proposal for Eco-Reserve Conference

The organizers of the Eco Reserve Conference have asked the Fir Island Nature Club near Victoria, BC, to put together a proposal to host the conference in 2017. To complete the proposal, you will **Organize the Content, Format Text, Add Graphics**, and **Add a Table of Contents and Cover Page**. FIGURE B-10 on page 37 shows the six pages of the completed proposal.

Organize the Content

You need to open the document containing the text of the proposal, and then organize the document in Outline view so you can get a clear sense of how the document is structured.

STEPS

1. **Start Word, open** PR B-01.docx **from the location where you store your Data Files, save it as** PR B-Eco-Reserve Conference Proposal, **then show formatting marks**

2. **Click the** VIEW tab, **then click the** Outline button **in the Views group**

   In Outline view, you designate levels for headings and subheadings. Text that is not a heading is designated as Body Text by default.

3. **Click** Introduction **at the top of the page, then click the** Promote to Heading 1 button **in the Outline Tools group as shown in** FIGURE B-1

   The text "Introduction" is designated as a Level 1 heading and the Heading 1 style is applied.

4. **Click the** Facilities **heading (about halfway down the screen), click** «‹ **, click** Accommodations **immediately below, click the** Promote button ‹ **in the Outline Tools group, then click the** Demote button → **in the Outline Tools group**

   The "Accommodations" heading is formatted as a Level 2 heading and the Heading 2 style is applied.

5. **Format the remaining headings in the document as described below**

Heading Text	Level to Apply	Heading Text	Level to Apply
Additional Accommodations	3	Access and Travel	1
Catering/Dining Facilities	2	Special Events	1
Meeting Venues	2	Conclusion	1
Audio/Visual Equipment and Internet	3		

6. **Scroll to the top of the document, click the** Show Level list arrow **in the Outline Tools group, then click** Level 2 **to see the structure of the document as shown in** FIGURE B-2

7. **Click** Meeting Venues, **click the** Move Up button ▲ **in the Outline Tools group, then double-click the** Expand button ➕ **to the left of Special Events**

   All the text associated with the Special Events heading is now visible. You can collapse and expand headings and subheadings in Outline view to organize your content.

8. **Click** Opening Reception, **press [Tab] to create a Level 2 heading, click** Activities, **press [Shift][Tab] to move the heading from body text to Level 2, then compare the outline to** FIGURE B-3

9. **Click the** Close Outline View button **in the Close group, press [Ctrl][Home] to move to the top of the document, then save the document**

FIGURE B-1: Promoting "Introduction" to Level 1 in Outline view

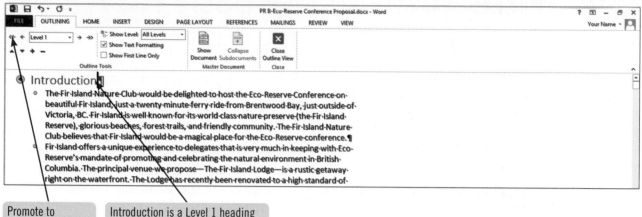

Promote to Heading 1 button

Introduction is a Level 1 heading formatted with the Heading 1 style

FIGURE B-2: Document structure in Outline view

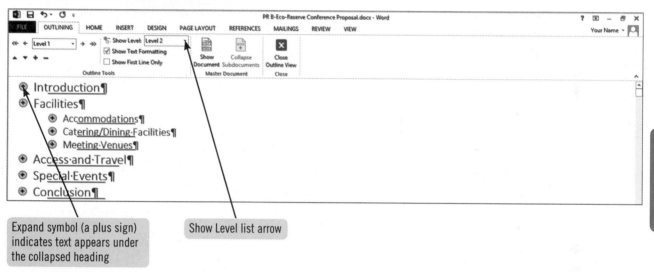

Expand symbol (a plus sign) indicates text appears under the collapsed heading

Show Level list arrow

FIGURE B-3: Completed outline

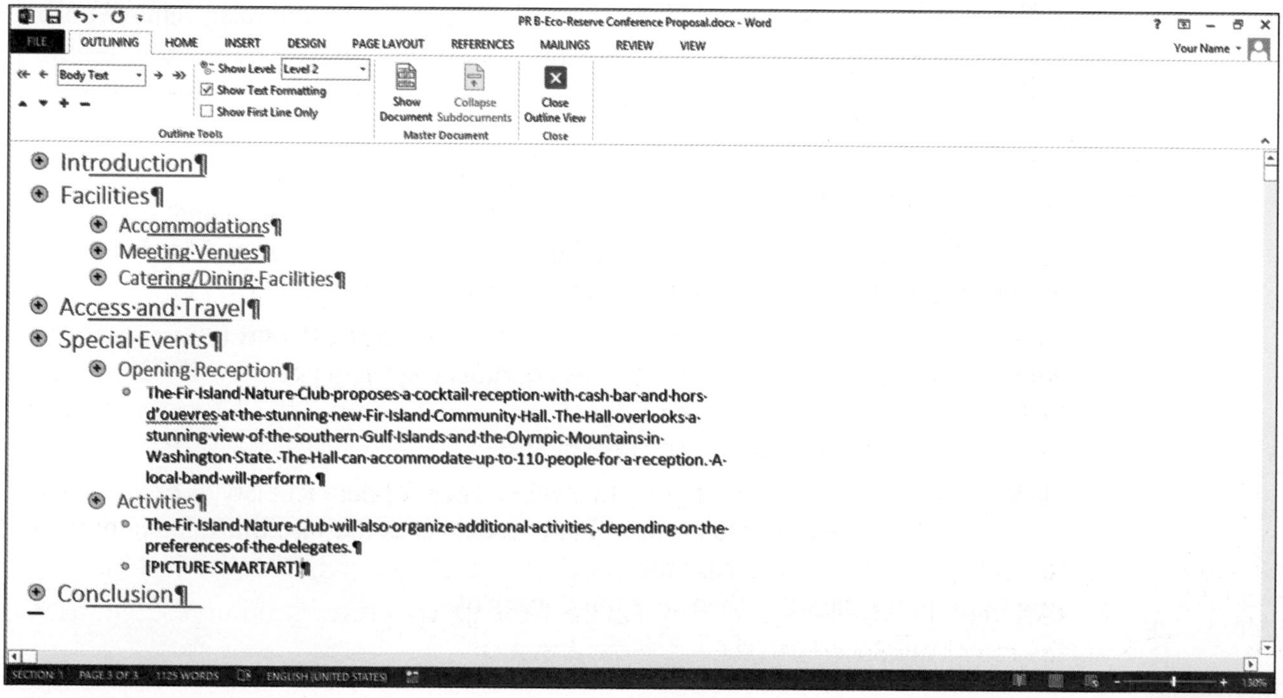

Multipage Proposal (continued)

Format Text

By default, the document is formatted with the Office 2013 Style Set. You change the theme, apply a new Style Set, modify the formats associated with the Heading 1 and Heading 2 styles, then go through the document to modify formatting and update additional styles as needed.

STEPS

TROUBLE
If a border appears around the word instead of the paragraph, click the Undo button ⤺ on the Quick Access toolbar, then repeat step 2 and be sure to select the paragraph mark.

HINT
You can modify a style by updating it to match selected text or by changing options in the Modify Style dialog box.

HINT
When you update the Normal style, all text formatted with that style is updated, even if you made changes to the formatting.

HINT
If you want headings in row one to repeat when a table breaks across two pages, click the Repeat Header Rows check box in the Data group.

1. Click the DESIGN tab, click the Themes button in the Document Formatting group, select the Celestial theme, click the More button ⯆ in the Document Formatting group, then select the Minimalist Style Set (last selection in the first row)

2. Select INTRODUCTION including the paragraph mark, click the HOME tab, click the Change Case button Aa ▾ in the Font group, click Capitalize Each Word, click the Borders list arrow ⊞, click Borders and Shading, click the Color list arrow, click Red, Accent 6, Darker 25%, click the left side of the Preview as shown in FIGURE B-4, then click OK

3. Right-click Heading 1 in the Styles gallery, click Update Heading 1 to Match Selection as shown in FIGURE B-5, click away from the heading, right-click Heading 2 in the Styles group, click Modify, change the font size to 14 pt, click the Automatic list arrow, click Red, Accent 6, Darker 25%, then click OK

4. Scroll down and select the text from "22 rooms" to "$209" below the Accommodations paragraph, click 4 on the Ruler bar, click the Increase Indent button ⧉ in the Paragraph group once, click the Line and Paragraph Spacing button ⧏▾ in the Paragraph group, then click Remove Space After Paragraph

5. Click anywhere in the paragraph below the tabbed list, click the Line and Paragraph Spacing button ⧏▾, click Add Space Before Paragraph, right-click Normal in the Styles group, then click Update Normal to Match Selection

   Notice that the formatting you applied to the tabbed list in step 4 has been removed.

6. Select the four lines of tabbed text again, click ⧉, click 4 on the ruler, remove both the Before and the After paragraph spacing, double-click the tab marker at 4" on the ruler, click 4 in the list of tab stops, click the 3 option button, click OK, then compare the tabbed list to FIGURE B-6

7. Scroll to the Additional Accommodations subheading, select Additional Accommodations, change the font size to 12 pt and the font color to Red, Accent 6, Darker 25%, select the Capitalize Each Word option from the Change Case button, then update Heading 3 to match the selection

8. Select the text from the line containing Accommodation and Rooms (you may need to scroll down) to the line starting with "Waves Hideaway" and ending with "8723", click the INSERT tab, click Table in the Tables group, click Convert Text to Table, verify that the number of columns is 4, then click OK

9. With the table still selected, click the More button ⯆ in the Table Styles group, select the Grid Table 2, Accent 6 table style (Red), double-click the far right table border to autofit the table contents, click the TABLE TOOLS LAYOUT tab, click the Sort button in the Data group, click OK, then save the document

Word Projects II

FIGURE B-4: Borders and Shading dialog box

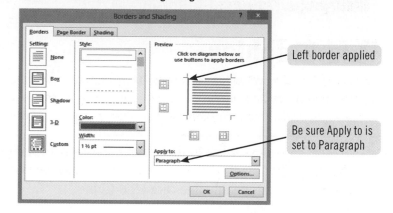

Left border applied

Be sure Apply to is set to Paragraph

FIGURE B-5: Updating a style based on applied formats

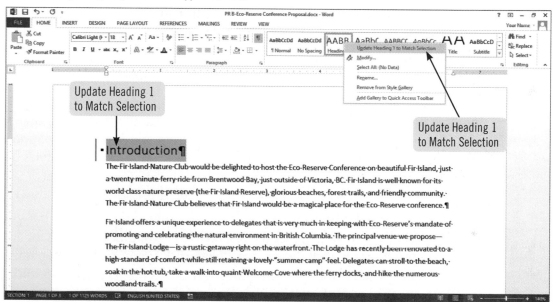

Update Heading 1 to Match Selection

Update Heading 1 to Match Selection

FIGURE B-6: Tabbed text formatted

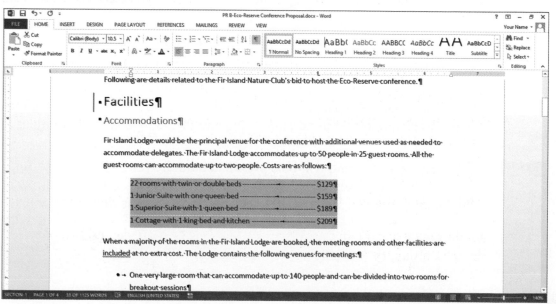

Add Graphics

You insert a photograph with a caption, create a SmartArt graphic that contains three additional pictures, and enhance the bulleted lists with colored bullets using a different symbol.

STEPS

1. Press [Ctrl][Home], click to the left of paragraph 1 (begins "The Fir Island Nature Club..."), click the INSERT tab, click Pictures, navigate to the location where you store your Data Files, then double-click PR B-02.jpg

TROUBLE

If you do not see the alignment guides, click the PAGE LAYOUT tab, click the Align list arrow in the Arrange group, then click Use Alignment Guides. A check mark should appear next to Use Alignment Guides for the feature to be active.

2. Select the contents of the Width box in the Size group, type 3.5, press [Enter], click the Wrap Text button in the Arrange group, click Square, then use the mouse and the green alignment guides to position the picture as shown in FIGURE B-7

3. Click Picture Effects in the Picture Styles group, point to Bevel, click 3-D Options, enter settings as shown in FIGURE B-8, then close the Format Picture pane

4. With the picture still selected, click the REFERENCES tab, click Insert Caption in the Captions group, verify that "Figure 1" appears, type a colon (:), press [Spacebar], type View from Fir Island Lodge, then click OK

5. Select all the text in the caption, including Figure 1, click the HOME tab, change the font color to Red, Accent 6, Darker 50%, click the Line and Paragraph Spacing button, click Remove Space Before Paragraph, click the More button ⬇ in the Styles group, right click Caption in the Styles Gallery, then click Update Caption to Match Selection
   Now every caption you add to a picture will be formatted with the updated style.

6. Scroll to the bulleted list below the Accommodations subheading (the first bullet begins with "One very large room..."), click the first bulleted item, click the Bullets list arrow ▤ ▾ in the Paragraph group, click Define New Bullet, click Symbol, click the Font list arrow, select Wingdings, select the Character Code text box contents , type 216, click OK, click Font, change the font color to Red, Accent 6, Darker 25%, click OK, then click OK
   All the bulleted items in the document are now formatted with the new bullet symbol.

HINT

You can use the Navigation Pane to move quickly to headings and sub-headings in a multi-page document.

7. Click the VIEW tab, click the Navigation Pane check box in the Show group, click Activities to go directly to the Activities subheading, then select the placeholder [PICTURE SMARTART] but not the paragraph mark

8. Click the INSERT tab, click SmartArt in the Illustrations group, click Picture, select the Bending Picture Blocks SmartArt style, click OK, then click the top left picture block

9. Click Browse next to From a file, navigate to the location where you store your Data Files, double-click PR B-03.jpg, click the caption box, type Storm Watching, then fill the remaining picture blocks using PR B-04.jpg and PR B-05.jpg and add captions as shown in FIGURE B-9

TROUBLE

Be sure to click the border of each text box to select the text box.

10. Click the Storm Watching text box, press and hold the [Ctrl] key, click the Surfing and Nature Walks text boxes, click the right mouse button, click the Fill list arrow on the Mini toolbar, click Red, Accent 6, Darker 50%, then save the document

FIGURE B-7: Positioning the picture using alignment guides

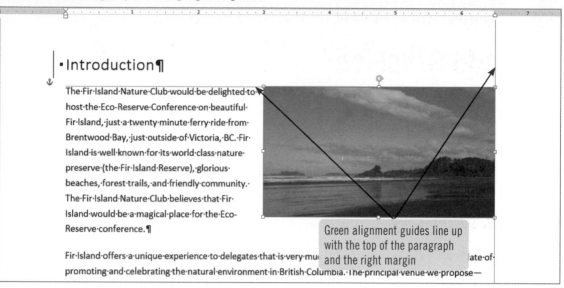

· Introduction¶

The·Fir·Island·Nature·Club·would·be·delighted·to·
host·the·Eco-Reserve·Conference·on·beautiful·
Fir·Island,·just·a·twenty·minute·ferry·ride·from·
Brentwood·Bay,·just·outside·of·Victoria,·BC.·Fir·
Island·is·well·known·for·its·world·class·nature·
preserve·(the·Fir·Island·Reserve),·glorious·
beaches,·forest·trails,·and·friendly·community.·
The·Fir·Island·Nature·Club·believes·that·Fir·
Island·would·be·a·magical·place·for·the·Eco-
Reserve·conference.¶

> Green alignment guides line up with the top of the paragraph and the right margin

Fir·Island·offers·a·unique·experience·to·delegates·that·is·very·much [...] ate·of·
promoting·and·celebrating·the·natural·environment·in·British·Columbia.·The·principal·venue·we·propose—

FIGURE B-8: 3D Format settings

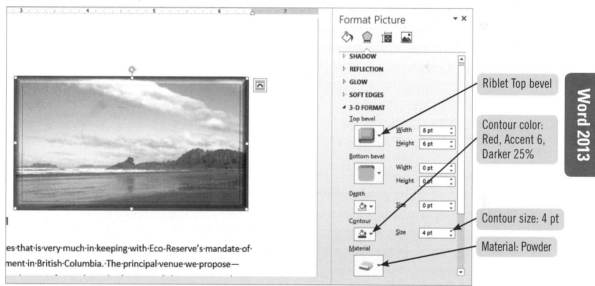

> Riblet Top bevel

> Contour color: Red, Accent 6, Darker 25%

> Contour size: 4 pt

> Material: Powder

FIGURE B-9: Pictures and captions for the SmartArt diagram

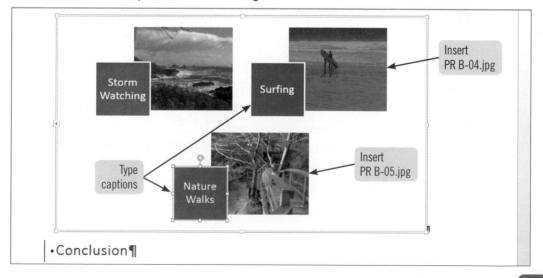

> Insert PR B-04.jpg

> Insert PR B-05.jpg

> Type captions

· Conclusion¶

Create the Table of Contents and Cover Page

First, you insert a footer containing a page number and the text you want to appear on each page of the proposal text. You also insert a section break above the first page of the proposal text and generate a table of contents, then insert a cover page.

STEPS

1. Click Introduction in the Navigation pane, close the Navigation pane, click the INSERT tab, click the Footer button in the Header & Footer group, click Blank, press [Ctrl][R], click the Page Number button, point to Current Position, click Accent Bar 2, then click the Close Header and Footer button in the Close group

2. Click the PAGE LAYOUT tab, click Breaks, click Next Page, press [Ctrl][Home], click the HOME tab, then click the Clear All Formatting button in the Font group

   The document contains two sections: Section 1 is the blank page and Section 2 is the rest of the document.

3. Press [Enter] three times, press the ↑ once to position the insertion point at the second paragraph mark, click the REFERENCES tab, click Table of Contents in the Table of Contents group, select Automatic Table 2, then scroll up to view the table of contents

   The table of contents is generated based on the styles you applied to the various headings.

4. Press [Ctrl][Home], click the INSERT tab, click Cover Page in the Pages group, scroll to and click Semaphore, double-click the vertical bar in the document, click the Shape Fill list arrow, then click Red, Accent 6, Darker 25%

HINT
You need to type the subtitle text, which is "Submitted by the Fir Island Nature Club" and delete the company and address controls.

5. Click the [DATE] control, click the selection handle (the control turns dark blue), press [Delete], scroll down and click [DOCUMENT TITLE], then enter text and delete placeholders as shown in the completed document in FIGURE B-10

6. View the page in One Page view, click the Document Title control, drag the top middle sizing handle down to just above the Title tag to make room to insert a picture, click at the top of the document above the Page Break, insert the picture file PR B-06.jpg, increase the width to 6.5", then add the caption On the Ferry to Fir Island

7. Return to 130% view, scroll to page 2 (contains the Table of Contents), double-click in the Footer area, click the Page Number button in the Header & Footer group, click Format Page Numbers, click the Number format list arrow, click i, ii, iii, then click OK

8. Click the Next button in the Navigation group two times to move to the footer for Section 2, click the Link to Previous button in the Navigation group to deselect it, click the Page Number button, click Format Page Numbers, click the Start at option button, verify that 1 appears in the Start at text box, click OK, then exit the footer

   You deselected the Link to Previous buttons in Section 2 to ensure that changes you made to the page number in Section 2 does not affect the page number in Section 1.

MORE PRACTICE
For more practice with the skills presented in this project, complete Independent Challenge 1.

9. Scroll through the document, add a page break at the paragraph that begins "When a majority … ", scroll up and right-click the table of contents, click Update Field, click the Update entire table option button, click OK, save the document, submit a copy to your instructor, then close the document

FIGURE B-10: Completed Proposal

Figure 1: On the Ferry to Fir Island

ECO-RESERVE CONFERENCE PROPOSAL
SUBMITTED BY FIR ISLAND NATURE CLUB

YOUR NAME

Table of Contents

Introduction

The Fir Island Nature Club would be delighted to host the Eco-Reserve Conference on beautiful Fir Island, just a twenty minute ferry ride from Brentwood Bay, just outside of Victoria, BC. Fir Island is well known for its world class nature preserve (the Fir Island Reserve), glorious beaches, forest trails, and friendly community. The Fir Island Nature Club believes that Fir Island would be a magical place for the Eco-Reserve conference.

Figure 2: View from Fir Island Lodge

Fir Island offers a unique experience to delegates that is very much in keeping with Eco-Reserve's mandate of promoting and celebrating the natural environment in British Columbia. The principal venue we propose—The Fir Island Lodge—is a rustic getaway right on the waterfront. The Lodge has recently been renovated to a high standard of comfort while still retaining a lovely "summer camp" feel. Delegates can stroll to the beach, soak in the hot tub, take a walk into quaint Welcome Cove where the ferry docks, and hike the numerous woodland trails.

Following are details related to the Fir Island Nature Club's bid to host the Eco-Reserve conference.

Facilities

Accommodations

Fir Island Lodge would be the principal venue for the conference with additional venues used as needed to accommodate delegates. The Fir Island Lodge accommodates up to 50 people in 25 guest rooms. All the guest rooms can accommodate up to two people. Costs are as follows:

22 rooms with twin or double beds	$129
1 Junior Suite with one queen bed	$159
1 Superior Suite with 1 queen bed	$189
1 Cottage with 1 king bed and kitchen	$209

When a majority of the rooms in the Fir Island Lodge are booked, the meeting rooms and other facilities are included at no extra cost. The Lodge contains the following venues for meetings:

> One very large room that can accommodate up to 140 people and can be divided into two rooms for breakout sessions
> One suite that can accommodate 20 people
> One board room that can accommodate 20 people

Additional Accommodations

In addition to the accommodation offered at Fir Island Lodge, delegates can choose from the bed and breakfast establishments listed below, each of which is within walking distance of the Fir Island Lodge.

Accommodation	Rooms	Cost	Contact
Evergreen Bed and Breakfast	5	$125 - $235	250-555-1266
Heron Point Guest House	4	$145-$235	250-555-5789
Laurel Hideaway	4	$150	250-555-8823
Lighthouse Point Bed and Breakfast	4	$210 - $340	250-555-1276
Pacific Sands Bed and Breakfast	4	$135	250-555-3465
Seastrand House	4	$125	250-555-9340
Seaview Bed and Breakfast	3	$125	250-555-7895
Sunset Bed and Breakfast	4	$125 - $165	250-555-1800
Waves Hideaway	4	$190	250-555-8723

Meeting Venues

As noted above, the principal meeting venue would be at the Fir Island Lodge which can accommodate up to four breakout sessions—large room divided into two that can accommodate up to 70 people each and two rooms that can accommodate 20 people each. In addition, Seastrand House (five minute walk) can accommodate a meeting of up to 30 people and the Fir Island Community Hall (a 15 minute walk or short bus ride from the Lodge) can accommodate up to 75 people.

The venues available on Fir Island are not conventional hotel meeting rooms. Delegates may need to move around to different locations. However, we feel this activity is part of the charm of coming to Fir Island for the Eco-Reserve conference. A shuttle bus will be available as needed.

Audio/Visual Equipment and Internet

The Fir Island Lodge has free Wi-Fi throughout the facility. In addition, the Lodge has two 50" TV screens, a large pull down screen and a sound system. The Fir Island Nature Club can provide two projectors at a nominal additional charge.

Catering/Dining Facilities

The Fir Island Lodge can provide catering for the entire conference – up to 140 people seated at tables. We anticipate the following schedule for food service:

> Friday Reception: Reception hosted by the Fir Island Nature Club held at the Fir Island Community Hall—a stunning venue overlooking the Pacific Ocean. The reception will include a cash bar, hors d'oeuvres, and musical entertainment. Following the reception, delegates who are staying on Fir Island can either go to one of the five restaurants on the island or arrangements can be made for a buffet dinner at Fir Island Lodge.
> Saturday Breakfast: Buffet breakfast at the Lodge
> Saturday Lunch: Buffet lunch at the Lodge
> Saturday Banquet: Banquet at the Lodge

In addition, the Lodge can provide snacks during breaks. Delegates who go to other venues for breakout sessions will also be provided with snacks arranged through one of the local cafes.

Access and Travel

Getting to Fir Island is half the attraction of any visit to the Island. The Queen of Georgia from Brentwood Bay outside Victoria runs almost hourly beginning at 5:00 am with the last ferry leaving Fir Island at 10 pm. The ride is just twenty minutes past some of the most breathtaking marine scenery in western Canada. Delegates who live in Victoria can easily commute to Fir Island for the conference events. A walk-on passenger pays $9.10 and a passenger with a vehicle $32.65. We recommend that delegates walk onto the ferry instead of bringing cars. Parking is limited near the Lodge and in Welcome Cove. The Fir Island Nature Club can arrange to pick up people who need assistance. The Lodge also provides a shuttle service.

Special Events

Opening Reception

The Fir Island Nature Club proposes a cocktail reception with cash bar and hors d'ouevres at the stunning new Fir Island Community Hall. The Hall overlooks a stunning view of the southern Gulf Islands and the Olympic Mountains in Washington State. The Hall can accommodate up to 110 people for a reception. A local band will perform.

Activities

The Fir Island Nature Club will also organize additional activities, depending on the preferences of the delegates.

Storm Watching

Surfing

Nature Walks

Conclusion

Fir Island is a special place. The people who live here love to share the island with visitors. Every weekend, notices for nature walks, concerts, art openings, garden walks, plant sales, and other community events crowd the bulletin boards. At the same time, Fir Island is a great place to just relax and enjoy the view. Delegates looking for a lively night life won't find it on Fir Island. What they will find is a level of tranquility and quiet that has become all too rare in our modern lives.

The Fir Island Nature Club welcomes the opportunity to host delegates from all over British Columbia. Delegates will experience the unique charm that has made Fir Island a magnet for environmentalists and nature lovers from all over the world while also enjoying the opportunity to network with fellow delegates in surroundings that are truly spectacular – rain or shine!

Six-Panel Program Brochure

You have been asked to create the six-panel brochure shown in **FIGURE B-13** and **FIGURE B-14** on pages 41 and 43 of the text to advertise a one-year intensive training program in French language skills. Page 1 of the document consists of the inside three panels of the brochure (panels 2, 3, and 4), and page 2 consists of the folded-over panel, the back panel, and the front panel (panels 5, 6, and 1). To create the brochure, you need to **Set Up the Brochure**, **Create Page 1**, and then **Create Page 2**.

Set Up the Brochure

You set up the brochure in Landscape orientation, create a header and a footer for Page 1 (panels 2, 3 and 4), and then insert and modify a clip art picture in the footer.

STEPS

TROUBLE
If Heading 1 formatting is displayed, click the Undo button ↰ on the Quick Access toolbar, then right-click Heading 1 and modify the style per the instructions in step 2.

HINT
You press and hold the [Shift] key while you draw the line to keep the line straight.

1. Open a new document in Word, click the PAGE LAYOUT tab, change to Landscape orientation, click the Margins button in the Page Setup group, use the Custom Margins option to change all four margins to 0.3", click OK, then save the document as PR B-French Language School Brochure

2. Click the DESIGN tab, apply the Wisp theme, click the HOME tab, right-click Heading 1 in the Styles gallery, click Modify, click Format, click Border, click the Shading tab, select Green, Accent 6, Lighter 80% as the fill color, click OK, click Format, click Paragraph, change the After Spacing to 6 pt, click OK, select the Green, Accent 6, Darker 50% Font color, then click OK

3. Click the VIEW tab, click Page Width in the Zoom group, click the INSERT tab, click Header in the Header & Footer group, click Blank, then click the Different First Page check box in the Options group to select it

4. Click the INSERT tab, click the Shapes button in the Illustrations group, click the Line icon, hold down [Shift], draw a straight line about 2" long, select the contents of the Width text box in the Size group, type 10.4, then press [Enter]

5. Click the Shape Outline list arrow in the Shape Styles group, click Green, Accent 6, Darker 25%, click the Shape Outline list arrow again, point to Weight, click 4½ pt, click the Shape Effects button in the Shape Styles group, point to Shadow, click the Offset Bottom shadow style (top row, middle selection in the Outer category), start the line at the left margin and create a blank line under the horizontal line as shown in FIGURE B-11

6. Click the HEADER & FOOTER TOOLS DESIGN tab, click the Go to Footer button in the Navigation group, click the Online Pictures button in the Insert group, then type France map in the Office.com Clip Art search box and press [Enter]

7. Click the green map of France, then click Insert

8. Enter .5 in the Height text box, press [Enter], press [Ctrl][R] to move the picture to the right margin, click the Wrap Text button in the Arrange group, then click Behind Text
   The picture appears in the footer as shown in FIGURE B-12.

9. Click the Color button in the Adjust group, click Green, Accent color 6 Dark (second row, last column), exit the footer, then save the document

FIGURE B-11: Straight line drawn from the left to the right margin in the header

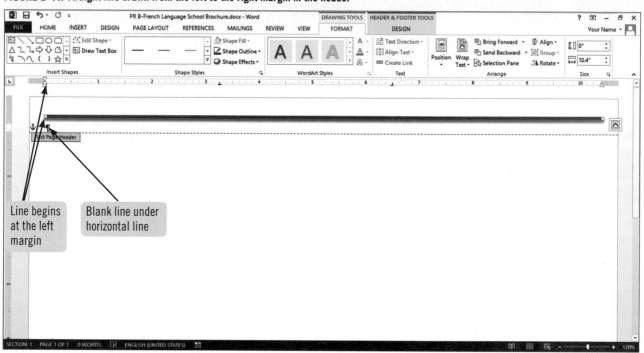

Line begins at the left margin

Blank line under horizontal line

FIGURE B-12: First page footer

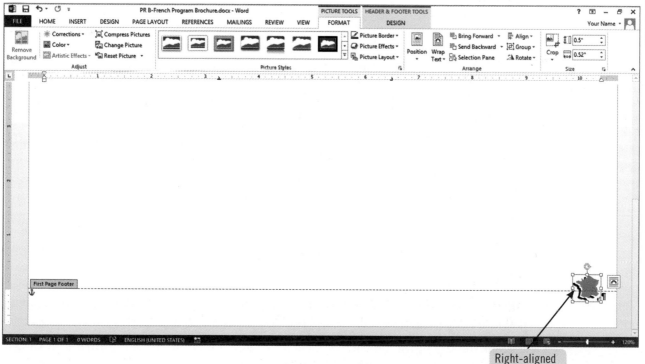

Right-aligned clip art picture

Word 2013

Six-panel Brochure (continued)

Create Page 1

To simplify the brochure creation process, you use a table form to contain the information required for each brochure panel. You need to create a table consisting of 5 columns—one column for each of the three panels and two columns for the space between columns. Next, you insert and format the brochure text and create an attractive graphic.

STEPS

HINT

If gridlines are not visible, click the TABLE TOOLS LAYOUT tab, then click View Gridlines in the Table group.

1. **Press [Ctrl][Home], press [Enter], click the** INSERT **tab, click** Table **in the Tables group, drag to create a table of 5 columns and 1 row, click the** Table Move Handle ⊞, **click the** Borders list arrow **in the Borders group, then click** No Border

   The width of the page is 11" and your margins are .3". As a result, you have 10.4" to divide into three wide columns and two narrow columns. The correct proportions are 3.2" for each panel and .4" for each space.

2. **Click in the first cell in the table, select the contents of the** Width text box **in the Cell Size group, type 3.2, press [Enter], press [Tab], change the width of the second column to .4", then resize the remaining three columns to 3.2", .4" and 3.2"**

3. **Select the table, click** Properties **in the Table group, click the** Row tab, **click the** Specify height text box, **enter 6.8, click the** Row height is list arrow, **click** Exactly, **click the** Table tab, **click the** Around option **in the Text wrapping section, then click** OK

4. **Click in the first cell, click the** HOME **tab, click** Heading 1 **in the Styles group, type** Program Overview, **then press [Enter]**

   The text for the brochure is in another file. You copy and paste text as needed for the three panels.

5. **Open** PR B-07.docx **from the location where you store your Data Files, save it as** PR B-French Program Text, **select the first two paragraphs (to "university level"), copy them, return to the Program brochure, click the** Paste button, **click anywhere in the first paragraph, click the** PAGE LAYOUT **tab, change the After spacing to 6 pt, click the** HOME **tab, right-click** Normal **in the Styles group, then click** Update Normal to Match Selection

6. **Click at the end of the second paragraph, press [Enter], click the** INSERT **tab, click the** Pictures button, **double-click** PR B-08.jpg, **click the** Rotate button, **click** Rotate Right 90°, **select the contents of the** Height text box, **type 3.2, press [Enter], click the** Wrap Text button, **then click** Behind Text

7. **With the picture still selected, click** Artistic Effects, **click the** Pencil Sketch effect **(top row, fourth column), click** Color, **click the** Dark Red, Accent color 1 Light color **(bottom row, second column), click** Corrections, **then click** Brightness +40%, Contrast -40% **(top right selection)**

8. **Move the mouse toward the top left corner of the picture to show the** 🔆, **then drag to position the picture as shown in** FIGURE B-13

TROUBLE

Copy and paste text for one column at a time.

9. **Click at the top of the second wide column, copy text, paste it, and format it as shown in** FIGURE B-13, **then save the document**

   Format the headings with the Heading 1 style, adjust column widths in the table to show two columns, apply the Grid Table 2 - Accent 6 table style, then deselect the First Column check box.

Program Overview

The Intensive French Program offered by the Chicago Language School prepares students for study, travel or business in the French-speaking world. This program is designed for professionals and students who need to communicate in French with colleagues, instructors and clients. The program trains students to an advanced level of French proficiency in conversation and an intermediate level in written French. The program culminates with a one-month stay in France. Students then have the option to stay in France to take further training or to travel.

Upon successful completion of the Chicago Language School program, graduates receive a certificate recognized as equivalent to 18 credits at the university level.

Admission Procedures

Applicants must have an intermediate level of French for acceptance into the program. This level is determined during an interview with the Program Coordinator and completion of a one-hour written exam. In addition, applicants must have completed high school. Upon acceptance into the program, a non-refundable $500 administration fee is payable.

To apply for the program, call the Chicago Language School at (312) 555-3321.

Program Content

The Chicago Language program is divided into two 4-month terms followed by one month in France for a total program length of nine months.

Term 1	Term 2
Intermediate Conversation	Advanced Conversation
Reading Comprehension I	Reading Comprehension II
French Business Writing	Living and Working in France
French Creative Writing	French Cooking

Course Descriptions

Intermediate Conversation: Ask questions, give simple descriptions, use present tense, use past tense with avoir.

Reading Comprehension I: Develop grammar skills, understand travel documents and newspaper articles.

French Business Writing: Study typical business situations and develop business correspondence in French.

French Creative Writing: Develop a flair for French through writing short vignettes, poems, and stories in French and through study of selected French literary classics.

Advanced Conversation: Express yourself easily, use all the main structures and tenses in French accurately, develop good aural comprehension.

Living and Working in France: Understand French regulations, identify job opportunities, learn French geography and culture.

Reading Comprehension II: Develop grammar skills, read and understand business contracts, read and understand journal articles and books.

French Cooking: Learn French cooking (in French) from a French chef.

Create Page 2

As shown in FIGURE B-14, page 2 contains panels 5, 6, and 1 of the completed brochure. Panel 1 is the cover and panel 6 is the back panel when the brochure is folded.

STEPS

1. Click at the end of the French Cooking entry in the fifth column, press [Tab] to start a new row on the following page, select the new row, then click the Clear All Formatting button ✦ in the Font group on the HOME tab

2. From the Brochure Text document, copy the remaining text, paste it in the first table cell, format the heading with the Heading 1 style, then format the table with the Grid Table 2 - Accent 6 table style with the First Column check box deselected

HINT
Use the line wrap in the table in the figure to judge column width.

3. With the table still selected, click the HOME tab, click the Line and Paragraph Spacing button in the Paragraph group, click Remove Space After Paragraph, then adjust column widths as shown in the completed page in FIGURE B-14

4. Click below the table, press [Enter] two times, click the INSERT tab, click the Table button in the Table group, then click the top left table cell to insert a table consisting of just one cell

5. Fill the table cell with Green, Accent 6, Darker 50%, change the font color to White, then enter and format the text shown in FIGURE B-14

   You need to increase the font size of "Contact Us" to 24 pt, the Before spacing to 24 pt, bold all the text, and change the font color of the hyperlink to White. To enter the address text, press [Shift][Enter] after lines as needed to remove the After paragraph spacing.

6. Click in the middle table cell, type and format the return address as shown in FIGURE B-14 (use [Shift][Enter] as needed), press [Enter] twice, type your name followed by placeholders for the recipient address as shown in FIGURE B-14, select all six lines of text, click the TABLE TOOLS LAYOUT tab, click the Text Direction button in the Alignment group two times, scroll down, select the block of text that includes your name, click the HOME tab, then click the Increase Indent button ≢≣ six times

   You could insert mail merge fields instead of placeholders to send the brochure to a mailing list.

7. Click in the final panel, type Chicago Language School, center it, enhance it with the Green, Accent 6, Darker 50% font color, bold, and 36 pt, press [Enter] following the title, insert the picture PR B-09.jpg, increase the width to 2", click the Crop list arrow in the Size group, point to Crop to Shape, then click the Oval shape

8. Click Picture Effects in the Picture Styles group, point to Soft Edges, select 5 point, type French Program under the picture, then enhance it with Green, Accent 6, Darker 25%, bold, and 16 pt

MORE PRACTICE
For more practice with the skills presented in this project, complete Independent Challenge 2.

9. Center all content on the panel, adjust spacing above and below the photo to match the figure, delete the [Type here] placeholder in the header, exit the header, save the document and submit a copy to your instructor, then close both documents

   If possible, print the brochure on two sides of the same sheet of paper. If you cannot do so, place the two printed pages back to back, staple them, then fold them so that "Chicago Language School" appears on the front panel and the mailer information appears on the back panel.

Study Trip to France

Following the completion of Term 2, students fly to Paris and embark on a one-month stay in France that includes one week in each of four locations:

Week	Home Base	Highlights
One	Paris	World class museums, French cafes, walks along the Seine
Two	Tours	Chateaux of the Loire Valley
Three	Sarlat	Prehistoric sites and medieval towns in the Dordogne
Four	Aix en Provence	Sun, scenery, and the sweet life in Provence

Contact Us

Chicago Language School
200 Madison Street
Chicago, IL 60605

(312) 555-3321
www.chicagolanguage.org

Chicago Language School
200 Madison Street
Chicago, IL 60605

Your Name
Recipient Address
City, State, Zip

French Program

Chicago Language School

One-Page Résumé for Sharon Lee

Sharon Lee recently earned a Business Administration Certificate from Madison College in Tulsa, Oklahoma. Now, she needs to create an attractive one-page résumé to include with her job applications. For this project, you will **Create and Enhance the Résumé** The completed résumé is shown in FIGURE B-15.

Create and Enhance the Résumé

You need to set up the résumé heading, modify styles, and then create a table to contain the résumé text. Finally, you need to enter and format the text.

STEPS

HINT
Sharon's name is enhanced with 18 pt and bold.

1. Open a new document in Word, change the Left and Right margins to 1.2", type and center the name and address as shown in FIGURE B-15 (press [Shift][Enter] between each line), press [Enter] following the e-mail address, click the Align Text Left button ≡ in the Paragraph group, type Objective, press [Enter], then save the résumé as PR B-Sharon Lee Résumé to the location where you save the files for this book

HINT
In the Modify Style dialog box, click Format, Font to modify all the Font settings, click Format, Border to modify the borders and shading, then click Format, Paragraph to modify the Before and After spacing.

2. Click the DESIGN tab, select the Shaded Style Set, click the HOME tab, then modify the Heading 1 style as follows: 14 pt, bold, italic, black font color, and Small Caps, bottom border only with a width of 1½ pt and black, no shading, the Before Spacing set to 12 pt, and the After Spacing set to 3 pt

3. Apply the Heading 1 style to "Objective", press [Enter], type the text for the objective as shown in FIGURE B-15, press [Enter], then insert a table consisting of 2 columns and 10 rows

4. Select the table, click the TABLE TOOLS LAYOUT tab, click Properties in the Table group, click the Column tab, click the Next Column button, enter 1.5 as the preferred width of column 1, click the Next Column button, enter 4.8 as the preferred width of column 2, then click OK

5. Click the TABLE TOOLS DESIGN tab, select the table, click the Borders list arrow in the Borders group, then click No Border

6. Select the cells in the first row of the table, click the TABLE TOOLS LAYOUT tab, then click the Merge Cells button in the Merge group

7. Using FIGURE B-15 as your guide, type Education in the merged row, apply the Heading 1 style, press [Tab], type 2014-2016 in column 1 of the new row, press [Tab], type Madison College, Tulsa, OK in column 2, press [Enter], then type and format the text that appears under "Madison College"
   You will need to format "Madison College" with bold, format "Business Administration Certificate" with italic, and apply bullets to the list of skills.

8. Press [Tab] to go to the next row, type 2012 as shown, then complete the résumé as shown in FIGURE B-15
   Remember to merge the rows that contain headings (e.g., "Work Experience"), to apply the Heading 1 style to the headings, and to apply bold, italic, and bullets where required.

MORE PRACTICE
For more practice with the skills presented in this project, complete Independent Challenge 3.

9. Check the spelling and grammar, adjust spacing where necessary, type your name in the document footer, save the résumé, submit a copy to your instructor, then close it

Sharon Lee

120 Hamilton Street
Tulsa, OK 74015
(918) 555-3400 / sharonlee@webplace.org

OBJECTIVE

An Office Administrator position in a fast-paced environment where I can apply my expert level computer skills to streamline systems

EDUCATION

2014-2016	**Madison College**, Tulsa, OK
Business Administration Certificate

- Business Computing: Word, Excel, PowerPoint, Access, In Design, Dreamweaver
- Business Communications and Organizational Behavior
- Accounting and Bookkeeping: Simply Accounting
- Project Management
- Supervisory Skills

2012	**Elm View High School**
Graduated Grade 12, with honors

WORK EXPERIENCE

2012-2014	**Weston Bookkeeping**, 2300 Maple Street, Tulsa
Office Assistant (part time)
Responsibilities include:

- Maintain company records
- Format documents in Word 2013
- Organize company database with Access 2013

2010-2012	**Lakeside Camp**, Braggs, OK
Camp Counselor (summers)
Responsibilities included:

- Supervised groups of 10 campers aged 9 to 11
- Organized crafts and sports activities
- Assisted with general office duties

2011-2012	**Mario's Pizza**, Tulsa
Pizza waiter and cashier (part time)

VOLUNTEER EXPERIENCE

2014-2016	**Madison College Business Technology Department**
Student Activities Coordinator
2011-2012	**Food Bank**, Tulsa

Your Name

Independent Challenge 1

Write a multiple-page proposal that requests a significant change in a course, program, or company procedure. For example, you could request more hours of computer training as part of a college course or propose the setting up of a day care facility at your company. Alternatively, you could write a proposal to purchase new computer equipment or to establish a more equitable procedure for allocating holiday time. If you are a student, you may want to request that more classroom time be allocated to a specific topic such as the Internet or computerized accounting. If you are in the workplace, you could propose a new marketing strategy for a particular product or you could request new computer software (such as the latest Office upgrade). The possibilities are endless! Fill in the boxes provided below with information about your proposal and then follow the steps to create and format the proposal, a title page, and a table of contents page. The completed proposal should consist of approximately three pages of text (excluding the title page and table of contents).

1. Determine the subject of your proposal. To help you focus on a subject, ask yourself what changes you would like to see happen in your own workplace or at college. Write the principal request that your proposal will make in the box below:

Proposal Request: _____
_____
_____
_____

2. Determine the three or four principal sections of your proposal in addition to the introduction and conclusion. These sections will form the basis of your outline. For example, suppose you decide to write a proposal that requests changes to a college course on computer applications that you have just taken. You could organize your proposal into the following three sections:
   I. Recommended Software
   II. Laboratory Hours
   III. Learning Materials
   Under each of these headings you would describe the current situation in the course and then offer your recommendations for improvement. Write the three principal sections of your proposal in the box below:

I. _____

II. _____

III. _____

3. After each of the principal topics you listed above, add subheadings that further organize your proposal. Limit the number of additional headings to one or two for each section.
4. Start a new document in Word, switch to Outline view, then enter the headings and subheadings for your proposal. Remember to assign Level 1 to top level headings that will be formatted with the Heading 1 style and Levels 2 and 3 to lower level headings. A Level 2 heading is formatted with the Heading 2 style and a Level 3 heading is formatted with the Heading 3 style.
5. Save the proposal as **PR B-My Proposal** to the location where you save the files for this book.
6. In Outline view you can also choose to enter text under each heading. You assign the Body Text level to text that you want to appear as regular text below a heading or subheading. As you write, try to visualize your reader. What information does your reader need to make an informed decision concerning your request? How will your request directly affect your reader? What benefits will your reader gain by granting your request? What benefits will other people gain? All of these questions will help you to focus on communicating the information your reader needs in order to respond positively to the principal request your proposal makes.

Independent Challenge 1 (continued)

7. Once you are satisfied that your proposal includes all the required headings and subheadings, and most of the text required for the proposal, switch to Print Layout view.

8. Enter the remaining text for the proposal as needed. Make sure you include at least one table.

9. Apply a theme to your document, then select a new Style Set.

10. Modify the Heading 1 and Heading 2 styles (and the Heading 3 style if used) to use the formats of your choice. Experiment until you are satisfied that the document headings are clear, easy to read and reflect your own sense of design.

11. Modify the Normal style as needed to ensure the proposal text is spaced the way you want it.

12. Include at least two pictures in your proposal. Add captions to both pictures and modify the Caption style.

13. Apply picture effects to at least one of the pictures; experiment with the many ways in which you can change the appearance of a picture.

14. Apply an appropriate table style to each table in your proposal. Make sure you use a consistent style.

15. If you included a bulleted list, format the bullet character to use a different symbol and change the color of the bullet symbol.

16. Include a SmartArt graphic in an appropriate section of your proposal. For example, you could include a Target diagram that shows the steps toward a specific goal related to your proposal.

17. Insert a footer that includes your name at the left margin and the page number at the right margin.

18. Insert a Next Page section break above page 1 of your proposal, clear formatting, then generate a table of contents.

19. Insert a cover page using the style of your choice. Add text to controls and delete controls as needed. The cover page should, at a minimum, include a title and your name.

20. Change the page numbering style on the Table of Contents page to lowercase Roman numerals that start at "i", then click the Different First Page check box to select it.

21. Go to the first page of the proposal and set the page number to start at "1", then update the table of contents.

22. View the proposal in Multiple Pages view, make any spacing adjustments required, check spelling and grammar, save the document, submit a copy to your instructor, then close the document.

Independent Challenge 2

Create a two-page, six-panel brochure that advertises the products or services sold by a company (real or fictitious) of your choice. For example, you could create a brochure to advertise the programs offered by a public television station or to present the products sold by Quick Buzz, a company that sells high-energy snack foods. If you are involved in sports, your brochure could describe the sports training programs offered by a company called Fitness Forever, or if you are interested in art, your brochure could list the products sold by an art supply store called Painting Plus. For ideas, check out the pictures available on Office.com Clip Art. A particular clip art picture or photograph may provide you with an idea for a brochure subject.

1. Determine the name of your company and the products or services that it sells. Think of your own interests and then create a company that reflects these interests.

2. Select two or three products or services that your brochure will highlight. For example, a brochure for a landscaping company called Greenscapes could present information about bedding plant sales, landscaping design, and garden maintenance services.

3. Determine the information required for the two pages and six panels of your brochure. Remember that page 1 includes panels 2, 3, and 4 of the brochure (the inside panels) and page 2 includes the panel that folds into the center of the brochure, the back cover, and the front cover (panels 5, 6, and 1). You may wish to allocate one of the three inside panels for each of the products or services you have selected. For example, if you want to create a brochure for the Painting Plus art supply store, you could devote one panel to each of the three main types of products sold: painting supplies, papers and canvases, and drawing supplies. On panel 5, you could include a price list. Allocate panel 6 as a mailer panel that will include the return address of your company and placeholder text for recipient addresses.

4. Before you start creating the brochure in Word, sketch the brochure layout on two blank pieces of paper. Put the sketch back-to-back and fold the brochure so that you can see how it will appear to readers. The more time you spend planning your brochure, the fewer problems you will encounter when you start creating your brochure in Word.

5. Refer to the brochure you created in Unit B Project 2. If you wish, you can adapt this brochure to advertise programs at a different educational establishment.

6. In Word, start a new document, select Landscape orientation, then set the four margins to .3".

7. Select a theme for the brochure text, then modify the Heading 1 style so it uses the colors and spacing you prefer. Remember you can always adjust the Heading 1 style as you work.

8. Create an attractive header, footer, or both that appears only on page 1 of the brochure, then save the brochure as **PR B-My Brochure** to the location where you save the files for this book.

9. Press [Enter] once at the top of the page to leave some space, then create a table consisting of five columns. Set the widths of columns 1, 3, and 5 at 3.2" and columns 2 and 4 at .35".

10. Remove the border lines, then in the Table Properties dialog box, set the row height at exactly 6.8" and the Text wrapping on the Table tab to Around.

11. Enter the headings, text, tables, and any other enhancements for the three panels on page 1 of the brochure.

12. Include on either page of your brochure a photograph that appears partially behind the text. Experiment with the many ways you can use Picture Effects to create an interesting graphic that reinforces the message of your brochure.

13. Press [Tab] in the fifth column to create a new table row on page 2 of the brochure, then clear the formatting.

14. Make the center panel on page 2 (the back cover) a mailer panel with the text rotated. Refer to the brochure you created for Project 2 for a sample mailer.

15. On the front cover of the brochure, include a heading and a picture that will attract the reader's attention and inspire him or her to open the brochure to read its contents. Keep the design simple but compelling.

16. View the brochure in Multiple Pages view, check the spelling and grammar, make any spacing adjustments required, add your name in the mailer on panel 6, save the document, submit a copy to your instructor, then close the document.

Independent Challenge 3

Create or modify your own résumé. To help you determine the information required for your résumé, fill in the boxes below and then create the résumé in Word as directed.

1. Determine your objective. What kinds of positions are you looking for that will match your qualifications and experience? How will your skills help the company that employs you? Refer to the objective you typed in Unit B Project 3, then enter your objective in the box below:

Résumé Objective:

_____

_____

2. In the table below, list the components related to your educational background, starting with your most recent school or college. Note the name of the institution, the certificate or degree you received, and a selection of the courses relevant to the type of work you are seeking.

Year(s):	Institution:	Certificate/Degree:	Courses:

3. In the table below, list the details related to your work experience. Use parallel structure when listing your responsibilities; that is, make sure that each element uses the same grammatical structure. For example, you can start each point with a verb, such as "maintain," "manage," or "use," and then follow it with the relevant object, for example, "maintain company records" and "use Microsoft Word 2013 to create promotional materials." Make sure you use the appropriate tense: present tense for your current position and past tense for former positions.

Year(s):	Company or Institution:	Responsibilities:

Independent Challenge 3 (continued)

4. In the table below, describe any volunteer experience you have, awards you have received and, if you wish, your hobbies and interests:

Year(s):	Focus of Additional Information	Examples
	Volunteer Experience	
	Awards	
	Hobbies/Interests	

5. Set up your résumé in Word as follows:

  a. Type your name and format it attractively, then enter and enhance the appropriate contact information. Don't forget to include your e-mail address.

  b. Save the résumé as **PR B-My Résumé** to the location where you save the files for this book.

  c. Create a new style called **Résumé Heading Style** based on the Normal style with formatting you choose.

  d. Enter **Objective** formatted with the new Résumé Heading Style, then type your objective.

  e. Create a table consisting of two columns, then enter the headings and text required for your résumé. Refer to Unit B Project 3 for ideas.

  f. Fit the résumé to one page, check spelling and grammar, save the document, submit a copy to your instructor, then close the document.

Independent Challenge 4 - Team Project

To further explore how you can develop a wide range of documents with Word 2013, you will work with two other people to complete a team project. The subject of the team project is the assessment of a college program of your choice. The program should be one that all team members are familiar with. A good choice is a course or program that all team members have taken. Follow the guidelines provided below to create the three documents required for the team project. When you have completed the project, the team will submit a document containing information about the project, as well as three files related to the project: a program proposal, a program brochure, and a team résumé.

Project Setup

1. As a team, work together to complete the following tasks.

   - Share e-mail addresses among all three team members.
   - Set up a time (either via e-mail, an online chat session, Internet Messaging, or face to face) when you will get together to choose the program or venture you will assess and assign roles.
   - At your meeting, complete the table below with information about your team and the program you selected.

Team Name (last names of the team member or another name that describes the project; for example, "Lee-Tzerin-Jefferson" or "Marketing Program").
Team Members 1. 2. 3.
Program Title
Program Purpose (for example, to provide students with business skills or training in theater production, etc.)
Team Roles: Indicate who is responsible for each of the following three files (one file per team member) Program Proposal: Program Brochure: Team Résumé:
Document Formatting: Select a theme, Style Set, and color scheme that will be used to format all of the documents created for the Team Project. Theme: Style Set: Color Scheme:

Independent Challenge 4 - Team Project (continued)

Document Development

Individually, complete the tasks listed below for the file you are responsible for. You need to develop appropriate content, and format the file attractively. Be sure team members use the same theme, style set, and color scheme when creating the documents as detailed in the table above. Include the team name on all documents.

Program Proposal

This document is a multipage proposal that identifies a specific change that you and your team members feel would improve some aspect of the program you have selected. For example, you could write a proposal that requests a work experience component or a module on social networking in a communications course, or the development of a job database. Think about the program you have selected and how it could be improved. Refer to the guidelines provided in Independent Challenge 1 to help you identify the principal sections of your proposal. Limit the number of principal sections to three. Create the proposal as follows:

1. Create a new Word document and save it as **PR B-Team Project_Program Proposal** to the location where you save files for this book, then apply the document theme, Style Set, and color scheme selected by your team.
2. In Outline view, enter the headings and subheadings for the proposal. Remember to assign Level 1 to top level headings that will be formatted with the Heading 1 style and Levels 2 and 3 to lower level headings.
3. Enter text for the proposal either in Outline view or in Print Layout view. Include tables and bulleted lists as needed to communicate information clearly. The text for your proposal, including headings, tables, and bulleted lists should be about three pages, not including the cover page and table of contents.
4. Ensure the completed proposal includes the following components:
   - Modified heading styles and/or Normal style
   - At least one picture that includes a caption and has been modified with Picture Effects
   - At least one table formatted with a table style
   - At least one bulleted list that uses a bullet symbol other than the default symbols
   - At least one SmartArt graphic
   - A Table of Contents on a separate page with "i" page numbering in the footer
   - A Cover page using one of the Cover page styles that you modify in some way
5. Insert a section break between the Table of Contents page and the first page of the proposal text. In the footer, include a page number and the name of your team. Make sure the page number on the Table of Contents page is formatted as "i" and the page numbers for the proposal text start at "1".
6. Save the document and submit it to your instructor along with the other documents created by your team members.

Program Brochure

This document describes the program your team has chosen in a brochure that could be distributed to prospective students. The purpose of the brochure is to provide information about the program and to "sell" the program. The completed brochure should be printed on two sides of an 8 1/2 × 11" piece of paper in landscape orientation folded in thirds. Create the program brochure as follows:

1. On a blank piece of paper, sketch the panels of the brochure and determine what information you want to include in each panel. Refer to the brochure you created in this unit for design ideas. Refer to program information on your college Web site, for ideas regarding the content for the program brochure.

Independent Challenge 4 (continued)

2. Create a new Word document and save it as **PR B-Team Project_Program Brochure** to the location where you save files for this book, then apply the document theme, Style Set, and color scheme selected by your team.

3. Set up the document so that it prints in landscape orientation with .3" margins, press [Enter] once at the top of the page to create some space, then create a table consisting of five columns. Set the widths of columns 1, 3, and 5 at 3.2" and columns 2 and 4 at .4". Remove the border lines, then in the Table Properties dialog box, set the row height at exactly 6.8" and the Text wrapping on the Table tab to Around.

4. Enter the headings, text, tables and any other enhancements for the six panels of the brochure (three panels on each page).

5. Ensure the completed brochure includes the following components:
   - Modified heading styles and/or Normal style
   - At least one picture that has been modified and appears partially or wholly behind text
   - A header or a footer (or both) that appears only on page 1 of the brochure (the three inside panels)
   - A compelling cover panel

6. You can also choose to include a mailer as the back panel or you can use the back panel to contain contact information about the program.

7. View the brochure in Multiple Pages view, then make adjustments to the spacing so the program prints correctly.

8. Print a copy of the brochure, double-sided if possible, check that the spacing is correct when the program is folded, then make adjustments as needed.

9. Save the document and submit it to your instructor along with the other documents created by your team members.

Team Résumé

1. Sketch a one-page team résumé that summarizes information about each of the three team members. Use a table form with a section for each team member.

2. Create a new Word document and save it as **PR B-Team Project_Team Résumé** to the location where you save files for this book, then apply the document theme, Style Set, and color scheme selected by your team.

3. Adapt the résumé you created for Project 3 for use as a team résumé. Instead of an individual's name at the top of the document, you will include the name of the team and contact information for one person. Instead of headings such as "Work Experience" and "Education," include the name of each team member.

4. For each team member, include about ten lines of information describing the member's education and work experience. Use bulleted lists if you wish.

5. Format the text attractively so the completed document is contained on one page and provides readers with a clear and easy-to-read summary of each team member's experience and education.

6. Save the document and submit it to your instructor along with the other documents created by your team mates.

▶ Project Summary

As a team, complete the project summary as follows.

1. Open PR B-10.docx from the location where you save your Data Files, then save it to your **PR B-Team Project_Summary**.

2. Read the directions in the document, then ensure that each team member enters his or her name in one of the tables along with a short description of the skills used and the challenges faced by each member while creating the Word document.

3. Save the document, then submit all four documents to your instructor.

Visual Workshop

As part of a report you've prepared for Cedarview Designs about the launch of its new Web development strategy, you need to create the Cover page shown in **FIGURE B-16**. Start Word and create a new blank document. Select the Retrospect Cover Page style and the Depth theme. Delete the second page that was automatically inserted when you inserted the cover page. Change the color of the large bottom rectangle to Light Turquoise, Background 2, Darker 50%. (Note: The white space between the boxes is removed when the bottom box is no longer selected.) Add text to the placeholders as shown in **FIGURE B-16**, then delete unused placeholders. Click anywhere in the white space to select the text box that contains the Title and Subtitle controls, then drag the bottom of the text box up to position the Document Title and Subtitle controls toward the top of the page as shown in the figure and to create room to insert a picture. Double-click below the Subtitle content control (you will see several paragraph marks if show formatting marks is active), then click at any of the new paragraph marks and insert the picture file **PR B-11.jpg**. Change the text wrapping to Square, increase the height to 6", then position the picture as shown in the figure. Modify the picture with the following settings: Brightness: +40% Contrast: -20%, Color: Aqua, Accent color 1 Light, Artistic Effect: Photocopy. Save the cover page as **PR B-Web Development Cover Page** to the location where you save the files for this book, submit the file to your instructor, then close the document.

FIGURE B-16

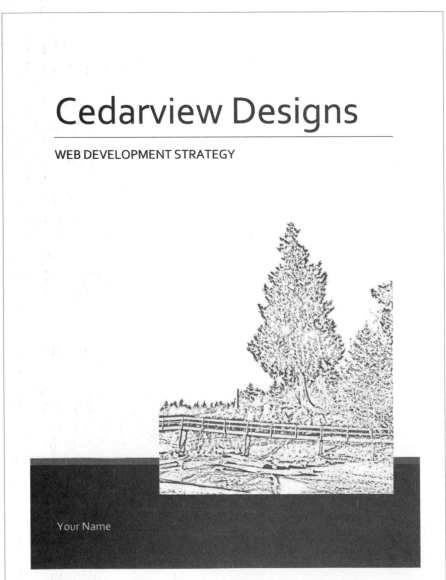

Excel Projects I

Projects

In this unit you will create the following:

Personal Budget

Set up the worksheet • Apply a theme • Format and align cells • Change column width • Use AutoFill • Use formulas • Enter absolute and relative values • Enter cell references between worksheets • Answer what-if questions • Create sparklines • Select non-adjacent cells • Adjust row height • Set print options (*Skills also practiced in Independent Challenge 1*)

Invoice Form and Tracker

Apply cell borders • Insert clip art • Apply cell formatting • Name sheet tabs • Copy/paste worksheets • Enter cell references between worksheets • Convert a table to a range • Group worksheets • Create a custom header • Format a table • Use the IF function • Filter table rows (*Skills also practiced in Independent Challenge 2*)

Loan Amortization Schedule

Apply text wrapping • Indent cell content • Use the PMT function • Edit a table • Create a custom header • Use the SUM function (*Skills also practiced in Independent Challenge 3*)

Team Project

Files You Will Need

PR C-01.docx

Personal Budget

One of the most useful ways in which you can use Excel in your daily life is to create a budget to keep track of your income and expenses. You can then use your budget to identify and track trends. For example, you can determine if you spend a consistent amount each month on entertainment or if you spend less in some months than in others. You can also use the budget to ask "what-if" questions to identify how best to allocate your resources. To create the personal budget, you **Enter and Enhance Labels**, **Calculate Totals**, **Ask What-If Questions**, and **Format and Print the Budget**. The completed budget appears in **FIGURE C-10** on page 63.

Enter and Enhance Labels

You create a worksheet, enter and enhance the worksheet title, then add the labels for the months of the year and the income and expense categories.

STEPS

1. Start Excel and open a new blank workbook, type Personal Six Month Budget, press [Enter], type the labels in cells A2 to A7 as shown in FIGURE C-1, then save the workbook as PR C-Personal Budget to the location where you save the files for this book

2. Click cell A1, click the PAGE LAYOUT tab, click Themes in the Themes group, click Slice, click the HOME tab, click the Font Size list arrow ⑪ ▾ in the Font group, change the font size to 20 pt, then click the Bold button Ⓑ in the Font group

3. Click cell A2, then change the font size to 16 pt

4. Select cells A1:H2, right-click the selection, click Format Cells, click the Alignment tab, click the Horizontal list arrow, click Center Across Selection, then click OK

5. Select cells A1:H1, click the Fill Color list arrow 🖌 ▾ in the Font group, click Dark Green, Accent 3, Darker 25%, click the Font Color list arrow 🅰 ▾ in the Font group, then click White, Background 1

6. Click cell B3, type JAN, move the pointer over the lower-right corner to show the Fill Handle pointer ✚, drag ✚ to cell G3, click the Center button ≡ in the Alignment group, click cell H3, then type Totals

   The labels for the months from January to June are added and centered.

7. Click B on the worksheet frame, click and drag to select columns B to H as shown in FIGURE C-2, click Format in the Cells group, click Column Width, type 14, then click OK

8. Click cell A9, then enter the labels required for cells A9:A23 as shown in FIGURE C-3

9. Click the REVIEW tab, click the Spelling button in the Proofing group, click Yes if prompted, correct any spelling errors, then save the workbook

FIGURE C-1: Labels for Cells A1 to A7

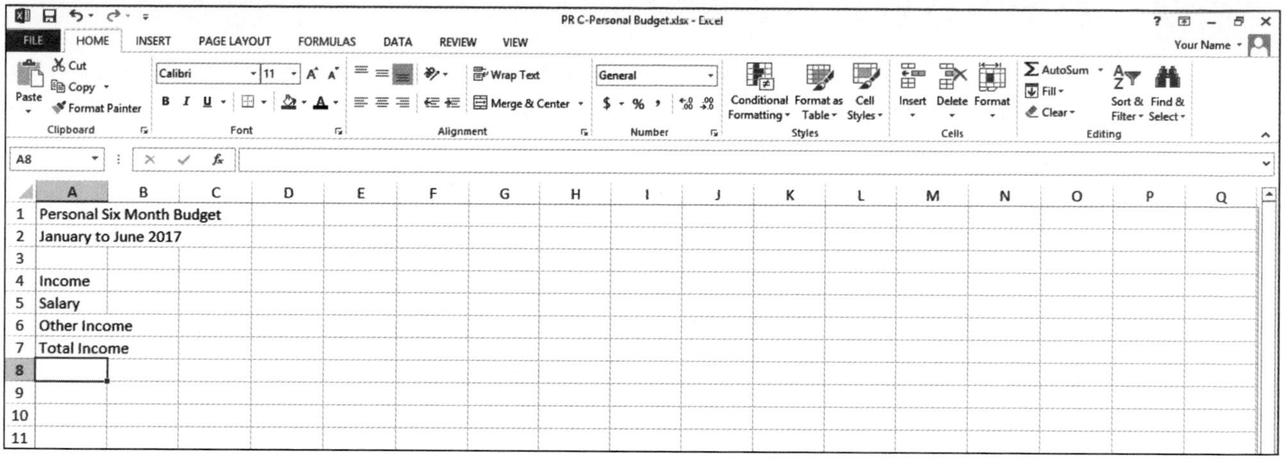

FIGURE C-2: Selecting columns

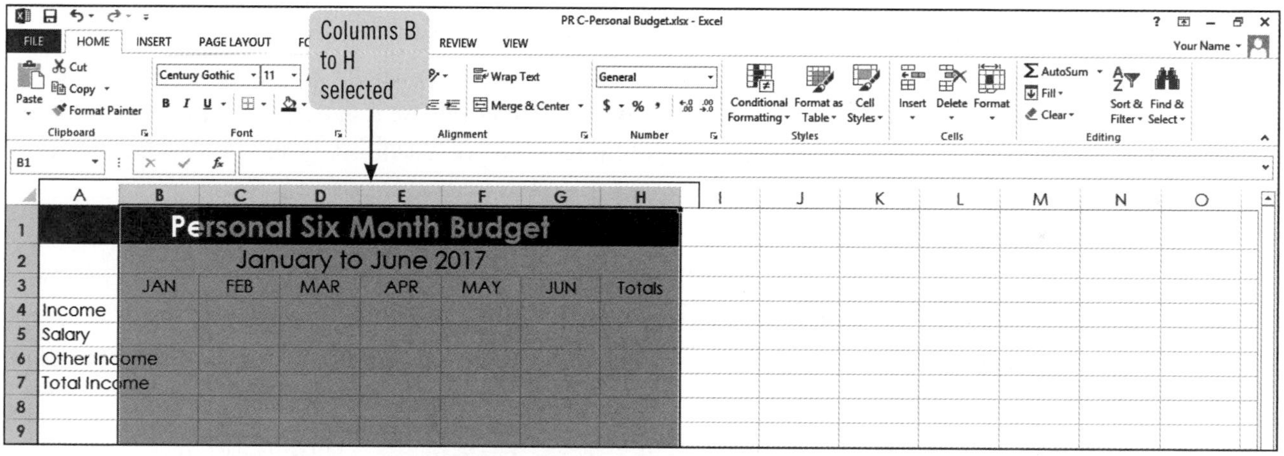

FIGURE C-3: Labels for Cells A9 to A23

	A	B	C	D
7	Total Income			
8				
9	Expenses			
10	Housing			
11	Grocery			
12	Car Payment			
13	Home Phone			
14	Cell Phone			
15	Internet			
16	Cable TV			
17	Utilities			
18	Entertainment			
19	Student Loan			
20	Savings			
21	Total Expenses			
22				
23	Cash Available			
24				

Labels for cells A9 to A23

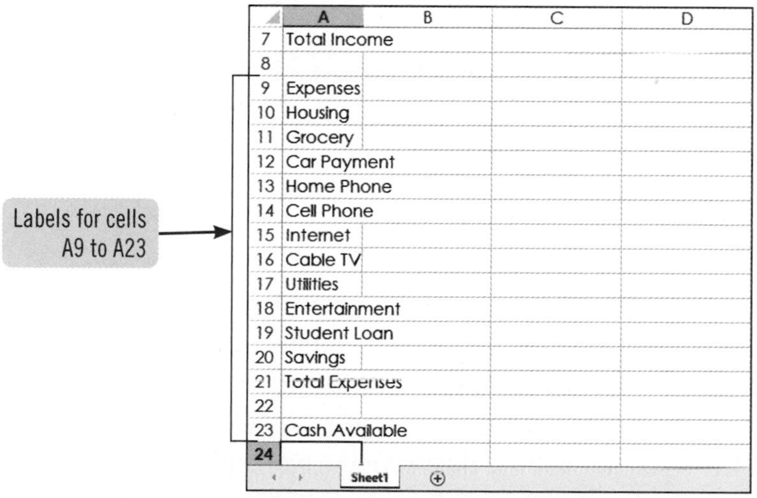

Merging cells

A merged cell is created by combining two or more cells into a single cell. The cell reference for the merged cell is the upper-left cell of the originally selected range. When you merge a range of cells containing data, only the data in the upper-left cell of the range is included in the merged cell. If you want to merge cells in a single row quickly, use the Merge and Center button in the Alignment group on the HOME tab and then adjust the alignment as needed. If you want to merge cells in several consecutive rows, use the Alignment tab in the Format Cells dialog box.

Calculate Totals

You need to enter the income and expenses for the first six months of the year. Then, you need to calculate self-employment income, total income, and expenses.

STEPS

1. Double-click the column divider between columns A and B on the worksheet frame to increase the width of column A to fit all the labels, click cell B10, enter the values for January as shown in FIGURE C-4, select cells B10:B20, position the pointer over the lower-right corner of cell B20, then drag ＋ to cell G20

HINT
You use a new worksheet to avoid cluttering the first worksheet with data that will not be printed.

2. Double-click the Sheet1 tab at the bottom of the worksheet, type Budget, press [Enter], click ⊕, double-click the Sheet2 tab, type Other Income, then press [Enter]

   In addition to your salary, you have earned income from Web site design work and garden work.

3. Type Hours in cell A1, press [Enter], select cells A1:G1, click the HOME tab, click the Merge & Center button in the Alignment group, fill the merged cell with Dark Green, Accent 3, Lighter 80%, click the Bold button B, click cell B2, type January, fill the range C2:G2 with the remaining months, then bold and center the labels

4. Using FIGURE C-5 as a guide, enter and format the labels and values in cells A3 to G11, widening column A as needed

   Your worksheet should look like FIGURE C-5.

5. Click cell B6, enter the formula =B3*B10, press [Enter], then copy the formula to cell G6

   Oops! Cells C6 through G6 contain no values. Why? When you copied the formula, Excel changed the cell references in the copied formula because the formulas contained relative references. You need to enter a formula in cell B6 that uses an absolute reference for cell B10 (the rate of pay for Web work). When you use an absolute cell reference, the value associated with the absolute cell reference remains constant no matter where the formula is copied to in the worksheet.

HINT
If your computer supports the use of function keys, press [F4] or [Fn][F4] to insert the dollar signs in the selected cell reference.

6. Click cell B6, select B10 in the formula bar, type $B$10, press [Enter], click cell B6 again, then drag ＋ to fill cells C6:G6 with the revised formula

7. Click cell B7, enter the formula =B4*$B$11, copy the formula to cell G7, select the range B6:G8, then click the AutoSum button in the Editing group

   In January and February, $ -, is displayed in cells B7 and C7 because no hours were worked during those months.

8. Click the Budget tab, click cell B6, type =, click the Other Income tab, click cell B8, press [Enter], then drag ＋ in cell B6 to fill the range C6:G6

9. Click cell B5, type 2650, use the fill handle to copy the value to the range C5:G5, select the range B5:H7, click the AutoSum button in the Editing group, select the range B10:H21, click the AutoSum button, then save the workbook

   The total income displayed in cell H7 is 19050 and the total expenses shown in cell H21 are 15780 as shown in FIGURE C-6 (shown in 90% zoom).

FIGURE C-4: Values for cells B10 to B20

	A	B	C	D
7	Total Income			
8				
9	Expenses			
10	Housing	1000		
11	Grocery	300		
12	Car Payment	350		
13	Home Phone	40		
14	Cell Phone	75	←	Values for January expenses
15	Internet	40		
16	Cable TV	50		
17	Utilities	75		
18	Entertainment	200		
19	Student Loan	300		
20	Savings	200		
21	Total Expenses			
22				
23	Cash Available			
24				

Sheet1 ⊕

FIGURE C-5: Labels and values for the Other Income sheet

	A	B	C	D	E	F	G	H
1				Hours				
2		January	February	March	April	May	June	
3	Web	15	10	20	10	5	5	
4	Garden	0	0	5	10	10	10	
5				Total Pay				
6	Web							
7	Garden							
8	Total Pay							
9								
10	Web Rate	$ 35.00						
11	Garden Rate	$ 25.00						
12								

FIGURE C-6: Worksheet completed with totals

	A	B	C	D	E	F	G	H	I	J	K	L	M	N	O
1				Personal Six Month Budget											
2				January to June 2017											
3		JAN	FEB	MAR	APR	MAY	JUN	Totals							
4	Income														
5	Salary	2650	2650	2650	2650	2650	2650	15900							
6	Other Income	$ 525.00	$ 350.00	$ 825.00	$ 600.00	$ 425.00	$ 425.00	$ 3,150.00							
7	Total Income	3175	3000	3475	3250	3075	3075	19050							
8															
9	Expenses														
10	Housing	1000	1000	1000	1000	1000	1000	6000							
11	Grocery	300	300	300	300	300	300	1800							
12	Car Payment	350	350	350	350	350	350	2100							
13	Home Phone	40	40	40	40	40	40	240							
14	Cell Phone	75	75	75	75	75	75	450							
15	Internet	40	40	40	40	40	40	240							
16	Cable TV	50	50	50	50	50	50	300							
17	Utilities	75	75	75	75	75	75	450							
18	Entertainment	200	200	200	200	200	200	1200							
19	Student Loan	300	300	300	300	300	300	1800							
20	Savings	200	200	200	200	200	200	1200							
21	Total Expenses	2630	2630	2630	2630	2630	2630	15780							
22															
23	Cash Available														

Total income is 19050

Total expenses is 15780

Budget   Other Income   ⊕

READY

Understanding relative and absolute references

By default, Microsoft Excel considers all values entered in formulas as relative values. That is, Excel automatically changes all cell addresses in a formula when you copy the formula to a new location. If you do not want Excel to change the cell address of a value when you copy it, you must make the value absolute. To do this, you enter a dollar sign ($) before both the column and the row designation in the address. For example, $C$26 tells Excel that the reference to cell C26 must not change, even if you copy the formula to a new location in the worksheet. If your computer supports the use of Function keys, you can click the cell reference and then press [F4] or [Fn][F4] to insert the $.

Ask What-If Questions

You need to calculate how much cash is available each month, and then perform the calculations required to answer several what-if questions. You also create sparklines to provide a quick visual review of monthly variations in income, expenses, and cash flow.

STEPS

1. **Click cell B23 on the Budget tab, enter the formula =B7-B21, press [Enter], then copy the formula across to cell H23**

   The total cash available at the end of six months, given the current level of income and expenses is 3270. The first what-if question is "What if you raise the hourly rate charged for Web Design work to $50?"

2. **Click the Other Income tab, click cell B10, type 50, press [Enter], widen columns if ## marks appear, then click the Budget tab**

   By changing the amount charged for Web Design work, you answer the what-if question and see that your total profit in cell G23 increases to 4245. Next, you want to know, "What if an increase in the hourly rate for Web design work results in a 40-percent drop in the number of hours worked from January to June?"

3. **Click the Other Income tab, click 4 on the worksheet frame to select row 4, click the Insert button in the Cells group (a new row appears above "Garden"), click cell A4, type 40%, click cell B4, enter the formula =B3-(B3*$A$4) as shown in FIGURE C-7, press [Enter], then copy the formula to the range C4:G4**

4. **Click cell B7, select B3 in the formula bar, type B4, press [Enter], copy the revised formula to cell G7, then click the Budget tab**

   The new total in cell H23 is 2945—quite a reduction from 4245! Perhaps you shouldn't raise the hourly rate if the result is a 40-percent drop in the number of hours worked.

5. **Click the Undo button ↶ until the extra row is removed from the Other Income sheet and the value in cell B10 is again $35.00 (you will click the Undo button about ten times), then return to the Budget sheet**

   The value in cell H23 is again 3270. Next, you want to know, "What if Housing costs increase to $1,200/month?" starting in March?

6. **Click cell E10 in the Budget sheet, type 1200, then drag the fill handle to cell G10**

   If you increase your housing cost, you reduce your total available cash (cell H23) to 2670. You can experiment endlessly with entering various combinations of values for income and expenses to see the effect on the "bottom line."

7. **Click cell I3, type Trend, press [Enter], click cell I7, click the INSERT tab, click Column in the Sparklines group, move the Create Sparklines dialog box down as needed so you can see row 7, select the range B7:G7, then click OK**

   You insert a Column sparkline to provide a visual representation of the variation in income over the six months covered by the budget.

8. **Click the High Point check box in the Show group, click the HOME tab, click the Copy button in the Clipboard group, click cell I21, click the Paste button, click cell I23, then click the Paste button**

9. **Modify values as shown in the highlighted cells in FIGURE C-8, verify that 2230 appears in cell H23, then save the workbook**

Excel Projects I

FIGURE C-7: Calculating a reduction in hours worked

Formula in cell B4

	A	B	C	D	E	F	G	H	I
1				Hours					
2		January	February	March	April	May	June		
3	Web	15	10	20	10	5	5		
4	40%	=B3-(B3*$A$4)							
5	Garden	0	0	5	10	10	10		
6				Total Pay					
7	Web	$ 750.00	$ 500.00	$1,000.00	$ 500.00	$ 250.00	$ 250.00		
8	Garden	$ -	$ -	$ 125.00	$ 250.00	$ 250.00	$ 250.00		
9	Total Pay	$ 750.00	$ 500.00	$1,125.00	$ 750.00	$ 500.00	$ 500.00		
10									
11	Web Rate	$ 50.00							
12	Garden Rate	$ 25.00							
13									
14									
15									
16									
17									
18									
19									
20									
21									

VLOOKUP — fx =B3-(B3*$A$4)

Budget | Other Income

FIGURE C-8: Values to modify in the Budget sheet

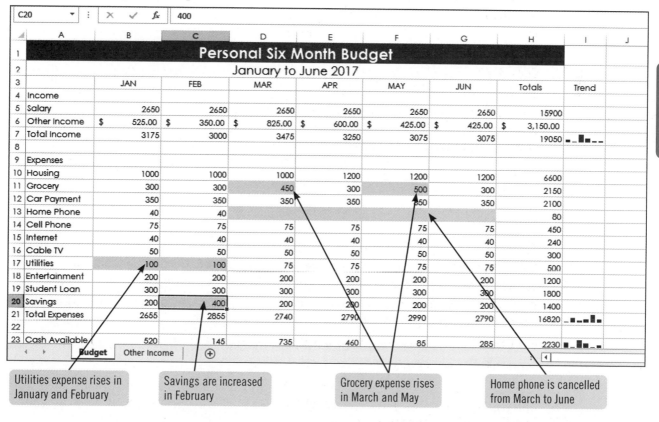

C20 — fx 400

	A	B	C	D	E	F	G	H	I	J
1				Personal Six Month Budget						
2				January to June 2017						
3		JAN	FEB	MAR	APR	MAY	JUN	Totals	Trend	
4	Income									
5	Salary	2650	2650	2650	2650	2650	2650	15900		
6	Other Income	$ 525.00	$ 350.00	$ 825.00	$ 600.00	$ 425.00	$ 425.00	$ 3,150.00		
7	Total Income	3175	3000	3475	3250	3075	3075	19050		
8										
9	Expenses									
10	Housing	1000	1000	1000	1200	1200	1200	6600		
11	Grocery	300	300	450	300	500	300	2150		
12	Car Payment	350	350	350	350	350	350	2100		
13	Home Phone	40	40					80		
14	Cell Phone	75	75	75	75	75	75	450		
15	Internet	40	40	40	40	40	40	240		
16	Cable TV	50	50	50	50	50	50	300		
17	Utilities	100	100	75	75	75	75	500		
18	Entertainment	200	200	200	200	200	200	1200		
19	Student Loan	300	300	300	300	300	300	1800		
20	Savings	200	400	200	200	200	200	1400		
21	Total Expenses	2655	2855	2740	2790	2990	2790	16820		
22										
23	Cash Available	520	145	735	460	85	285	2230		

Budget | Other Income

Utilities expense rises in January and February

Savings are increased in February

Grocery expense rises in March and May

Home phone is cancelled from March to June

Format and Print the Budget

To make the worksheet easier to read, you need to add border lines and fills to selected cells, format values using either the Accounting Number Format or the Comma Style (depending on their location in the worksheet), and then use a variety of Page Setup features.

STEPS

1. Select cells A3:I3 on the Budget tab, click the Border list arrow ⊞ ▾ in the Font group, click More Borders, then refer to FIGURE C-9: click the single thick border in the Style list, click the Color list arrow, click Dark Green, Accent 3, Darker 25%, click the Top Border button, click the Bottom border button, click OK, then apply bold

HINT
To complete these steps, use the completed budget in FIGURE C-10 as a guide.

2. Select cells A5:A6, fill them with Dark Green, Accent 3, Lighter 60%, fill the range B5:H6 with Dark Green, Accent 3, Lighter 80%, then format the Expenses cells with Red, Accent 6, Lighter 60% and Lighter 80% and the Cash Available row with Dark Blue, Text 2, Lighter 60% and Lighter 80%

3. Click cell A4, press and hold the [Ctrl] key, click cells A7, A9, A21, and A23, then apply Bold

   You use the [Ctrl] key to select a series of nonadjacent cells.

4. Select the range B5:H23, then click the Comma Style button ⁹ in the Number group

5. Select the range B5:H5, press and hold the [Ctrl] key, select the range B7:H7, B10:H10 B21:H21 and B23:H23, then click the Accounting Number Format button $ in the Number group

6. Select cells A1:I1, click the Merge & Center button in the Alignment group, then merge and center cells A2:I2

   When you add columns to a worksheet, you sometimes need to adjust how cells are merged so the worksheet appears balanced.

7. Click 7 on the worksheet frame, press and hold [Ctrl], select row 21 and row 23, click the Format button in the Cells group, click Row Height, type 30, click OK, select and fill cells A8:I8 with Dark Green, Accent 3, Darker 25%, then repeat for cells A22:I22, select row 8 and row 22, then set the row height at 8

   With an increased row height, the sparklines are more visible. The narrow rows look like border lines which gives the worksheet a finished look.

8. Click the FILE tab, click Print, click Portrait Orientation, click Landscape Orientation, click the Page Setup link at the bottom of the Print pane, click the Margins tab, click to select the Horizontally and Vertically check boxes, click the Header/Footer tab, click Custom Header, type Personal Budget in the left section, press [Tab] twice, type your name in the right section, click OK, then click OK again

9. Click the No Scaling list arrow, click Fit Sheet on One Page, then compare the completed worksheet to FIGURE C-10

MORE PRACTICE
For more practice with the skills presented in this project, complete Independent Challenge 2.

10. Click ◀ to exit Backstage view, save the file and submit it to your instructor, then close the workbook

FIGURE C-9: **Format Cells dialog box**

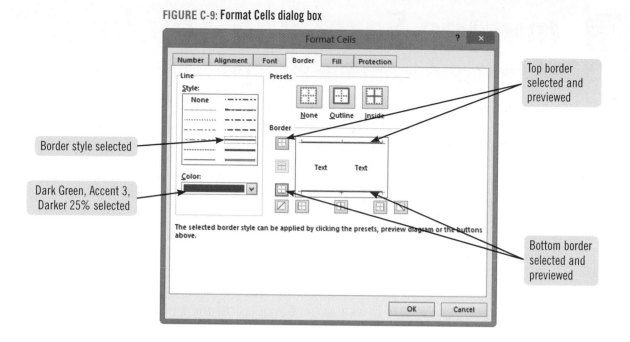

Top border selected and previewed

Border style selected

Dark Green, Accent 3, Darker 25% selected

Bottom border selected and previewed

FIGURE C-10: **Completed budget**

Personal Budget   Your Name

Personal Six Month Budget
January to June 2017

		JAN		FEB		MAR		APR		MAY		JUN		Totals	Trend
Income															
Salary	$	2,650.00	$	2,650.00	$	2,650.00	$	2,650.00	$	2,650.00	$	2,650.00	$	15,900.00	
Other Income		525.00		350.00		825.00		600.00		425.00		425.00		3,150.00	
Total Income	$	3,175.00	$	3,000.00	$	3,475.00	$	3,250.00	$	3,075.00	$	3,075.00	$	19,050.00	
Expenses															
Housing	$	1,000.00	$	1,000.00	$	1,000.00	$	1,200.00	$	1,200.00	$	1,200.00	$	6,600.00	
Grocery		300.00		300.00		450.00		300.00		500.00		300.00		2,150.00	
Car Payment		350.00		350.00		350.00		350.00		350.00		350.00		2,100.00	
Home Phone		40.00		40.00										80.00	
Cell Phone		75.00		75.00		75.00		75.00		75.00		75.00		450.00	
Internet		40.00		40.00		40.00		40.00		40.00		40.00		240.00	
Cable TV		50.00		50.00		50.00		50.00		50.00		50.00		300.00	
Utilities		100.00		100.00		75.00		75.00		75.00		75.00		500.00	
Entertainment		200.00		200.00		200.00		200.00		200.00		200.00		1,200.00	
Student Loan		300.00		300.00		300.00		300.00		300.00		300.00		1,800.00	
Savings		200.00		400.00		200.00		200.00		200.00		200.00		1,400.00	
Total Expenses	$	2,655.00	$	2,855.00	$	2,740.00	$	2,790.00	$	2,990.00	$	2,790.00	$	16,820.00	
Cash Available	$	520.00	$	145.00	$	735.00	$	460.00	$	85.00	$	285.00	$	2,230.00	

Invoice Form and Tracker

Vista Landscaping provides gardening and landscaping services to homes in Palm Springs, California. The owner of the company has asked you to create a simple invoice form that she can use to bill her customers. She also wants you to create a worksheet that she can use to keep track of the invoices she sends out. To create the invoice and invoice tracker, you **Create the Invoice Form**, **Enter Invoice Information**, and **Develop the Invoice Tracker**. The completed invoice form is shown in FIGURE C-13 and the completed invoice tracker appears in FIGURE C-17 on page 69.

Create the Invoice Form

You need to create an invoice form that includes labels for all the information the owner and customers require, is easy to read and understand, and prints on one page.

STEPS

1. Open a new workbook in Excel, apply the Parallax theme, type Vista Landscaping in cell A1 and INVOICE in cell H1, select the range A1:H1, fill the cells with Lime, Accent 2, Darker 25%, change the font color to white, then with the cells still selected, increase the font size to 24 pt and apply bold

2. Click cell H1, click the Align Right button ☰ in the Alignment group, then save the workbook as PR C-Invoice Form and Tracker to the location where you save the files for this book

3. Select column A, click the Format button in the Cells group, set the width of the column at 18, set the column width of column H to 14, then enter and format the labels as shown in FIGURE C-11

4. Select cells B7:D9, click the Borders list arrow 🔲 ▾, click Outside Borders, select the range H6:H9, then click the Borders button 🔲

5. Click cell A11, type Quantity, press [Tab], type Unit, press [Tab], type Description, click cell G11, type Unit Price, press [Tab], then type Amount

6. Select the range C11:F11, click the Merge & Center button in the Alignment group, select the range A11:H11, apply bold and center alignment, then fill the cells with Lime, Accent 2, Lighter 60%

7. Select the range C12:F12, click the Merge & Center button, click the lower-right corner of cell F12, then drag ➕ to cell F25

   The cells under the Description heading are wider, allowing more room for the description.

8. Select the range A12:H25, click the Borders list arrow 🔲, click All Borders, then complete the bottom of the form so that it appears as shown in FIGURE C-12

9. Click cell E1, click the INSERT tab, click Online Pictures, click in the Office.com Clip Art search box, type palm tree, press [Enter], click the palm tree shown in FIGURE C-13, then click Insert

10. Click the picture in the worksheet, select the contents of the Height text box in the Size group, type 1, press [Enter], use your mouse to position the picture so that it appears to the left of INVOICE as shown in FIGURE C-13, then save the workbook

FIGURE C-11: Labels entered and enhanced

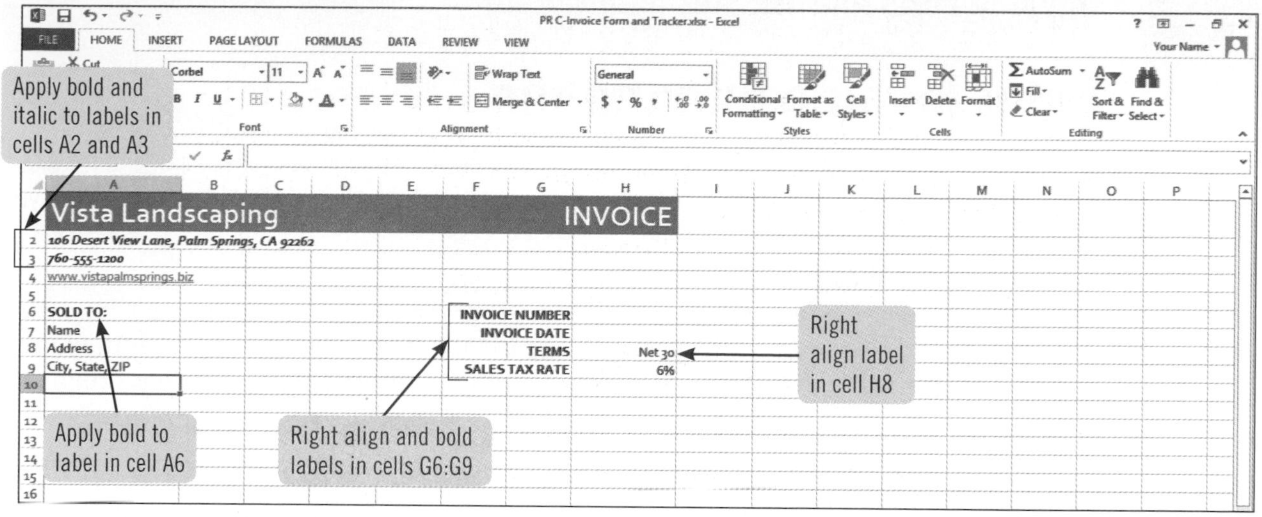

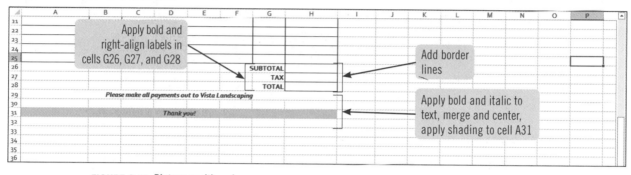

Apply bold and italic to labels in cells A2 and A3
Apply bold to label in cell A6
Right align and bold labels in cells G6:G9
Right align label in cell H8
Vista Landscaping
INVOICE
106 Desert View Lane, Palm Springs, CA 92262
760-555-1200
www.vistapalmsprings.biz
SOLD TO:
Name
Address
City, State, ZIP
INVOICE NUMBER
INVOICE DATE
TERMS
SALES TAX RATE
Net 30
6%

FIGURE C-12: Labels for rows 26 to 31

Apply bold and right-align labels in cells G26, G27, and G28
Add border lines
Apply bold and italic to text, merge and center, apply shading to cell A31
SUBTOTAL
TAX
TOTAL
Please make all payments out to Vista Landscaping
Thank you!

FIGURE C-13: Picture positioned

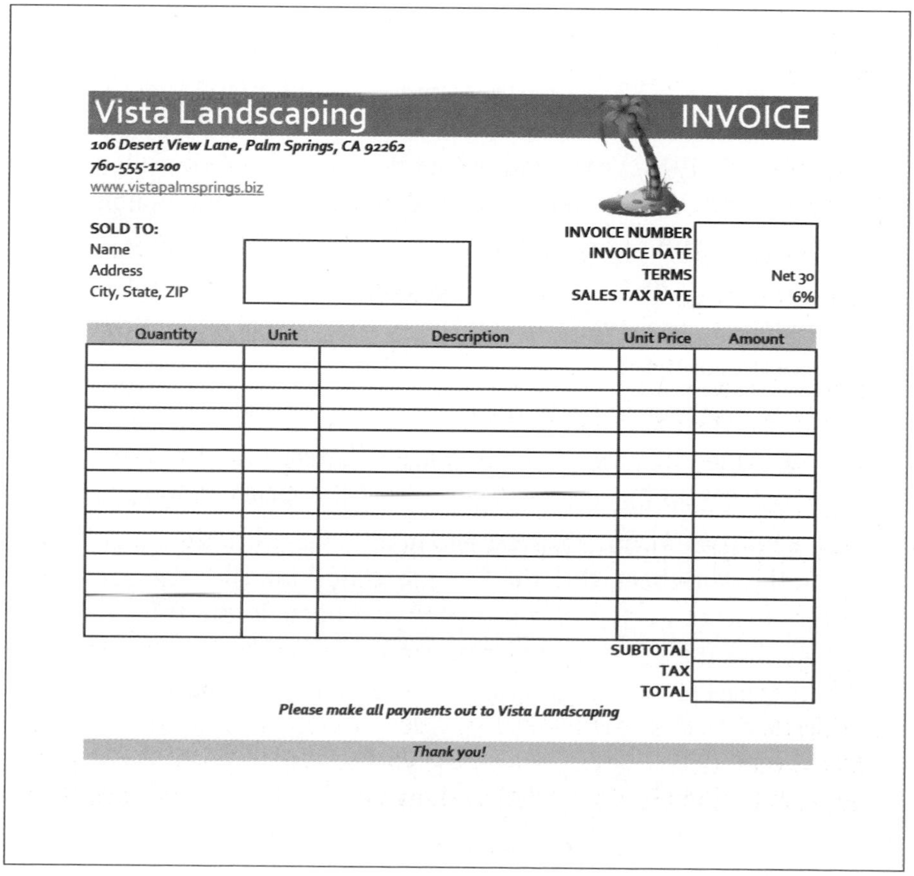

Vista Landscaping
INVOICE
106 Desert View Lane, Palm Springs, CA 92262
760-555-1200
www.vistapalmsprings.biz
SOLD TO:
Name
Address
City, State, ZIP
INVOICE NUMBER
INVOICE DATE
TERMS
SALES TAX RATE
Net 30
6%
Quantity
Unit
Description
Unit Price
Amount
SUBTOTAL
TAX
TOTAL
Please make all payments out to Vista Landscaping
Thank you!

Excel 2013

Enter Invoice Information

A useful form is one into which you only need to enter variable information such as the name of the client and the various items they purchased. First, you enter formulas into the blank form and then you complete the form for three different clients.

STEPS

HINT

No values are displayed in cells H12:H25 because you have not yet entered values in the cells associated with the formulas.

1. Click cell H12, type =A12*G12, press [Enter], use the fill handle to copy the formula to cell H25, then click the Accounting Number Format button $ in the Number group

2. Click cell H26, type =SUM(H12:H25), press [Enter], enter the formula =H26*H9 to calculate the sales tax based on the values in cells H26 and H9, press [Enter], enter the formula =H26+H27, then press [Enter]

3. Select the range G12:G25, click the Accounting Number Format button $, select the range C12:C25, then click the Align Left button ≣

4. Double-click the Sheet1 tab, type Invoice Form, press [Enter], click ⊕, name the new sheet 101, then add two more sheets named 102 and 103 respectively

   You will keep one copy of the invoice form in the Invoice Form tab, and then create three new invoices—one invoice per tab. By keeping all invoices together in one workbook, the owner of Vista Landscaping simplifies her billing procedures.

5. Click the Invoice Form tab, click the Select All button ◢ at the top left corner of the worksheet frame to select the entire worksheet, click the Copy button, click the 101 tab, click the Paste button, click the 102 tab, click the Paste button, then paste the invoice form in the 103 sheet

HINT

Remember to enter the correct invoice number in cell H6 in each invoice. Check Invoice 101 or **FIGURE C-14** for hourly rates for consultation and site preparation.

6. Go to the 101 sheet, complete invoice 101 as shown in FIGURE C-14, verify that the total value in cell H28 is $2,082.90, then enter data in tab 102 and 103 according to the following information:

   On May 20, 2016, Vista Landscaping did 25 hours of consultation work for Martha Lalonde of 34 Western Road in Palm Springs (92265) and bought 10 plants (assorted shrubs) at a cost of $25 each.

   On May 28, 2016, Vista Landscaping did 5 hours of landscape design and consultation for Peter Ng of 100 Sunrise Place in Palm Springs (92266) and 45 hours of site preparation.

7. Verify that the total in sheet 102 is $2,252.50 and the total in 103 is $2,544.00

8. Click ⊕, name the new tab Tracker, press [Enter], drag the tab to the right of Invoice Form, then set up the Tracker sheet so that it appears as shown in FIGURE C-15

HINT

Use the ScreenTips to find the Insert Sheet Name button.

9. Click the Invoice Form tab, press and hold [Shift], click the 103 tab to select all five tabs in the worksheet, click the FILE tab, click Print, click Page Setup, click the Header/Footer tab, click Custom Header, enter your name in the Left section, click in the Right section, click the Insert Sheet Name button, click OK, click OK, then save the workbook

   By selecting multiple tabs, you group them into one worksheet so you that you create the header for all five worksheets at the same time.

FIGURE C-14: Completed Invoice 101

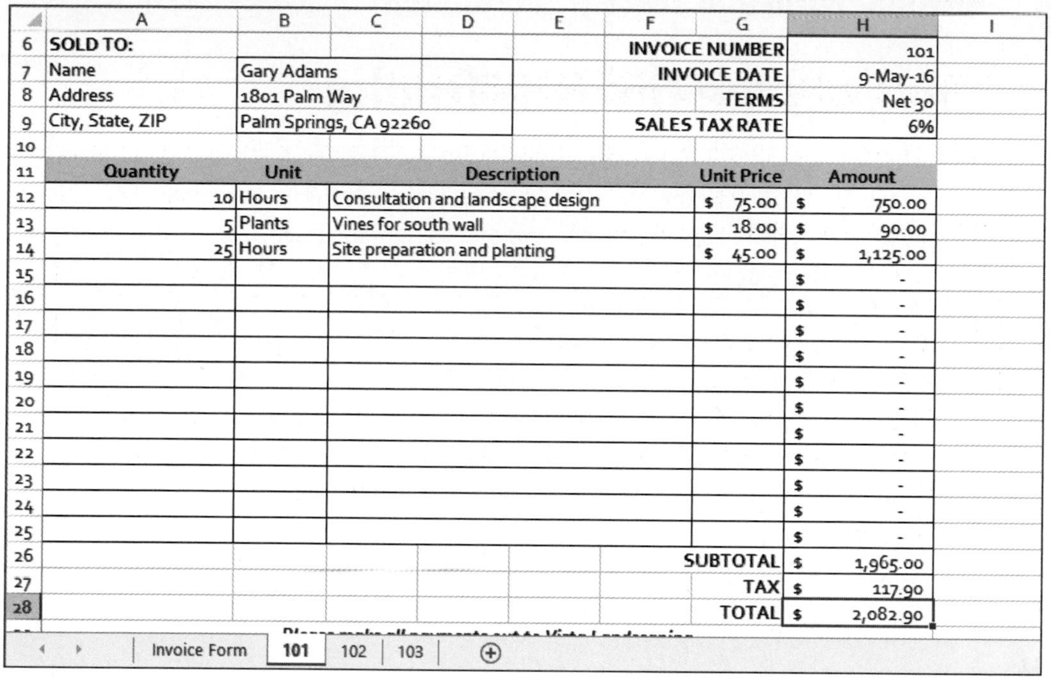

	A	B	C	D	E	F	G	H	I
6	SOLD TO:					INVOICE NUMBER		101	
7	Name	Gary Adams				INVOICE DATE		9-May-16	
8	Address	1801 Palm Way				TERMS		Net 30	
9	City, State, ZIP	Palm Springs, CA 92260				SALES TAX RATE		6%	
10									
11	Quantity		Unit		Description		Unit Price	Amount	
12	10		Hours	Consultation and landscape design			$ 75.00	$ 750.00	
13	5		Plants	Vines for south wall			$ 18.00	$ 90.00	
14	25		Hours	Site preparation and planting			$ 45.00	$ 1,125.00	
15								$ -	
16								$ -	
17								$ -	
18								$ -	
19								$ -	
20								$ -	
21								$ -	
22								$ -	
23								$ -	
24								$ -	
25								$ -	
26							SUBTOTAL	$ 1,965.00	
27							TAX	$ 117.90	
28							TOTAL	$ 2,082.90	

Invoice Form | **101** | 102 | 103 | (+)

Excel 2013

FIGURE C-15: Labels for the Invoice Tracker

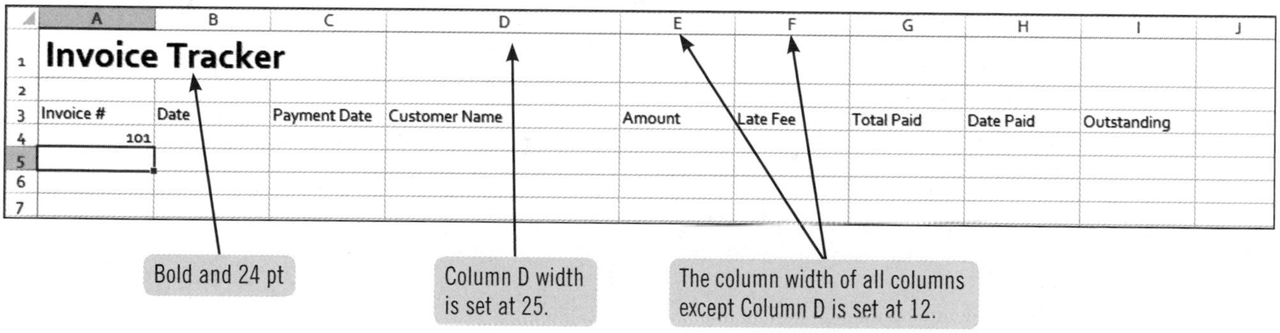

	A	B	C	D	E	F	G	H	I	J
1	**Invoice Tracker**									
2										
3	Invoice #	Date		Payment Date	Customer Name	Amount	Late Fee	Total Paid	Date Paid	Outstanding
4	101									
5										
6										
7										

Bold and 24 pt

Column D width is set at 25.

The column width of all columns except Column D is set at 12.

Develop the Invoice Tracker

You can use Excel to automate so many common business tasks including keeping track of invoices in one easy to read list. You format the Invoice Tracker as a table that will list information about each of the three invoices you have created and then enter invoice data from the three Invoice tabs. The completed Invoice Tracker is shown in **FIGURE C-17**.

1. **In the Invoice Tracker, select the range A3:I20, click** Format as Table **in the Styles group, select** Table Style Medium 6 (pink), **click the** My table has headers check box **to select it, click** OK, **click the** Banded Rows check box **in the Table Style Options group to deselect it, click** Convert to Range **in the Tools group, then click** Yes

   You've formatted the Invoice Tracker as a tables so that you can quickly apply border lines and shading. You then convert the table to a range so that you can turn off the calculated columns feature. When you are entering cell references from other sheets into a table with the calculated columns feature active, you can get unexpected results when you copy formulas.

2. **Click cell A5, type 102, select cells A4 and A5, then drag the fill handle from cell A5 to cell A20 to fill all the cells with invoice numbers in sequential order**

   You set up the sequence by entering 101 and then 102. If you copied only 101, you would fill the column with 101, rather than with the sequential numbers: 101, 102, 103, and so on.

3. **Enter the values from invoice 101 in the tracker as follows: click cell B4, type =, click the 101 tab, click cell H7, press [Enter], click cell C4, type = B4+30, press [Enter], click cell D4, type =, click the 101 tab, click cell B7, press [Enter], click cell E4, type =, click the 101 tab, click cell H28 to select the invoice total, press [Enter], then enter 2000 in cell G4 and June 15, 2016 in cell H4**

4. **Select the range F4:G20, press and hold the [CTRL] key, select the range I4:I20, then apply the** Accounting Number style

   Now you are ready to enter formulas to calculate the late fee and outstanding balance.

TROUBLE

Be sure to type 0 (zero) for the False value.

5. **Click cell F4, click the** Insert Function button f_x **on the formula bar, click** IF, **click** OK, **type H4, type >, type C4, press [Tab], type 5, press [Tab], type 0, then compare the Function Arguments dialog box to FIGURE C-16**

   The IF function enters $5.00 in cell F4 (Late Fee) IF the date in cell H4 (Date Paid) is later than the date in cell C4 (Payment Date).

6. **Click** OK, **click cell I4, type =E4-G4+F4, then press [Enter]**

TROUBLE

You will use AutoFill to enter the remaining data in a later step.

7. **Click cell B5, enter the cell address for the invoice date from invoice 102, enter the cell address for the customer name in cell D5, enter the total invoice amount from invoice 102 in cell E5, click cell G5, type =E5 to enter the amount paid, then type June 1, 2016 for the Date Paid**

8. **Repeat Step 7 for invoice 103, but this time enter the Total Paid as 1500 and the Date Paid as July 13, 2016, then fill cells with the formulas from row 4 so that each invoice includes a Payment Date, a Late Fee (if applicable) and an Outstanding Balance**

MORE PRACTICE

For more practice with the skills presented in this project, complete Independent Challenge 2.

9. **On** Invoice 102, **change the name to** Martha Grant **and the consultation hours to** 20, **return to the Tracker, compare it to FIGURE C-17, set it up to print in Landscape orientation on one page, submit copies of all five worksheets to your instructor, then save and close the workbook**

FIGURE C-16: **Function Arguments dialog box**

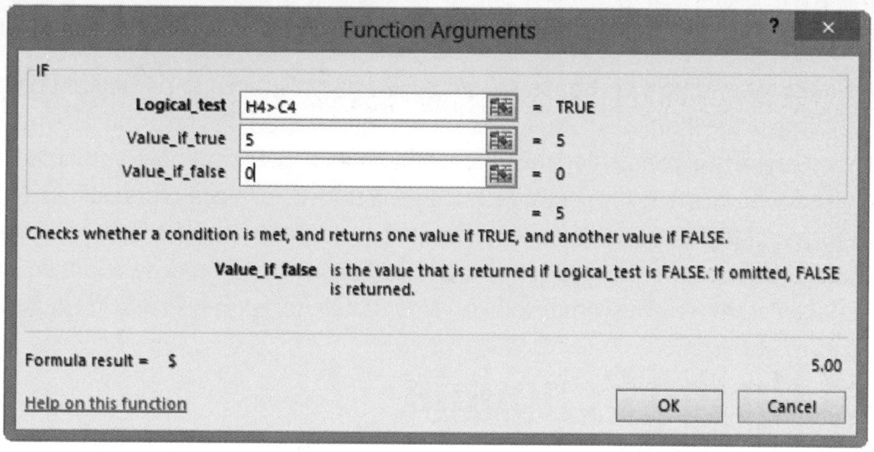

FIGURE C-17: **Completed and updated Invoice Tracker**

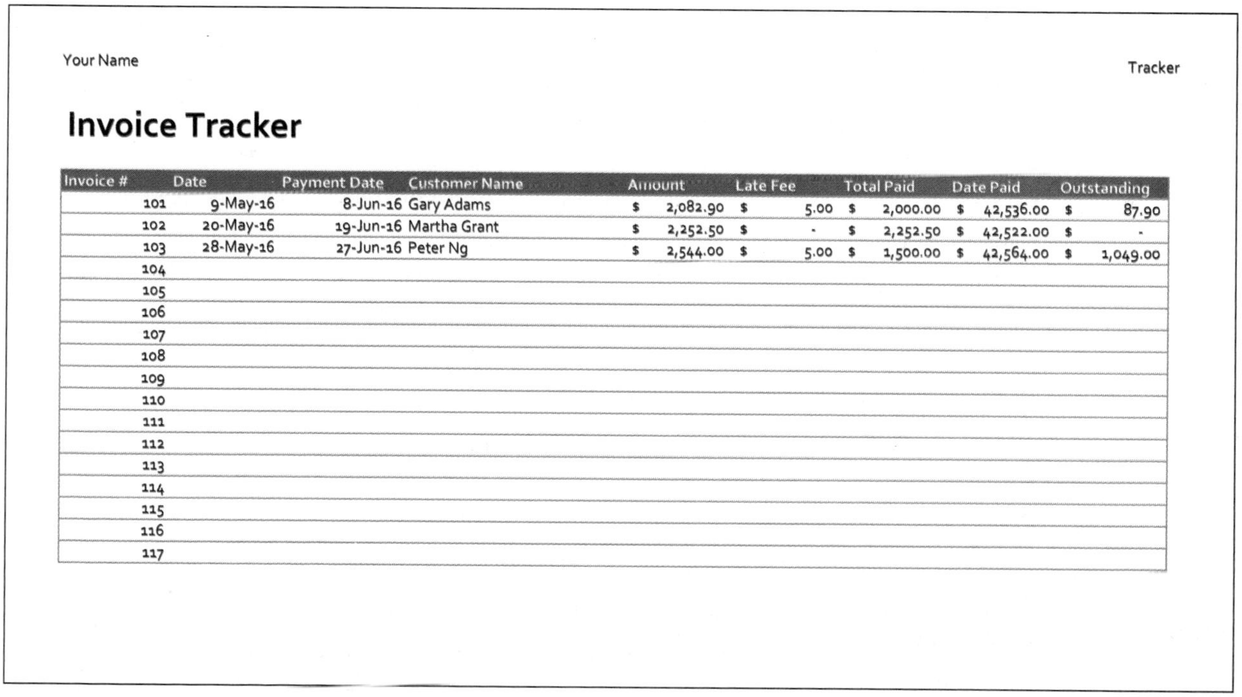

Your Name   Tracker

Invoice Tracker

Invoice #	Date	Payment Date	Customer Name	Amount		Late Fee		Total Paid		Date Paid		Outstanding
101	9-May-16	8-Jun-16	Gary Adams	$	2,082.90	$	5.00	$	2,000.00	$	42,536.00	$ 87.90
102	20-May-16	19-Jun-16	Martha Grant	$	2,252.50	$	-	$	2,252.50	$	42,522.00	$ -
103	28-May-16	27-Jun-16	Peter Ng	$	2,544.00	$	5.00	$	1,500.00	$	42,564.00	$ 1,049.00
104												
105												
106												
107												
108												
109												
110												
111												
112												
113												
114												
115												
116												
117												

Loan Amortization Schedule

Borrowing money usually costs money because you generally need to pay interest on the money that you borrow. One of the most useful ways in which you can use Excel is to help you determine the cost of a loan, including payments, interest, and the total cost of borrowing. For example, you can set up a loan amortization schedule to calculate the cost of a car loan or a student loan or a mortgage on a house. You use functions such as PMT to set up an amortization schedule that includes a table detailing all the payments involved in the loan. For this project you need to **Set up the Schedule** and then **Enter Formulas to Calculate Payments**. The completed loan amortization schedule is shown in FIGURE C-22 on page 73.

Set Up the Schedule

1. Create a blank workbook in Excel, select the Depth theme, then save the workbook as PR C-Loan Amortization Schedule

2. Select columns A to I, then set the column width at 12

3. Enter and format labels for the worksheet as shown in FIGURE C-18, selecting the colors of your choice for the shaded areas

4. Select the range B4:B8, click the Increase Indent button in the Alignment group two times, then increase the indent two times for the range F4:F5

5. Click cell A10, enter just the labels shown in FIGURE C-19 (your labels will not yet wrap, be bold, or be formatted as a table)

6. Select the range A10:I22, click Format as Table in the Styles group, select Table Styles Light 16 (teal), click the My table has headers check box, then click OK

7. Select columns A to I on the worksheet frame, reset the column width at 12, select the range A10:I10, then click Wrap Text in the Alignment group

   When you format cells as a table, the column widths are sometimes adjusted and you need to readjust them. By default, filter arrows appear in the header row of a table so that you can filter table entries. You can remove these arrows.

8. With row 1 of the table still selected, click the TABLE TOOLS DESIGN tab, click the Filter Button check box in the Table Style Options group to deselect it, then click away from the table

9. Click cell D4, enter and format values related to a loan for $10,000 (widen columns as needed) as shown in FIGURE C-20, double-click the Sheet1 tab, name the sheet Loan Schedule, then save the workbook

   To calculate loan payments you need the loan amount ($10,000), the interest rate being charged (4%), and the number of years over which you plan to pay off the loan (1). In the next lesson, you can enter these values into the PMT function to determine your monthly payment.

FIGURE C-18: Labels for cells A1 to H8

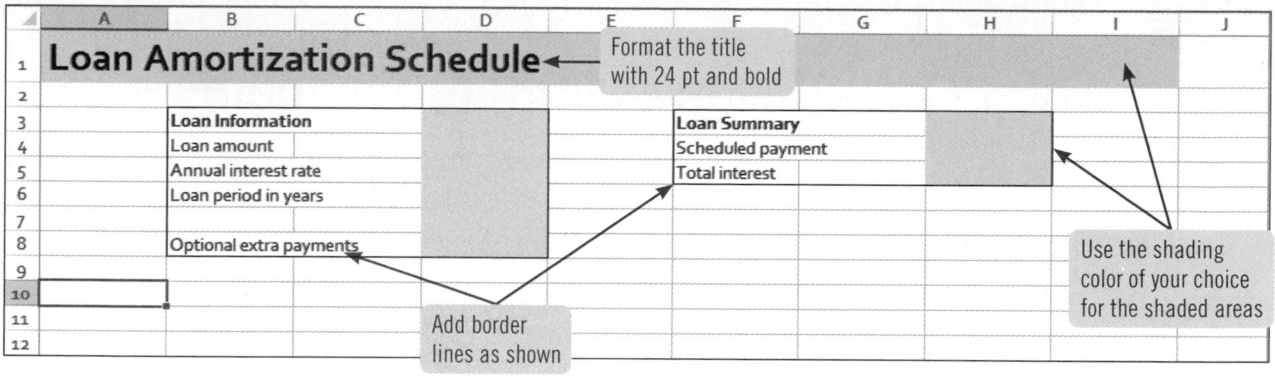

	A	B	C	D	E	F	G	H	I	J
1	**Loan Amortization Schedule** ←				Format the title with 24 pt and bold					
2										
3		**Loan Information**				**Loan Summary**				
4		Loan amount				Scheduled payment				
5		Annual interest rate				Total interest				
6		Loan period in years								
7										
8		Optional extra payments								
9										
10										
11										
12										

Add border lines as shown

Use the shading color of your choice for the shaded areas

FIGURE C-19: Labels for row 10

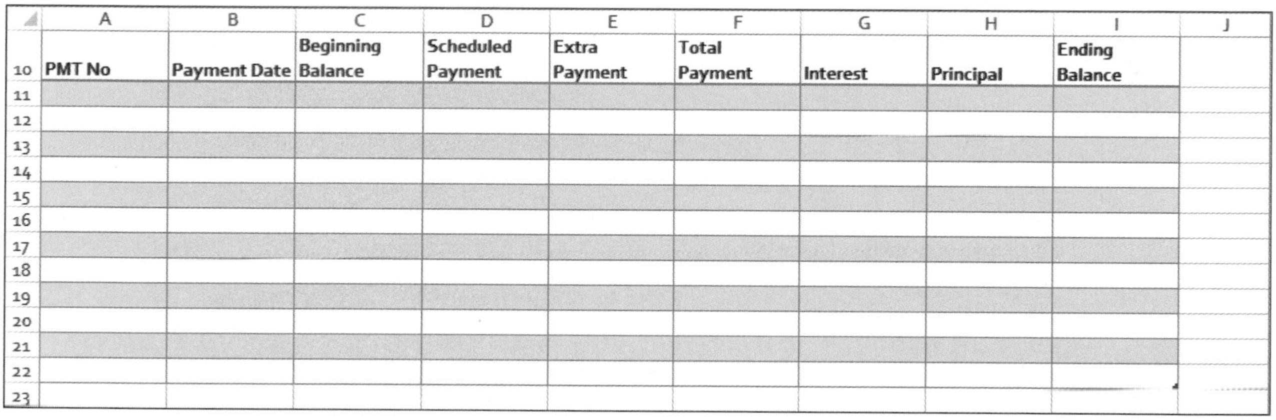

	A	B	C	D	E	F	G	H	I	J
10	PMT No	Payment Date	Beginning Balance	Scheduled Payment	Extra Payment	Total Payment	Interest	Principal	Ending Balance	
11										
12										
13										
14										
15										
16										
17										
18										
19										
20										
21										
22										
23										

FIGURE C-20: Formatted table and loan information

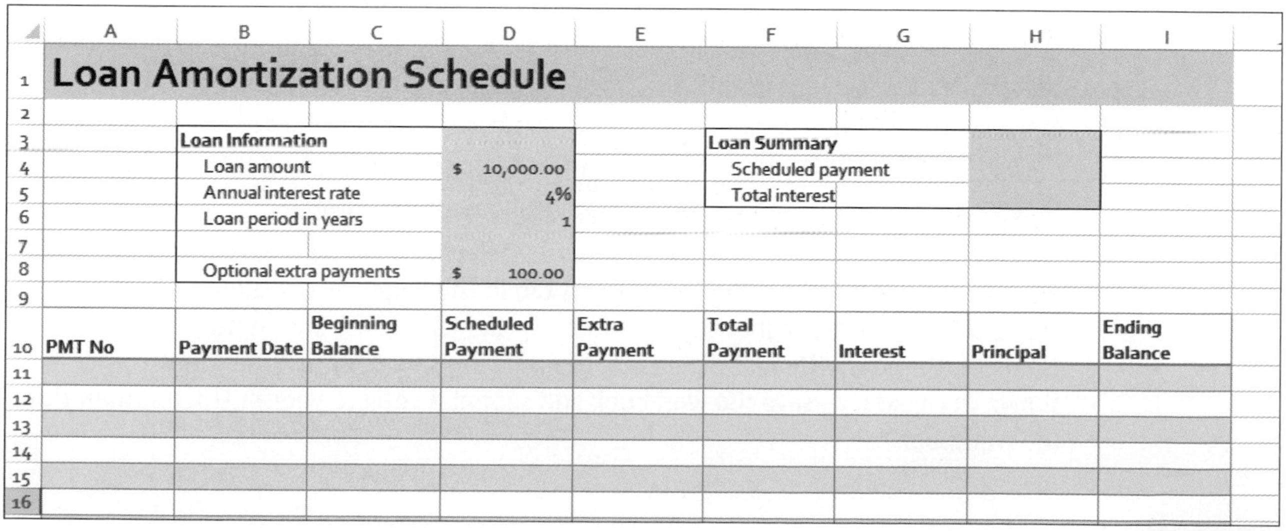

	A	B	C	D	E	F	G	H	I
1	**Loan Amortization Schedule**								
2									
3		**Loan Information**				**Loan Summary**			
4		Loan amount		$ 10,000.00		Scheduled payment			
5		Annual interest rate		4%		Total interest			
6		Loan period in years		1					
7									
8		Optional extra payments		$ 100.00					
9									
10	PMT No	Payment Date	Beginning Balance	Scheduled Payment	Extra Payment	Total Payment	Interest	Principal	Ending Balance
11									
12									
13									
14									
15									
16									

Enter Formulas to Calculate Payments

You use the PMT function to calculate loan payments and then you can enter payments in the table. Once you have entered the required values for the PMT function and the function itself, you can use the Loan Amortization Schedule as a template for a wide range of loans, adding rows as needed. The completed schedule is shown in **FIGURE C-22**.

STEPS

1. Click cell **H4**, click the Insert Function button f_x on the Formula bar, type **PMT**, press **[Enter]**, click **OK**, type **$D$5/12** in the Rate text box

   You will be copying the PMT function so you need to make the values required for the function absolute. You divide the interest rate by 12 to determine the monthly interest rate.

2. Click in the Nper box, type **$D$6*12**, click in the PV box, enter **-$D$4**, then compare the Function Arguments dialog box to **FIGURE C-21**

   You multiply the loan period by 12 to determine the number of months you will be paying off the loan. The PV is the loan amount. You make this value a negative value because it is money owed. After exiting the Function Arguments dialog box, you should see $851.50. If you do not, click the Insert Function button to return to the dialog box and compare it closely to **FIGURE C-21**.

3. Click **OK**, click cell **A11**, type **1**, type **2** in cell **A12**, select cells **A11** and **A12**, fill the remaining rows in the table (to cell A22) with sequential numbers, click cell **B11**, type **January 1, 2016**, press **[Enter]**, type **February 1, 2016** in cell **B12**, then fill the remaining rows in the table with the dates from March 1, 2016 to December 1, 2016

4. Click cell **C11**, type **=D4** to enter the beginning balance ($10,000), press **[Enter]**, click the Undo button to remove the extra entries, click cell **D11**, type **=$H$4**, press **[Enter]**, click , click cell **E11**, type **=$D$8**, press **[Enter]**, then click

5. In cell **F11**, enter the formula to add the Scheduled Payment to the Extra payment (**=D11+E11**), in cell **G11**, enter the formula **=C11*($D$5/12)**, then in cell **H11**, enter the formula to subtract the Interest from the Total Payment (**=F11-G11**)

6. In cell **I11**, enter the formula **=C11-F11** (the Total Payment subtracted from the Beginning Balance), click cell **C12**, type **=I11**, then use AutoFill to fill the remaining cells in each column

   The Amortization table appears as shown in **FIGURE C-22**.

7. Click cell **D4**, type **5000**, press **[Enter]**, change the interest rate to **2%**, then delete the optional extra payment in cell **D8**

   Notice how the scheduled payment is now $421.19 and the values in the table have updated.

8. Click cell **H5**, type **=SUM(**, select the range **G11:G22**, type a closed bracket **)**, press **[Enter]**, click cell **H5**, then apply the Accounting Number format

9. Click the **FILE** tab, click **Print**, click **Page Setup**, select **Landscape** orientation, center the worksheet **horizontally** (using the Margins tab in the Page Setup dialog box), then create a custom header showing your name in the left corner and using the Insert Sheet Name button in the Header dialog box to insert the sheet name in the right corner as shown in **FIGURE C-23**, save the workbook and submit a copy to your instructor, then close the workbook

FIGURE C-21: Data for the PMT function

Function Arguments

PMT

Rate	$D$5/12		= 0.003333333
Nper	$D$6*12		= 12
Pv	-$D$4		= -10000
Fv			= number
Type			= number

= 851.499042

Calculates the payment for a loan based on constant payments and a constant interest rate.

FIGURE C-22: Completed Loan Amortization Schedule

Loan Amortization Schedule

Loan Information

Loan amount	$ 10,000.00
Annual interest rate	4%
Loan period in years	1
Optional extra payments	$ 100.00

Loan Summary

Scheduled payment	$851.50
Total interest	

PMT No	Payment Date	Beginning Balance	Scheduled Payment	Extra Payment	Total Payment	Interest	Principal	Ending Balance
1	1-Jan-16	$ 10,000.00	$851.50	$ 100.00	$ 951.50	$ 33.33	$ 918.17	$ 9,048.50
2	1-Feb-16	$ 9,048.50	$851.50	$ 100.00	$ 951.50	$ 30.16	$ 921.34	$ 8,097.00
3	1-Mar-16	$ 8,097.00	$851.50	$ 100.00	$ 951.50	$ 26.99	$ 924.51	$ 7,145.50
4	1-Apr-16	$ 7,145.50	$851.50	$ 100.00	$ 951.50	$ 23.82	$ 927.68	$ 6,194.00
5	1-May-16	$ 6,194.00	$851.50	$ 100.00	$ 951.50	$ 20.65	$ 930.85	$ 5,242.50
6	1-Jun-16	$ 5,242.50	$851.50	$ 100.00	$ 951.50	$ 17.48	$ 934.02	$ 4,291.01
7	1-Jul-16	$ 4,291.01	$851.50	$ 100.00	$ 951.50	$ 14.30	$ 937.20	$ 3,339.51
8	1-Aug-16	$ 3,339.51	$851.50	$ 100.00	$ 951.50	$ 11.13	$ 940.37	$ 2,388.01
9	1-Sep-16	$ 2,388.01	$851.50	$ 100.00	$ 951.50	$ 7.96	$ 943.54	$ 1,436.51
10	1-Oct-16	$ 1,436.51	$851.50	$ 100.00	$ 951.50	$ 4.79	$ 946.71	$ 485.01
11	1-Nov-16	$ 485.01	$851.50	$ 100.00	$ 951.50	$ 1.62	$ 949.88	$ (466.49)
12	1-Dec-16	$ (466.49)	$851.50	$ 100.00	$ 951.50	$ (1.55)	$ 953.05	$ (1,417.99)

Loan Schedule

FIGURE C-23: Revised Loan Amortization Schedule

Your Name   Loan Schedule

Loan Amortization Schedule

Loan Information

Loan amount	$ 5,000.00
Annual interest rate	2%
Loan period in years	1
Optional extra payments	

Loan Summary

Scheduled payment	$421.19
Total interest	$ 53.67

PMT No	Payment Date	Beginning Balance	Scheduled Payment	Extra Payment	Total Payment	Interest	Principal	Ending Balance
1	1-Jan-16	$ 5,000.00	$421.19	$ -	$ 421.19	$ 8.33	$ 412.86	$ 4,578.81
2	1-Feb-16	$ 4,578.81	$421.19	$ -	$ 421.19	$ 7.63	$ 413.56	$ 4,157.61
3	1-Mar-16	$ 4,157.61	$421.19	$ -	$ 421.19	$ 6.93	$ 414.26	$ 3,736.42
4	1-Apr-16	$ 3,736.42	$421.19	$ -	$ 421.19	$ 6.23	$ 414.97	$ 3,315.22
5	1-May-16	$ 3,315.22	$421.19	$ -	$ 421.19	$ 5.53	$ 415.67	$ 2,894.03
6	1-Jun-16	$ 2,894.03	$421.19	$ -	$ 421.19	$ 4.82	$ 416.37	$ 2,472.83
7	1-Jul-16	$ 2,472.83	$421.19	$ -	$ 421.19	$ 4.12	$ 417.07	$ 2,051.64
8	1-Aug-16	$ 2,051.64	$421.19	$ -	$ 421.19	$ 3.42	$ 417.77	$ 1,630.45
9	1-Sep-16	$ 1,630.45	$421.19	$ -	$ 421.19	$ 2.72	$ 418.48	$ 1,209.25
10	1-Oct-16	$ 1,209.25	$421.19	$ -	$ 421.19	$ 2.02	$ 419.18	$ 788.06
11	1-Nov-16	$ 788.06	$421.19	$ -	$ 421.19	$ 1.31	$ 419.88	$ 366.86
12	1-Dec-16	$ 366.86	$421.19	$ -	$ 421.19	$ 0.61	$ 420.58	$ (54.33)

Independent Challenge 1

Create your own personal budget for the next six months, then ask a series of what-if questions to help you make decisions regarding how you will spend your money. To help you get started, fill in the boxes below with the required information, then set up your budget in an Excel worksheet and perform the calculations required to answer several what-if questions. If you wish, adapt the workbook you created in Unit C Project 1 to show labels and values relevant to your own situation.

1. You need to determine the goal of your budget. Even a personal budget should be created for a specific purpose. For example, you may wish to save for a vacation or to buy a car, or you may just want to live within a set income. Identify the goal of your budget in the box below:

Budget goal: _____
_____
_____

2. Determine your sources of income. You may receive money from a paycheck, from investment dividends, or from a student loan. Each income source requires a label and a row on your budget worksheet. In the box below, list the income labels you will require:

Income labels:

1. _____
2. _____
3. _____
4. _____
5. _____

3. Determine your expenses. At the very least, you will probably need to list your rent, food, utilities, phone, and transportation costs such as car payments, gas, insurance, and bus fares. In addition, include labels for entertainment, clothing, incidentals, and savings. In the box below, list the expense labels you have identified:

Expense labels:

1. _____   6. _____
2. _____   7. _____
3. _____   8. _____
4. _____   9. _____
5. _____   10. _____

4. Create a new workbook in Excel, save it as **PR C-My Personal Budget** to the location where you save the files for this book, then set up your budget in Excel as follows:
   a. Select a theme, then enter and enhance a title for your budget in cell A1.
   b. Enter the period covered by the budget in cell A2. Merge and center the cells in each row (1 and 2) so the labels appear centered over all the columns used for the budget.
   c. Use AutoFill to enter the six months covered by the budget starting in cell B3, then enter the Income and Expenses labels and appropriate subcategory labels in column A.
   d. Enter the values associated with your income and expenses categories. Adjust expenses according to the time of year. For example, your utilities costs will probably be less in the summer than in the winter if you live in the north, while your entertainment and travel expenses may occur mostly in the summer.

Independent Challenge 1 (continued)

e. Calculate your total income and expenses.

f. Add a row to the worksheet with a label and cells that calculate the Cash Available after expenses are subtracted.

g. Create Sparklines for the Total Income, Total Expenses, and Cash Available rows. You can choose the Line or Column Sparkline styles. Show the High Point for each of the three sparklines.

h. Increase the height of the rows containing Sparklines so that they are easy to read.

i. Name Sheet1 **Budget**, then format the worksheet attractively using shading and border lines. Experiment with different looks.

j. In the Page Setup dialog box, change the page orientation to Landscape, fit the entire worksheet to one page, center the worksheet vertically and horizontally, then create a Custom Header containing your name at the left margin and the sheet name at the right margin. (*Hint*: Click the Sheet Name button.)

k. Add a new worksheet, name the new sheet **What If** then copy the Budget worksheet to the What If worksheet.

l. Below the copied worksheet, set up a series of five questions and space for answers to show how the answers to the questions affect the total cash available. **FIGURE C-24** shows a sample setup. Make sure you enter questions that will help you plan your finances to achieve the goal you set.

FIGURE C-24

	A	B	C	D	E	F	G	H
24								
25	**What If Questions**							
26	What if I move to a new apartment where my rent is $100 less than the current rent starting in April?							
27		Answer:						
28	What if I join a fitness club with monthly dues of $60/month starting in February?							
29		Answer:						
30	What if I put 15% of my income into savings each month starting in March?							
31		Answer:						
32	What if I start taking cello lessons at $150/ month starting in January?							
33		Answer:						
34	What if I get rid of my cell phone starting in May?							
35		Answer:						
36								

m. Make the necessary calculations and modifications to the copy of your budget to answer your five questions. For each question, enter the total Cash Available next to Answer. Note that you must enter this value by typing it, not by entering a cell address because the value will change each time you enter new data.

n. Save the workbook and submit a copy to your instructor, then close the workbook.

Independent Challenge 2

You can transfer the skills you used to create the invoice form to create other types of business forms such as expense forms, order forms, work orders, etc. The key is to sketch the components of the form on paper first to determine how best to organize the labels and spaces for users to enter information. For ideas on form design, click the FILE tab, click New, enter Form in the Search box, then scroll through the hundreds of form templates available. You can use these form designs as starting points for your own forms. For this Independent Challenge, create a form to keep track of travel expenses for three consecutive months. Then prepare an expense tracker which lists the total expenses in each category for each month in a table.

1. On a sheet of paper, sketch out a design for the expense form. Determine the travel categories needed; for example, accommodations, transportation, fuel/mileage (determine the mileage rate your company will pay; e.g., $.25/mile or $.16/kilometer), meals, entertainment, and miscellaneous (or other) expenses. The purpose of the form is to provide you with an easy-to-use format for entering and totaling travel expenses incurred each day. If you wish, you can adapt the basic design shown in **FIGURE C-25**.

2. Set up Sheet1 with a theme and an attractive heading including the name and address of the company as well as labels for dates and each expense category. Name the sheet tab **Expense Form**.

Independent Challenge 2 (continued)

3. Include formulas to calculate total expenses for each day and total expenses for each category, the subtotal, any advances, and the total. Be sure to include a label to identify each value.
4. Make sure the form includes a value for mileage reimbursement as shown in **FIGURE C-25**. This value is entered as a cell address to calculate fuel costs when you use your car for business purposes.

FIGURE C-25

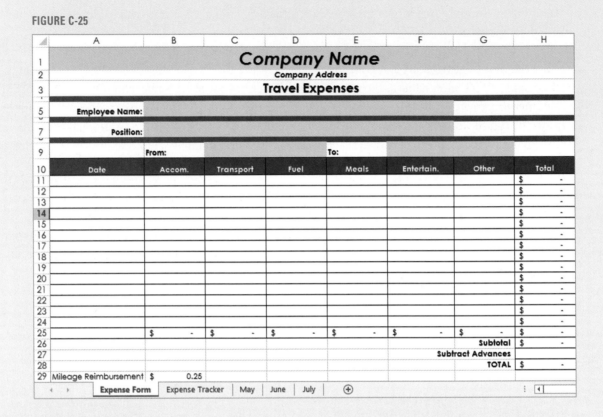

5. Copy your expense form to three new worksheets, then name the sheet tabs with the months you traveled (e.g., **March, April, May**).
6. Save the workbook as **PR C-My Travel Expense Form** to the location where you save the files for this book.
7. Enter expenses for at least three days of travel in each month. You can travel three separate days or one trip of three or more days. Assume that each time you fly, you drive your own car to the airport from your home town. Include the mileage calculation. If you wish, enter a value for any advances you received in the Subtract Advances cells, then in the Total cell subtract this value from the subtotal and verify that the total is correct. (Note: An advance is money received before you go on the trip to help cover trip expenses. You subtract advances from the total expenses because an advance is money you have already received for expenses.)
8. Add a new worksheet, name it **Expense Tracker**, then move it to the right of the Expense Form tab.
9. In the Expense Tracker sheet, set up an expense tracker that you can use to enter category totals for each month. **FIGURE C-26** shows sample labels for an expense tracker.

FIGURE C-26

	A	B	C	D	E	F	G	H	I
1				**Expense Tracker**					
2	Month	Accom.	Transport	Fuel	Meals	Entertain.	Other	Total	
3									
4									

Independent Challenge 2 (continued)

10. Apply a table style to the row containing the labels and at least six more rows, then convert the table into a range so that the cell addresses can be entered correctly.

11. Use cell addresses in the tracker so that expense categories are updated automatically.

12. Verify that the total expenses for each month match the appropriate worksheet. Note that for each month, you can enter the cell address for the first category (for example, Accommodations), then copy the address across to the total column. The correct totals will be entered so long as the order of categories in the Expense Tracker is the same as the order of categories in the expense forms.

13. In the last row of the table, calculate the total amount spent in each category and the total amount spent on all travel for the three months.

14. Add a new column to the right of the Total column called **Bonus.** (Note: In this company, a bonus is given if the travel expenses for a month are less than a set criteria.) Insert an IF function that multiplies the value in the Total cell next to the first month by 15% IF the value in the Total cell is less than a value you choose (in this case, 2000) or displays 0 if the criteria is not met. For example, if the total expenses for May are $5,000 and the number that triggers a bonus is $2,000, then the value entered in the Bonus cell will be 0 because the May expenses are more than the trigger amount. However, if the total expenses in May are $1,000, then $150 (15% of $1000) will be displayed in the Bonus cell. Copy the IF function to the Bonus cells for the other months.

15. Click the Expense Form tab, press and hold [Shift], click the last worksheet tab, then set up the document to print in Landscape orientation, centered horizontally, and with your name and the sheet name in a custom header. By using the Shift key to group all five worksheets, you only need to identify the print settings for the sheets once.

16. Save workbook and submit a copy of all five sheets to your instructor, then close the workbook.

Independent Challenge 3

Use the Loan Amortization Schedule you created in Project 3 to calculate a loan for a project of your choice.

1. Open PR C-Loan Amortization Schedule, then save it as **PR C-My Loan Information**.

2. Change the theme applied to the worksheet.

3. In row 2, enter the purpose of the loan; for example, to purchase a car, pay off a student loan, etc. Format the label attractively with a large font size and shading.

4. Enter the amount of the loan (a different amount from the amount currently entered).

5. Enter the annual interest rate and the loan period in years. Make the loan payment longer than one year.

6. Enter any extra payments you wish to make. You may decide to make extra payments only in some months.

7. Extend the number of months covered by the table to match the number of years you selected. For example, if you entered 5 as the number of years, the table will need to extend over 60 rows (5 years × 12 months per year). Notice that the item may be paid off a few months early, particularly if you enter extra payments. Make sure all the values are entered for each payment for each month entered. Use the Fill command as needed to populate the table.

8. Note when the loan is paid off. You will see entries in the Ending Balance column formatted with brackets which indicate negative amounts. Use a different shading color to highlight the row showing the first negative balance. Notice how this row changes, depending on how many extra payments you have made. You can quickly see that making an extra payment occasionally can significantly reduce the amount of interest you pay on a loan. Delete any remaining rows that contain negative ending balances.

9. In cell H5, enter the total interest paid for your loan.

10. Format the worksheet attractively to print over one or two pages. Note that the worksheet may extend over two pages depending on how many payments you entered in the table.

11. Be sure your name appears in the worksheet header, save the workbook and submit a copy to your instructor, then close the workbook.

Independent Challenge 4 - Team Project

To further explore how you can develop a wide range of workbooks with Excel 2013, you will work with two other people to complete a team project. The subject of the team project is the planning of a trip involving up to five people. The trip should be for a business or class purpose (not a family trip) that includes individuals—each of whom will be billed separately. Follow the guidelines provided below to create the three workbooks required for the team project. When you have completed the project, the team will submit a document containing information about the project, as well as three files related to the project: a trip budget, trip statements (including expenses tabs and a tracker), and trip financing.

▶ Project Setup

1. As a team, work together to complete the following tasks.
   - Share e-mail addresses among all three team members.
   - Set up a time (either via e-mail, an online chat session, Internet Messaging, or face to face) when you will get together to choose your topic and assign roles.
   - At your meeting, complete the table below with information about your team and the event you are creating documents for.

Team Name (last names of the team member or another name that describes the project; for example, "Jones-Cho-Knorr" or "Concert Fundraiser").
Team Members 1. 2. 3.
Trip type (for example, business trip, class trip, attendance at a conference, etc.)
Trip purpose (for example, attendance of three co-workers at a work-related conference, class field trip to Hawaii to study the geology of volcanoes, business trip to visit clients in another country, etc.)
Trip location and dates (for example, New York from March 10 to March 15)
Trip financing sources (for example, personal, organization/business contribution, loan). Make one of the financing sources a loan.
Team Roles: Indicate who is responsible for each of the following three files (one file per team member) Trip Budget: Trip Statements (includes an expenses tab for each team member and a tracker): Trip Financing:
Workbook Formatting: Select a theme and color scheme that will be used to format all of the workbooks created for the Team Project. Theme: Color Scheme:

Independent Challenge 4 - Team Project (continued)

► Workbook Development

Individually, complete the tasks listed below for the file you are responsible for. You need to develop appropriate content and format the file attractively. Be sure team members use the same theme and color scheme when creating the workbook as detailed in the previous table. Include the team name on all workbooks.

Trip Budget

This workbook contains a budget for the trip and includes sources of income for the trip and categories for all expected expenses. Create the workbook as follows:

1. Create a new Excel workbook and save it as **PR C-Team Project_Trip Budget** to the location where you save files for this book, then apply the workbook theme and color scheme selected by your team.
2. In cell A1, enter **Trip Budget** followed by the location or purpose of your trip (for example, Trip Budget: Sustainability Conference).
3. In cell A2, enter the location and dates of the trip (for example, New York City, March 10 to 15).
4. Format the labels attractively with larger font sizes, shading, and/or border lines.
5. Enter **Expenses** in cell A3, then include labels for **Unit, Unit Cost, Number, People**, and **Total**. Note that a unit would be a ticket, a room, a day, etc. The Total column contains a formula that multiplies the Unit Cost by the Number of the People. For example, if the trip extended over five nights for three people, the line for the Accommodations expense would contain Night as the Unit, $250 as the Unit Cost (the per night cost), 5 for the Number of nights, 3 for the people, and $3,750 for the Total. (Note: Some entries such as car rental may not include the number of people if they all share one car. You will need to adjust formulas as needed.)
6. Enter labels for the trip expenses; for example, airline tickets, car rental, accommodations, conference fees, attractions, meals, etc. Include a line for miscellaneous expenses.
7. In the Total column, include calculations for the subtotal, a contingency amount of 10% of the Subtotal, and the Total Expenses, which is the Subtotal added to the Contingency Expense. (Note: A contingency is generally expressed as a percentage of the total expenses and is included to account for unforeseen expenses.)
8. Enter values for the various expense categories. Be realistic; you may wish to check typical airfares to your trip location and typical costs for hotels. Ensure that the formulas calculate correctly.
9. Name the worksheet **Expenses**, then create a new worksheet called **Revenue**.
10. In the Revenue worksheet, enter labels for income sources (e.g., personal contributions, company contribution, loans). Include formulas to calculate total revenues.
11. In the Revenue sheet, enter values for the various income categories, then create a Sparkline that provides a visual representation of how much revenue is generated from each revenue source. Indicate the High Point. Increase the height of the row containing the Sparkline so that it is easy to read.
12. In the Expenses worksheet, add an entry for **Revenue** below Total Expenses and another entry for **Surplus/Deficit**. In the Revenue cell, enter the cell address of the total revenues entered in the Revenue sheet and in the Surplus/Deficit cell enter the formula to subtract the revenue expenses from the revenue to determine if you have sufficient revenue to cover all the expenses.
13. View the Expenses worksheet and verify that the revenue and surplus/deficit cells contain values.
14. Work with the expenses and revenue sources until you are satisfied that you have a realistic budget with little or no deficit or surplus.
15. Group the two worksheets (use [Shift], then click the Expenses tab and then the Revenue tab), then set up the worksheets for printing: add a custom header that includes your Team name at the left margin, your name in the middle, and the sheet name at the right margin; scale both worksheets to fit on one page, and center the worksheets horizontally.
16. Save the workbook and submit it to your instructor along with the other workbooks created by your team members.

Independent Challenge 4 - Team Project (continued)

Trip Statements (Expenses and Tracker Tabs)

This workbook contains a form for recording the expenses generated by each person who goes on the trip (up to three people), completed forms for each individual, and a statement tracker. View the other forms you've created in this unit (the invoice form for Project 2 and the expense form for Independent Challenge 2), then create the workbook as follows:

1. Sketch the trip expense statement form on a piece of paper to determine how best to organize the labels and spaces for entering data.

2. Create a new Excel workbook and save it as **PR C-Team Project_Trip Statements** to the location where you save files for this book, then apply the workbook theme and color scheme selected by your team.

3. Create the form in a worksheet called **Statement Form**. In cell A1, enter **Trip Expenses** and the trip location or purpose and in cell A2 enter the location and dates of the trip. Use lines and shading to make the form as easy to read as possible. You should include sufficient rows to cover the duration of the trip. Make sure the form includes labels for all the expense categories. See **FIGURE C-25** in Independent Challenge 2 for a sample.

4. Include a clip art picture in an appropriate area of the statement form. The picture should relate in some way to the location of the trip. For example, you could insert a clip art picture of the Eiffel Tower if the trip destination is Paris.

5. Once you are satisfied with the appearance of the statement form, create a tab for each of the people who are going on the trip (three people, one for each team member), then copy the form to each of the tabs.

6. Consult with the team member who is creating the overall trip budget for information about trip expenses such as hotel costs and airline tickets, then enter realistic expenses into the trip statements. Note that the actual expenses entered do not need to match exactly the budgeted expenses. The purpose of the trip statements is to record the expenses actually incurred. The purpose of the budget is to predict expenses. However, the values entered in both should be similar.

7. Create a Trip Tracker worksheet and move it so it appears to the right of the Statement worksheet. Set up the worksheet so that you can enter cell addresses from each of the individual worksheets. Format the tracker information as a table that you convert to a range. (*Hint*: Click in the table, then click Convert to Range in the Tools group on the TABLE TOOLS DESIGN tab.) Note that the purpose of the Trip Tracker is to provide a snapshot of all of the expenses incurred by all of the people who went on the trip.

8. On the Trip Tracker, calculate the total expenses incurred by all of the trip participants.

9. Group the worksheets, then set up the worksheets for printing: select Landscape orientation, add a custom header that includes your Team name at the left margin, your name in the middle, and the sheet name at the right margin; scale worksheets to fit on one page, and center the worksheets horizontally.

10. Save the workbook and submit it to your instructor along with the other workbooks created by your team members.

Independent Challenge 4 - Team Project (continued)

Trip Financing

1. Open the PR C-Loan Amortization Schedule file that you created for Project 3, then save it as **PR C-Team Project_Trip Financing**.

2. Change the theme and color scheme to those selected by the team. Adjust the shading colors as needed so the workbook is easy to read.

3. In row 2, enter a subtitle that describes the purpose of the loan (for example, "Financing Travel to the Sustainability Conference in New York").

4. Consult with the team member who is working on the budget to determine the portion of budget costs to be covered by a loan, then enter this amount in the appropriate area of the Trip Financing workbook.

5. Research the current interest rates for a short term loan of six months, then enter this rate and 6 as the loan period.

6. View the PMT function entered in the Scheduled Payment cell (click the Insert Function button to open the Function Arguments dialog box), then modify entries to take into account that the loan is for six months (not one year). Think carefully about the changes you need to make.

7. Modify the table to show only six payments.

8. Enter up to three optional payments, then highlight the row containing the ending balance closest to 0.

9. In cell H5, enter the total interest paid for the loan.

10. Add a custom header that includes your Team name at the left margin, your name in the middle, and the sheet name at the right margin.

11. Save the workbook and submit it to your instructor along with the other workbooks created by your team members.

▶ Project Summary

As a team, complete the project summary as follows.

1. Open PR C-01.docx from the location where you save your Data Files, then save it to your **PR C-Team Project Summary**.

2. Read the directions in the document, then ensure that each team member enters his or her name in one of the tables along with a short description of the skills used and the challenges faced by each member while creating the Word document.

3. Save the document, then submit all four documents to your instructor.

Visual Workshop

Create the six-month budget shown in FIGURE C-27 for Sun Power, a small consulting company that advises consumers and businesses about solar power options. Set up the workbook in Landscape orientation; apply the Berlin theme, fill cell A1 with Orange, Accent 1, Lighter 80%; enter values as shown in FIGURE C-27; enter formulas to calculate total revenue, total expenses, and profit/loss; apply the Comma or Accounting styles to cells as shown; then add shading using variations of Orange, Accent 1 for revenue, Green, Accent 3 for expenses, and Lavender, Accent 5 for Profit/Loss. Save the budget as **PR C-Sun Power Budget** to the location where you save the files for this book, then answer the following What-If questions or make up your own What-If questions and apply them to the worksheet:

1. In February, you estimate that three new businesses will ask for consultations at an average rate of $1,200 per consultation. These contracts are in addition to the current revenue for consultations. You project that the contract revenue generated in February will increase by 5 percent in March, 10 percent in April, then 20 percent for May and June. Calculate all increases based on February revenue. *Hint*: The formula for cell D6 is =$C$6*1.05. Remember to use absolute cell references when you copy the formula and to change the percentages. What is the total revenue for consulting in cell H6? Enter the cell address H6 in cell B20.

2. Make the salaries expense for both May and June $5,000. What is the total salaries expense in cell H11? Enter the cell address of the value in cell B21.

3. Increase the advertising costs for March by 30% of the costs for February. *Hint*: The required formula is =C14*1.3.

4. Make the equipment leases for March four times the current equipment leases for February. What is the total projected profit in cell H18? Enter the cell address of the value in cell B23.

Save the workbook, preview it, make sure the worksheet fits on one page in Landscape orientation and is centered horizontally, add your name to the center section of the header, save the workbook and submit a copy to your instructor, then close the workbook and Excel.

FIGURE C-27

▲	A	B	C	D	E	F	G	H	I
1				Sun Power					
2				Six-Month Budget: January to June, 2016					
3									
4		January	February	March	April	May	June	Totals	
5	REVENUE								
6	Consultant Fees	$ 8,000.00	$10,000.00	$10,000.00	$10,000.00	$10,000.00	$10,000.00	$58,000.00	
7	Product Sales	900.00	1,200.00	1,300.00	1,500.00	1,900.00	2,000.00	8,800.00	
8	Total Revenue	$ 8,900.00	$11,200.00	$11,300.00	$11,500.00	$11,900.00	$12,000.00	$66,800.00	
9									
10	EXPENSES								
11	Salaries	$ 3,000.00	$ 3,000.00	$ 3,000.00	$ 3,000.00	$ 3,000.00	$ 3,000.00	$18,000.00	
12	Rent	3,000.00	3,000.00	3,000.00	3,000.00	3,000.00	3,000.00	18,000.00	
13	Equipment Leases	1,000.00	1,000.00	1,000.00	1,000.00	1,000.00	1,000.00	6,000.00	
14	Advertising	2,000.00	2,000.00	2,000.00	2,000.00	2,000.00	2,000.00	12,000.00	
15	Operating Costs	1,200.00	1,200.00	1,200.00	1,200.00	1,200.00	1,200.00	7,200.00	
16	Total Expenses	$10,200.00	$10,200.00	$10,200.00	$10,200.00	$10,200.00	$10,200.00	$61,200.00	
17									
18	PROFIT/LOSS	$ (1,300.00)	$ 1,000.00	$ 1,100.00	$ 1,300.00	$ 1,700.00	$ 1,800.00	$ 5,600.00	
19									
20	Question 1 Answer								
21	Question 2 Answer								
22	Question 3 Answer								
23	Question 4 Answer								
24									

Excel Projects II

Projects

In this unit you will create the following:

Sales Forecast

Change tab color • Apply cell formatting • Adjust column width • Use AutoFill • Use formulas • Create a what-if analysis scenario • Use the Scenario Manager • Adjust maximum value in chart value axis • Create a column chart from non-adjacent cells (*Skills also practiced in Independent Challenge 1*)

Customer Profile

Apply a table format • Wrap text • Name a table • Use the SUM function • Use the COUNTA and COUNTIF functions • Sort a table on two fields • Specify criteria to filter a table • Identify a Subtotal list • Create a PivotTable • Create a PivotChart • Add labels to a pie chart (*Skills also practiced in Independent Challenge 2*)

Sales Report

Adjust cell styles • Apply conditional formatting • Create a PivotTable • Collapse/Expand PivotTables • Work with the Slicer (*Skills also practiced in Independent Challenge 3*)

Team Project

Files You Will Need

PR D-01.xlsx	PR D-04.xlsx
PR D-02.jpg	PR D-05.docx
PR D-03.xlsx	PD D-06.xlsx

Microsoft® product screenshots used with permission from Microsoft® Corporation.

Sales Forecast for City Transitions Consulting

You work for Transitions Consulting, a small consulting firm that advises businesses and delivers workshops on how to develop environmentally friendly and sustainable work environments through the use of recycling programs, walk-to-work initiatives, sustainable business practices, and so on. Business is good, so the owner wants to move from a home office to a commercial office space and hire a workshop facilitator and a sales representative. To help the owner decide what course of action he should take, you use scenarios in Excel to perform different what-if analyses. For this project, you **Set up the Workbook**, **Create Current Scenarios**, **Create Best and Worst Case Scenarios**, and **Format the Scenarios**. The completed reports showing the Best Base and Worst Case scenarios are shown in **FIGURE D-8** and **FIGURE D-9** on page 91.

Set Up the Workbook

You need to enter the labels and values for the six-month revenue and expenses statement for Transitions Consulting, and then calculate the total revenue, expenses, and net income.

STEPS

HINT
Enter the expenses for July, then use the Fill handle to fill the remaining months.

1. **Start Excel, open a new blank workbook, apply the Ion theme, then enter data and format the worksheet as shown in FIGURE D-1**
   - Column A: set the width to **21**
   - Columns B:H: Set the width to **12**
   - Row 1: Format with **24 pt**, **bold**, and filled with **Purple, Accent 6, Lighter 60%**
   - Row 2: Format with **14 pt** and **bold**
   - Row 4: Apply **bold** to all column heads
   - Cells A5, A8, A10, A16, A18: Format with **all caps** and **bold**

2. **Save the workbook as PR D-Transitions Consulting Sales Forecasts to the location where you save your files for this book**

3. **Double-click the Sheet1 tab, type Forecasts, right-click Forecasts, point to Tab Color, then click Purple, Accent 6, Lighter 40%**

4. **Select cells B6:H8, click the AutoSum button in the Editing group, then verify that 48000 appears in cell H8**

5. **Select cells B11:H16, click the AutoSum button, then verify that 43800 appears in cell H16**

6. **In cell B18, enter a formula that subtracts the total expenses in cell B16 from the total revenue in cell B8 (1700)**

7. **Fill cells C18:H18 with the formula in cell B18**
   The total net profit for July to December 2016 is 4200 in cell H18.

8. **Select cells B6:H6, click the Accounting Number Format button $ in the Number group, select cells B7:H7, then click the Comma Style button ' in the Number group**

HINT
You can use the Ctrl key to select nonadjacent rows to speed up the process.

9. **Refer to FIGURE D-2 to format the remaining rows with the appropriate formats, then save the document**

	A	B	C	D	E	F	G	H
1	**Transitions Consulting**							
2	**Revenue and Expenses: July to December 2016**							
3								
4		July	August	September	October	November	December	Totals
5	**REVENUE**							
6	Workshop Fees	5000	3000	3000	4000	4000	3000	
7	Consulting Fees	4000	6000	4000	5000	5000	2000	
8	**TOTAL REVENUE**							
9								
10	**EXPENSES**							
11	Salaries	6000	6000	6000	6000	6000	6000	
12	Rent	500	500	500	500	500	500	
13	Advertising	300	300	300	300	300	300	
14	Equipment Lease	200	200	200	200	200	200	
15	Operating Costs	300	300	300	300	300	300	
16	**TOTAL EXPENSES**							
17								
18	**NET PROFIT**							
19								
20								

Sheet1

	A	B	C	D	E	F	G	H
1	**Transitions Consulting**							
2	**Revenue and Expenses: July to December 2016**							
3								
4		July	August	September	October	November	December	Totals
5	**REVENUE**							
6	Workshop Fees	$ 5,000.00	$ 3,000.00	$ 3,000.00	$ 4,000.00	$ 4,000.00	$ 3,000.00	$ 22,000.00
7	Consulting Fees	4,000.00	6,000.00	4,000.00	5,000.00	5,000.00	2,000.00	26,000.00
8	**TOTAL REVENUE**	$ 9,000.00	$ 9,000.00	$ 7,000.00	$ 9,000.00	$ 9,000.00	$ 5,000.00	$ 48,000.00
9								
10	**EXPENSES**							
11	Salaries	$ 6,000.00	$ 6,000.00	$ 6,000.00	$ 6,000.00	$ 6,000.00	$ 6,000.00	$ 36,000.00
12	Rent	500.00	500.00	500.00	500.00	500.00	500.00	3,000.00
13	Advertising	300.00	300.00	300.00	300.00	300.00	300.00	1,800.00
14	Equipment Lease	200.00	200.00	200.00	200.00	200.00	200.00	1,200.00
15	Operating Costs	300.00	300.00	300.00	300.00	300.00	300.00	1,800.00
16	**TOTAL EXPENSES**	$ 7,300.00	$ 7,300.00	$ 7,300.00	$ 7,300.00	$ 7,300.00	$ 7,300.00	$ 43,800.00
17								
18	**NET PROFIT**	$ 1,700.00	$ 1,700.00	$ (300.00)	$ 1,700.00	$ 1,700.00	$ (2,300.00)	$ 4,200.00
19								
20								

Forecasts

Excel 2013

Create Current Scenarios

You create scenarios so you can engage in what-if analysis, which is the process of changing values in selected cells so you can see how the changes affect formula results, such as total revenue, total expenses, and total profit. A scenario is a set of values that you name and save. You can apply various combinations of scenarios to see how formula results are affected. In this project, you will create three sets of scenarios: Current, Best Case, and Worst Case. First, you highlight the cells that contain the values you plan to change when you create the three scenario sets. Although highlighting the cells is not a required step when you create scenarios, you do so in order to quickly and easily identify which rows contain the data that will change when you show different scenarios. Second, you use the Scenario Manager to create scenarios that represent the current values for workshops, rent, salaries, and operating costs.

STEPS

1. **Select cells B6:G6, press and hold [Ctrl], select cells B11:G12, then select cells B15:G15**

   You have selected the cells containing the values you will include in the set of Current scenarios.

2. **Click the Fill Color list arrow ⬛ ⋅ in the Font group, click Yellow in the Standard Colors area, then click cell B6**

   The cells for Workshop Fees, Salaries, Rent, and Operating Costs are filled with yellow, as shown in **FIGURE D-3** so you can easily see which values change each time you show a new scenario.

3. **Select cells B6:G6, click the DATA tab, click the What-If Analysis button in the Data Tools group, click Scenario Manager, then click Add**

   In the Add Scenario dialog box, you enter a name for the scenario and designate which cells will change when you add new data.

4. **Type Current Workshop Fees, then click OK to accept B6:G6 as the cells to change**

   In the Scenario Values dialog box, you can keep values currently entered or you can enter new values.

5. **Click OK again to accept the values currently entered in cells B6:G6**

   The Current Workshop Fees scenario consists of the values currently entered in cells B6:G6.

6. **Click Add, type Current Salaries, click the Collapse Dialog Box button 🔲 at the far right of the Changing cells text box, then select cells B11:G11 in the worksheet**

   These cells contain the values for the current salaries being paid each month from July to December.

7. **Click the Expand Dialog Box button 🔲, verify that $B$11:$G$11 appears in the Changing Cells box, click OK, then click OK to accept the values currently entered in cells B11:G11**

8. **Add a scenario called Current Rent based on cells B12:G12, then add a scenario called Current Operating Costs based on cells B15:G15**

9. **Compare the Scenario Manager dialog box to FIGURE D-4, click Close to exit the Scenario Manager dialog box, then save the workbook**

FIGURE D-3: Scenario cells highlighted

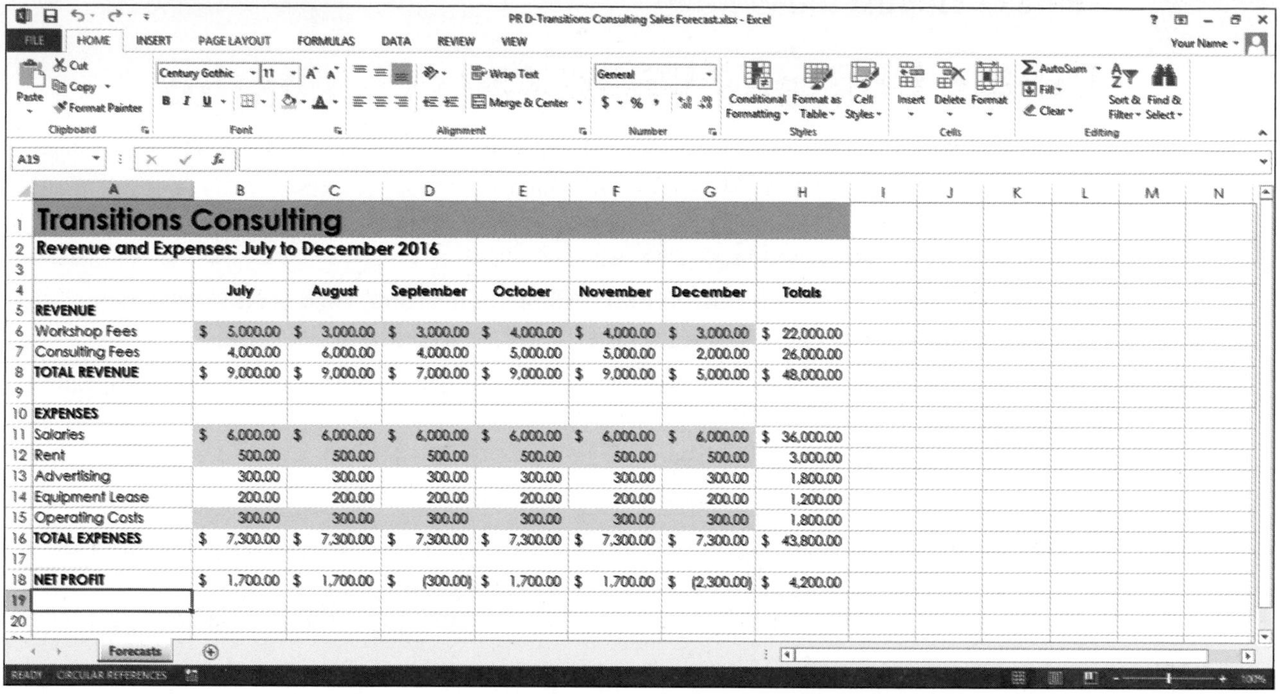

	A	B	C	D	E	F	G	H
1	Transitions Consulting							
2	Revenue and Expenses: July to December 2016							
3								
4		July	August	September	October	November	December	Totals
5	REVENUE							
6	Workshop Fees	$ 5,000.00	$ 3,000.00	$ 3,000.00	$ 4,000.00	$ 4,000.00	$ 3,000.00	$ 22,000.00
7	Consulting Fees	4,000.00	6,000.00	4,000.00	5,000.00	5,000.00	2,000.00	26,000.00
8	TOTAL REVENUE	$ 9,000.00	$ 9,000.00	$ 7,000.00	$ 9,000.00	$ 9,000.00	$ 5,000.00	$ 48,000.00
9								
10	EXPENSES							
11	Salaries	$ 6,000.00	$ 6,000.00	$ 6,000.00	$ 6,000.00	$ 6,000.00	$ 6,000.00	$ 36,000.00
12	Rent	500.00	500.00	500.00	500.00	500.00	500.00	3,000.00
13	Advertising	300.00	300.00	300.00	300.00	300.00	300.00	1,800.00
14	Equipment Lease	200.00	200.00	200.00	200.00	200.00	200.00	1,200.00
15	Operating Costs	300.00	300.00	300.00	300.00	300.00	300.00	1,800.00
16	TOTAL EXPENSES	$ 7,300.00	$ 7,300.00	$ 7,300.00	$ 7,300.00	$ 7,300.00	$ 7,300.00	$ 43,800.00
17								
18	NET PROFIT	$ 1,700.00	$ 1,700.00	$ (300.00)	$ 1,700.00	$ 1,700.00	$ (2,300.00)	$ 4,200.00

FIGURE D-4: Scenario Manager dialog box

Excel 2013

Sales Forecast (continued)

Create Best and Worst Case Scenarios

You need to change the values in the worksheet to reflect best case projections, and then you need to change the values again to reflect worst case projections.

1. Click the What-If Analysis button in the Data Tools group, click Scenario Manager, click Current Workshop Fees, click Add, type Best Case Workshop Fees, then click OK

2. Type 10000, press [Tab], enter the values for cells C6:G6 in the Scenario Values dialog box as shown in FIGURE D-5, then click OK

These values represent the revenue the owner hopes to generate from delivering workshops if he moves to a commercial space and hires additional help.

3. Click Current Salaries, click Add, type Best Case Salaries, click OK, type 12000, press [Tab], enter 12000 for cells C11:G11, then click OK

The monthly salaries expense will double when a new workshop facilitator and sales representative are hired.

4. Click Current Rent, add a scenario called Best Case Rent that changes all the values in cells B12:G12 to 1500, click Current Operating Costs, then add a scenario called Best Case Operating Costs that changes all the values in cells B15:G15 to 800

The owner hopes to obtain office space for $1,500 a month and generate operating costs of no more than $800 a month.

5. Click Best Case Workshop Fees, click Show, click Best Case Salaries, click Show, show the remaining Best Case scenarios, then click Close

The value in cell H18 is $8,200. This value represents the company's net profit after six months if the owner moves to a commercial space and hires new personnel. But what happens if the move takes place and things don't go as planned?

6. Click the What-If Analysis button in the Data Tools group, click Scenario Manager, click Current Workshop Fees, click Add, type Worst Case Workshop Fees, click OK, type 9000, press [Tab], enter the values for cells C6:G6 for Worst Case Workshop Fees as shown in FIGURE D-6, then click OK

7. Add the Worst Case Salaries, Worst Case Rent, and Worst Case Operating Costs scenarios based on the values displayed below:

Worst Case Salaries	13000
Worst Case Rent	2000
Worst Case Operating Costs	900

8. Show all the Worst Case scenarios, then close the Scenario Manager dialog box

The total net income displayed in cell H18 is now $(22,400.00) as shown in FIGURE D-7. The Worst Case scenarios are based on your projection of lower revenue from workshop fees paired with higher expenses for salaries, rent, and operating costs.

9. Click What-If Analysis in the Data Tools group, click Scenario Manager, click Current Workshop Fees, click Show, show all the remaining Current scenarios, click Close, then fill cell H18 with yellow and apply Bold

You should see $4,200.00 in cell H18.

FIGURE D-5: Best Case Workshop Fees values

Best Case Workshop Fees values for cells C6:G6

Scenario Values

Enter values for each of the changing cells.

1: $C$6   12000
2: $D$6   12000
3: $E$6   13000
4: $F$6   14000
5: $G$6   10000

OK   Cancel

The dialog box displays five values at a time; scroll up to see the value for B6

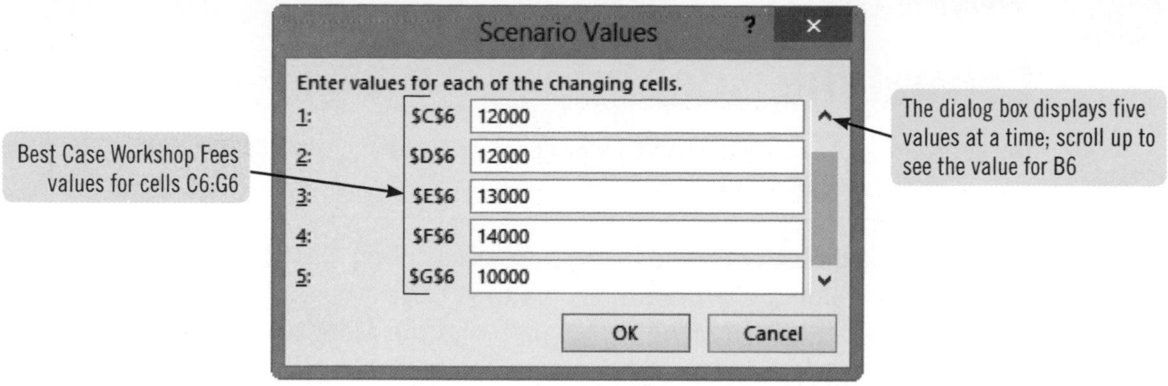

FIGURE D-6: Worst Case Workshop Fees values

Worst Case Workshop Fees for cells C6:G6

Scenario Values

Enter values for each of the changing cells.

1: $C$6   8000
2: $D$6   9000
3: $E$6   9000
4: $F$6   7000
5: $G$6   8000

OK   Cancel

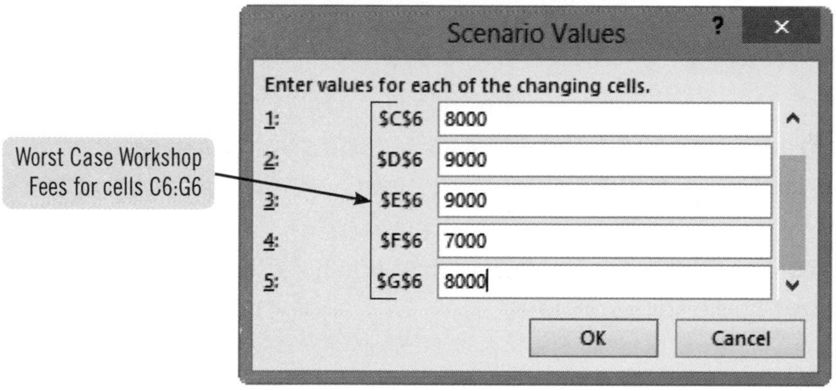

FIGURE D-7: Worksheet with Worse Case Scenarios shown

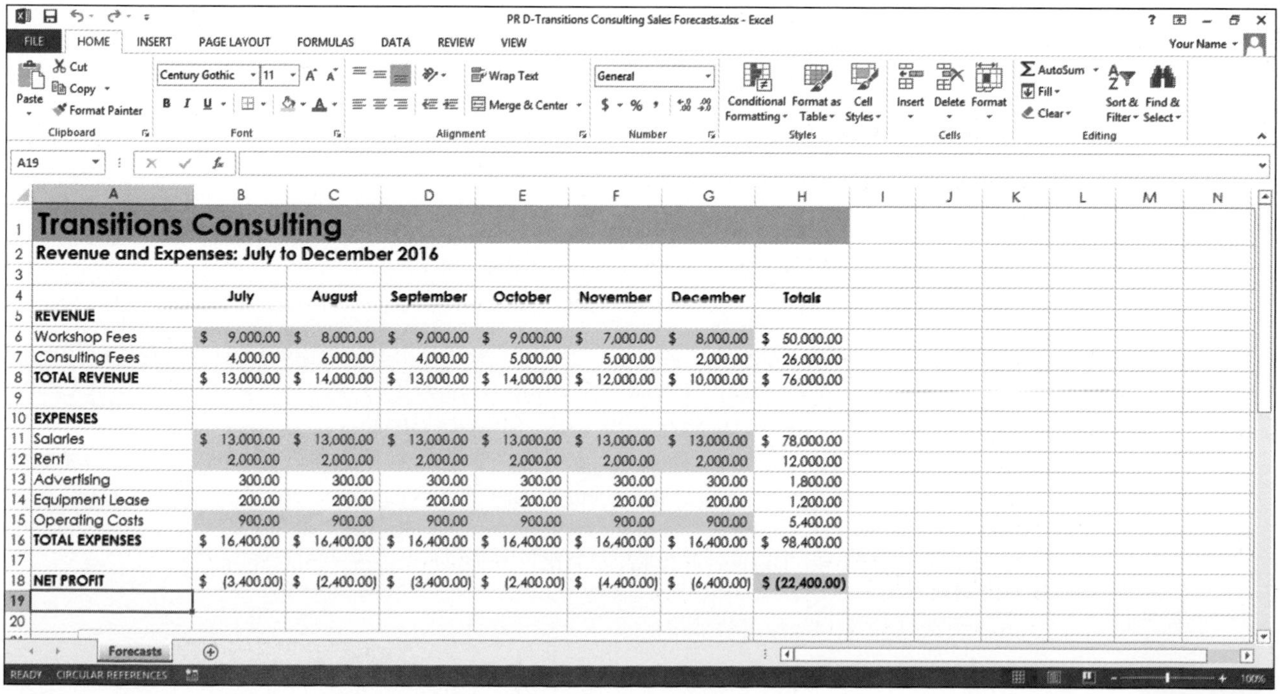

PR D-Transitions Consulting Sales Forecasts.xlsx - Excel

Transitions Consulting
Revenue and Expenses: July to December 2016

	July	August	September	October	November	December	Totals
REVENUE							
Workshop Fees	$ 9,000.00	$ 8,000.00	$ 9,000.00	$ 9,000.00	$ 7,000.00	$ 8,000.00	$ 50,000.00
Consulting Fees	4,000.00	6,000.00	4,000.00	5,000.00	5,000.00	2,000.00	26,000.00
TOTAL REVENUE	$ 13,000.00	$ 14,000.00	$ 13,000.00	$ 14,000.00	$ 12,000.00	$ 10,000.00	$ 76,000.00
EXPENSES							
Salaries	$ 13,000.00	$ 13,000.00	$ 13,000.00	$ 13,000.00	$ 13,000.00	$ 13,000.00	$ 78,000.00
Rent	2,000.00	2,000.00	2,000.00	2,000.00	2,000.00	2,000.00	12,000.00
Advertising	300.00	300.00	300.00	300.00	300.00	300.00	1,800.00
Equipment Lease	200.00	200.00	200.00	200.00	200.00	200.00	1,200.00
Operating Costs	900.00	900.00	900.00	900.00	900.00	900.00	5,400.00
TOTAL EXPENSES	$ 16,400.00	$ 16,400.00	$ 16,400.00	$ 16,400.00	$ 16,400.00	$ 16,400.00	$ 98,400.00
NET PROFIT	$ (3,400.00)	$ (2,400.00)	$ (3,400.00)	$ (2,400.00)	$ (4,400.00)	$ (6,400.00)	$ (22,400.00)

Format the Scenarios

You decide to create a column chart and then print worksheets to show the three sets of scenarios.

STEPS

1. Select cells B4:G4, press and hold [Ctrl], select cells B18:G18, click the INSERT tab, click the Insert Column Chart button ![icon] in the Charts group, click the Clustered Column button (far-left selection in the top row), click the More button ![icon] in the Chart Styles group, then select Style 6 (sixth column, top row)

2. Click Chart Title, type Current Monthly Net Profit, press [Enter], click the Change Colors button in the Chart styles group, scroll down the gallery, then select any one of the Color 10 boxes (lavender color)

3. Click the frame that encloses the chart, drag the chart down to row 21, then resize the chart so the upper-left corner starts at the midpoint of cell A21 and the lower-right corner ends in cell G41

4. Click away from the chart to deselect it, click the DATA tab, open the Scenario Manager dialog box, show all the Best Case scenarios, close the Scenario Manager dialog box, then verify that $5,000 appears as the top value of the value axis (y-axis)

5. Show all the Current scenarios again, close the Scenario Manager, right-click the value axis (contains the dollar amounts), click Format Axis, select the contents of the Maximum text box in the Format Axis pane, type 5000, then close the Format Axis pane
   You change the top value of the value axis to match the top value ($5,000) of the value axis when the Best Case scenarios are active to ensure the column charts provide a meaningful comparison among the scenarios.

6. Click away from the chart to deselect it, click the FILE tab, click Print, click Page Setup, click the Fit to option button to fit the worksheet on one page, click the Margins tab, click the Horizontally check box to select it, click the Header/Footer tab, click Custom Header, type Current Scenarios at the left and your name at the right, click OK, click OK, then click Print

7. Open the Scenario Manager dialog box, show all the Best Case scenarios, close the dialog box, then verify that $8,200 appears in cell H18

8. Click the chart title, click in the formula bar, type Best Case Forecast, click outside the chart, click the PAGE LAYOUT tab, click the Print Titles button in the Page Setup group, click the Header/Footer tab, click the Custom Header button, change the custom header text to Best Case Scenarios, then print a copy
   FIGURE D-8 shows a printout of the worksheet with the Best Case scenarios active.

9. Show all the Worst Case scenarios, verify that $(22,400.00) appears in cell H18, change the chart title to Worst Case Forecast, change the custom header to show Worst Case Scenarios, print a copy, then save and close the workbook
   FIGURE D-9 shows a printout of the worksheet with the Worst Case scenarios active. Now that you have created scenarios, you can mix and match them to view new predictions. For example, you could show the Current Salaries and Current Operating Costs scenarios along with the Best Case Rent scenario and Worst Case Sales scenario. The net profit in cell H18 changes with each combination.

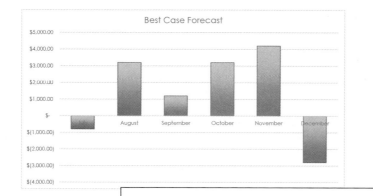

Best Case Scenarios   Your Name

Transitions Consulting
Revenue and Expenses: July to December 2016

	July	August	September	October	November	December	Totals
REVENUE							
Workshop Fees	$ 10,000.00	$ 12,000.00	$ 12,000.00	$ 13,000.00	$ 14,000.00	$ 10,000.00	$ 71,000.00
Consulting Fees	4,000.00	6,000.00	4,000.00	5,000.00	5,000.00	2,000.00	26,000.00
TOTAL REVENUE	$ 14,000.00	$ 18,000.00	$ 16,000.00	$ 18,000.00	$ 19,000.00	$ 12,000.00	$ 97,000.00
EXPENSES							
Salaries	$ 12,000.00	$ 12,000.00	$ 12,000.00	$ 12,000.00	$ 12,000.00	$ 12,000.00	$ 72,000.00
Rent	1,500.00	1,500.00	1,500.00	1,500.00	1,500.00	1,500.00	9,000.00
Advertising	300.00	300.00	300.00	300.00	300.00	300.00	1,800.00
Equipment Lease	200.00	200.00	200.00	200.00	200.00	200.00	1,200.00
Operating Costs	800.00	800.00	800.00	800.00	800.00	800.00	4,800.00
TOTAL EXPENSES	$ 14,800.00	$ 14,800.00	$ 14,800.00	$ 14,800.00	$ 14,800.00	$ 14,800.00	$ 88,800.00
NET PROFIT	$ (800.00)	$ 3,200.00	$ 1,200.00	$ 3,200.00	$ 4,200.00	$ (2,800.00)	$ 8,200.00

Best Case Forecast

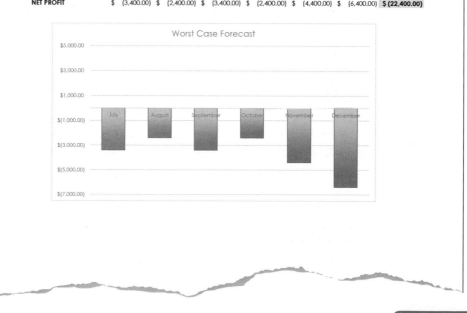

Worst Case Scenarios   Your Name

Transitions Consulting
Revenue and Expenses: July to December 2016

	July	August	September	October	November	December	Totals
REVENUE							
Workshop Fees	$ 9,000.00	$ 8,000.00	$ 9,000.00	$ 9,000.00	$ 7,000.00	$ 8,000.00	$ 50,000.00
Consulting Fees	4,000.00	6,000.00	4,000.00	5,000.00	5,000.00	2,000.00	26,000.00
TOTAL REVENUE	$ 13,000.00	$ 14,000.00	$ 13,000.00	$ 14,000.00	$ 12,000.00	$ 10,000.00	$ 76,000.00
EXPENSES							
Salaries	$ 13,000.00	$ 13,000.00	$ 13,000.00	$ 13,000.00	$ 13,000.00	$ 13,000.00	$ 78,000.00
Rent	2,000.00	2,000.00	2,000.00	2,000.00	2,000.00	2,000.00	12,000.00
Advertising	300.00	300.00	300.00	300.00	300.00	300.00	1,800.00
Equipment Lease	200.00	200.00	200.00	200.00	200.00	200.00	1,200.00
Operating Costs	900.00	900.00	900.00	900.00	900.00	900.00	5,400.00
TOTAL EXPENSES	$ 16,400.00	$ 16,400.00	$ 16,400.00	$ 16,400.00	$ 16,400.00	$ 16,400.00	$ 98,400.00
NET PROFIT	$ (3,400.00)	$ (2,400.00)	$ (3,400.00)	$ (2,400.00)	$ (4,400.00)	$ (6,400.00)	$ (22,400.00)

Worst Case Forecast

Excel 2013

Excel 2013
UNIT D

Customer Profile for Walk Europe

As the Sales Manager of Walk Europe, an online travel company that organizes self-guided walking tours in Europe, you create a Customer Profile that analyzes data about clients who have purchased tours in July of 2016. To create the Customer Profile, you will **Set Up the Customer List**, **Analyze the List**, and then **Format the Customer Profile** as shown in FIGURE D-17 on page 97.

Set Up the Customer List

You open a workbook containing a list of clients, format the list as a table, calculate totals, and use COUNT functions to determine the number and percentage of clients who are 60 years of age or over.

STEPS

1. **Open** PR D-01.xlsx **from the location where you store your files, save it as** PR D-Customer Profile for Walk Europe, **then apply the** Parallax theme

   > **HINT**
   > When you format a list as a table, each column is assigned a name based on the label in the header.

2. **Select the range** A1:J45, **click the** HOME **tab, click the Format as Table button in the Styles group, select** Table Style Light 12 (one of the red selections), **click OK, select Table1 in the Table Name text box in the Properties group, type** JulyList, **then press [Enter]**

3. **On the worksheet frame, click** D, **press and hold [Ctrl], click** I, **verify only columns D and I are selected, click the** HOME **tab, click the Wrap Text button in the Alignment group, reduce the width of columns D and I to 10, click the Wrap Text button twice more, then verify that the header text in columns D and I wraps as shown in** FIGURE D-10

4. **Click cell** J2, **enter a formula to multiply the value in cell C2 by the value in cell I2, then format the values in the** Per Person Cost **and** Total Cost **cells using the** Accounting Number Format

5. **Using** FIGURE D-11 **as a guide, click cell** L1, **enter and format the labels in cells L1:L6 and the shading in cells M2:M6, then widen column L**

6. **Click cell** M2, **type** =SUM(, **select the range** J2:J45 (you will see =SUM(JulyList[Total Cost] in the formula bar), **type**), **press [Enter], then apply the Accounting Number Format style**

7. **Click cell** M3, **then enter a** SUM **formula to add all the values in the Guests column**

   > **HINT**
   > When you click the Go button, the function name will be selected in the Select a function list in the Insert Function dialog box.

8. **Click cell** M4, **click the** Insert Function button fx **on the formula bar, type** COUNTA, **click Go, click OK, select the range** A2:A45, **compare the Function Arguments dialog box to** FIGURE D-12, **click OK, then verify that 44 appears in cell M4**

   The COUNTA function counts every cell containing an entry in any form, regardless of whether it is a label or a value.

9. **Click cell** M5, **click the** Insert Function button fx, **type** COUNTIF, **click Go, click OK, complete the Function Arguments dialog box as shown in** FIGURE D-13, **then click OK**

   The COUNTIF function counts all the values in a range that conform to specific criteria. In this case, you counted all entries in the Average Age column that were greater than or equal to 60. You should see 16 in cell M5.

10. **Click cell** M6, **enter the formula** =M5/M4, **press [Enter], click cell M6, click the** Percent Style button % **in the Number group, then save the workbook**

Excel Projects II

FIGURE D-10: Columns resized and text wrapped

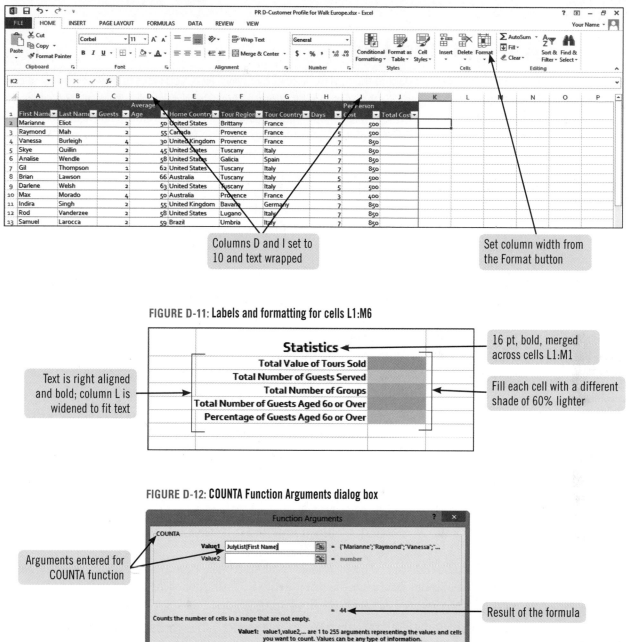

Columns D and I set to 10 and text wrapped

Set column width from the Format button

FIGURE D-11: Labels and formatting for cells L1:M6

16 pt, bold, merged across cells L1:M1

Text is right aligned and bold; column L is widened to fit text

Fill each cell with a different shade of 60% lighter

FIGURE D-12: COUNTA Function Arguments dialog box

Arguments entered for COUNTA function

Result of the formula

FIGURE D-13: COUNTIF Function Arguments dialog box

Arguments entered for COUNTIF function; you can select the range in the worksheet, enter the cell addresses, or enter the name of the table and range

Enter >=60 as the Criteria

Customer Profile (continued)

Analyze the List

You want to analyze the data in the JulyList table in two ways. First, you want to view a list only of clients aged 60 or over and then use the Subtotals function to show the breakdown of these clients according to the Tour Country they visited (France, Italy, and so on.). Second, you want to know the total amount spent on tours by clients in each of the home countries (United States, Canada, and so on). You create a PivotTable to calculate the total amount spent by each group of clients from each home country and then use the data in the PivotTable to create a pie chart.

1. **Double-click the** Sheet1 **tab, type** List, **press [Enter], add a new worksheet called** Analysis, **then add another new worksheet called** Customer Profile

2. **Click the** List **sheet tab, click the Filter button** ▼ **in the Average Age cell (cell D1), point to** Number Filters, **then click** Greater Than Or Equal To

3. **Type** 60 **in the Custom AutoFilter dialog box, then click** OK

    The table is filtered to show only client groups with an average age of 60 or older.

4. **Select the range** A1:J45, **click the** Copy **button in the Clipboard group, click the** Analysis **sheet tab, click cell** A1, **click the** Paste **button, then widen columns as needed**

5. **Click the** DATA **tab, click the** Sort **button in the Sort & Filter group, click the** Sort by list arrow, **click** Tour Country, **click** Add Level, **click the** Then by list arrow, **click** Tour Region, **compare the Sort dialog box to** FIGURE D-14, **then click** OK

    You sort a list before you create a Subtotal list so that all related rows in the category you want to subtotal are together.

6. **Click** Subtotal **in the Outline group, click the** At each change in list arrow, **scroll to and click** Tour Country, **verify that** Sum **appears in the Use function text box and the** Total Cost **check box is selected as shown in** FIGURE D-15, **click** OK, **then widen the** Total Cost **column**

    The Subtotals list calculates the total amount spent in each tour country by groups of guests who are 60 or older. You can see at a glance that this group spent $10,350.00 on walking tours in France.

7. **Click the** List **sheet tab, click the** Filter **button in the Sort & Filter group to remove the filter, click the** INSERT **tab, click** PivotTable **in the Tables group, click the** Existing Worksheet option button, **click the** Analysis **sheet tab, scroll down and click cell** A25, **then click** OK

8. **Click the** Home Country **check box in the PivotTable Fields pane, scroll down the PivotChart Fields pane to see the** Total Cost **field, drag the** Total Cost **field to the** VALUES area, **then scroll down the worksheet window to view the PivotTable as shown in** FIGURE D-16

    The PivotTable calculates the amount spent by groups of guests from each of the home countries.

9. **Select the range** B26:B33, **click the** HOME **tab and apply the** Accounting Number Format **style, click the** PIVOTTABLE TOOLS ANALYZE **tab, click** PivotChart **in the Tools group, click** Pie, **click** OK, **move the pie chart down so it starts in cell** D25, **then save the workbook**

FIGURE D-14: Sort dialog box

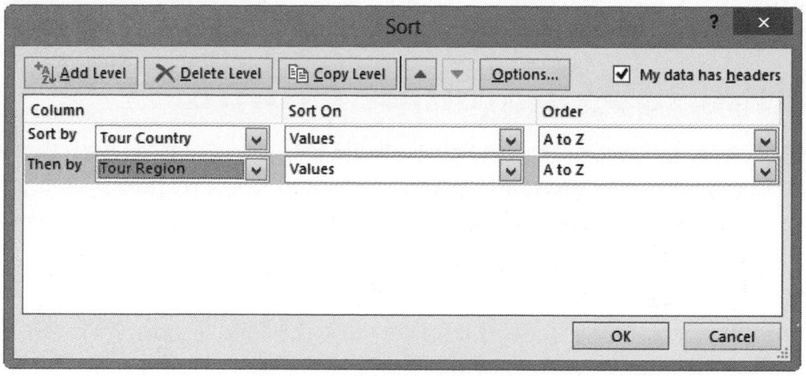

FIGURE D-15: Subtotals dialog box

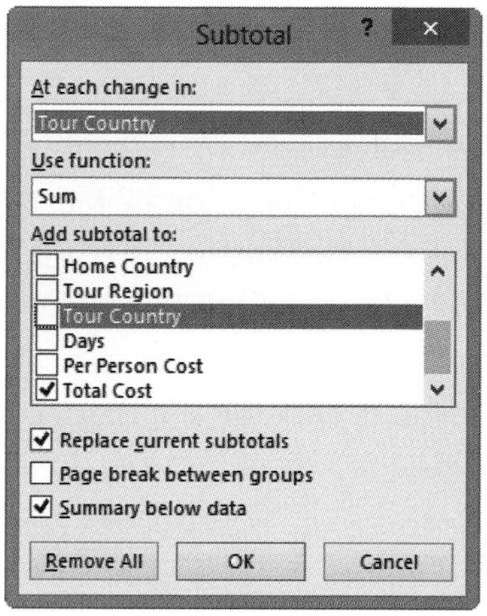

FIGURE D-16: Creating the PivotTable

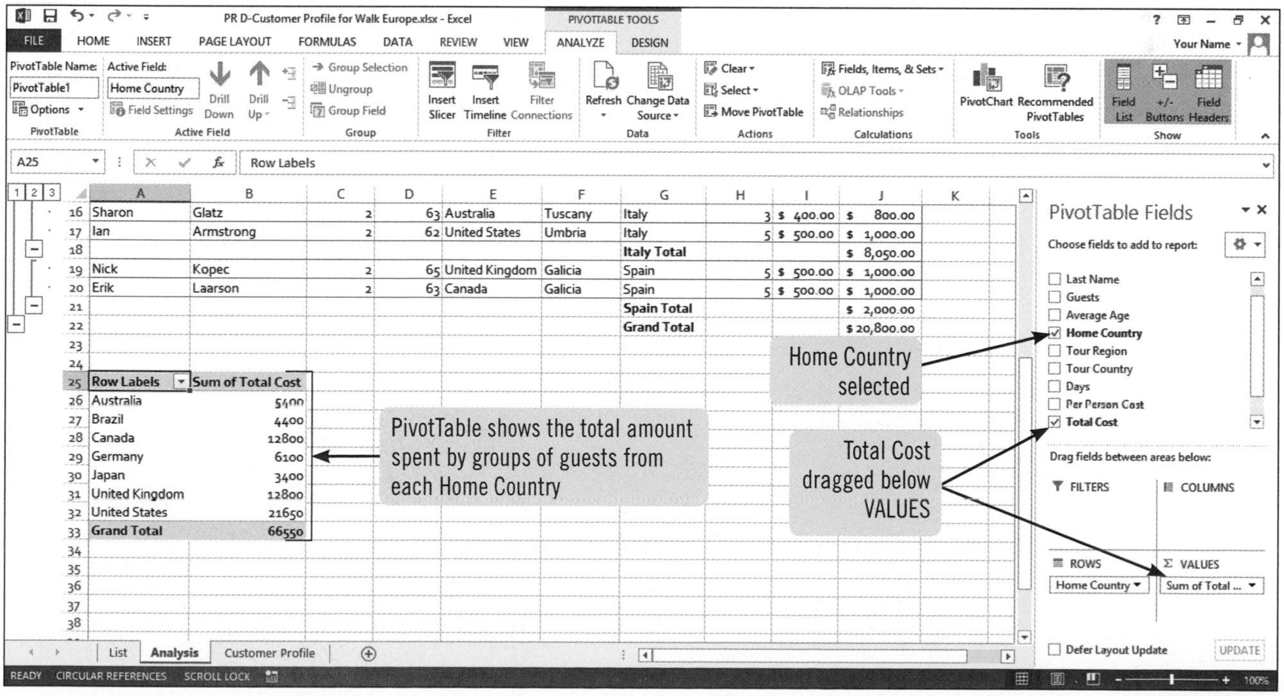

Excel 2013

Customer Profile (continued)

Format the Customer Profile

You copy the components you want to include in the Customer Profile from the Analysis tab, paste them into the Customer Profile sheet, and then format them, add text boxes, then format the worksheet for printing on one page. The completed Customer Profile is shown in **FIGURE D-17**.

STEPS

1. Click the Customer Profile sheet tab, click the INSERT tab, click the Text Box button in the Text group, draw a text box from cell A1 to J6, then apply 24 pt and bold to Walk Europe, and 16 pt and bold to the subtitle as shown in FIGURE D-17

2. Right-click the text box, click Format Shape (the Format Shape pane opens), click FILL, click the Picture or texture fill option button, click File, navigate to the location where you store files for this book, then double-click PR D-02.jpg

3. Click the PICTURE TOOLS FORMAT tab, click the Artistic Effects button in the Adjust group, then select the Line Drawing effect (top row, last column)

TROUBLE
Be sure Column A is still selected when you click the Wrap Text button.

4. Click the List sheet tab, select the range L2:M6, copy it, click the Customer Profile sheet tab, click cell A8, click the Paste button, increase the width of Column A to 16, click the Wrap Text button in the Alignment group, then increase the width of column B to show the total

5. Click the Analysis sheet tab, click the pie chart, copy it, then paste it in cell D8 on the Customer Profile sheet tab

6. Change the chart title to Revenue by Client Country, click the PIVOTCHART TOOLS DESIGN tab, click Add Chart Element, point to Legend, click None, click Add Chart Element, point to Data Labels, click More Data Label Options, click the Category Name check box, then click the Outside End option button

7. Close all open panes, drag the lower right corner handle of the pie chart to cell J20, then apply Chart Style 9

8. Click the Analysis sheet tab, select the range A1:J22, copy the range, paste it in cell A23 of the Customer Profile sheet, then refer to FIGURE D-17: widen columns as needed, wrap the "Tour Country" label, merge and center cells A22:J22, enter the text shown in row 22, apply bold, then fill the cell with Red, Accent 4, Lighter 80%

9. Click the text box at the top of the document, click the FILE tab, click Print, click No Scaling, click Fit Sheet on One Page, then add a custom footer that includes your name in the Center section

MORE PRACTICE
For more practice with the skills presented in this project, complete Independent Challenge 2.

10. Return to the worksheet, save the workbook, submit a copy to your instructor, then close the workbook

   When printed, your worksheet should appear similar to **FIGURE D-17**.

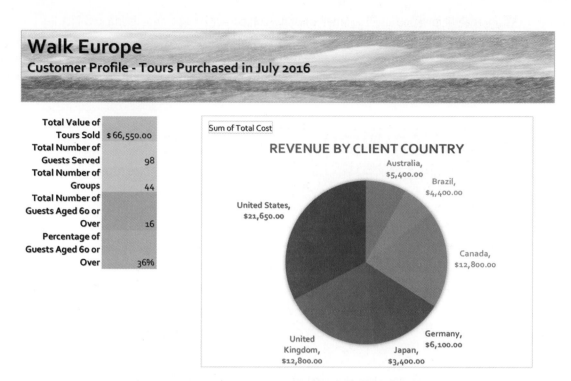

Walk Europe
Customer Profile - Tours Purchased in July 2016

Total Value of Tours Sold	$ 66,550.00
Total Number of Guests Served	98
Total Number of Groups	44
Total Number of Guests Aged 60 or Over	16
Percentage of Guests Aged 60 or Over	36%

Sum of Total Cost

REVENUE BY CLIENT COUNTRY

- Australia, $5,400.00
- Brazil, $4,400.00
- Canada, $12,800.00
- Germany, $6,100.00
- Japan, $3,400.00
- United Kingdom, $12,800.00
- United States, $21,650.00

France is the most popular tour country with client groups with an average age of 60 or older.

First Name	Last Name	Guests	Average Age	Home Country	Tour Region	Tour Country	Days	Per Person Cost	Total Cost
Deborah	Klein	2	65	Germany	Loire Valley	France	5	$ 500.00	$ 1,000.00
Laurie	Black	2	66	Canada	Loire Valley	France	7	$ 850.00	$ 1,700.00
Jolene	Terry	2	67	Canada	Loire Valley	France	7	$ 850.00	$ 1,700.00
Alex	Wigham	2	70	United States	Provence	France	7	$ 850.00	$ 1,700.00
Vince	Shad	3	69	United States	Provence	France	7	$ 850.00	$ 2,550.00
Pat	Rhinehart	2	73	Germany	Provence	France	7	$ 850.00	$ 1,700.00
						France Total			$ 10,350.00
Sofia	Guthenberg	1	60	Canada	Bavaria	Germany	3	$ 400.00	$ 400.00
						Germany Total			$ 400.00
Gil	Thompson	1	62	United States	Tuscany	Italy	7	$ 850.00	$ 850.00
Brian	Lawson	2	66	Australia	Tuscany	Italy	5	$ 500.00	$ 1,000.00
Darlene	Welsh	2	63	United States	Tuscany	Italy	5	$ 500.00	$ 1,000.00
Ellen	Cronan	2	68	Canada	Tuscany	Italy	7	$ 850.00	$ 1,700.00
Miguel	Piggott	2	70	United Kingdom	Tuscany	Italy	7	$ 850.00	$ 1,700.00
Sharon	Glatz	2	63	Australia	Tuscany	Italy	3	$ 400.00	$ 800.00
Ian	Armstrong	2	62	United States	Umbria	Italy	5	$ 500.00	$ 1,000.00
						Italy Total			$ 8,050.00
Nick	Kopec	2	65	United Kingdom	Galicia	Spain	5	$ 500.00	$ 1,000.00
Erik	Laarson	2	63	Canada	Galicia	Spain	5	$ 500.00	$ 1,000.00
						Spain Total			$ 2,000.00
						Grand Total			$ 20,800.00

Your Name

Sales Report for Food Style

As an analyst for Food Style, a small catering company, you use an existing product list to produce a report that analyzes sales over three years. The report includes two worksheets—one with conditional formatting that provides a visual comparison of product sales, and the other with a PivotTable, column chart, and Slicer that arrange and summarize product data to allow for comparisons and trend analysis. To create the Sales Report, you need to **Apply Conditional Formatting** and **Filter and Chart Results**.

Apply Conditional Formatting

You open the product list, use conditional formatting to highlight trends, then create a PivotTable that shows yearly sales by product category. **FIGURE D-19** shows conditional formatting applied to the data.

STEPS

1. Start Excel, open PR D-03.xlsx from the location where you store your Data Files, save it as PR D-Food Style Sales Analysis to the location where you save the files for this book, then apply the Slice theme

2. Click cell F1, type Total, use the SUM function to calculate the total number of products sold in all three years, then use the Fill handle to copy the formula for all products

    The worksheet contains the total menu items that Food Style sold in its catering business in each year from 2014 to 2016. Each product is allocated a category such as "Appetizer" or "Dessert."

3. Select cells A1:F1, click the HOME tab, click the Cell Styles button in the Cells group, click Accent 1 in the Themed Cell Styles section, then bold and center the headings

4. Select the range F2:F30, click the Conditional Formatting button in the Styles group, point to Data Bars, click Blue Data Bar in the Solid Fill area, increase the width of the Total column to 15, then click cell G1

    The Conditional Formatting shows that Tropical Salad is the most popular product as shown in **FIGURE D-18**.

5. Select the range B2:B30, click the Conditional Formatting button, point to Highlight Cells Rules, click Text That Contains, notice that Salad is selected, then click OK

    All instances of "Salad" in the range are formatted with a red font color and light red fill.

6. Click the Conditional Formatting button again, point to Highlight Cells Rules, click Text That Contains, type Dessert, click the with list arrow, click Custom Format, click the Fill tab, click one of the lighter Lime green color boxes (such as 8th column, 2nd row), click OK, then click OK

7. Repeat Step 6 to format Main Course with a light blue fill and Appetizer with a light orange fill, click cell A1, then compare the list to **FIGURE D-19**

8. Name Sheet1 Sales Data, add a new sheet called Product Sales, select A1:F30 in the Sales Data sheet, click the INSERT tab, click PivotTable in the Tables group, click the Existing Worksheet option button, click the Product Sales sheet tab, click cell A1, then click OK

    The PIVOTTABLE TOOLS ANALYZE and DESIGN tabs are now available and the PivotTable Fields pane opens on the right side of the window.

9. In the Product Sales sheet, click the Product check box in the PivotTable Fields pane, click each of the remaining check boxes in the PivotTable Fields pane, then save the workbook

    All the data from the list is added to the PivotTable, with each product assigned to a different row.

FIGURE D-18: **Data bars applied to the Total column**

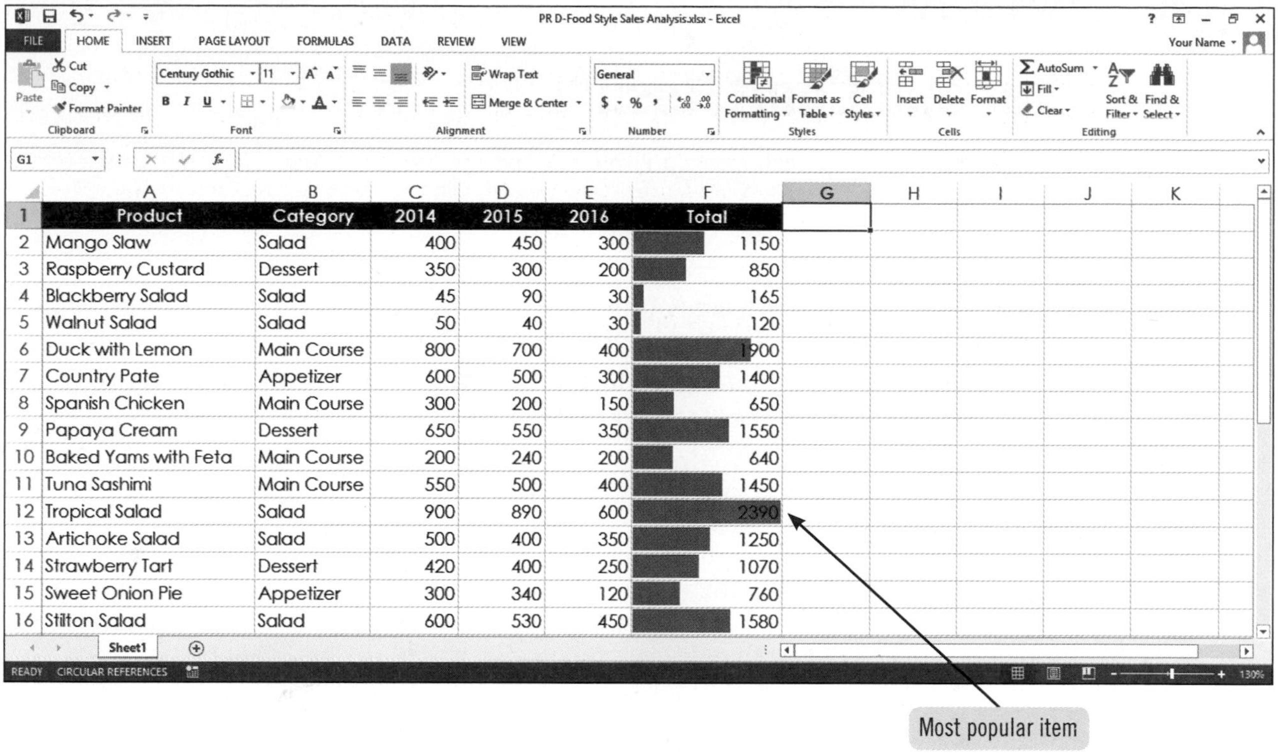

	A	B	C	D	E	F	G
1	Product	Category	2014	2015	2016	Total	
2	Mango Slaw	Salad	400	450	300	1150	
3	Raspberry Custard	Dessert	350	300	200	850	
4	Blackberry Salad	Salad	45	90	30	165	
5	Walnut Salad	Salad	50	40	30	120	
6	Duck with Lemon	Main Course	800	700	400	1900	
7	Country Pate	Appetizer	600	500	300	1400	
8	Spanish Chicken	Main Course	300	200	150	650	
9	Papaya Cream	Dessert	650	550	350	1550	
10	Baked Yams with Feta	Main Course	200	240	200	640	
11	Tuna Sashimi	Main Course	550	500	400	1450	
12	Tropical Salad	Salad	900	890	600	2390	
13	Artichoke Salad	Salad	500	400	350	1250	
14	Strawberry Tart	Dessert	420	400	250	1070	
15	Sweet Onion Pie	Appetizer	300	340	120	760	
16	Stilton Salad	Salad	600	530	450	1580	

Most popular item

FIGURE D-19: **List with conditional formatting for Category entries**

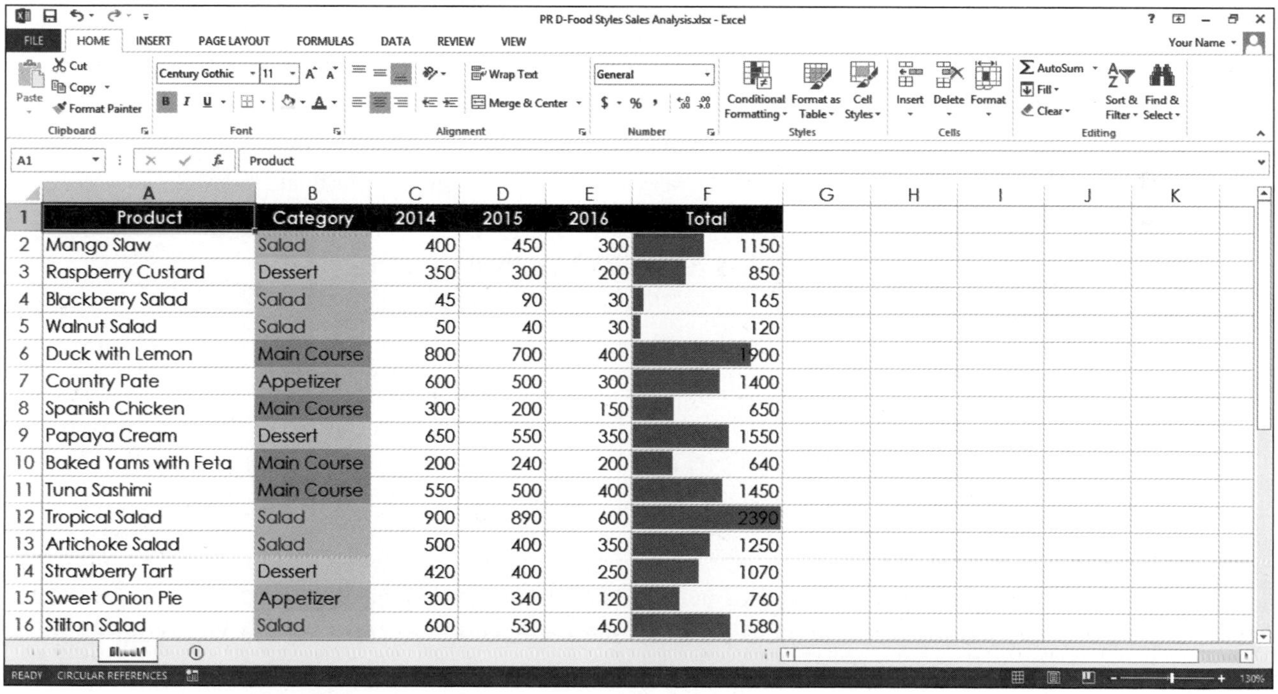

	A	B	C	D	E	F	G
1	Product	Category	2014	2015	2016	Total	
2	Mango Slaw	Salad	400	450	300	1150	
3	Raspberry Custard	Dessert	350	300	200	850	
4	Blackberry Salad	Salad	45	90	30	165	
5	Walnut Salad	Salad	50	40	30	120	
6	Duck with Lemon	Main Course	800	700	400	1900	
7	Country Pate	Appetizer	600	500	300	1400	
8	Spanish Chicken	Main Course	300	200	150	650	
9	Papaya Cream	Dessert	650	550	350	1550	
10	Baked Yams with Feta	Main Course	200	240	200	640	
11	Tuna Sashimi	Main Course	550	500	400	1450	
12	Tropical Salad	Salad	900	890	600	2390	
13	Artichoke Salad	Salad	500	400	350	1250	
14	Strawberry Tart	Dessert	420	400	250	1070	
15	Sweet Onion Pie	Appetizer	300	340	120	760	
16	Stilton Salad	Salad	600	530	450	1580	

Filter and Chart Results

You modify the PivotTable, then create a PivotChart and use the Slicer. The completed sales report is shown in **FIGURE D-22**.

1. Click Product in the ROWS area of the PivotTable Fields pane, click Move Down to sort and summarize the products by category, insert a new row above row 1 and type Food Style Sales Report, press [Enter], apply the Title style to cell A1, then click in the PivotTable to show the PivotTable Fields pane

2. Click the Collapse button ⊟ to the left of Appetizer to collapse the list of appetizers as shown in FIGURE D-20, then click ⊟ next to Dessert, Main Course, and Salad so all four categories are collapsed

3. Click the INSERT tab, click the Insert Column Chart button ▉▼ in the Charts group, click Clustered Column, drag the chart to position its upper-left corner in cell A10, then deselect the 2015 check box and the Total check box in the PivotTable Fields pane

   Only data for 2014 and 2016 is shown. As you can see, Food Style experienced a significant reduction in sales of all four product categories between 2014 and 2016.

HINT
The Slicer provides you with a quick and easy way to show only the data you want to study.

4. Click in the PivotTable, click the PIVOTTABLE TOOLS ANALYZE tab, click Insert Slicer in the Filter group, click the Category check box, click OK, click Dessert in the Slicer, then move the Slicer so you can see the chart and PivotTable as shown in FIGURE D-21

   Only the sales of items in the Dessert category are shown in the PivotTable and the chart.

5. Click the Clear Filter button ▥ to the right of Category in the Slicer to restore the Slicer, click anywhere in the PivotTable, click Product in the lower-left corner of the chart, click the (Select All) check box to deselect it, click the check box next to "Apricot Cobbler," "Asparagus Salad," and "Blackberry Salad," click OK, click the Expand button ⊞ next to "Dessert" in the PivotTable, then click ⊞ next to "Salad"

   You can quickly compare the drop in sales for any combination of products and categories.

6. Click the Collapse button ⊟ next to "Dessert," click ⊟ next to "Salad," click Product in the chart, click the (Select All) check box, then click OK

   The chart again compares the sales for 2014 and 2016 in all four categories.

7. Click the Sales Data sheet tab, click cell E4, type 200, press [Enter], notice how the width of the blue bar in cell F4 increases, click the Product Sales sheet tab, click the PIVOTTABLE TOOLS ANALYZE tab, then click the Refresh button in the Data group

   Each time you change the data used to build the PivotTable, you need to refresh the PivotTable.

8. Click the chart, click the Field Buttons list arrow in the Show/Hide group, then click Hide All

MORE PRACTICE
For more practice with the skills presented in this project, complete Independent Challenge 3.

9. Show the Sales Data worksheet, press and hold [Shift], click the Product Sales sheet, set up both worksheets to print on one page, centered horizontally, with your name in the Left section of the Header and the sheet name in the Right section, submit the workbook to your instructor, then close the workbook

   The completed Sales Report appears as shown in FIGURE D-22.

FIGURE D-20: Collapsing the Appetizer group

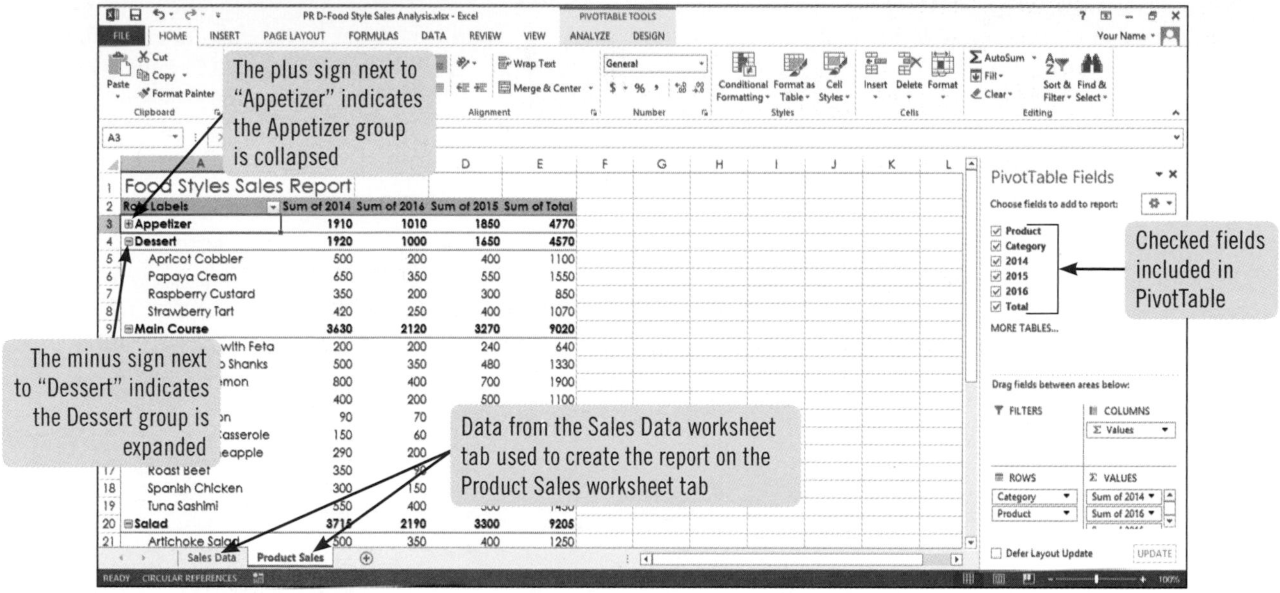

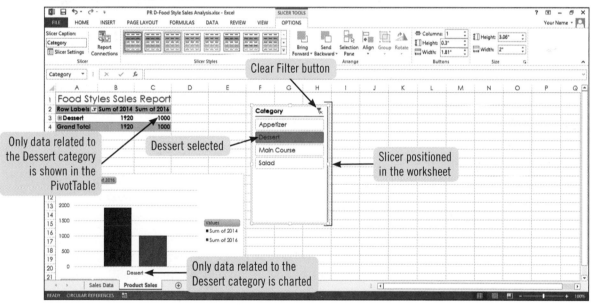

FIGURE D-21: Positioning the Slicer

FIGURE D-22: Product Sales

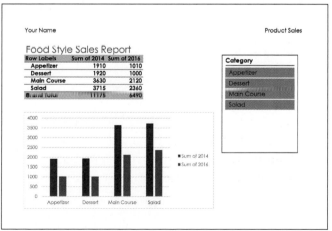

Independent Challenge 1

As the owner of a small business, you decide that you need to expand your operations in order to generate more income. To help you make an informed decision, you use the Scenario Manager to see the effect of your plans on a current revenue and expenses worksheet.

1. Determine the name of your company, the type of business it conducts, and your plans for expansion. For example, you could run a home-based catering service that has grown big enough to warrant moving the business out of your home and into a commercial location. Alternatively, you could run a snow removal business from a small commercial office and decide to move into a larger office and buy several new pieces of snow removal equipment. Write the name of your company and a short description of your expansion plans in the box below:

Company Name: _____

Description of Expansion Plans: _____

_____

2. Create a worksheet that shows your revenue and expenses over a six-month period. Include labels for each of six months (e.g., for July to December), insert labels for the various types of revenue you generate (e.g. Catering Sales and Consulting), and insert labels for your various expenses (e.g. Rent, Salaries, Advertising, Equipment, and Operating Costs). Calculate your monthly revenue and expenses and your total profit/loss for each month and at the end of six months.
3. Format the worksheet attractively, then save the workbook as **PR D-My Predictions** to the location where you save the files for this book.
4. Fill the rows containing the data you plan to change when you create your Best and Worst Case scenarios with the color of your choice.
5. Use the Scenario Manager to create Current scenarios from the data currently entered in the worksheet. Note that you only need to create scenarios for the rows that contain the values you will change when you create Best Case scenarios and Worst Case scenarios.
6. Select a Current scenario, click Add, rename the Current Scenario as the **Best Case Scenario** for that category, then change values using the Scenario Manager to reflect your best case predictions should you carry out your expansion plans. For example, if you decide to move to a new office, your Rent expense may increase, and if you hire an assistant, your Salaries expense will increase. Make sure you also increase your income to reflect the increased revenue that you expect to make as a result of expanding your operations.
7. Repeat Step 6, but this time enter values to reflect your worst case predictions, should your expansion plans fail to proceed as well as you hope.
8. Show the Best Case scenarios, create a column chart or bar chart that displays the Best Case monthly income, apply the chart style of your choice, add **Best Case Forecast** as the chart title, then format and print a copy of the worksheet. Make sure you include your name and text that identifies this report as the Best Case Forecast in the header along with similar descriptive text in the subtitle on the worksheet.
9. Make a note of the upper limit of the value axis (y-axis) in the chart. You need this information because you want the printed charts with the Current, Best, and Worst Case scenarios worksheets to display the same upper limit on the value axis so that the differences in the three charts are readily apparent.

Independent Challenge 1 (continued)

10. Show the Current scenarios, change the subtitle on the worksheet and the title of the chart to reflect the current scenarios, change the upper limit on the value axis (as noted in step 9) to the same upper limit displayed in the Best Case column chart, change the header to reflect the worksheet content, then print a copy of the worksheet.

11. Show the Worst Case scenarios, change the subtitle on the worksheet and the title of the chart to reflect the worst case scenarios, change the upper limit on the value axis (as noted in step 9) to the same upper limit displayed in the Best Case chart, change the header to reflect the worksheet content, then print a copy.

12. Save and close the workbook, then submit your files to your instructor.

Independent Challenge 2

Create a list of 30 or 40 customers and the products or services they have purchased from a company of your choice. When you have completed the list, ask questions about the data and then use PivotTable, AutoFilter, and Subtotal functions to create an attractively formatted Customer Profile that provides an easy-to-understand summary of the data that answers the questions.

1. Determine the name of your company and the type of products it sells. For example, you could run an adventure tour company called Dynamism Tours that sells hiking, cycling, and kayaking tour packages in the Pacific Northwest.

2. In Excel, create a list of 30 to 40 customers who have purchased your product or service in the past month. For example, the list of customers who have purchased tours from Dynamism Tours could include fields such as Customer Name, Age Range (e.g., Under 30, 30 to 50, Over 50, and so on), Number of Guests, Tour Duration, Tour Category (e.g., Hiking, Cycling, Kayaking, and so on), Tour Location, Amount Spent, and so on. The field names you include will depend upon the type of information you wish to feature in your customer profile. For example, if you want to find out how much money was spent by in a specific age range on Hiking tours, you will need to include field names for Age Range, Tour Category, and Amount.

3. Save the workbook as **PR D-My Customer Profile**, select the theme of your choice, then set up the workbook with three sheet tabs named **List**, **Analysis**, and **Customer Profile**.

4. Format the completed list as a table that contains headers, name the table, then adjust column widths (wrap text if needed) so the list is easy to read.

5. Include a column called **Total**, then calculate the total amount each person in the list spent on the product or service.

6. Set up a portion of the worksheet with labels for specific data such as "Number of Guests Under 30," or "Total Number of Guests," and so on. Include at least three labels for different information.

7. Use the COUNTA, SUM, and COUNTIF functions as needed to enter the totals required for the labels you entered.

8. In the List sheet tab, use filtering to show only those records (rows) that conform to specific criteria (for example, only customers who took cycling tours), then copy the filtered list to the Analysis sheet.

9. Sort the filtered list so that all records of a certain category (for example, all records for "Under 30" or "Hiking tours") are together.

10. Use the Subtotal function to calculate the total amount spent in each category.

11. Return to the List sheet tab, remove the filter, create a PivotTable that appears below the filtered list in the Analysis sheet tab, then select fields in the PivotTable Fields pane to develop a PivotTable that shows the information you want. For ideas, click the Recommended PivotTables button and view the various ways in which you can view data from your list.

Independent Challenge 2 (continued)

12. Create a chart from the PivotTable, then format it attractively.
13. In the Customer Profile sheet, create a text box to contain the name of the company and the subtotal "Customer Profile" followed by the month of data being analyzed (e.g., June 2016). Fill the text box with a picture and modify the Color effects as needed so the text box presents a striking image for your company.
14. Copy the various components of your customer profile into the Customer Profile worksheet (the statistics, Subtotal list, and PivotChart), arrange them attractively on one page, then add text as needed to explain the various components.
15. Group all three worksheets, set each sheet up to print on one page with a header containing your name in the Left section and the sheet name in the Right section, then save the workbook and submit a copy to your instructor.

Independent Challenge 3

As the manager of a local video store, you have decided to evaluate the popularity of a selection of the Best Picture Oscar winners your clientele rents and buys. The data you need is already included in an Excel file. You open this file and then use Conditional Formatting to highlight trends and the PivotTable tool to create a report and chart that analyzes the data.

1. Start Excel, open **PR D-04.xlsx** from the location where you store your Data Files, save it as **PR D-Oscar Winners Report** to the location where you save the files for this book, name the Sheet1 tab **Unit Sales and Rentals**, then add a new sheet named **Report**.
2. Select a new theme of your choice for the workbook, then format the Unit Sales and Rentals worksheet so that the header row is formatted with the Heading 1 cell style. Adjust column widths as needed.
3. Sort the table in ascending order by Year.
4. Apply Conditional Formatting to the 2016 Unit Rentals column using the Data Bar option of your choice.
5. For column C, create a Conditional Formatting rule that fills any cell containing "Drama" with the shading color of your choice, any cell containing "Comedy" with a different color, and any cell containing "Musical" with a different color.
6. Create a PivotTable in cell A3 of the Report worksheet from the data, then add all the fields to the PivotTable by clicking each of the check boxes in the PivotTable Fields pane.
7. Move Title below Genre in the Row Labels area.
8. Enter **Selected Oscar Winners** as the title in cell A1 and **Rentals by Genre** as the subtitle in cell A2. Merge and center the titles across columns A to D, then apply the Title cell style to cell A1 and the Heading 1 cell style to cell A2.
9. Collapse the list so only the genres appear, check only the Title, Genre, and 2016 Unit Rentals boxes in the PivotTable Fields pane, then create a pie chart that shows the breakdown of Unit Rentals by genre.

Independent Challenge 3 (continued)

10. Format the chart attractively using a chart style of your choice. Include **Breakdown of Rentals by Genre** as the chart title.

11. Show the Slicer, then use it to view the total rentals of each title in the Musical genre. (*Hint:* Remember to expand the Musical Genre in the PivotTable to see the rentals by title.) Experiment with some other views and notice how the pie chart changes, depending on which data you select. Remove the filter from the Slicer, then click Genre and (Select All) so that all three legend entries appear in the chart.

12. In the Unit Sales and Rentals worksheet, change the 2016 Unit Rentals for My Fair Lady to **250**, then refresh the PivotTable in the Report worksheet.

13. Set up both sheets in the workbook so they are centered horizontally and include Your Name and the sheet name in the header, save the workbook, submit a copy to your instructor, then close the workbook.

Independent Challenge 4 - Team Project

To further explore how you can develop a wide range of workbooks with Excel 2013, you will work with two other people to complete a team project. The subject of the team project is the analysis of a small business of your choice. The business should be one that sells products or services to a range of clients that can be arranged into categories (for example, by age group, geographical location, or some other criteria). In addition, the products or services should be divisible into categories. Follow the guidelines provided below to create the three workbooks required for the team project. When you have completed the project, the team will submit a document containing information about the project, as well as the three files related to the project: company forecasts, a customer profile, and a sales report.

Project Setup

1. As a team, work together to complete the following tasks.
   - Share e-mail addresses among all three team members.
   - Set up a time (either via e-mail, an online chat session, Internet Messaging, or face to face) when you will get together to choose your topic and assign roles.
   - At your meeting, complete the table that follows with information about your team and the company you are creating documents for.

Team Name (last names of the team member or another name that describes the project; for example, "Wong-Harrison-Starr" or "Celebrity Tours").
Team Members 1. 2. 3.
Company name
Company products/services and categories (for example, the product could be Video Games and the categories Sports, Action, Strategy, and so on). Include no more than 5 categories.
Client categories (for example, age group, location, gender, and so on). Include up to three client categories.
Current revenue categories (up to two) and values over six months: Current expense categories (up to six) and values over six months:
Team Roles: Indicate who is responsible for each of the following three files (one file per team member). Company Forecasts: Customer Profile: Sales Report:
Workbook Formatting: Select a theme and color scheme that will be used to format all of the workbooks created for the Team Project. Theme: Color Scheme:

Independent Challenge 4 - Team Project (continued)

➤ Workbook Development

Individually, complete the tasks listed below for the file you are responsible for. You need to develop appropriate content, and format the file attractively. Be sure team members use the same theme and color scheme when creating the workbook as detailed in the table above. Include the team name in the left section of the header on all workbooks. In the center section include the individual name and in the Right section include the worksheet name.

Company Forecasts

This workbook contains a statement of revenues and expenses for a time frame such as six months along with values entered for revenue and expenses for three scenarios: Current, Best Case, and Worst Case. These scenarios can be used to determine the consequences of a specific course of action such as relocating to a new office or hiring new staff. Create the workbook as follows:

1. Create a new Excel workbook and save it as **PR D-Team Project_Company Forecasts** to the location where you save files for this book, then apply the workbook theme and color scheme selected by your team.

2. Enter the name of the company in cell A1, a subtitle providing more information about the information on the worksheet, and the months covered by the revenue and expenses starting in column B (for example, in cell B4). In column A, enter revenue sources (up to two) and expense categories (up to six). Calculate the total revenue from all sources, the total expenses, and the net profit. See **FIGURE D-7** for a layout example.

3. Select at least one revenue source and up to three expenses that you will use as the basis for three scenarios: Current, Best Case, and Worse Case. Fill these rows with a color to differentiate them from the other rows in the worksheet.

4. Use the Scenario Manager to create Current scenarios from the data currently entered in the selected rows.

5. Create Best Case scenarios that show positive consequences of a specific action such as moving to a new location. The Best Case scenarios should show increased revenue, along with expenses that reflect the change (for example, a higher Rent expense if the company is moving from a home office to a commercial location), from the Current scenarios.

6. Create Worst Case scenarios that show negative consequences of the change.

7. Show all the Best Case scenarios, then create a column chart that displays the Best Case monthly income, apply the chart style of your choice, then note the upper limit of the value axis (y-axis) in the chart. You want the printed charts with the Current, Best, and Worst Case scenarios worksheets to display the same upper limit on the value axis so that the differences in the three charts are readily apparent. Change the title of the chart to reflect the information displayed in the chart.

8. Show the Current scenarios, then change the upper limit on the value axis to the same upper limit displayed in the Best Case column chart. Change the title of the chart to reflect the information displayed in the chart.

9. Show the Worst Case scenarios, change the title of the chart to reflect the information displayed in the chart, then change the upper limit on the value axis to the same upper limit displayed in the Best Case chart.

10. Format the workbook for printing: set it up to print in Landscape orientation on one page and centered horizontally, enter the Team name in the Left section, your name in the Center section, and the text "Worst Case Scenarios" in the Right section. Save the workbook and submit it to your instructor along with the other workbooks created by your team members.

Independent Challenge 4 - Team Project (continued)

Customer Profile

This workbook contains an analysis of a list of 30 to 40 customers and the products or services purchased during a specific time frame from your team's company. Make sure you've agreed with team members regarding product/service categories and the types of customers who purchase your company's product or service, then create the workbook as follows:

1. Create a new Excel workbook and save it as **PR D-Team Project_Customer Profile** to the location where you save files for this book, then apply the workbook theme and color scheme selected by your team.

2. Set up the workbook with three sheet tabs named **List**, **Analysis**, and **Profile**.

3. Create a list of 30 to 40 customers who have purchased your product or service in the past month. Include up to ten fields in the first row—the header row. Sample fields include Customer Name, Age Range (e.g., Under 30, 30 to 50, Over 50, and so on), Location (e.g., home state or neighborhood), Product Category, Amount Spent, and so on. The field names you include will depend upon the type of information you wish to feature in your customer profile. For example, if you want to find out how much money was spent by people in a specific neighborhood on a specific product, you will need to include field names for Neighborhood, Product Category, and Amount. Make sure you include data that can be used in calculations to determine the total amount spent by each customer.

4. Format the completed list as a table that contains headers, name the table, then adjust column widths (wrap text if needed) so the list is easy to read.

5. Include a column named **Total**, then calculate the total amount each person in the list spent.

6. Set up a portion of the worksheet with labels for specific data such as "Number of Guests in Colorado," or "Total Number of Guests." Include at least three labels for different information.

7. Use the COUNTA, SUM, and COUNTIF functions as needed to enter the totals required for the labels you entered.

8. In the List sheet tab, use filtering to show only the records (rows) that conform to specific criteria (for example, only customers who live in California), then copy the filtered list to the Analysis sheet.

9. Sort the filtered list so that all records of a certain category (for example, all records for "cities in California") are together.

10. Use the Subtotal function to calculate the total amount spent in each category.

11. Return to the List sheet tab, remove the filter, create a PivotTable that appears below the filtered list in the Analysis sheet tab, select fields in the PivotTable Fields pane to develop a PivotTable that shows the information you want. For ideas, click the Recommended PivotTables button and view the various ways in which you can view data from your list.

12. Create a chart from the PivotTable, then format it attractively with an appropriate title.

13. In the Profile sheet tab, create a text box to contain the name of the company and the subtitle **Customer Profile** followed by the month defining the data being analyzed (e.g., September 2016). Fill the text box with a picture and adjust effects as needed so the text box presents a striking image for your team's company.

14. Copy the various components of your customer profile into the Profile sheet (the statistics, Subtotal list, and PivotChart), arrange them attractively on one page, then add text as needed to explain the various components.

15. Group all three worksheets, set each sheet up to print on one page with a header containing your team name in the Left section, your name in the Center section, and the sheet name in the Right section.

16. Save the workbook and submit it to your instructor along with the other workbooks created by your team members.

Independent Challenge 4 - Team Project (continued)

Sales Report

This workbook contains a list of your team company's products or services sorted into three to four categories and then a report on sales. Make sure you've agreed with team members regarding product/service categories. You can determine the numbers for the sales. Create the workbook as follows:

1. Create a new Excel workbook and save it as **PR D-Team Project_Sales Report** to the location where you save files for this book, then apply the workbook theme and color scheme selected by your team.
2. Set up the workbook with two sheet tabs named **Unit Sales** and **Report**.
3. Create a list of at least 30 products or services in up to four categories. Include labels for three years of sales and a column for totals.
4. Enter values for the number of product/services sold in each category over the three years.
5. Use Conditional Formatting to highlight differences in the Total column in order to show sales trends.
6. Use Conditional Formatting to fill each cell containing a category label with a different fill color so you can see at a glance the breakdown of product/services by category.
7. Create a PivotTable in the Report sheet, then add fields as needed to analyze the sales data in the Unit Sales sheet. Check the Recommended PivotTables button for ideas.
8. Create a pie chart from the PivotTable, format the chart attractively with an appropriate title, then experiment with various ways in which you can show data from the PivotTable in the PivotChart.
9. Show the Slicer and use it to view the data in various ways. Your goal is to use the PivotTable and Slicer tools to reveal trends in sales of your team company's products or services.
10. Format all the data in the Report attractively on one page.
11. Group the two worksheets, set each sheet up to print on one page with a header containing your team name in the Left section, your name in the Center section, and the sheet name in the Right section.
12. Save the workbook and submit it to your instructor along with the other workbooks created by your team members.

▶ Project Summary

As a team, complete the project summary as follows.

1. Open **PR D-05.docx** from the location where you save your Data Files, then save it to your **PR D-Team Project_Summary**.
2. Read the directions in the document, then ensure that each team member enters his or her name in one of the tables along with a short description of the skills used and the challenges faced by each member while creating the Word document.
3. Save the document, then submit all four documents to your instructor.

Visual Workshop

You work for The Learning Place, a home-based business that distributes learning toys all over the country. The toys are created for three age groups (Toddler, Preschool, and School Age) and in four categories (Construction, Art, Academic, and Character). A list of the units sold of each product is contained in PR D-06.xlsx. Open the workbook, save it as **PR D-The Learning Place** to the location where you save files for this book, then insert a new worksheet called **Report**. Format the Data worksheet using the Heading 2 cell style for the header rows, calculate totals, and apply conditional formatting as shown in **FIGURE D-23** (use the color of your choice for the bars and a selection of shading colors for the age groups). In the Report sheet, create the PivotTable, PivotChart and Slicer as shown in **FIGURE D-24**. Go to the Data sheet, change the quantity of Science Plus Card Sets to **100** and the quantity of Math Cards to **150**, then refresh the PivotTable. Set up both worksheets to print on one page centered horizontally with your name in the Left section of the header and the sheet name at the Right section. Save the workbook, submit a copy to your instructor, then close the workbook.

FIGURE D-23

	A	B	C	D	E	F	G
1	Product Name	Category	Age Group	Quantity	Price	Total	
2	Big Block Builders	Construction	Preschool	25	$ 25.00	$ 625.00	
3	Annie Anatomy Doll	Character	Toddler	60	$ 30.00	$ 1,800.00	
4	Mechanix	Construction	School Age	45	$ 45.00	$ 2,025.00	
5	Chatty Friends	Character	Toddler	20	$ 15.00	$ 300.00	
6	Science Plus Card Sets	Academic	School Age	80	$ 15.00	$ 1,200.00	
7	Prehistoric Adventures	Academic	School Age	40	$ 45.00	$ 1,800.00	
8	Jake the Builder	Character	Preschool	45	$ 20.00	$ 900.00	
9	Rock Collection	Academic	School Age	25	$ 40.00	$ 1,000.00	
10	Soft Blocks	Construction	Toddler	60	$ 20.00	$ 1,200.00	
11	Math Cards	Academic	School Age	72	$ 15.00	$ 1,080.00	
12	My First Painting	Art	Toddler	35	$ 25.00	$ 875.00	
13	Modeling Kit	Art	School Age	12	$ 25.00	$ 300.00	
14							

FIGURE D-24

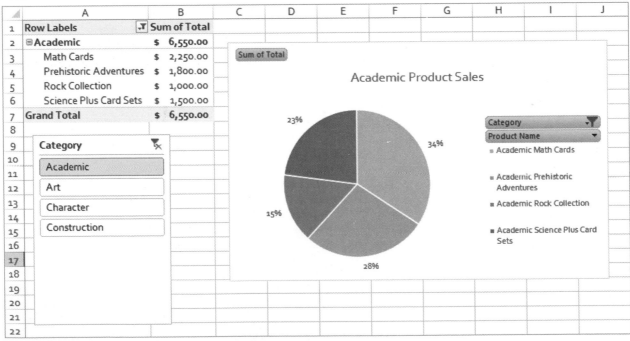

Integration Projects I

Projects

In this unit you will create the following:

Performance Review

Set margins • Modify styles • Format tables • Add the DEVELOPER tab • Insert Rich Text, Combo Box, Date, and Legacy Tools form controls • Set up a worksheet • Insert a recommended chart • Set the value axis • Copy Excel data and paste it as a Linked Microsoft Excel Object in Word • Edit link sources • (*Skills also practiced in Independent Challenge 1*)

Sales Report

Set up an Excel worksheet • Create scenarios • Use Goal Seek • Create a chart by selecting data • Add a data series to a chart • Modify the decimal places in a chart axis • Copy Excel data and paste it as a Linked Microsoft Excel Object in Word • Copy a chart and paste it in Word • Draw call-out shapes in Word • Update data in Excel and verify linked data updates in Word (*Skills also practiced in Independent Challenge 2*)

Marketing Update

Crop a picture to a shape • Add a WordArt object • Create a screen clipping • Copy and paste an Excel chart as a Linked Microsoft Excel Object in Word • Copy and paste Excel data into Word as Unformatted Text (*Skills also practiced in Independent Challenge 3*)

Team Project

Files You Will Need

PR E-01.docx
PR E-02.docx

Performance Reviews

Sally Lee and Paul Hopper are due for a job performance review at Go Discover Holidays. As their supervisor, you need to create a form to compile the results of each review. To complete the performance reviews, you **Create the Form in Word**, **Add Form Content Controls in Word**, **Compile Results in Excel**, and then **Link the Form and Results** for each employee.

Create the Form in Word

You set up the performance review form in Word and create a table to contain the data for the form.

STEPS

HINT
Use the PAGE LAYOUT tab to change margins, and use the DESIGN tab to apply a document theme and style.

1. Start a new blank document in Word, set the top and bottom margins to .6", apply the Droplet theme, select the Centered document style, then save the document as PR E-Performance Review Form to the location where you save the files for this book

2. Type Go Discover Holidays, press [Enter], type Performance Review, press [Enter], select Go Discover Holidays, click the HOME tab, click Title in the Styles gallery, select Performance Review, then apply the Subtitle style

3. Select Go Discover Holidays, change the font size to 26, click the PAGE LAYOUT tab, enter 6 for the After spacing, press [Enter], click the HOME tab, right-click Title in the Styles gallery, then click Update Title to Match Selection

4. Click the blank line below "Performance Review", click the INSERT tab, click Table, click Insert Table, type 4, press [Tab], type 12, click OK, then type the text for the table as shown in FIGURE E-1

HINT
You use the [Ctrl] key to select non-adjacent rows in a table quickly so that you can apply formatting all at once.

5. Click to the left of row 1 (contains "Employee Information") to select the entire row, press and hold [Ctrl], click to the left of "Rankings", click to the left of "Ranking Summary", "Ranking Chart", and "Written Evaluation" to select them, then release [Ctrl]

6. Click the TABLE TOOLS DESIGN tab, click the Shading list arrow in the Table Styles group, select Lime, Accent 3, Darker 25%, click the HOME tab, click the Font Color list arrow ▲▾ in the Font group, click the White, Background 1 color, then click the Increase Font Size button A˄ in the Font group two times

HINT
Use CTRL to select and center all the merged rows at once.

7. Select row 1, click the TABLE TOOLS LAYOUT tab, click the Merge Cells button in the Merge group, click the HOME tab, click the Center button ☰, then use FIGURE E-2 as your guide to merge cells and center text

8. Move the mouse to the left of the border between "Job Title" and "Review Period" to show the Insert control, click the Insert control ⊕ to insert a new row, then enter Department in the first cell and Manager in the third cell

9. Use [Ctrl] to select rows 1 through 6 ("Employee Information" through "Rankings"), and the rows containing "Ranking Summary", "Ranking Chart", and "Written Evaluation", click the TABLE TOOLS LAYOUT tab, click Properties in the Table group, click the Row tab, click the Specify height check box, type .3 in the Specify height text box, click the Cell tab, click the Center option in the Vertical alignment section, click OK, then save the document

The document appears as shown in **FIGURE E-2**.

Integration Projects I

FIGURE E-1: Table text

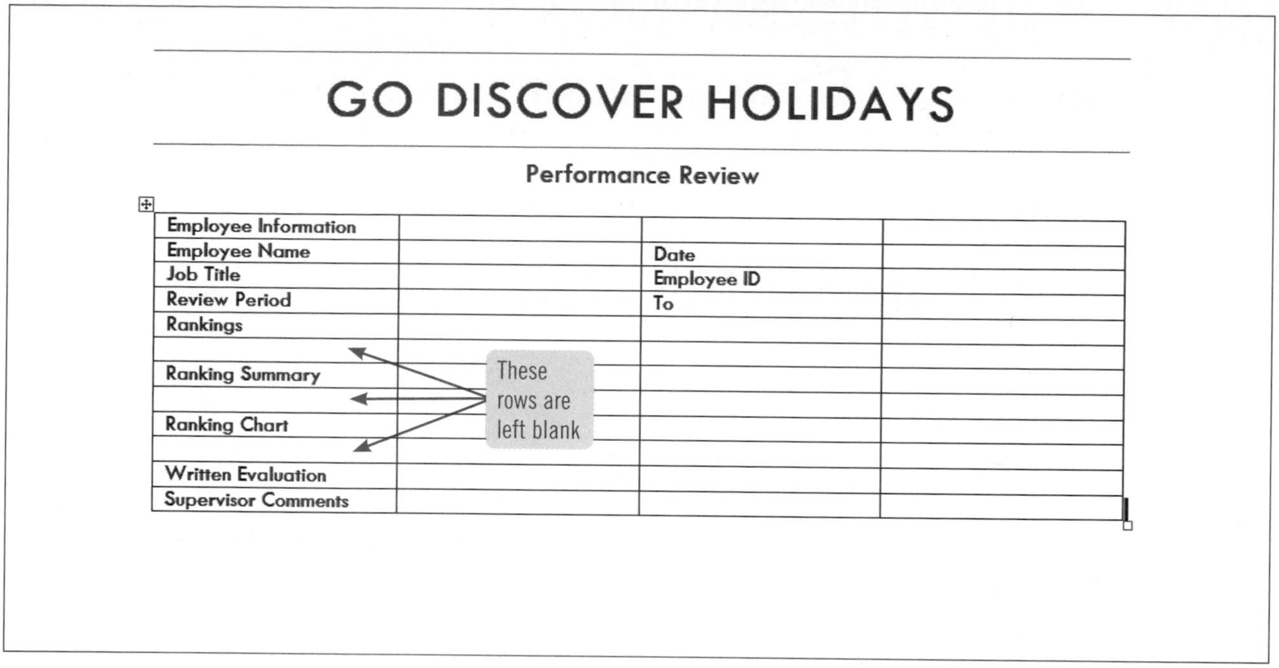

GO DISCOVER HOLIDAYS

Performance Review

Employee Information			
Employee Name		Date	
Job Title		Employee ID	
Review Period		To	
Rankings			
Ranking Summary			
Ranking Chart			
Written Evaluation			
Supervisor Comments			

These rows are left blank

FIGURE E-2: Table cells merged and formatted

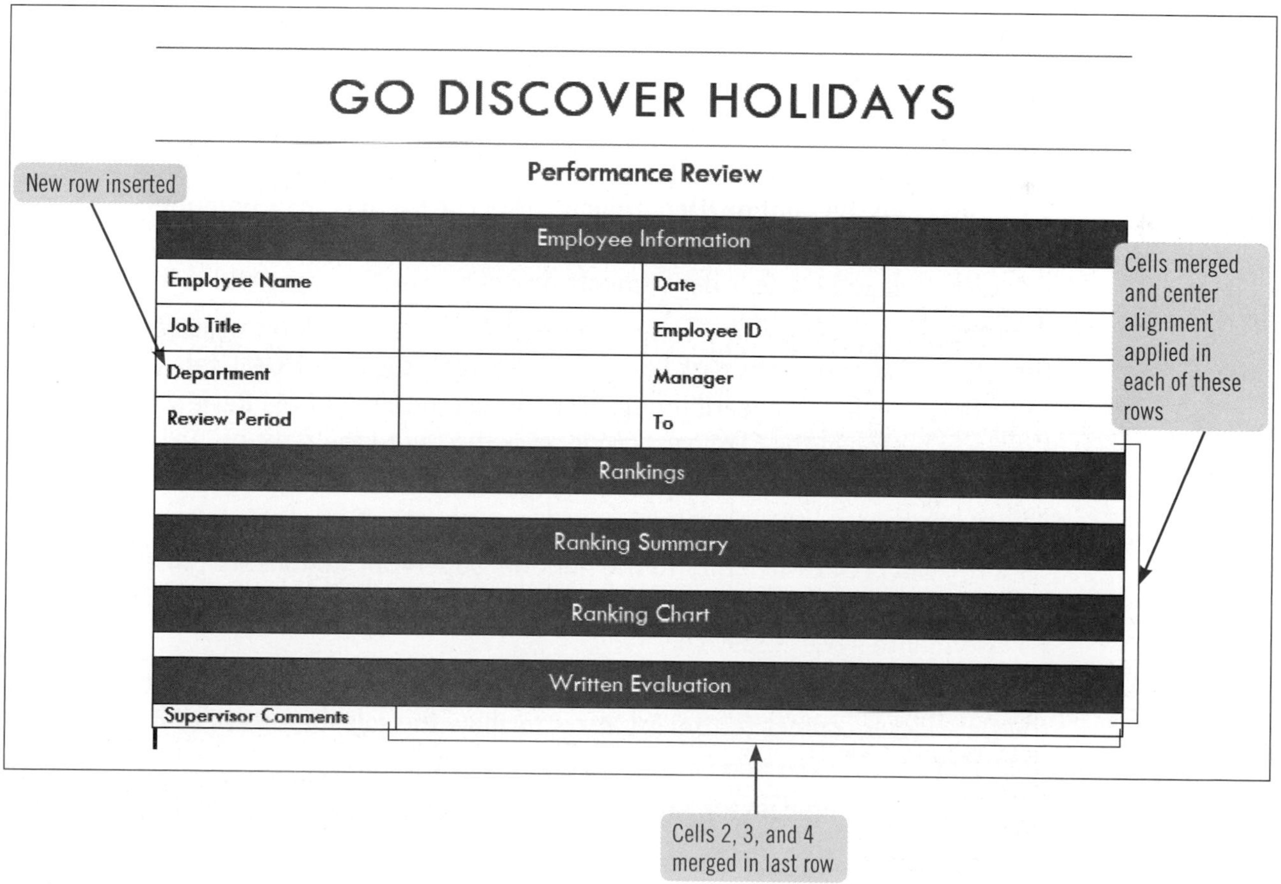

GO DISCOVER HOLIDAYS

Performance Review

New row inserted

Employee Information			
Employee Name		Date	
Job Title		Employee ID	
Department		Manager	
Review Period		To	
Rankings			
Ranking Summary			
Ranking Chart			
Written Evaluation			
Supervisor Comments			

Cells merged and center alignment applied in each of these rows

Cells 2, 3, and 4 merged in last row

Integration 2013

Add Form Content Controls in Word

You plan to use the same performance review form to record the performance reviews of numerous employees. You want the form to be an electronic one that you can complete on the computer. To make the form reusable, you need to insert form content controls. Your first step is to show the DEVELOPER tab so you can access the tools used to create forms.

STEPS

1. Click the FILE tab, click Options, click Customize Ribbon, click the Developer check box in the list of Main Tabs to select it, click OK, then click the cell to the right of "Employee Name"

2. Click the DEVELOPER tab, then click the Rich Text Content Control button Aa in the Controls group to insert a Rich Text content control as shown in FIGURE E-3

3. Press [Tab] twice to move to the blank cell to the right of "Date", click the Date Picker Content Control button in the Controls group, click the Properties button in the Controls group, select the date format that corresponds to July 31, 2016, then click OK

   When you fill in the form, you will only be able to enter a date in the cell to the right of "Date".

4. Click the cell to the right of "Employee ID", click the Legacy Tools button in the Controls group, click the Text Form Field control button abl, double-click the shaded area to open the Text Form Field Options dialog box, click the Type list arrow, click Number, select the contents of the Maximum Length text box, type 4, compare the Text Form Field Options dialog box to FIGURE E-4, then click OK

   When you fill in the form, you will only be able to enter up to four digits in the cell to the right of Employee ID.

5. Add a Rich Text content control in the cells to the right of "Job Title" and "Manager", click the cell to the right of "Department", click the Combo Box Content Control button in the Controls group, click Properties, click Add, type Administration, click OK, click Add, add the four departments shown in FIGURE E-5, then click OK

6. Click the Date Picker content control to the right of Date, click the selection handle to the left of "Click" (it turns dark blue when selected), click the HOME tab, click the Copy button in the Clipboard group, click the cell to the right of "Review Period", click the Paste button in the Clipboard group, click the cell to the right of "To", then click the Paste button

   You can copy and paste fields that contain special formatting to save time.

7. Click the DEVELOPER tab, click to the right of "Supervisor Comments", insert a Rich Text content control, save the document, then save the document again as PR E-Performance Review_Sally Lee

HINT
You can also type the date in the Date Picker content control.

8. Click the cell to the right of "Employee Name", type Sally Lee, press [Tab] twice, click the Date Picker content control list arrow to show the calendar, scroll to April 2016, then click 18

9. Enter the remaining data for Sally Lee as shown in FIGURE E-6, then save the document

FIGURE E-3: Rich Text content control inserted

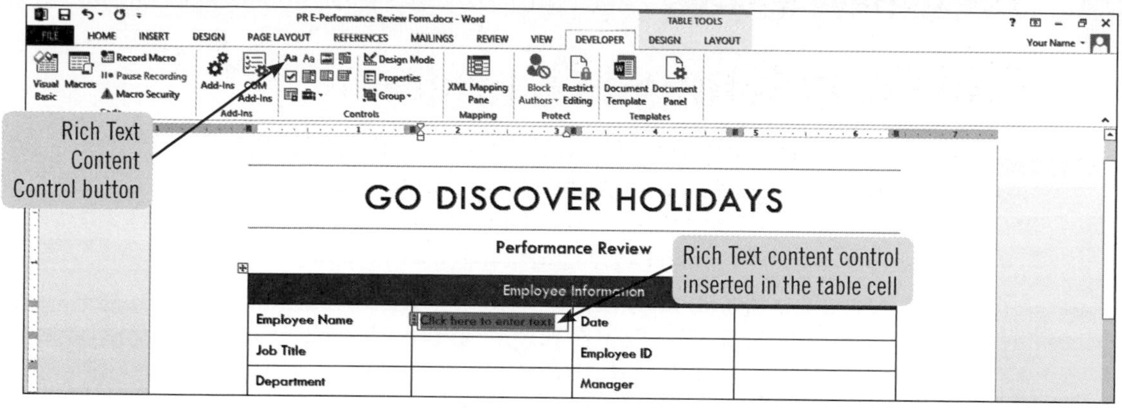

PR E-Performance Review Form.docx - Word
TABLE TOOLS
FILE
HOME
INSERT
DESIGN
PAGE LAYOUT
REFERENCES
MAILINGS
REVIEW
VIEW
DEVELOPER
DESIGN
LAYOUT
Your Name
Record Macro
Pause Recording
Macro Security
Visual Basic
Macros
Add-Ins
COM Add-Ins
Design Mode
Properties
Group
Controls
XML Mapping Pane
Mapping
Block Authors
Restrict Editing
Protect
Document Template
Document Panel
Templates
Rich Text Content Control button
GO DISCOVER HOLIDAYS
Performance Review
Rich Text content control inserted in the table cell
Employee Information
Employee Name
Click here to enter text.
Date
Job Title
Employee ID
Department
Manager

FIGURE E-4: Text Form Field Options dialog box

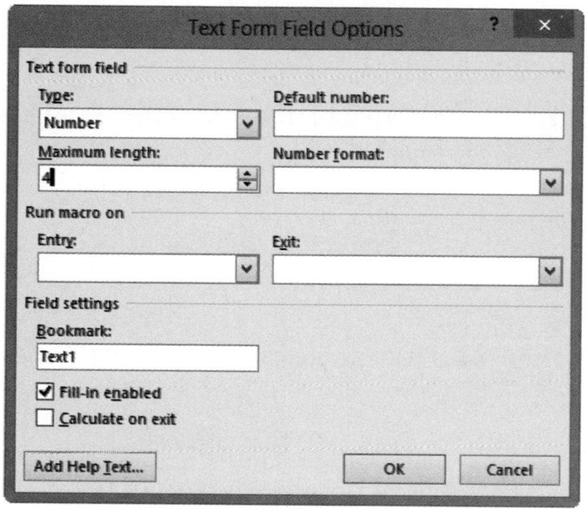

Text Form Field Options
Text form field
Type:
Number
Default number:
Maximum length:
4
Number format:
Run macro on
Entry:
Exit:
Field settings
Bookmark:
Text1
Fill-in enabled
Calculate on exit
Add Help Text...
OK
Cancel

FIGURE E-5: Drop-Down List Properties

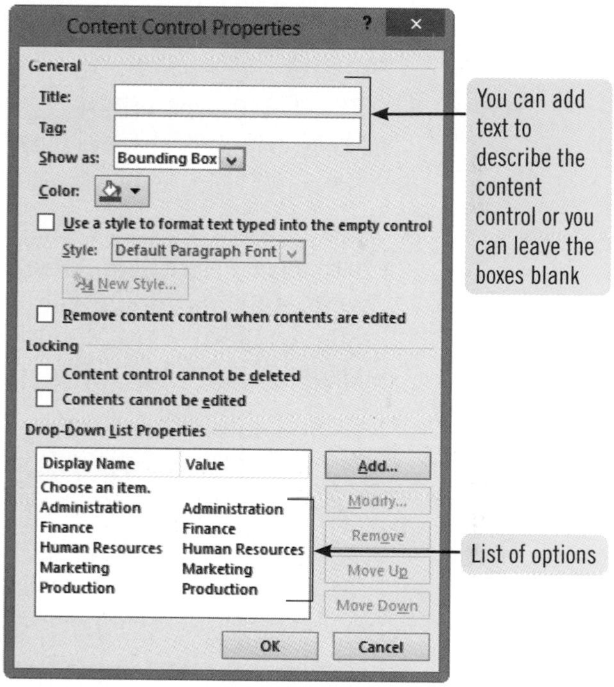

Content Control Properties
General
Title:
Tag:
Show as:
Bounding Box
Color:
Use a style to format text typed into the empty control
Style:
Default Paragraph Font
New Style...
Remove content control when contents are edited
Locking
Content control cannot be deleted
Contents cannot be edited
Drop-Down List Properties
Display Name
Value
Choose an item.
Administration
Administration
Finance
Finance
Human Resources
Human Resources
Marketing
Marketing
Production
Production
Add...
Modify...
Remove
Move Up
Move Down
OK
Cancel
You can add text to describe the content control or you can leave the boxes blank
List of options

FIGURE E-6: Form text for Sally Lee

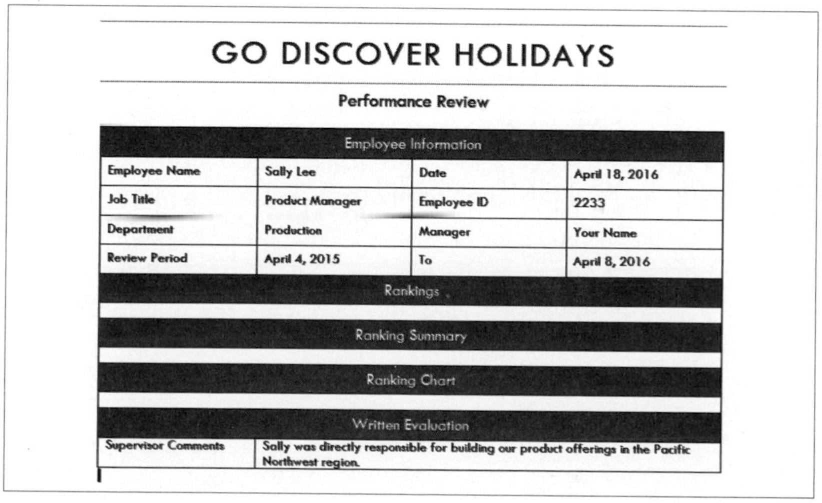

GO DISCOVER HOLIDAYS
Performance Review
Employee Information
Employee Name
Sally Lee
Date
April 18, 2016
Job Title
Product Manager
Employee ID
2233
Department
Production
Manager
Your Name
Review Period
April 4, 2015
To
April 8, 2016
Rankings
Ranking Summary
Ranking Chart
Written Evaluation
Supervisor Comments
Sally was directly responsible for building our product offerings in the Pacific Northwest region.

Integration 2013

Performance Reviews (continued)

Compile Results in Excel

You need to create a worksheet in Excel into which you can enter the numerical results of the performance review. You also need to create a chart in Excel that summarizes the results.

STEPS

HINT
Use Copy and Paste to minimize typing time.

1. Start a new blank workbook in Excel, type Supervisor Rating in cell A1, select cells A1:B1, click the Merge and Center button in the Alignment group, apply bold, enter and enhance the text and adjust column widths as shown in FIGURE E-7, add your name to cell A17, then save the workbook as PR E-Performance Reviews to the location where you are saving the files for this book

2. Double-click the Sheet1 tab, type Sally, press [Enter], click cell B8, click the AutoSum button in the Editing group, press [Enter], then click cell E8 and use AutoSum to add the range E2:E7

3. Click cell B10, type =(B2+E2)/2, press [Enter], click cell B10, then drag the fill handle to fill cells B11:B15 with the formula in cell B10

   This formula determines the average score between the Supervisor Rating and the Peer Rating.

4. Select cells A10:B15, click the INSERT tab, click the Recommended Charts button in the Charts group, click OK to accept Clustered Column, click the Quick Layout button in the Chart Layouts group, click Layout 3, click the More button ▼ in the Chart Styles group, select Style 16, click the Chart Title, press [Delete], click the Legend ("Series1" below the chart), then press [Delete]

5. Size and position the chart so that it extends from cell D10 through cell J26

6. Right-click the value axis (y-axis), click Format Axis, select the contents of the Maximum text box in the Format Axis pane, type 5, press [Enter], verify that Reset appears to the right, then click ✕ to close the Format Axis pane

   By retyping the value, you set the maximum scale for the value axis at 5 so that the scale remains the same regardless of the data entered in the chart.

7. Click the New sheet button ⊕ next to the Sally tab, double-click the Sheet2 tab, type Paul, press [Enter], click the Sally tab, click the Select All button ◢ to the left of the "A" in the upper-left corner of the worksheet frame to select the entire worksheet, click the Copy button in the Clipboard group, click the Paul tab, then click the Paste button in the Clipboard group

8. Enter values for Paul in cells B2:B7 and cells E2:E7 as shown in FIGURE E-8, then verify that the totals are updated

9. Right-click the chart, click Select Data, click the Collapse button 📧 next to "Chart data range", click the Paul tab, then verify that cells A10:B15 are selected

   When you copy the chart from the Sally worksheet to the Paul worksheet, the chart still references the cells in the Sally worksheet. You change the reference so that the chart shows data related to Paul's rankings.

10. Click the Expand button 🖼, click OK, then save the workbook

    The chart appears as shown in FIGURE E-9.

FIGURE E-7: Worksheet labels and values

	A	B	C	D	E	F
1	Supervisor Rating			Peer Rating		
2	Knowledge	5		Knowledge	4	
3	Work Quality	5		Work Quality	3	
4	Attendance	4		Attendance	4	
5	Initiative	5		Initiative	4	
6	Communication	3		Communication	1	
7	Dependability	4		Dependability	4	
8						
9	Average Rating					
10	Knowledge					
11	Work Quality					
12	Attendance					
13	Initiative					
14	Communication					
15	Dependability					
16						

FIGURE E-8: Values for Paul

	A	B	C	D	E	F
1	Supervisor Rating			Peer Rating		
2	Knowledge	2		Knowledge	1	
3	Work Quality	3		Work Quality	1	
4	Attendance	1		Attendance	3	
5	Initiative	1		Initiative	2	
6	Communication	2		Communication	2	
7	Dependability	2		Dependability	1	
8		11			10	

FIGURE E-9: Paul's chart updated

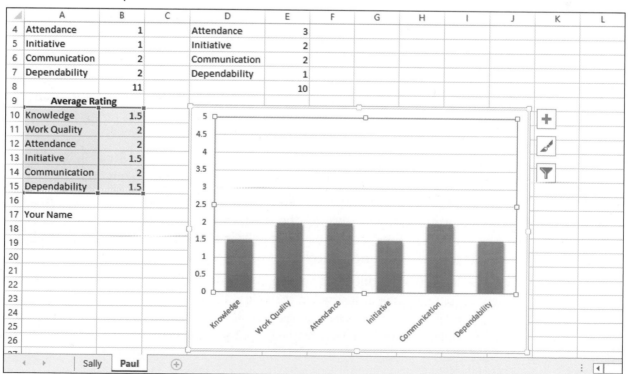

Performance Reviews (continued)

Link the Form and Results

You need to copy Sally's performance results from Excel and paste them into the Word form as linked objects. After completing and saving Sally's performance review form, you need to save the document as Paul's, edit the text to reflect Paul's information, and then change the source for the Excel performance results so the linked objects reflect Paul's information.

STEPS

1. Click the Sally tab, select cells A1:E8, click the Copy button in the Clipboard group, switch to Word, click the cell below "Rankings", click the Paste list arrow in the Clipboard group, click Paste Special, click the Paste link option button, click Microsoft Excel Worksheet Object, then click OK

2. Switch to Excel, select cells A9:B15, copy them, switch to Word, click the cell below "Ranking Summary", click the Paste list arrow, click Paste Special, click the Paste link option button, click Microsoft Excel Worksheet Object, then click OK

3. Switch to Excel, click the chart, copy it, switch to Word, click the cell below "Ranking Chart", click the Paste list arrow, click the Use Destination Theme & Link Data button 📊 in the selection of Paste Options, click the chart, click the CHART TOOLS FORMAT tab, click the launcher 🖼 in the Size group, click the Lock aspect ratio check box to select it, select the contents of the Height text box, type 2.3, then click OK

> **TROUBLE**
> If the value for attendance is not 5, right-click the object under "Rankings", click Update Link, right-click the object under Ranking Summary, then click Update Link.

4. Switch to Excel, change Sally's ranking for Attendance to 5 in both the Supervisor and the Peer cells (cell B4 and cell E4), verify the value for Attendance is "5" in the charts under Rankings and the top of the Attendance column in the chart is even with "5" on the value axis in Word, save the document, then save and close the Excel workbook

    Sally's rankings for Attendance and the column chart are both updated in the Word document because the data is linked to the Excel workbook.

> **TROUBLE**
> The values in the Excel objects will not yet match **FIGURE E-10**.

5. Use Save As on the FILE tab to save the document again as PR E-Performance Review_ Paul Hopper, scroll to and click the Employee Name table cell, press [Tab], then enter text for Paul in the Employee Information and Written Evaluation sections as shown in the completed form in FIGURE E-10

6. Click the FILE tab, click Edit Links to Files in the lower-right corner under Related Documents, click the top link in the Links dialog box, click Change Source, click Item, select Sally and type Paul as shown in FIGURE E-11, then click OK

7. Navigate to the location of PR E-Performance Reviews.xlsx in the list of files, click PR E-Performance Reviews.xlsx, click Open, repeat the process to change the source for the second link listed in the Links dialog box, then click OK

> **HINT**
> Excel opened when you clicked Open in step 7.

8. Click ⬅ to exit Backstage view, click the chart, click the CHART TOOLS DESIGN tab, click Select Data in the Data group, select Sally in the Select Data Source dialog box, type Paul, click OK, then close Excel

>
> **MORE PRACTICE**
> For more practice with the skills presented in this project, complete Independent Challenge 1.

9. Save the document, submit a copy of the Excel workbook and both performance review documents to your instructor, then close the document

    The completed performance review for Paul appears as shown in **FIGURE E-10**. If you wish to make changes to a Word document linked to an Excel workbook, open the Excel workbook first. Then, open the Word document and click Yes in response to the message that appears asking if you wish to maintain the link between the document and the workbook.

GO DISCOVER HOLIDAYS

Performance Review

Employee Information			
Employee Name	Paul Hopper	Date	April 18, 2016
Job Title	Sales Agent	Employee ID	5566
Department	Marketing	Manager	Your Name
Review Period	April 4, 2015	To	April 8, 2016

Rankings

Supervisor Rating		**Peer Rating**	
Knowledge	2	Knowledge	1
Work Quality	3	Work Quality	1
Attendance	1	Attendance	3
Initiative	1	Initiative	2
Communication	2	Communication	2
Dependability	2	Dependability	1
	11		10

Ranking Summary

Average Rating	
Knowledge	1.5
Work Quality	2
Attendance	2
Initiative	1.5
Communication	2
Dependability	1.5

Ranking Chart

Written Evaluation

Supervisor Comments	Paul needs to develop a more conventional work ethic.

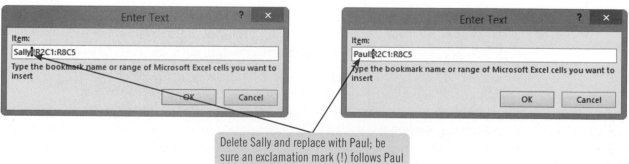

Delete Sally and replace with Paul; be sure an exclamation mark (!) follows Paul

Integration 2013

Sales Report for Evergreen Resorts

Evergreen Resorts manages a chain of hotels on four islands off the coast of British Columbia: Bowen Island, Galiano Island, Saltspring Island, and Pender Island. As the sales manager for the chain, you want to attract more guests to the hotels in the spring months of April, May, and June in order to ensure that those months are profitable. You need to determine the number of rooms to rent during these spring months in order to show a profit. For this project, you need to **Summarize Sales**, **Calculate Projected Sales**, and **Create the Sales Report**. The completed sales report appears as shown in **FIGURE E-18** on page 125.

Summarize Sales

You need to enter labels and values in an Excel worksheet and then calculate total sales.

STEPS

1. **Start a new workbook in Excel, enter and enhance the labels and values so that the worksheet appears as shown in** FIGURE E-12, **then save the workbook as** PR E-Evergreen Resorts Sales Data **to the location where you save the files for this book**

2. **Click cell** B8, **enter the formula to multiply the** Average Cost per Room **by the** Total Number of Rooms Rented, **then copy the formula through cell** E8, **widening columns as needed**

   As you complete the required calculations, refer to **FIGURE E-13** to verify your totals.

3. **Click cell** B13, **enter the formula to multiply the** Number of Rooms Available **by the** Operating Cost per Room, **then copy the formula through cell** E13

   Note that the value for the Operating Cost per Room is based on the cost over a three-month period.

4. **Click cell** B15, **enter the formula to add the** Total Operating Costs **to the** Advertising Costs, **then copy the formula through cell** E15

5. **Calculate the Net Revenue in cell** B17 **as the** Total Expenses **subtracted from the** Total Room Rental Revenue, **then copy the formula through cell** E17, **widening columns as needed**

   The hotels on Bowen Island and Galiano Island lost money during the spring months of April, May, and June. Only the Saltspring Island and Pender Island hotels made a profit.

6. **Select cells** B7:F8, **click the** AutoSum button **in the Editing group, then widen** Column F **as needed to fit content**

7. **Select cells** B13:F17, **click the** AutoSum button, **then verify that** $(8,400.00) **appears in cell F17 as shown in** FIGURE E-13

8. **Select cells** B7:E7, **click the** DATA tab, **click** What-If Analysis **in the Data Tools group, click** Scenario Manager, **click** Add, **type** 2016 Rentals, **click** OK, **click** OK, **then click** Close

   You create a scenario to preserve the existing data because in the next lesson you will change the data in order to calculate projected sales.

9. **Apply borders and shading to the worksheet so that it appears as shown in** FIGURE E-13, **then save the workbook**

FIGURE E-12: Worksheet setup

	A	B	C	D	E	F	G
1	**Evergreen Resorts**						
2	*Sales Summary for April, May, June, 2016*						
3							
4		**Bowen Island**	**Galiano Island**	**Saltspring Island**	**Pender Island**	**Totals**	
5	**REVENUE**						
6	Average Cost per Room	$ 150.00	$ 125.00	$ 175.00	$ 175.00		
7	Total Number of Rooms Rented	200	300	700	400		
8	Total Room Rental Revenue						
9							
10	**EXPENSES**						
11	Number of Rooms Available	20	30	50	30		
12	Operating Cost per Room	$ 2,000.00	$ 2,000.00	$ 2,000.00	$ 2,000.00		
13	Total Operating Costs						
14	Advertising Costs	$ 1,200.00	$ 2,000.00	$ 3,000.00	$ 2,200.00		
15	Total Expenses						
16							
17	**NET REVENUE**						
18							
19							

Annotations:
- 24 pt, bold (pointing to "Evergreen Resorts")
- 14 pt, bold (pointing to "Sales Summary for April, May, June, 2016")
- Wrap text in columns B to E, then adjust column widths as needed
- Apply Accounting Number formatting and bold as shown

FIGURE E-13: Worksheet complete with calculations and formatting

	A	B	C	D	E	F	G
1	E ...orts						
2	Sa... l, May, June, 2016						
3							
4		**Bowen Island**	**Galiano Island**	**Saltspring Island**	**Pender Island**	**Totals**	
5	**REVENUE**						
6	Average Cost per Room	$ 150.00	$ 125.00	$ 175.00	$ 175.00		
7	Total Number of Rooms Rented	200	300	700	400	1600	
8	Total Room Rental Revenue	$ 30,000.00	$ 37,500.00	$122,500.00	$70,000.00	$260,000.00	
9							
10	**EXPENSES**						
11	Number of Rooms Available	20	30	50	30		
12	Operating Cost per Room	$ 2,000.00	$ 2,000.00	$ 2,000.00	$ 2,000.00		
13	Total Operating Costs	$ 40,000.00	$ 60,000.00	$100,000.00	$60,000.00	$260,000.00	
14	Advertising Costs	$ 1,200.00	$ 2,000.00	$ 3,000.00	$ 2,200.00	$ 8,400.00	
15	Total Expenses	$ 41,200.00	$ 62,000.00	$103,000.00	$62,200.00	$268,400.00	
16							
17	**NET REVENUE**	$(11,200.00)	$(24,500.00)	$ 19,500.00	$ 7,800.00	$ (8,400.00)	
18							
19							

Annotations:
- Blue, Accent 5, Lighter 80%; cells are merged and centered, then left aligned
- Blue, Accent 5, Darker 25% with White text
- Border lines added to ranges A4:F8, A10:F15 and A17:F17
- Gold, Accent 4, Lighter 80%

Sales Report (continued)

Calculate Projected Sales

You use the Goal Seek feature to determine how many rooms you should rent at the Bowen Island and Galiano Island hotels to increase the net revenue from these hotels, then create a bar chart to compare current and projected income from the rental of rooms at the Bowen Island and Galiano Island hotels.

STEPS

1. Click cell B17 (the net revenue for the Bowen Island hotel), click What-If Analysis in the Data Tools group on the DATA tab, click Goal Seek, click the text box next to "To value:", type 10000 (four zeroes), press [Tab], type B7 as shown in FIGURE E-14, click OK, then click OK again

   The value needed, 341.3333333, appears in cell B7.

2. Click cell C17, click What-If Analysis, click Goal Seek, enter 8000 as the To value and C7 as the cell to change, click OK, click OK, select B7:F7, click the HOME tab, apply the Comma style, then click the Decrease Decimal button ⬚ twice

   Over the three months, you need to rent 341 rooms at the Bowen Island hotel to make a profit of $10,000, and you need to rent 560 rooms at the Galiano Island hotel to make a profit of $8,000.

3. Click the DATA tab, click What-If Analysis, click Scenario Manager, click Add, type Projected Rentals, enter B7:C7 as the changing cells, click OK, click OK, then click Close

4. Double-click the Sheet1 tab, type 2016 Rentals, click the Select All button ◢ in the upper-left corner of the worksheet frame to select all the data, click the HOME tab, click the Copy button in the Clipboard group, add a new worksheet, click the Paste button in the Clipboard group, then name the new sheet tab Projected Rentals

5. Show the 2016 Rentals worksheet, click the DATA tab, click What-If Analysis, click Scenario Manager, click 2016 Rentals, click Show, click Close, then click cell A1

   The net revenue in cell F17 of the 2016 Rentals sheet is again $ (8,400.00).

6. Go to the Projected Rentals worksheet, click cell A20, click the INSERT tab, click the Insert Bar Chart button ⬚ ▾ in the Charts group, click Clustered Bar (the upper-left selection), click Select Data in the Data group, click the Chart data range Collapse button ⬚, click the 2016 Rentals tab, select cells B4:E4, press and hold [Ctrl], select cells B8:E8, click the Chart data range Expand button ⬚, then click OK

7. Move the chart down so that it starts at cell A20, resize it so that it extends to cell G40, click Select Data in the Data group, click Edit, type 2016 Rentals as shown in FIGURE E-15, click OK, click Add, type Projected Rentals, click the Series values Collapse button ⬚, select cells B8:E8 on the Projected Rentals tab, click the Expand button ⬚, click OK, then click OK

8. Click Add Chart Element in the Chart Layouts group, point to Chart Title, click Above Chart, type Comparison of Current and Projected Room Rentals, press [Enter], click Add Chart Element, point to Legend, then click Bottom

9. Right-click the value axis (x-axis) in the bar chart, click Format Axis, scroll down the Format Axis pane, click NUMBER, select the contents of the Decimal places text box, type 0, click ✖ to close the Format Axis pane, then save the workbook

   The chart is shown in FIGURE E-16.

FIGURE E-14: Goal Seek dialog box

Goal Seek ? ×

Set cell: B17
To value: 10000
By changing cell: B7

OK   Cancel

FIGURE E-15: Edit Series dialog box

Edit Series ? ×

Series name:
2016 Rentals   Select Range
Series values:
='2016 Rentals'!$B$8:$E$8   = $30,000.00 , ...

OK   Cancel

FIGURE E-16: Chart comparing current rentals with projected rentals

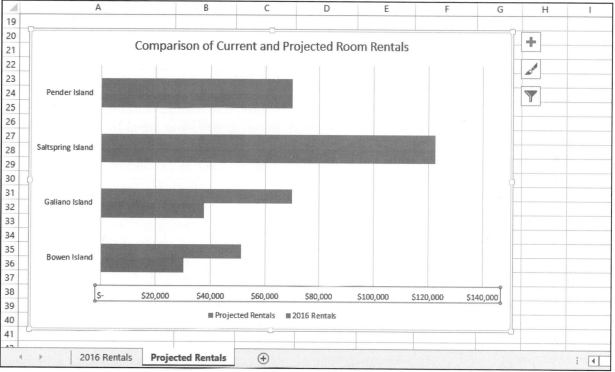

Using Goal Seek

You use Goal Seek when you know the result you want a formula to produce, but you don't know what value you need to include in the formula to get the result. For example, suppose you want to make $1000 a month from a part-time job. You know you can make $15/hour, but you need to know how

many hours a month you need to work to make $1000. You set up a worksheet with Hours Worked, Hourly Rate, and Total. The total cell must include a formula—in this case Hours Worked X Hourly Rate. You use Goal Seek to set the Total to $1000 by changing the Hours Worked. **FIGURE E-17** shows the result.

FIGURE E-17: Goal Seek Example

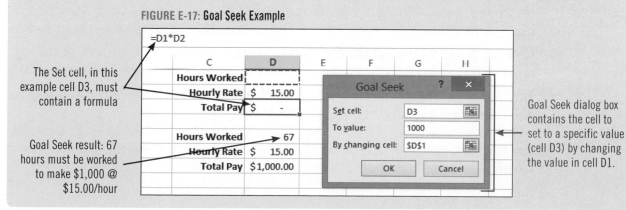

The Set cell, in this example cell D3, must contain a formula

=D1*D2

	C	D	E	F	G	H
	Hours Worked					
	Hourly Rate	$ 15.00				
	Total Pay	$ -				
	Hours Worked	67				
	Hourly Rate	$ 15.00				
	Total Pay	$1,000.00				

Goal Seek ? ×

Set cell: D3
To value: 1000
By changing cell: $D$1

OK   Cancel

Goal Seek result: 67 hours must be worked to make $1,000 @ $15.00/hour

Goal Seek dialog box contains the cell to set to a specific value (cell D3) by changing the value in cell D1.

Create the Sales Report

You need to compile all the data from the Excel workbook in a report you create in Word. The completed report is shown in FIGURE E-18.

STEPS

1. Start Word, open a new blank document, type Sales Report for Evergreen Resorts, press [Enter], apply the Title style to the text, click the DESIGN tab, select the Slice theme, select the Casual Style Set, then save the document as PR E-Evergreen Resorts Sales Report to the location where you save the files for this book

2. Click the Colors button in the Document Formatting group, scroll to and select the Red Orange color set, type the subtitle, then type the first paragraph of text as shown in the completed sales report in FIGURE E-18

3. Switch to Excel, select cells A1:F17 in the Projected Rentals worksheet, click the Copy button in the Clipboard group, switch to Word, verify you are at the end of the paragraph you just typed, press [Enter], click the HOME tab, click the Paste list arrow, click Paste Special, click the Paste link option button, click Microsoft Excel Worksheet Object, then click OK

4. Right-click the copied worksheet object in Word, click Format Object, click the Size tab, set the Width of the object to 6", click OK, double-click below the worksheet object, type the paragraph of text under the copied worksheet object as shown in FIGURE E-18, then press [Enter]

5. Double-click the copied worksheet object, click cell A2, select Summary in the formula bar, type Projections, select 2016, type 2017, then press [Enter]

6. Scroll to the chart, click the chart, click the Copy button, switch to Word, click below the last paragraph of text, click the Paste list arrow, click the Use Destination Theme & Link Data button 🗐, set the Height of the chart to 3.1" and the Width to 6.1", switch to Excel, change the cost of the Saltspring Island rooms (cell D6) to 150, return to Word, scroll to verify that the Saltspring Island room cost was updated to $150, then click anywhere in the text above the chart

   By selecting the Use Destination Theme & Link Data option, you ensure that the chart uses the color scheme and theme associated with the Word document, not the original Excel workbook.

TROUBLE
If the room rate was not updated, right-click the worksheet object, then click **Update Link**.

TROUBLE
You will need to drag the yellow diamond handle to move the tail to the left side of the callout. You may need to drag and move several times to get the callout to look like you want.

7. Click the INSERT tab, click Shapes in the Illustrations group, click the Rounded Rectangular Callout shape in the Callouts section, draw a shape above the chart, click the More button ⬇ in the Shape Styles gallery, click Subtle Effect - Gold, Accent 2, type Increase to 341 rooms, then resize and position the callout as shown in FIGURE E-18

8. Click the border of the callout box, copy and paste the callout box, then enter the required text and position the callout box next to Galiano Island as shown in FIGURE E-18

MORE PRACTICE
For more practice with the skills presented in this project, complete Independent Challenge 2.

9. Save and close the document, switch to Excel, add your name below the chart, save and close the workbook, then submit both files to your instructor

   If you wish to make changes to the Word document linked to the Excel workbook, open the Excel workbook first. Then, open the Word document and click Yes in response to the message that appears asking if you wish to maintain the link between the document and the workbook.

Sales Report for Evergreen Resorts
Prepared by Your Name

In April, May, and June of 2016, both the Bowen Island and Galiano Island resorts lost money. To increase revenue at the Bowen Island resort, we need to rent 341 rooms instead of the current 200 rooms. To increase revenue at the Galiano Island resort, we need to rent 560 rooms instead of the current 300 rooms. By so doing, we increase the Bowen Island resort revenue to $10,000 and the Galiano Island resort revenue to $8,000.

Evergreen Resorts

Sales Projections for April, May, June, 2017

	Bowen Island	Galiano Island	Saltspring Island	Pender Island	Totals
REVENUE					
Average Cost per Room	$ 150.00	$ 125.00	$ 150.00	$ 175.00	
Total Number of Rooms Rented	341	560	700	400	2,001
Total Room Rental Revenue	$ 51,200.00	$ 70,000.00	$105,000.00	$ 70,000.00	$296,200.00
EXPENSES					
Number of Rooms Available	20	30	50	30	
Operating Cost per Room	$ 2,000.00	$ 2,000.00	$ 2,000.00	$ 2,000.00	
Total Operating Costs	$ 40,000.00	$ 60,000.00	$100,000.00	$ 60,000.00	$260,000.00
Advertising Costs	$ 1,200.00	$ 2,000.00	$ 3,000.00	$ 2,200.00	$ 8,400.00
Total Expenses	$ 41,200.00	$ 62,000.00	$103,000.00	$ 62,200.00	$268,400.00
NET REVENUE	$ 10,000.00	$ 8,000.00	$ 2,000.00	$ 7,800.00	$ 27,800.00

The bar chart shown below compares the current room rentals in April, May and June of 2016 with the projected room rentals in April, May, and June of 2017.

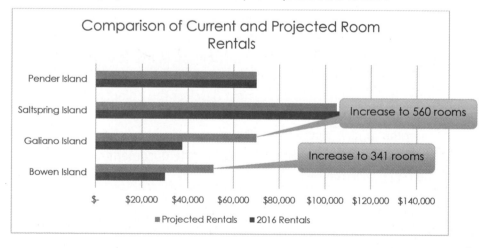

Marketing Update for Classic Tours

Classic Tours hosts four two-week tours of Mediterranean countries. As the office manager, you need to create a one-page marketing update that describes the tours offered by the company and summarizes current sales. You **Create the Update in Word** and then **Add Linked Data from Excel**. The completed document is shown in FIGURE E-22 on page 129.

Create the Update in Word

You need to enter the text for the marketing update, create an attractive header in another document and insert it as a screenshot into the update, then enter sales data in Excel.

STEPS

1. **Start Word, open a new blank document, change the top and bottom margins to .6", type the text as shown in FIGURE E-19, then save the document as PR E-Classic Tours Marketing Update to the location where you save the files for this book**
   As noted in FIGURE E-19, this document will contain linked data from Excel.

2. **Open PR E-01.docx from the location where you store files for this book, then save it as PR E-Classic Tours Header**
   This file contains a picture that you will use to create an attractive heading to insert into the Marketing Update as a screenshot.

3. **Click the picture, click the PICTURE TOOLS FORMAT tab, click the Crop list arrow, point to Crop to Shape, then click the Flowchart Document shape in the Flowchart section of shapes (7th selection in the first row of the Flowchart section)**

4. **Click the launcher ⌐ in the Size group, click the Lock Aspect Ratio check box to deselect it, enter 1.2 for the Absolute Height and 6 for the Absolute Width, click OK, then save the document**

HINT
Refer to
FIGURE E-20
for placement.

5. **Click the INSERT tab, click the WordArt button in the Text group, select the Fill - Gold, Accent 4, Soft Bevel style, type Classic Tours, drag the WordArt down to position it over the text box on the picture, then deselect the object and press [Enter] a few times to move the insertion point down**
   You move the insertion point down so it doesn't appear in the screen clipping.

6. **Show the PR E-Classic Tours Marketing Update document, add a blank line at the top of the page, click the blank line, click the INSERT tab, click Screenshot, then click Screen Clipping**

7. **Drag + from the upper-left corner of the image to the bottom-right corner to select the graphic as shown in FIGURE E-20**
   The graphic appears in the Word document.

HINT
Remember to calculate totals; do not type the values in cells B7 and C7.

8. **Start Excel, open a new blank workbook, apply the Slice theme, then enter and enhance the labels and values, calculate totals, and apply borders and shading as shown in FIGURE E-21**

9. **Name the Sheet1 tab Sales, add a new sheet and name it Chart, then save the workbook as PR E-Classic Tours Marketing Data to the location where you save the files for this book**

FIGURE E-19: Text for the marketing update

Classic Tours conducts tours in four categories each year to various destinations in the Mediterranean countries. The focus of each tour is the exploration of the remnants of ancient civilizations. The four tours are Greek Odyssey, Ancient Crete, Pillars of Hercules, and Roman Conquest. All of the tours run by Classic Tours are two weeks in duration.

Since its incorporation in 2004, Classic Tours has consistently sold virtually all of the Greek Odyssey and Roman Conquest tours. In most years, 80% of the Ancient Crete tours are sold. The Pillars of Hercules tours were first offered in 2015 and are steadily gaining in popularity. Shown below is a breakdown of tour sales by category.

In 2016, Classic Tours offered a total of xx tours and sold xx tours. The column chart shown below displays the number of tours sold in each category relative to the number of tours available. Greek Odyssey tours rank the highest in terms of the number of tours sold relative to the tours available.

> You will replace the "xx" references with values later

FIGURE E-20: Creating a screen clipping

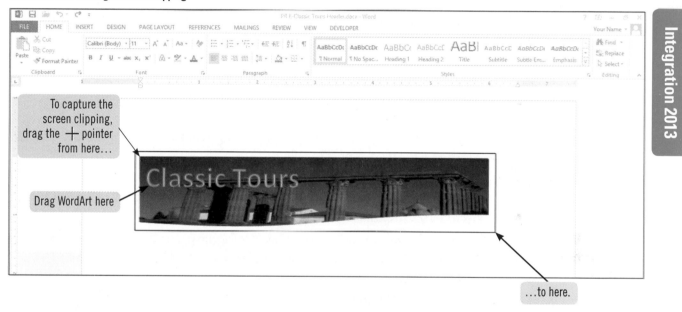

> To capture the screen clipping, drag the ✛ pointer from here...

> Drag WordArt here

> ...to here.

FIGURE E-21: Sales data in Excel

	A	B	C	D
1	**2016 Sales by Category**			
2	**Tour Name**	**Tours Available**	**Tours Sold**	
3	Greek Odyssey	40	36	
4	Ancient Crete	30	22	
5	Pillars of Hercules	20	10	
6	Roman Conquest	30	20	
7		120	88	
8				

> Bold, 16 pt with Dark Green, Accent 4, Lighter 80%

> Use AutoSum to calculate the values in cells B7 and C7

Marketing Update (continued)

Add Linked Data from Excel

You need to create a chart in Excel, and then copy the sales data and chart into Word as linked objects. The completed report is shown in **FIGURE E-22**.

STEPS

1. Select cells A2:C6 on the Sales tab, click the INSERT tab, click Recommended Charts, select the Clustered Column chart (fourth selection), click OK, click the Move Chart button in the Location group, click the Object in list arrow, click Chart, then click OK

2. Click the chart title and type Tours Sold Compared to Tours Available, size and position the chart so that it extends from cell A1 through cell J21, click the Sales tab, then save the workbook

3. Select cells A1:C7, copy them, switch to Word, click after "category" at the end of the second paragraph, press [Enter], click the Paste list arrow, then click the Link & Keep Source Formatting button 🖼

   The data is pasted into Word as a linked object that uses the formatting you applied in Excel.

4. Switch back to Excel, click the Chart tab, click the chart, copy it, switch to Word, click after "available" at the end of the last paragraph, press [Enter], click the Paste list arrow, then click the Keep Source Formatting & Link Data button 🖼

5. Click the chart, click the CHART TOOLS FORMAT tab, set the height of the chart at 3.2" and the width at 5.5", then center the chart

TROUBLE
Add a space after the value if needed.

6. Switch to Excel, show the Sales sheet, click cell B7, copy it, switch to Word, select the first xx in line 1 of paragraph 3, click the Paste list arrow, click Paste Special, click the Paste link option button, click Unformatted Text, then click OK

7. Copy cell C7 from Excel and paste it as a link (Unformatted Text) over the second xx in paragraph 3, switch to Excel, change the number of available tours for Roman Conquest in cell B6 to 25, switch to Word, then verify that the tours available are now 115 in the table and the paragraph, and that the blue Tours Available bar for Roman Conquest in the chart extends to the 25 line

8. Double-click the footer area below the chart, then type your name and right-align it

MORE PRACTICE
For more practice with the skills presented in this project, complete Independent Challenge 3.

9. Center the worksheet object and adjust the spacing of objects as needed so that all content fits on one page, save the document, switch to Excel, add your name to cell A10 in the Sales worksheet, save the workbook in Excel, submit all files to your instructor, then close all files

   If you wish to make changes to the Word document linked to the Excel workbook, open the Excel workbook first. Then, open the Word document and click Yes in response to the message that appears asking if you wish to maintain the link between the document and the workbook.

Classic Tours conducts tours in four categories each year to various destinations in the Mediterranean countries. The focus of each tour is the exploration of the remnants of ancient civilizations. The four tours are Greek Odyssey, Ancient Crete, Pillars of Hercules, and Roman Conquest. All of the tours run by Classic Tours are two weeks in duration.

Since its incorporation in 2004, Classic Tours has consistently sold virtually all of the Greek Odyssey and Roman Conquest tours. In most years, 80% of the Ancient Crete tours are sold. The Pillars of Hercules tours were first offered in 2015 and are steadily gaining in popularity. Shown below is a breakdown of tour sales by category.

2016 Sales by Category		
Tour Name	**Tours Available**	**Tours Sold**
Greek Odyssey	40	36
Ancient Crete	30	22
Pillars of Hercules	20	10
Roman Conquest	25	20
	115	88

In 2016, Classic Tours offered a total of 115 tours and sold 88 tours. The column chart shown below displays the number of tours sold in each category relative to the number of tours available. Greek Odyssey tours rank the highest in terms of the number of tours sold relative to the tours available.

Your Name

Integration 2013

Independent Challenge 1

Create a form in Word that you can use to record data related to a performance review for a position or situation of your choice. For example, you could create a form to review a course, a workshop, or an employee. Fill in the boxes below with the required information, then use the information in the boxes to set up the form in Word. You need to insert content controls to contain information that will change each time you fill in the form for a different evaluation. You then need to enter data related to the evaluation in an Excel worksheet and finally copy the data and paste it as a link in Word. The completed document in Word should also include a linked chart created from the Excel data. Use the performance reviews you created for Go Discover Holidays in Unit E Project 1 as your model.

1. Determine the company name and the position or situation that requires a performance review form. You also need to determine at least five categories to review. For example, if you are creating a form to review a series of workshops, the categories could be Registration Procedure, Instructor, Course Materials, Learning Outcomes, and Facilities. In the box below, write the name of your company and the five categories that you will rank in the performance review:

Company name: _____

Categories to review:

1. _____

2. _____

3. _____

4. _____

5. _____

2. In the box below, identify information about one individual, course, or workshop that you plan to review. If you're reviewing a person, include the name, department, and position. If you're reviewing a course or workshop, include the title, subject, instructor name, date, and location.

Review subject:

_____

_____

_____

_____

3. In Word, set up a document that includes a title and a subtitle, apply the Style Set of your choice, then modify the Normal style (for example, change the font size or font style). Select the theme of your choice.

4. Create an attractively formatted table to contain the performance review form. Use the performance review you created for Unit E Project 1 as your guide.

5. Insert form controls where required in the table form. Use at least three types of content controls such as the Rich Text, Combo Box, and Date Picker content controls. Remember that you can use the Legacy Tools form controls when you want to specify exactly how data should be entered in the cell. For example, if the form requires a course number, you can add a Text Form Field content control to specify that users enter only a 3-digit number for the course number. Type your name at the bottom of the page.

6. Save the form as **PR E-My Performance Review Form** to the location where you save the files for this book.

7. In Excel, enter labels for evaluation categories. For example, a course evaluation form could include categories such as "Instructor," "Course Materials," "Learning Outcomes," and so on.

8. Rename the sheet tab with a meaningful name, such as the name of the individual or course being reviewed, and enter rankings for one individual or course/workshop you are evaluating. Set up the worksheet attractively.

Independent Challenge 1 (continued)

9. Create a chart that illustrates some aspect of the data. For example, you could create a column chart that shows a ranking for each category. Remember to specify the maximum value of the value axis.

10. Enter your name below the form, then save the workbook as **PR E- My Performance Review Data** to the location where you save the files for this book.

11. In Word, enter appropriate information in the form fields related to the individual or course/workshop you are evaluating, then save the form as **PR E-My Performance Review 1** to the location where you save the files for this book.

12. In Word, copy data from the Excel worksheet and paste it as a linked Microsoft Excel Worksheet Object in an appropriate area of the form. Copy the chart and paste it as a link using the Use Destination Theme & Link Data option, resize the chart so the form fits on one page, then save the document.

13. In Excel, copy the worksheet (both the data and the chart) to a new worksheet, then replace the data with data related to a different individual, course, or workshop. Give the sheet tab a meaningful name to reflect the worksheet content.

14. Modify the chart so that it references data in the second worksheet. Make sure the maximum value on the value axis scale is the same on both charts to ensure a meaningful comparison between the charted results.

15. In Word, save the document as **PR E-My Performance Review 2** to the location where you save the files for this book, change the form information excluding the linked data and chart to reflect who or what is being reviewed, open the Edit Links to Files dialog box, then change the link so that it refers to the data in the second Excel worksheet.

16. Click the chart, click the CHART TOOLS DESIGN tab, click Select Data in the Data group, select the name currently entered in the Chart data range text box, type the correct reference, add your name below the chart on both worksheets, then save and close the Excel workbook.

17. Save the document, submit all files to your instructor, then exit Word and Excel.

Independent Challenge 2

In Excel, use the Goal Seek function to analyze a specific goal related to a company of your choice. In Word, create a sales report that includes data from Excel. For example, you could set a goal to increase your sales in two or three states or countries or increase the number of products of a certain type that you plan to sell. Refer to the sales report you created for Evergreen Resorts in Unit E Project 2 as your model.

1. In the box below, write the name of your company and a short description of your business goal. For example, you could name your company "Lavender Landscaping," and describe your goal as: To increase sales of perennials.

Company Name: _____

Description of Business Goal: _____
_____
_____

2. Set up a worksheet in Excel similar to the worksheet created for Evergreen Resorts in Unit E Project 2. Note that you need to include two or three products or locations, the income generated from sales, and your various expenses. Apply the theme of your choice.
3. Save the workbook as **PR E-My Sales Report Goals** to the location where you save the files for this book.
4. Create a current scenario of the data that you will use Goal Seek to change. For example, if you decide to increase the total number of bedding plants you sell in May, you need to create a current scenario of the sales data related to bedding plants.
5. Use Goal Seek to change the value in one of the cells. Note that the cell you wish to change must not contain a formula. However, the cell must be referenced in a formula contained in another cell, such as a total. You use Goal Seek to specify a set value for the cell containing the formula. For example, you can ask Goal Seek to calculate how many bedding plants you need to sell in May if you want your net income in May to equal $30,000.
6. Create a scenario from the projected data generated by Goal Seek, name the scenario **Projected**, then show the current scenario.
7. Copy the sales summary from the Current sheet into a new sheet called **Projected**, then show the Projected scenario sales summary.
8. In the Projected worksheet, create a bar chart (use the style of your choice) that compares the relevant values in the Current scenario (Sheet1) with the new values generated by Goal Seek and shown as the Projected scenario (Sheet2).
9. Format the bar chart attractively.
10. In Word, create a new document that includes the name of the company as a heading. Enter text that describes the company and summarizes the sales data. Leave placeholders for data you'll copy from Excel.
11. Save the report as **PR E-My Sales Report** to the location where you save the files for this book.
12. Copy data as needed to replace placeholder text and paste as links using Unformatted Text in the Paste Options dialog box.
13. Copy the data in the Projected worksheet, and paste it as a link into the Word report, using the Microsoft Excel Worksheet Object option in the Paste Special dialog box.
14. Copy the chart from the Projected worksheet, and paste it as a link into the Word report using the Keep Source Formatting and Link Data option. Enter a paragraph above the chart that summarizes the information in the chart.
15. Draw a callout to highlight each value in the chart that represents projected sales.
16. In Excel, change some of the data, then check that the data is updated correctly in the Word document.
17. Add your name to the worksheets, save and close the workbook, include your name in the sales report, submit a copy to your instructor, then save and close the document.

Independent Challenge 3

Create a one-page summary in Word that provides information about the sales and marketing efforts for a company of your choice. Use the marketing update you created for Classic Tours in Unit E Project 3 as your model. The summary should include an appropriate screen clipping of a header you create in Word using a photograph of your choice combined with a WordArt object.

1. In Excel, enter data related to your product line and create an appropriate chart in a second worksheet.
2. In Word, write a few paragraphs of text summarizing information about sales and marketing efforts.
3. From Excel, copy data into the document as a linked object, then copy the chart and paste it as a link into the Word document using the Keep Source Formatting & Link Data paste option.
4. Copy additional links into the body of the report using the Unformatted Text option in the Paste Special dialog box.
5. Make changes to the data in Excel, then update the links in Word.
6. In a separate Word document, create an attractive header for your document that combines a picture and a WordArt object. Crop the picture to a shape. Save the header as **PR E-My Update Header** to the location where you save the files for this book.
7. From the update, create a screen clipping of the header and size and position it attractively in the document.
8. Save the workbook as **PR E-My Update Data** to the location where you save the files for this book and the document as **PR E-My Update Report** to the same location. Select a different theme for the Word document and the Excel workbook so that when you use the "Use Source Formatting & Link Data" paste option, the formatting of the objects copied from the Excel workbook is retained.
9. Include your name on the Word document, save and close both files, then submit a copy of both files to your instructor.

Independent Challenge 4 - Team Project

To further explore how you can integrate Word and Excel to meet a wide range of business needs, you will work with two other people to complete a team project. The subject of the team project is the development and marketing of a non-profit organization of your choice. The organization should provide a range of services and engage in activities that generate revenue in the form of membership dues, fundraisers, sales, and so on. Follow the guidelines provided below to create the files required for the team project. When you have completed the project, the team will submit a document containing summary information about the project, as well as the Word and Excel files related to the project reviews, sales report, and marketing update.

▶ Project Setup

1. As a team, work together to complete the following tasks.
   - Share e-mail addresses among all three team members.
   - Set up a time (either via e-mail, an online chat session, Internet Messaging, or face to face) when you will get together to choose your topic and assign roles.
   - At your meeting, complete the table below with information about your team and the non-profit organization you are creating documents and workbooks for.

Team Name (last names of the team member or another name that describes the project; for example, "Martin-Donovan-Ng" or "Lakeview Recycling").
Team Members 1. 2. 3.
Organization Name
Organization services or activities (for example, the organization could offer music workshops to disadvantaged children).
Organization revenue sources (for example, membership dues, fundraisers, ticket sales, product sales, and so on).
Team Roles: indicate who is responsible for each of the following sets of files (one set per team member) Reviews (Use Unit E Project 1 as your model): Sales Report (Use Unit E Project 2 as your model): Marketing Report (Use Unit E Project 3 as your model):
File Formatting: Select a theme and color scheme that will be used to format all of the documents and workbooks created for the Team Project. Theme and Color Scheme: Applied to Word files: Applied to Excel files:

Independent Challenge 4 - Team Project (continued)

▶ File Development

Individually, complete the tasks listed below for the file set you are responsible for. You need to develop appropriate content and format each file you create attractively. Be sure team members use the same theme and color scheme when creating files as detailed in the previous table. On all workbooks, include the team name in the left section of the header, the individual name in the Center section, and the worksheet name in the Right section. On all documents, include the team name in the left side of the footer and the individual name in the right side of the footer.

Reviews

This set of files contains a form that can be used to evaluate some aspect of the non-profit organization. For example, if the organization sponsors workshops to teach music to disadvantaged children, the form could be a workshop evaluation form that children or parents complete following a workshop. In addition, you need to create evaluation data in an Excel workbook and then two Word documents containing two separate reviews. Each Word document is linked to a different sheet tab in the Excel workbook. Use Unit E Project 1 as your model to create the files as follows:

1. Create a new Word document, save it as **PR E-Team Project_Reviews** to the location where you save files for this book, then apply the theme and color scheme selected by your team.

2. Set up the document with a title and subtitle, apply the Style Set of your choice, then modify the Normal style.

3. Create a table to contain the review form. Make sure you include space for ranking information you will copy from Excel. Use the review form you created for Unit E Project 1 as your guide.

4. Insert at least three types of form controls (for example, Rich Text, List Box, and Date Picker). You can also use the Text Form Field control from the Legacy Tools if you want to limit the number of characters users can enter into a form cell.

5. Start a workbook in Excel, apply the theme and color scheme selected by your team, then save it as **PR E-Team Project_Review Data**. Enter labels for categories. For example, a workshop evaluation form could include categories such as "Instructor," "Workshop Materials," "Learning Activities," and so on.

6. Give the sheet tab a meaningful name; for example, the name of an individual, a workshop, or some other activity that is being reviewed, then enter appropriate rankings.

7. Create and format a chart to illustrate some aspect of the data. For example, you could create a column chart that shows a ranking for each category. Set a maximum value for the value axis.

8. Copy the sheet to a new worksheet, modify the data for a second review (for example, another workshop or activity), then modify the chart so that it references data in the second worksheet. Make sure the maximum value on the value axis scale is the same on both charts to ensure a meaningful comparison between the charted results.

9. Resave the Word form as **PR E-Team Project_Review1**, then enter appropriate information in the form fields related to the activity or individual being reviewed.

10. Copy data from the Excel worksheet and paste it as a linked Microsoft Excel Worksheet Object in an appropriate area of the form. Copy the chart and paste it as a link using the Use Destination Theme & Link Data option, resize the chart so the form fits on one page, then save the document.

11. Resave the document as **PR E-Team Project_Review2**, then change the form information excluding the linked data and chart to reflect who or what is being reviewed, open the Edit Links to Files dialog box, then change the link so that it refers to the data in the second Excel worksheet.

12. Edit the chart reference.

13. Group the two worksheets (see Unit C), add your name, team name, and worksheet name to the custom header as described in the Team Project overview, then save and close the workbook.

14. Ensure your name and team name appear in the footer on all three Word documents, then save and close all documents.

15. Submit all files to your instructor along with the files created by your team members.

Independent Challenge 4 - Team Project (continued)

Sales Report

This set of files includes an Excel workbook containing data about some aspect of the organization's revenue goals and a Word document that explains the data and includes data copied and pasted as links from the Excel workbook. You need to use the Goal Seek function to analyze a specific goal related to the organization. For example, you may wish to know how many members paying membership dues of $100 your organization needs in order to make a specific revenue target. Include at least two uses of Goal Seek. Use Unit E Project 2 as your model to create the files as follows:

1. Create a new Excel workbook and save it as **PR E-Team Project_Sales Report Data** to the location where you save files for this book, then apply the workbook theme and color scheme selected by your team.
2. Set up the workbook with data about the revenue streams for your organization; for example, membership dues, fundraising events, and product sales. Adapt the worksheet you created in Project 2, using only the data relevant for your organization. Your goal is to identify up to four income streams so that you can then use Goal Seek to determine how to improve the "bottom line."
3. Create a current scenario of the data that you will use Goal Seek to change.
4. Use Goal Seek to determine projected data for at least two components in your worksheet.
5. Create a projected scenario of the data generated by Goal Seek.
6. Copy the worksheet to a new worksheet and name both sheet tabs appropriately.
7. In the Projected worksheet, create a chart that compares the relevant values in the two worksheets.
8. In Word, create a new document saved as **PR E-Team Project_Sales Report**, apply the document theme and color scheme selected by your team, then enter appropriate text and copy data and the chart from Excel.
9. Format the sales report so it fills one page attractively.
10. Include callouts on the chart to highlight data changed by Goal Seek.
11. Group the two worksheets (see Unit C), add your name, team name, and worksheet name to the custom header as described in the Team Project overview, then save and close the workbook.
12. Ensure your name and team name appear in the footer on the Word document, then save and close the document.
13. Submit both files to your instructor along with the files created by your team members.

Independent Challenge 4 - Team Project (continued)

Marketing Update

This set of files includes a one-page summary in Word that provides information about some aspect of the organization's activities. For example, you could summarize the success of the programs offered by a non-profit organization dedicated to helping seniors or inner city kids or some other group. The summary is accompanied by data you enter in an Excel worksheet and then copy into the Word document. For example, the data could be a comparison of participant numbers in five programs over two or three years. Use Unit E Project 3 as your model to create the files as follows:

1. Create a Word document, then apply the document theme and color scheme selected by your team.

2. Enter information related to your organization and its activities and programs. Your goal is to summarize the current state of the organization in terms of revenue production, people served, and so on.

3. Save the file as **PR E-Team Project_Marketing Update**.

4. In a separate document, create an attractive header for your Word summary that consists of a picture and a WordArt object. Crop the picture to a shape and place the WordArt object on top. Experiment until you have created a striking header.

5. Save the document as **PR E-Team Project_Marketing Header**.

6. From the principal Word document, create a screen clipping of the header.

7. Create a new Excel worksheet and save it as **PR E-Team Project_Marketing Data**, then enter data related to the activities you wish to analyze.

8. Create a chart in a second worksheet and name both sheet tabs appropriately.

9. Copy data to the PR E-Team Project_Marketing Update Word document and paste it as links. Include the chart, a worksheet object and individual values. Remember to paste the values as Unformatted Text from the Paste Special dialog box.

10. Group the two worksheets (see Unit C), add your name, team name, and worksheet name to the custom header as described in the Team Project overview, then save and close the workbook.

11. Ensure your name and team name appear in the footer on both Word documents, then save and close the documents.

12. Submit all files to your instructor along with the files created by your team members.

Project Summary

As a team, complete the project summary as follows.

1. Open **PR E-02.docx** from the location where you save your Data Files, then save it to your **PR E-Team Project_Summary**.

2. Read the directions in the document, then ensure that each team member enters his or her name in one of the table cells along with a short description of the skills used and the challenges faced while creating his or her set of files.

3. Save the document, then submit all files to your instructor.

Visual Workshop

Create the worksheet shown in FIGURE E-23 in Excel, then save it as **PR E-Action Apps Data** to the location where you save the files for this book. Calculate the total sales of each item by multiplying the Quantity by the Price, then calculate the total sales in cell D7. Create the text for the sales report in Word as shown in FIGURE E-24, using the Metropolitan theme and entering the values as links (Unformatted Text) copied from the Excel workbook. Save the document as **PR E-Action Apps Report** to the location where you save the files for this book. In Excel, create a column chart that appears similar to the completed chart shown in FIGURE E-24. Apply Style 5. Copy the chart from Excel, and paste it into the Word document using the Use Destination Theme & Link Data paste option. In Excel, change the unit price of Office Fit to **$4.99**, add your name to the worksheet, then save and close the workbook. Update the links in the sales report where needed, add your name under the chart, save the document, then submit both files to your instructor.

FIGURE E-23

⬜	A	B	C	D	E
1	**Title**	**Quantity**	**Price**	**Total**	
2	Office Fit	2400	$ 3.99		
3	Go Running	1500	$ 2.99		
4	Ultimate Muscle Tone	1500	$ 4.99		
5	Yoga Fit	1400	$ 4.99		
6	Jump Fit	2000	$ 2.99		
7					

FIGURE E-24

Action Apps Top Sellers

Sales of fitness apps have been brisk in 2016. Shown below are the unit sales of our top six fitness apps. Our best-selling app is Office Fit with sales in 2016 of 2400 units for a total of $9,576.00.

The chart shown below compares the sales of each of the top selling apps.

Your Name

Access Projects

Projects

In this unit you will create the following:

Inventory Database

Create tables • List field names in Design view • Use the Lookup Wizard to create a list of options • Apply the Hyperlink, Number, and Currency data types • Enforce Referential Integrity • Create a form • Add records to a form and a subform • Use the Query Wizard • Set criteria in a query • Use the Expression Builder to insert formulas into a query • Create a report • Group records • Add totals to a report • Modify control properties (*Skills also practiced in Independent Challenge 1*)

Author Database

Apply the Currency and Number data types • Apply the Comma Number Format to a field • Create a two-table query • Sort records in a query • Insert a logo into a report • Modify the properties of an inserted picture • Use the Count Records and Sum options in a report • Update a report with new data (*Skills also practiced in Independent Challenge 2*)

Tours Database

Use the Lookup Wizard • Apply the Long Date format • Apply the Attachment and Long Text data types • Add attachments to a table • Import a table from another Access database • Create and format reports (*Skills also practiced in Independent Challenge 3*)

Team Project

Files You Will Need

PR F-01.jpg	PR F-05.jpg
PR F-02.jpg	PR F-06.accdb
PR F-03.jpg	PR F-07.accdb
PR F-04.jpg	PR F-08.jpg

Inventory for Aquarius Arts

Access 2013 UNIT F

Aquarius Arts distributes hand-crafted items to gift shops and specialty stores. For this project, you **Set Up the Tables**, **Create Forms**, **Create Queries**, and then **Format and Print an Order Report**. The order report is shown in **FIGURE F-14** on page 147.

Set Up the Tables

You set up two tables: the Organizations table with records for the organizations that supply items and the Products table with records for 15 products.

STEPS

1. Start Access, click Blank desktop database, type PR F-Aquarius Arts Inventory in the File Name text box, click the Browse button, navigate to the location where you save the files for this book, click OK, then click Create

2. Click the View button in the Views group to switch to Design view, type Aquarius Arts Organizations as the table name, then click [OK]

HINT If you were setting up an Organizations table for a real business, you would also include the address, phone number(s), and Web site address of each organization.

3. Type Organization ID, press [↓] to move the insertion point to the line below Organization ID, type Organization Name, press [↓], type Email Address, press [Tab], click the Data Type list arrow, click Hyperlink, click the Close 'Aquarius Arts Organizations' button, then click Yes to save the table

4. Click the CREATE tab, click Table in the Tables group, click the HOME tab, click the View button to switch to Design view, type Aquarius Arts Products as the table name, press [Enter], type Product ID, press [↓], then enter the remaining field names as shown in FIGURE F-1

TROUBLE If a warning message appears when you click the Lookup Wizard, click Open.

5. Click the Region Data Type list arrow, click Lookup Wizard, click the "I will type in the values that I want." option button, click Next, press [Tab], type Central America, press [↓], enter the remaining regions as shown in FIGURE F-2, click Next, then click Finish

6. Click the Category Data Type list arrow, repeat Step 5 to enter the categories as shown in FIGURE F-3, click Next, then click Finish

HINT The Organizations table is the "one" table and the Products table is the "many" table, which means one organization can supply many products.

7. Click the Organization Name Data Type list arrow, click Lookup Wizard, click Next to accept that you want the values to come from an existing table, verify that Table: Aquarius Arts Organizations is selected, click Next, click Organization Name in the list of available fields, click the Select Single Field button >, click Next, click Next, click Next, click Finish, then click Yes

When you use the Lookup Wizard to create a relationship, Access automatically uses the Primary Key field (Organization ID) from the "one" table and changes the data type for the related field in the "many" table from Text to Number.

8. Click the Units in Stock Data Type list arrow, click Number, click the Unit Price Data Type list arrow, then click Currency

9. Close and save the table, click the DATABASE TOOLS tab, click Relationships in the Relationships group, double-click the line between the two tables, click the Enforce Referential Integrity check box to select it, click OK, compare the Relationships window to FIGURE F-4, then close the Relationships window

You enforce referential integrity so you can enter only the names of Organizations listed in the Organizations table into the Products table. An error message appears if you enter an organization name into the Products table that is not included in the Organizations table.

FIGURE F-1: Fields for Aquarius Arts Products table in Design view

Field Name	Data Type	De
Product ID	AutoNumber	
Product Name	Short Text	
Region	Short Text	
Category	Short Text	
Organization Name	Short Text	
Units in Stock	Short Text	
Unit Price	Short Text ▼	

FIGURE F-2: Values for the Region field

Lookup Wizard

What values do you want to see in your lookup field? Enter the number of columns you want in the list, and then type the values you want in each cell.

To adjust the width of a column, drag its right edge to the width you want, or double-click the right edge of the column heading to get the best fit.

Number of columns: 1

Col1
Central America
Africa
Southeast Asia
India

Cancel | < Back | Next > | Finish

FIGURE F-3: Values for the Category field

Lookup Wizard

What values do you want to see in your lookup field? Enter the number of columns you want in the list, and then type the values you want in each cell.

To adjust the width of a column, drag its right edge to the width you want, or double-click the right edge of the column heading to get the best fit.

Number of columns: 1

Col1
Household
Jewelry
Art
Instrument

Cancel | < Back | Next > | Finish

FIGURE F-4: One-to-Many relationship

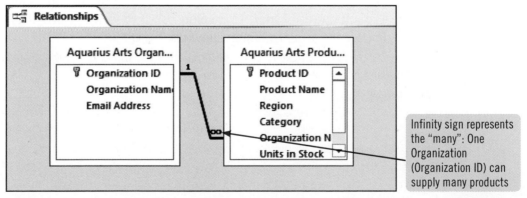

Relationships

Aquarius Arts Organ...
- Organization ID
- Organization Name
- Email Address

Aquarius Arts Produ...
- Product ID
- Product Name
- Region
- Category
- Organization N
- Units in Stock

Infinity sign represents the "many": One Organization (Organization ID) can supply many products

Create Forms

You need to create forms into which you can enter the data for the Aquarius Arts Organizations table and the Aquarius Arts Products table.

1. Click Aquarius Arts Organizations in the list of tables, click the CREATE tab, click Form in the Forms group, click the Themes button in the Themes group, then click Ion

   You have related the Organizations and Products tables in a one-to-many relationship. As a result, the form for the Organizations table appears on top and a subform for the Products table appears below. You can enter records for many products in this subform because one organization can supply many products.

2. Click the View button in the Views group to switch to Form view, press [Tab], type Helping Hands, press [Tab], then type sales@helpinghands.com

3. Double-click column dividers in the Product datasheet so all the field names are visible, click the blank cell below Product Name, type Ebony Bowl, press [Tab], type a to show Africa, press [Tab], type h to show household, press [Tab], type 15, press [Tab], type 150, then press [Enter]

   A new record is inserted. Notice how you can minimize typing time when you create lookup fields for as many of the fields as possible.

4. Enter data for four more products as shown in FIGURE F-5

5. Click the New (Blank) record button ▶* at the bottom of the form window (not the bottom of the Aquarius Arts Products subform) to show a new blank form for a new organization, click in the Organization Name text box, type Caring Circles, then enter sales@caringcircles.com as the Email Address

6. Enter the four products shown in FIGURE F-6 into the subform

7. Create another new blank form and enter Global Sustainability with the address sales@globalsustainability.com, enter the six products shown in FIGURE F-7, close the form, click Yes to save changes, then click OK to name the form

8. Double-click Aquarius Arts Organizations in the Tables section in the Objects pane to view the three organizations, then double-click Aquarius Arts Products in the Tables section to view the fifteen products

   When you entered the data into forms, the data was also entered into the tables.

9. Click the Aquarius Arts Organizations tab to show the Organizations table, then click the Expand button ⊞ next to Helping Hands to view the products associated with the Helping Hands organization as shown in FIGURE F-8

   The Expand button next to each organization name shows that each organization is the "one" in a "one-to-many" relationship.

10. Close both tables

FIGURE F-5: Completed form for Helping Hands

Product ID ▾	Product Name ▾	Region ▾	Category ▾	Units in Stock ▾	Unit Price ▾
1	Ebony Bowl	Africa	Household	15	$150.00
2	Jade Ring	Southeast Asia	Jewelry	8	$55.00
3	Talking Drum	Africa	Instrument	7	$68.00
4	Hand Pipes	Central America	Instrument	25	$80.00
5	Aztec Mask	Central America	Art	5	$125.00
*	(New)			0	$0.00

Record: I◄ ◄ 6 of 6 ► ►I ►☰ 🦢 No Filter Search

New (blank) record button moves to a new form to enter data for another organization

List of products carried by the Helping Hands organization appears in a subform

Record: I◄ ◄ 1 of 1 ► ►I ►☰ 🦢 No Filter Search

FIGURE F-6: Products for Caring Circles

Product ID ▾	Product Name ▾	Region ▾	Category ▾	Units in Stock ▾	Unit Price ▾
6	Lacquer Dinner Set	Africa	Household	5	$80.00
7	Hippo Carving	Africa	Art	15	$90.00
8	Jaguar Carving	Central America	Art	9	$150.00
9	Teak Bowl	Central America	Household	12	$90.00
*	(New)			0	$0.00

Number added automatically after each product is entered

FIGURE F-7: Products for Global Sustainability

Product ID ▾	Product Name ▾	Region ▾	Category ▾	Units in Stock ▾	Unit Price ▾
10	Woven Tapestry	Central America	Art	20	$200.00
11	Turquoise Pendant	Central America	Jewelry	8	$30.00
12	Blue Topaz Pendant	Southeast Asia	Jewelry	7	$300.00
13	Balinese Bells	Southeast Asia	Instrument	15	$100.00
14	Cane Basket	India	Household	18	$12.00
15	Elephant Wall Hanger	India	Household	9	$25.00

FIGURE F-8: Products for Helping Hands

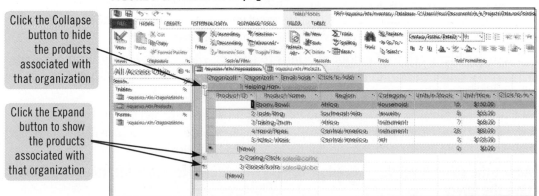

Click the Collapse button to hide the products associated with that organization

Click the Expand button to show the products associated with that organization

Create Queries

You create a query to find out how many products you have from Africa in the Household category, and then you create a query to determine the number of products with fewer than 10 items in stock. Finally, you enter formulas in the Expression Builder to calculate how many units you need to order and the total cost.

STEPS

HINT
To select a different table, click the Tables/Queries list arrow to the right of the Tables/Queries list box, then click the name of the table you want to use for the query.

1. **Click the CREATE tab, click the Query Wizard button in the Queries group, then click OK to accept Simple Query Wizard**

2. **Verify Table: Aquarius Arts Products is the table shown in the Tables/Queries list box**
   You select the table that contains the fields you want to include in your query.

3. **Click the Select All Fields button `>>` to select all the fields in the Available Fields list box, click Next, click Next to accept a Detail query, select the contents of the text box, type Africa Household as the query name, click the "Modify the query design." option button, then click Finish**

HINT
Use the column name and the row name to find the correct Criteria cell.

4. **Click the Region Criteria cell (see FIGURE F-9), type Africa, click the Category Criteria cell, type Household as shown in FIGURE F-9, then click the Run button in the Results group**
   The query results show that two of the products from Africa are from the Household category—the Ebony Bowl and the Lacquer Dinner Set.

5. **Click the Close 'Africa Household' button (upper-right corner of the datasheet), then click Yes to save the query**

6. **Click the CREATE tab, click the Query Wizard button in the Queries group, click OK, verify Table: Aquarius Arts Products is the table in the Tables/Queries list box, add all the fields, click Next, click Next, change the name to Items to Order, click the "Modify the query design." option button, then click Finish**

7. **Click the [Units in Stock] Criteria cell, type <10, then click the Run button in the Results group**
   The query results show a datasheet listing the 8 products currently with fewer than 10 units in stock.

TROUBLE
Enter the formula exactly as written including spaces. If the formula returns an error, carefully check the formula in the Expression Builder.

8. **Click the View button in the Views group, click in the blank cell to the right of [Unit Price] (you may need to scroll right), click Builder in the Query Setup group, type Units to Order: (10-[U to show the list of available field names as shown in FIGURE F-10, double-click [Units in Stock], type), then click OK**
   You select fields in the Builder to minimize typing errors. In this formula, "Units to Order" is the field name and is followed by a colon. The formula is enclosed in parentheses: (10-[Units in Stock]), which means that the value in the Units in Stock field will be subtracted from 10 because you want to always have at least 10 items in stock. Note that the Units in Stock field is contained in square brackets in the formula. Any time you reference a field in a formula, you must enclose it in square brackets.

9. **Click in the blank cell to the right of "Units to Order", click Builder, type Total: [Units to Order]*[U, select the Unit Price field, verify that the formula is Total: [Units to Order]*[Unit Price], click OK, then click the Run button**
   In this formula, "Total" is the name of the new field, and [Units to Order] and [Unit Price] both reference existing field names. The * symbol is the symbol used in all formulas for multiplication. This formula multiplies the value in the Units to Order field by the value in the Unit Price field.

10. **Adjust the column widths as needed, compare the query to FIGURE F-11, then close and save the query**

FIGURE F-9: Selecting Criteria

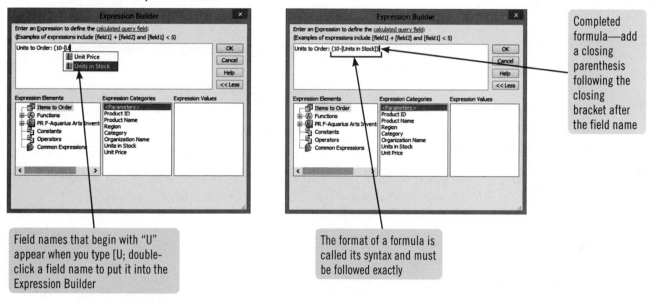

Field:	[Product ID]	[Product Name]	[Region]	[Category]	[Organization Name]	[Units in Stock]	[Unit Price]	
Table:	Aquarius Arts Produc	Aquarius Arts Produc	Aquarius Arts Produc	Aquarius Arts Produc	Aquarius Arts Produc	Aquarius Arts Produc	Aquarius Arts Produc	
Sort:								
Show:	☑	☑	☑	☑	☑	☑	☑	☐
Criteria:			"Africa"	Household				
or:								

Africa entered in the Region Criteria cell; quotation marks appear when you exit the cell

Household entered in the Category Criteria cell; quotation marks will appear when you exit the cell

FIGURE F-10: Formula in the Expression Builder

Expression Builder

Enter an Expression to define the calculated query field:
(Examples of expressions include [field1] + [field2] and [field1] < 5)

Units to Order: (10-[U

Unit Price
Units in Stock

OK
Cancel
Help
<< Less

Expression Elements
- Items to Order
- Functions
- PR F-Aquarius Arts Invent
- Constants
- Operators
- Common Expressions

Expression Categories
<Parameters>
Product ID
Product Name
Region
Category
Organization Name
Units in Stock
Unit Price

Expression Values

Field names that begin with "U" appear when you type [U; double-click a field name to put it into the Expression Builder

Expression Builder

Enter an Expression to define the calculated query field:
(Examples of expressions include [field1] + [field2] and [field1] < 5)

Units to Order: (10-[Units in Stock])

OK
Cancel
Help
<< Less

Expression Elements
- Items to Order
- Functions
- PR F-Aquarius Arts Invent
- Constants
- Operators
- Common Expressions

Expression Categories
<Parameters>
Product ID
Product Name
Region
Category
Organization Name
Units in Stock
Unit Price

Expression Values

Completed formula—add a closing parenthesis following the closing bracket after the field name

The format of a formula is called its syntax and must be followed exactly

FIGURE F-11: Datasheet view of query results

PR F-Aquarius Arts Inventory : Database- C:\Users\Your\Documents\A_A_Projects\Data and Solution Files\170329s_PRF\PR F-Aquarius Arts Inventory.accdb (Access 2007 - 2013 file format) - Access

FILE   HOME   CREATE   EXTERNAL DATA   DATABASE TOOLS

Your Name

Views | Clipboard | Sort & Filter | Records | Find | Text Formatting

All Access Obje... «

Search...

Tables
- Aquarius Arts Organizations
- Aquarius Arts Products

Queries
- Africa Household
- Items to Order

Forms
- Aquarius Arts Organizations

Items to Order

Product ID	Product Name	Region	Category	Organization Name	Units in Stock	Unit Price	Units to Or	Total
2	Jade Ring	Southeast Asia	Jewelry	Helping Hands	8	$55.00	2	$110.00
3	Talking Drum	Africa	Instrument	Helping Hands	7	$68.00	3	$204.00
5	Aztec Mask	Central America	Art	Helping Hands	5	$125.00	5	$625.00
6	Lacquer Dinner Set	Africa	Household	Caring Circles	5	$80.00	5	$400.00
8	Jaguar Carving	Central America	Art	Caring Circles	9	$150.00	1	$150.00
11	Turquoise Pendant	Central America	Jewelry	Global Sustainability	8	$30.00	2	$60.00
12	Blue Topaz Pendant	Southeast Asia	Jewelry	Global Sustainability	7	$300.00	3	$900.00
15	Elephant Wall Hanger	India	Household	Global Sustainability	9	$25.00	1	$25.00
*	(New)				0	$0.00		

Format and Print an Order Report

You format and print an Order report generated from the Items to Order query. The completed report is shown in FIGURE F-14

STEPS

TROUBLE
To switch to Layout view, click the View list arrow in the Views group, then click Layout View.

1. **Click Items to Order in the All Access Objects pane, click the CREATE tab, click the Report button in the Reports group, then switch to Layout View if that is not the active view**

   A report based on the Items to Order query is generated. You want to show the products grouped under the appropriate organization name.

2. **Click the Group & Sort button in the Grouping & Totals group if it is not already selected, click Add a group below the report grid, then click Organization Name**

   The three organizations are moved to the first column and their corresponding products are indented.

3. **Double-click in the header area, click after Order, add a hyphen (-) and Your Name following the report title, click the date, press [Delete], click the time, then press [Delete]**

4. **Scroll right, click $625 in the Total column, click Totals in the Grouping & Totals group, click Sum, then scroll to view the subtotal under each group of products and the grand total**

   You need to modify the height of the text boxes containing the totals and show them in Currency format.

HINT
All three subtotal boxes are selected when you select the first one.

5. **Click the total below $110.00 , use your mouse to increase the height so the value is visible (939) as shown in FIGURE F-12, right-click 939, click Properties, click the Format list arrow (not the Format tab), then click Currency**

6. **Scroll to view the grand total (2474), repeat Step 5 to modify the height and apply Currency formatting, click the text box to the left in the Unit Price column (contains $833.00), press [Delete], scroll down again, click the empty text box, click Solid next to Gridline Style Top, click the list arrow, click Transparent, then close the Property Sheet**

7. **Scroll up and click Product ID, click the REPORT LAYOUT TOOLS ARRANGE tab, click Select Column, then press the [Delete] key**

   After you generate a report you can easily delete columns you do not want to include.

8. **Click the REPORT LAYOUT TOOLS PAGE SETUP tab, click Landscape in the Page Layout group, then click Helping Hands (all the organization names are selected) and reduce the width of the text box to just fit "Global Sustainability"**

9. **Double-click the Units in Stock field name box, select Units in Stock, delete it, type Stock, change "Units to Order" to Order, then as shown in FIGURE F-13, reduce the width of each field so all eight fields fit on the page**

   When you create a report, you often need to adjust the width of fields so all the data fits on the page.

MORE PRACTICE
For more practice with the skills presented in this project, complete Independent Challenge 1.

10. **Click the REPORT LAYOUT TOOLS DESIGN tab, click the View button list arrow in the Views group, click Print Preview, compare the complete report to FIGURE F-14, submit a copy of the report to your instructor, exit Print Preview, close and save the report with the default name, then close the database**

FIGURE F-12: Adjusting the height of a text box content control

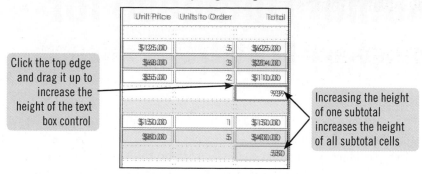

Click the top edge and drag it up to increase the height of the text box control

Increasing the height of one subtotal increases the height of all subtotal cells

Unit Price	Units to Order	Total
$1225.000	5	$6225.000
$68.000	3	$2204.000
$55.000	2	$1110.000
		9239
$150.000	11	$1150.000
$80.000	5	$4400.000
		$550

FIGURE F-13: Column widths adjusted in Layout view

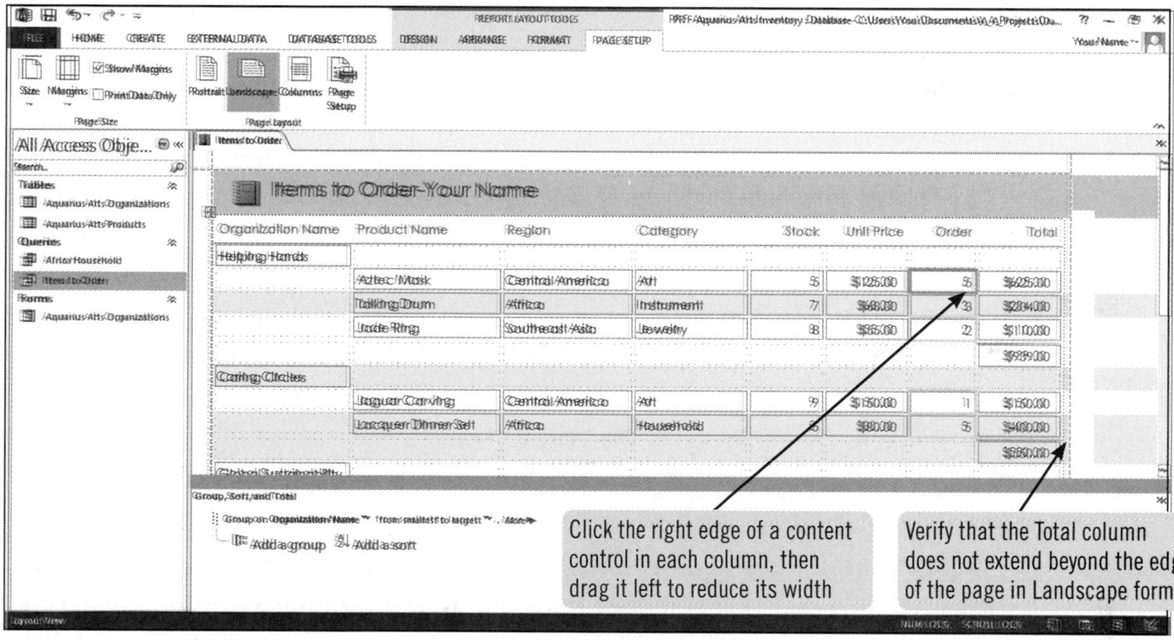

Click the right edge of a content control in each column, then drag it left to reduce its width

Verify that the Total column does not extend beyond the edge of the page in Landscape format

FIGURE F-14: Completed report in Print Preview

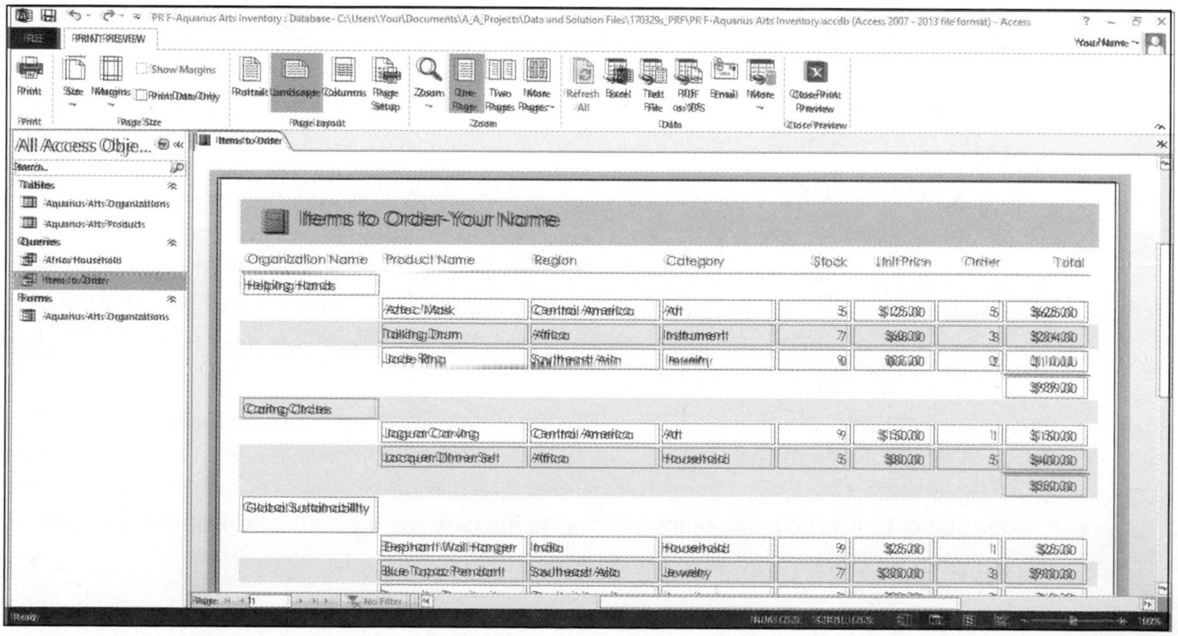

Access 2013

Author Database for Global Books

Global Books publishes nonfiction books that inspire people to action in the service of their communities. As the managing editor, you set up a database that you can use to identify the authors who have sold the most books, the titles that have earned revenues in excess of $150,000 during the last year, and the most popular topics purchased. For this project, you **Set Up the Tables**, **Enter Records and Create Queries**, and then **Create and Format a Report**. The completed report is shown in **FIGURE F-23** on page 153.

Set Up the Tables

You set up the Authors table and the Books table. Because one author can write many books, you set up the Authors table as the "one" table and the Books table as the "many" table.

STEPS

1. Start Access, click Blank desktop database, type PR F-Global Books, click the Browse button , navigate to the location where you save the files for this book, click OK, then click Create

2. Click the View button in the Views group, type Authors as the table name, press [Enter], enter the fields shown in FIGURE F-15 in Design view, then close and save the table

3. Click the CREATE tab, click the Table button in the Tables group, click the View button, type Books as the table name, then press [Enter]

4. In Design view, type the following fields: Book ID (to replace ID), Book Title, Author, Topic, Price, and Units Sold

   HINT
   You created a relationship between the Author table and the Books table because one author can write many books.

5. Click the Author Data Type list arrow, click Lookup Wizard, click Open if prompted, click Next to accept that you want the values to come from an existing table, click Next to accept the Authors table, click Last Name in the list of available fields, click the Select Single Field button ⸴ > ⸴, click Next, click Next, click Finish, then click Yes

   When you complete the Books table, the authors' last names will be available to you because you created a lookup table for the Author field that uses the Last Name field in the Authors table.

6. Click the Topic Data Type list arrow, click Lookup Wizard, click the "I will type in the values that I want." option button, click Next, press [Tab], type Diversity, press [↓], enter the remaining categories as shown in FIGURE F-16, click Next, then click Finish

7. Click the Price Data Type list arrow, click Currency, click the Units Sold Data type list arrow, then click Number

8. Close and save the table, click the DATABASE TOOLS tab, click Relationships in the Relationships group, double-click the line between the two tables, click the Enforce Referential Integrity check box to select it, click OK, then compare the Relationships window to FIGURE F-17

   Notice that the relationship is set up between the Author ID field in the Authors table and the Author field in the Books table. The Author ID field is used because each last name has a unique Author ID. When you selected the Last Name field in the Lookup Wizard, Access automatically created the relationship between the Author ID field (a unique number) in the Author table and the Author field in the Books table.

9. Close and save if prompted the Relationships window

FIGURE F-15: Fields for the Authors table

Field Name	Data Type	
🔑 Author ID	AutoNumber	
Last Name	Short Text	
First Name	Short Text	
Location	Short Text ▾	

FIGURE F-16: Values for the Topic field

Lookup Wizard

What values do you want to see in your lookup field? Enter the number of columns you want in the list, and then type the values you want in each cell.

To adjust the width of a column, drag its right edge to the width you want, or double-click the right edge of the column heading to get the best fit.

Number of columns: [1]

Col1				
Diversity				
Environment				
Globalization				
Sustainability				
*				

[Cancel] [< Back] [Next >] [Finish]

FIGURE F-17: One-to-Many relationship between author and books

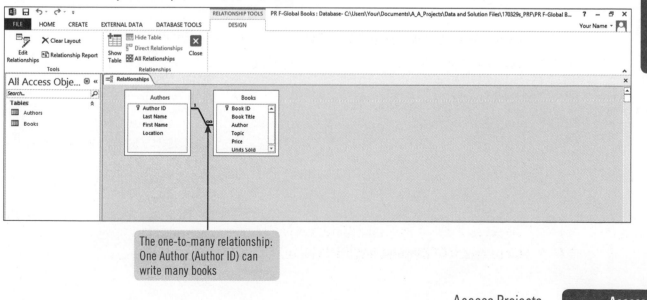

The one-to-many relationship: One Author (Author ID) can write many books

Author Database (continued)

Enter Records and Create Queries

Your market researchers have found that readers want more titles on the Globalization and Sustainability topics, so you decide to create a query that shows how many titles on these topics you have in stock. You then modify this query to list only those authors who sold more than $150,000 worth of books. Before you can create the query, you need to enter records for the Authors and Books tables.

STEPS

1. **Open the** Authors table, **enter the records shown in** FIGURE F-18, **adjust column widths as needed to fit content, then close and save the table**

2. **Open the** Books table, **click the** Units Sold field, **click the** TABLE TOOLS FIELDS tab, **click the** Apply Comma Number Format button ▸ **in the Formatting group, then click the** Decrease Decimals button ▸ **two times**

> **HINT**
> Remember that you can save time by typing only the first letter or two to show the required record for the Author and Topic fields.

3. **Enter the records shown in** FIGURE F-19 **and adjust column widths as needed, then close and save the table if prompted**

4. **Click the** CREATE tab, **click the** Query Wizard button **in the Queries group, click** OK, **select** Table: Authors **in the Tables/Queries list box, then add only the** Location field **to the Selected Fields list box**

5. **Click the** Tables/Queries list arrow, **click** Table: Books, **add all the fields except the Book ID field to the Selected Fields list box, click** Next, **click** Next **again, change the name of the query to** Popular Topics, **click the** "Modify the query design." **option button, then click** Finish

6. **Click the** Topic Sort cell, **click the** Sort cell list arrow, **click** Ascending, **then click the** Run button

   You can see at a glance that the two topics with the most available titles are Globalization and Sustainability.

> **HINT**
> The required formula is Total Sales: [Units Sold]*[Price].

7. **Switch to** Design view, **click the blank cell to the right of Units Sold, click** Builder **in the Query Setup group, enter a formula that will designate "Total Sales" as the field name and multiply the Units Sold by the Price, then click** OK

> **TROUBLE**
> If your query does not show seven results, recheck your Books table to be sure the entries match FIGURE F-19 then check to be sure your query criteria matches FIGURE F-20

8. **Click the** Topic Criteria cell, **type** Globalization, **click the** Total Sales Criteria cell, **type** >150000, **complete the criteria as shown in** FIGURE F-20, **then run the query**

   Seven books match the criteria.

9. **Close the Query Results window, then click** Yes **to save the modified query**

FIGURE F-18: Records for the Authors table

	Author ID	Last Name	First Name	Location	Click to Add
⊞	1	Lemieux	Gerald	Seattle, WA	
⊞	2	Ibrahim	Zane	Portland, OR	
⊞	3	Degrasso	Jule	Vancouver, BC	
⊞	4	Wilson	Ivy	London, England	
⊞	5	Pratt	Cheryl	Los Angeles, CA	
⊞	6	Howe	Marilyn	Dublin, Ireland	
⊞	7	Owen	Gary	Toronto, ON	
⊞	8	Ng	Jason	New York, NY	
*	(New)				

Plus signs indicate the table is related

FIGURE F-19: Records for the Books table

Book ID	Book Title	Author	Topic	Price	Units Sold	Click to Add
1	Green Living	Degrasso	Environment	$25.00	3,000	
2	The Planet's Way	Lemieux	Sustainability	$20.00	9,000	
3	Conservation Essentials	Lemieux	Sustainability	$25.00	6,000	
4	Celebration	Pratt	Diversity	$15.00	7,000	
5	Community Living	Howe	Globalization	$30.00	6,000	
6	Peace First	Howe	Globalization	$35.00	8,000	
7	Change for Tomorrow	Howe	Globalization	$40.00	9,000	
8	It Takes a Village	Ng	Globalization	$25.00	5,000	
9	Resource Stretching	Lemieux	Sustainability	$40.00	6,000	
10	Raising Citizens	Wilson	Globalization	$25.00	2,000	
11	Thriving Together	Wilson	Globalization	$30.00	9,000	
12	Earth Wise	Ng	Globalization	$35.00	8,000	
13	Staying Alive	Ibrahim	Sustainability	$35.00	3,000	
14	Building a Future	Owen	Diversity	$25.00	4,000	
15	Embracing Diversity	Pratt	Diversity	$20.00	3,000	
* (New)				$0.00	0	

FIGURE F-20: Selecting criteria

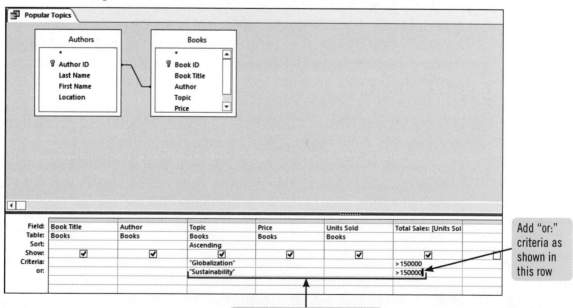

Criteria for Topic and Total Sales

Add "or:" criteria as shown in this row

Access 2013

Create and Format a Report

You need to create a report and then format it to present to your colleagues at a meeting. Your finished report will look similar to the one shown in **FIGURE F-23**.

STEPS

1. Verify that Popular Topics is selected in the list of queries, click the CREATE tab, click Report in the Reports group, apply the Slice theme, change the title of the report in the header area to Global Books - Your Name, then delete the date and time

HINT
When you insert a picture into the Logo control, you usually need to change the Size Mode to Stretch so the entire picture is visible.

2. Click the Logo button in the Header? Footer group, navigate to the location where you store files for this book, double-click PR F-01.jpg, click the Property Sheet button in the Tools group, click the Size Mode list arrow ("Clip" currently appears to the right of the Size Mode label), click Stretch to show the entire picture, then close the Property Sheet

3. Click the View list arrow in the Views group, click Design View, then as shown in FIGURE F-21, drag the blue header area down to increase its height to approximately 1"

   You work in Design view to change the size of report sections such as the Report Header and Detail sections.

4. Click the logo picture, then drag the lower-right size handle to increase the size of the logo to fit the height of the header area

TROUBLE
If Add a group is not available at the bottom of the window, click the Group & Sort button in the Grouping and Totals group.

5. Click the REPORT LAYOUT TOOLS DESIGN tab, switch to Layout View, click Add a group at the bottom of the window, then click Author

   The report records are grouped according to author so you can quickly see how many book titles belong to each author.

6. Click the REPORT LAYOUT TOOLS DESIGN tab, scroll to and click the Price label, click the Totals button in the Grouping & Totals group, click Count Records, click the Units Sold label, click the Totals button, click Sum, then click the Totals Sales label and sum the column

   The report now includes the total number of books written by each author, the total number of books sold by each author, and the total sales for each author.

7. Increase the height of the box containing "2" in the Price column so the summed values are visible, right-click the total (420000), click Properties, click the list box next to "Format", click the Format list arrow, click Currency, scroll to the bottom of the report, change the format of the grand total (1790000) to Currency, close the Property Sheet, then adjust the height and width of boxes as needed to fit content

8. Click the REPORT LAYOUT TOOLS PAGE SETUP tab, click Landscape, then modify the column widths so the report fits on one page as shown in FIGURE F-22

9. Close the report, click Yes, click OK, double-click Books in the All Access Objects pane to open the Books table, change the Units Sold for "The Planet's Way" (the second record) to 12,000, close the Books table, double-click the Popular Topics report, then click Refresh All in the Records group

   The total sales of Lemieux's books are now $480,000.

MORE PRACTICE
For more practice with the skills presented in this project, complete Independent Challenge 2.

10. Click the View list arrow, click Print Preview, click the Zoom list arrow in the Zoom group, click Fit to Window, compare the completed report to FIGURE F-23, submit a copy of the report to your instructor, then close the database

FIGURE F-21: Adjusting the height of a section in Design view

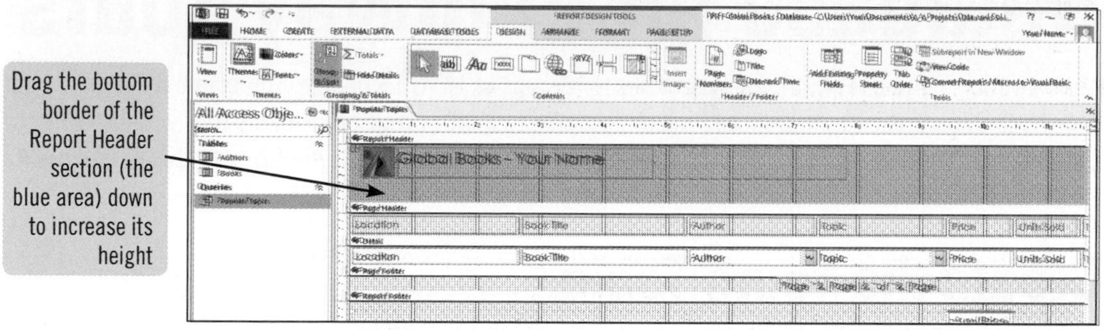

Drag the bottom border of the Report Header section (the blue area) down to increase its height

FIGURE F-22: Columns adjusted in Layout view

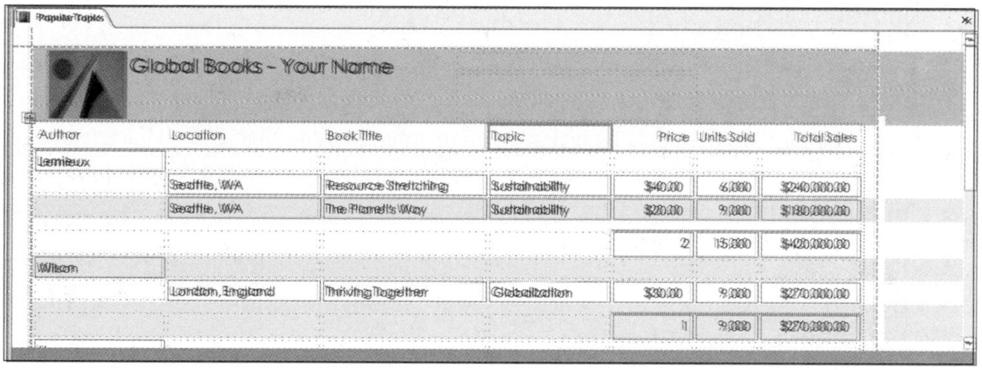

FIGURE F-23: Completed report in Print Preview

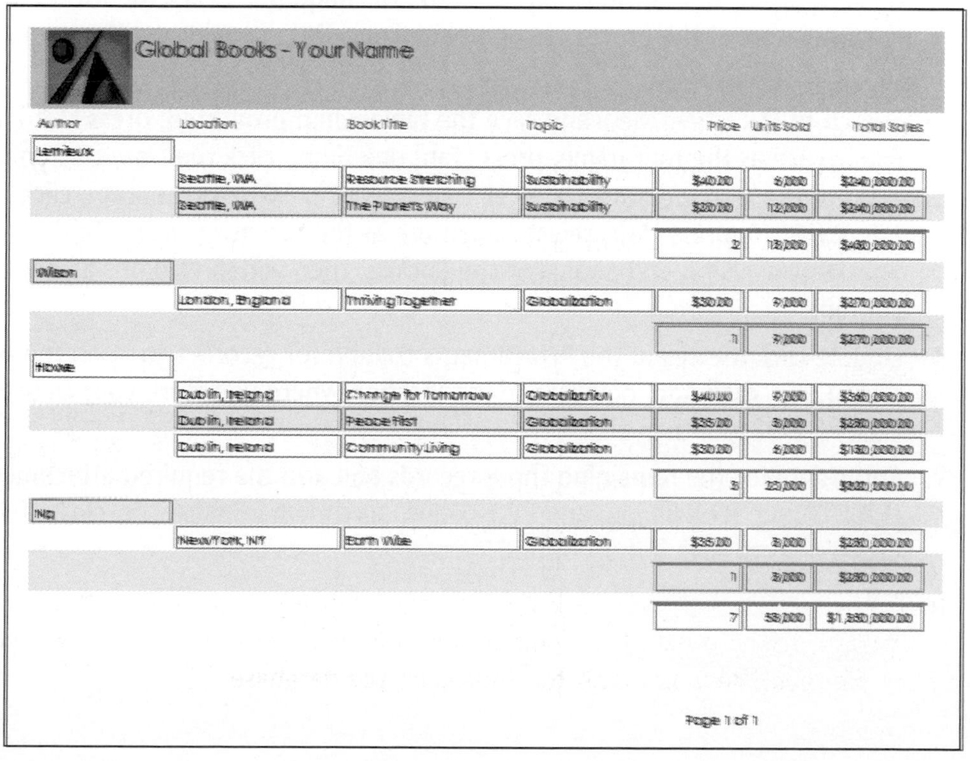

Access 2013

Database for Pathway Tours

Pathway Tours conducts North American tours for groups of 10 to 15 people. You create a database with information about each tour and then relate this table to a list of tour participants that you import from another database. For this project, you **Create the Tours Table**, and then you **Import the Participants Table**. The completed reports are shown in **FIGURES F-28** and **F-29** on page 157.

Create the Tours Table

You create the Pathway Tours database and then create the Tours table. The Tours table includes a field for pictures, which uses the Attachment data type.

STEPS

1. Start Access, then create a new database called PR F-Pathway Tours and save it to the location where you save the files for this book

2. Switch to Design view, save the table as Tours, then enter the field names and assign data types as shown in FIGURE F-24

   By default, a Short Text data type allows you to enter no more than 255 characters in a record. You select Long Text as the data type for "Description" so that you have the option to enter more than 255 characters.

3. Right click Description, click Insert Rows, then type Category in the new blank cell

4. Press [Tab], click the Category Data Type list arrow, click Lookup Wizard, then follow the steps in the Lookup Wizard to create a lookup column consisting of three entries: City, Cultural, and Adventure

5. Click Date/Time next to "Start Date", click in the cell next to "Format" in the Field Properties area below the fields list, then click the list arrow as shown in FIGURE F-25

   You can modify a wide range of properties related to a field, including its format, rules for how an entry is validated, and even whether an entry is required.

6. Click the Long Date format, click No next to "Required", click the list arrow and click Yes, then repeat the process to apply the Long Date format and the Required option to the End Date field

7. Switch to Datasheet view and save the table when prompted, press [Tab], type Peak Experience as the tour name, press [Tab] one time, click the Date button 📅 to the right of the selected Start Date cell, select July 11, 2016, press [Tab], click 📅 , select July 15, 2016, press [Tab] select Adventure as the category, press [Tab], type Spectacular hiking and cycling in the Rockies, then widen columns as needed to fit the content

8. Double-click the cell in the Attachments column for record 1 to open the Attachments dialog box, click Add, navigate to the location where you store your Data Files, double-click PR F-02.jpg, then click OK

9. Enter data for the remaining three records and add the required attachments (PR F-03.jpg, PR F-04.jpg, and PR F-05.jpg) as shown in FIGURE F-26, close the table, then answer Yes to save it if prompted

Access Projects

FIGURE F-24: Field list for the Tours table

	Field Name	Data Type
⮕	Tour ID	AutoNumber
	Tour Name	Short Text
	Start Date	Date/Time
	End Date	Date/Time
	Description	Long Text
	Pictures	Attachment

Ribbon: FILE | HOME | CREATE | EXTERNAL DATA | DATABASE TOOLS | TABLE TOOLS | DESIGN

PR F-Pathway Tours : Database- C:\Users\Y...

Views: View, Primary Key, Builder, Test Validation Rules | Tools | Insert Rows, Delete Rows, Modify Lookups | Property Sheet, Indexes | Show/Hide | Create Data Macros, Rename/Delete Macro | Field, Record & Table Events | Relationships, Object Dependencies | Relationships

All Access Obje... — Search... — Tables — Tours

FIGURE F-25: Changing the Date format

Field Name	Data Type	Description (Optional)
Tour ID	AutoNumber	
Tour Name	Short Text	
Start Date	Date/Time	
End Date	Date/Time	
Category	Short Text	
Description	Long Text	
Pictures	Attachment	

Field Properties

General | Lookup

Format	
Input Mask	
Caption	
Default Value	
Validation Rule	
Validation Text	
Required	
Indexed	
IME Mode	No Control
IME Sentence Mode	None
Text Align	General
Show Date Picker	For dates

General Date	11/12/2015 5:34:23 PM
Long Date	Thursday, November 12, 2015
Medium Date	12-Nov-15
Short Date	11/12/2015
Long Time	5:34:23 PM
Medium Time	5:34 PM
Short Time	17:34

Format list arrow

Long Date format

Design view. F6 = Switch panes. F1 = Help.

FIGURE F-26: Records for the Tours table

Tour ID	Tour Name	Start Date	End Date	Category	Description	🔗	Click to Add
1	Peak Experience	Monday, July 11, 2016	Friday, July 15, 2016	Adventure	Spectacular hiking and cycling in the Rockies	🔗(1)	
2	New York Bound	Monday, August 1, 2016	Friday, August 5, 2016	Cultural	Featuring city tours and four Broadway musicals	🔗(1)	
3	Red Rock Adventure	Monday, July 11, 2016	Monday, July 18, 2016	Adventure	Backpacking adventure in Arizona and Utah	🔗(1)	
4	Garden Delights	Tuesday, August 2, 2016	Friday, August 5, 2016	Cultural	Tour of special gardens in the Pacific Northwest	🔗(1)	
*	(New)					🔗(0)	

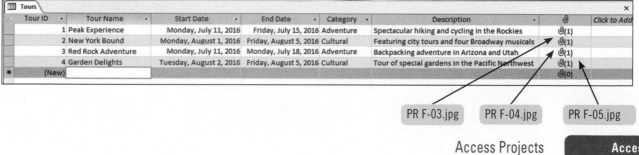

PR F-03.jpg   PR F-04.jpg   PR F-05.jpg

Access Projects

Access 2013

Import the Participants Table

You import the Participants table from another database, then create a relationship between the Tours table and the imported table. The relationship will be a one-to-many relationship because one tour can host many participants. The Tours table is the "one" table and the Participants table is the "many" table. Finally, you create two reports. One report shows all the tours and includes the picture of each tour, and the other report shows all the participants according to the tour they are taking.

STEPS

1. Click the EXTERNAL DATA tab, click Access in the Import & Link group, click Browse, navigate to the location where you store your Data Files, double-click PR F-06.accdb, click OK, click Tour Participants in the list of tables, click OK, then click Close

2. Double-click Tour Participants to open it, click Click to Add at the top of the first blank column, click Lookup & Relationship, click Next to accept that the lookup field will come from an existing table, click Table: Tours, click Next, click Tour Name, then click the Select Single Field button [>]

3. Click Next, click Next, click Next, type Tour as the lookup field name, click Finish, then as shown in FIGURE F-27, select a tour for each of the participants, widening the column as needed to fit the content

4. Close and save the table, click the DATABASE TOOLS tab, click Relationships in the Relationships group, double-click the line joining the two tables, click the Enforce Referential Integrity check box, click OK, then close the Relationships window

   By enforcing referential integrity, you ensure that a user can enter only tour names in the Tour Participants table that exist in the Tours table.

5. Click Tours, click the CREATE tab, click the Report button in the Reports group, apply the Organic theme, click Colors and select Green Yellow, then delete the date and time in the header

HINT
Be sure to move the page number text box so it is just to the left of the dotted line.

6. Modify the report title and adjust the column widths so all the data fits on the page as shown in FIGURE F-28, then close and save the report with the default name ("Tours")

7. Click the CREATE tab, click Query Wizard in the Queries group, click OK, create a query named Tours Query that includes the Tour Name field from the Tours table and the Last Name, First Name (in that order) and Country/Region fields from the Tour Participants table, finish the query, then close the query

8. Click Tours Query in the All Access Objects pane, click the Report button in the Reports group, apply the Organic theme and the Green Yellow color scheme, click the Group & Sort button in the Grouping & Totals group if it is not selected, click Add a group, click Tour Name, click Add a sort, then click Last Name

MORE PRACTICE
For more practice with the skills presented in this project, complete Independent Challenge 3.

9. Modify the report so that it appears as shown in FIGURE F-29 in Print Preview, making sure the page number is just to the left of the dotted line.

10. Close and save the report as Tour Participants, submit copies of both reports to your instructor, then close the database

FIGURE F-27: Matching tours with participants

ID	First Name	Last Name	Address	City	State/Provir	Code	Country/Region	Tour	Click
1	Alison	Leib	1803 Maple Drive	Vancouver	BC	V7H 1A7	Canada	Peak Experience	
2	Sal	Woodbury	18 Peak Road	Littleton	CO	80122	United States	New York Bound	
3	Kaiya	Grunwald	105 Independence Way	Boston	MA	02111	United States	New York Bound	
4	Ruth	Donwell	1200 Lake Street	Cincinnati	OH	45206	United States	Red Rock Adventure	
5	Corrine	Birkholz	230 Seaview Place	Halifax	NS	B9A 1P3	Canada	Peak Experience	
6	Annette	Grant	344 Cowan Road	Green Bay	WI	54311	United States	Garden Delights	
7	Stacey	Steinberg	122 West 40th Street	New York	NY	10010	United States	Garden Delights	
8	Malika	Gresch	890 Glenaden Drive	Toronto	ON	M5W 1E6	Canada	Red Rock Adventure	
9	Marco	Morales	67 Pacific Way	Santa Monica	CA	90405	United States	Peak Experience	
10	Parminder	Singh	80 The Mews	London		SW1X 8PZ	United Kingdom	Peak Experience	
11	Gino	Martelli	Via Principe Amedeo 1	Roma		00187	Italy	Red Rock Adventure	
12	Olive	Jefferson	678 Rainier Road	Seattle	WA	98110	United States	Garden Delights	
13	Laura	Tamblyn	34 Atlantic Street	Savannah	GA	31405	United States	Red Rock Adventure	
14	Julian	Fanning	230 Elm Road	Sacramento	CA	94822	United States	Peak Experience	
15	Marg	Seiler	400 High Park Road	Toronto	ON	M5E 3R5	Canada	Peak Experience	
*	(New)								

Press the first letter or two of each entry, then press the down arrow to quickly select the tour title and move to the next cell

FIGURE F-28: Tour report

Change the report title

Pathway Tours - Tour List

Tour ID	Tour Name	Start Date	End Date	Category	Description	Pictures
1	Peak Experience	Monday, July 11, 2016	Friday, July 15, 2016	Adventure	Spectacular hiking and cycling in the Rockies	
2	New York Bound	Monday, August 1, 2016	Friday, August 5, 2016	Cultural	Featuring city tours and four Broadway musicals	
3	Red Rock Adventure	Monday, July 11, 2016	Monday, July 18, 2016	Adventure	Backpacking adventure in Arizona and Utah	
4	Garden Delights	Tuesday, August 2, 2016	Friday, August 5, 2016	Cultural	Tour of special gardens in the Pacific Northwest	

4

Move the page number into the report

Page 1 of 1

Make sure the pictures do not extend beyond the dotted line

FIGURE F-29: Tour Participants report in Print Preview

Pathway Tours Participants - Your Name

Modify the report title and delete the date and time

Tour Name	Last Name	First Name	Country/Region
Garden Delights			
	Grant	Annette	United States
	Jefferson	Olive	United States
	Steinberg	Stacey	United States
New York Bound			
	Grunwald	Kaiya	United States
	Woodbury	Sal	United States
Peak Experience			
	Birkholz	Corrine	Canada
	Fanning	Julian	United States
	Leib	Alison	Canada
	Morales	Marco	United States
	Seiler	Marg	Canada
	Singh	Parminder	United Kingdom
Red Rock Adventure			
	Donwell	Ruth	United States
	Gresch	Malika	Canada
	Martelli	Gino	Italy
	Tamblyn	Laura	United States

15

Resize and position records as shown

Access Projects

Independent Challenge 1

Create a report based on tables that contain information about 20 to 30 products stocked by a company of your choice. You need to create a Products table that lists the products and then you need to create a Suppliers table that lists the companies or organizations that supply the products. Finally, you relate these two tables, make two queries, and then create a report.

1. Choose a name for your company and determine the type of products it sells. For example, you could call your company Golfways and describe it as a retail operation that sells golf equipment and accessories, such as golf clubs, bags, shoes, umbrellas, and clothing. Write the name of your company and a brief description of the products it sells in the box below:

    Company Name: _____

    Description: _____
    _____
    _____

2. Start Access, then create a database called **PR F-My Inventory**, and save it to the location where you save the files for this book.

3. Create a Suppliers table similar to the Organizations table you created for Unit F Project 1 that includes an ID field, a field for the name of the Supplier, and one or two additional fields such as an Email field or a Phone Number field.

4. Create a Products table similar to the table you created for Unit F Project 1. Include at least six fields, including the Supplier field and a Units in Stock field.

5. Identify fields that require a limited selection of responses. For example, a Category field for the Golf database could include the values "Shoes," "Accessories," "Clubs," "Clothing," and "Bags."

6. In the Products table, use the Lookup Wizard to create lookup values for the fields you identified, except for the values for the Supplier field.

7. Use the Lookup Wizard to identify the lookup values for the Supplier field in the Products table based on a field (such as Supplier Name) in the Suppliers table. (*Note*: When you identify the field in the Suppliers table (the "one" table) and make it available to the Products table (the "many" table), you create a relationship between the Suppliers table and the Products table.)

8. Open the Relationships window and enforce referential integrity so that you are not able to enter the name of any supplier not listed in the Suppliers table into the Products table.

9. Create a form for the Suppliers, then enter records for at least four Suppliers and the products each supplier carries. You should enter a minimum of 15 products spread across the suppliers.

10. In the box below, describe two queries you plan to make based on the Products and Suppliers tables. For example, you could ask which products are handled by a certain supplier, or which products are associated with a specific category, or which suppliers are located in a specific area. One of the queries should identify the items you need to order so that stock levels stay at 10 or above for all items.

    Query 1: _____
    _____
    _____

    Query 2: _____
    _____
    _____

11. Use the Query Wizard to create the queries. Make sure you specify the criteria for each query in Design view and then rename each query to reflect the contents.

Independent Challenge 1 (continued)

12. In the Items to Order query, use the Expression Builder to enter formulas to calculate the total value of each item you need to order. For example, if you decide you need to order items that have stock levels less than 10, you need to set the criteria for Units in Stock to <10 and enter two formulas. One formula subtracts 10 from the Units in Stock field, and the other formula multiplies the result by the Unit Price to determine the total cost of the units you need to order. Refer to the formulas you entered in Project 1 of this unit to ensure you use the correct syntax for the formulas.

13. Create a report that shows items you need to order based on your Items to Order query table.

14. Group the report by Supplier. Apply the theme of your choice, and adjust column widths until you are pleased with the appearance of the report. Note that you can choose to format the report in Landscape orientation.

15. Use the Totals button to add subtotals and totals so you can see at a glance how much each Supplier will receive for the products purchased from them. Use the Property sheet to format the totals with the Currency format.

16. Remove any totals that are not relevant; for example, the Unit Price total, then use the Property sheet to remove any formatting you do not want in the report.

17. Be sure the report title includes your name, remove the date and title from the header, submit a copy of the report to your instructor, and then close the database.

Independent Challenge 2

Create a database that contains information related to a company such as a publisher, an art gallery, or a talent agency that deals with people and the products they create. For example, you could create a database for a recording company that includes two tables—one table lists the recordings and the other table lists the recording artists. A database for an art gallery could include two tables—one for the artists and one for the paintings. Plan and then create the database as follows.

1. Start Access, then create a database called **PR F-My People List** and save it to the location where you save the files for this book.

2. Plan your database on paper by first listing all the fields you require. Here are some sample fields for an art gallery, in no particular order: Artist Name, Painting Title, Artist Phone Number, Painting Medium, Painting Size, Painting Genre, and Painting Price.

3. Divide the field names into two tables and determine the relationship between the two tables. For example, the fields for an art gallery database could be arranged into an Artists table and a Paintings table as follows:

   Artists Table: Artist ID, Artist Name, Phone Number

   Paintings table: Painting ID, Painting Title, Medium, Size, Genre, Price, and Artist Name

4. Determine the relationship between the two tables. In the example just presented, the Artists and Paintings tables are related through the Artist Name field because one artist can create many paintings.

5. Determine which fields require a limited selection of responses. For example, the Genre field in an Art Gallery database could include the values "Abstract," "Landscape," and "Photography."

6. Create the two tables in Access. Make sure you assign appropriate data types and that you use the Lookup Wizard to create lookup values for the fields you identified.

7. Use the Lookup Wizard to create a relationship between the two tables. For example, in an Art Gallery database, a relationship would be created between "Artist Name" in the Artists table (the "one" table) and "Artist Name" in the Paintings table (the "many" table). In this example, you only need to create the lookup values for the Artist Name field in the Artists table, and then use the Lookup Wizard to make that field available in the Paintings table.

8. Modify the relationship to enforce referential integrity so that you can enter only the names of artists included in the Artists table into the Paintings table.

9. Enter records for the two tables. You should enter a minimum of 15 records for the "many" table and four records for the "one" table.

10. View the relationship between the two tables.

Independent Challenge 2 (continued)

11. Determine two queries that you could make based on the data in the two tables. If appropriate, you could include a formula in one of the queries. For example, if artists sold multiple copies of reproductions, you could include a formula that multiplied the Units Sold by the Unit Price to determine the total revenue.

12. Select one query to use as the basis for a report. For example, you could create a report that lists only painters who have sold more than $15,000 worth of paintings. Ensure the query you choose includes at least one formula.

13. Create a report based on one of the query tables, group the records in the report using one field (for example the "Artist Name" field), then sort the records in ascending order using another field (for example, "Painting Name").

14. Use the Total command to create a subtotal for each of the sort categories (for example, a subtotal of the value of all products sold by each artist). Also include the grand total. Format all totals with the Currency format and increase the size and width of the controls as needed. Remove any controls you don't want.

15. Format the report attractively using the theme of your choice so all fields fit on one page. Note that you can use Landscape format if you wish.

16. In the header, use the Logo command to insert a picture of your choice. Change the Size Mode of the picture to Stretch, then increase the size of the header area and the picture.

17. Include your name in the report title, remove the date and time, then move the page indicator into the report if necessary.

18. Submit a copy to your instructor, then close the database.

Independent Challenge 3

Create a database called Canine Walkers that contains information about all the dogs and their human walkers at a small pet-walking service in your hometown. Follow the steps provided to create the database, create a Walkers table and a Pets table, and then create a report. Note that the relationship is created on the basis that one walker can walk many dogs. You enter records for the Walkers table, and then you import the Pets table from another database.

1. Start Access, then create a database called **PR F-Canine Walkers** and save it to the location where you save the files for this book.

2. Create a table named **Walkers**, then add fields as shown in FIGURE F-30.

FIGURE F-30

Walkers	
Field Name	Data Type
Walker ID	AutoNumber
First Name	Short Text
Last Name	Short Text
Cell Phone	Short Text

3. Click the Cell Phone Data Type cell, click Input Mask in the Field Properties section, click the launcher at the far right of the Input Mask text box (looks like three small dots), click Yes to save the table, then click Finish to accept the input mask settings in the Input Mask wizard for a phone number. You use the phone number Input Mask so that you can quickly enter just the numbers for the phone numbers. The Input Mask automatically inserted the brackets and the hyphen.

4. Switch to Datasheet view and save the table, then add a Lookup & Relationship field called **Region** that contains four values of your choice. (*Hint*: To add a Lookup & Relationship field in Datasheet view, click Click to Add, then click Lookup & Relationship and complete the wizard.) The lookup values should list four areas in your hometown (for example, "West Side," "Sunnybrook," "City Center," and "Riverview") where walkers are located. When you enter records for the Walkers table, you want to be able to assign a region to each walker. Enter **Region** as the field name.

Independent Challenge 3 (continued)

5. Enter data for four records as shown in FIGURE F-31, selecting the Region of your choice and entering phone numbers using the area code of your choice.

FIGURE F-31

Walker ID	First Name	Last Name	Region	Cell Phone	Click to Add
1	Jane	Adams	West Side	(206) 555-7889	
2	Gareth	George	Sunnybrook	(206) 555-7223	
3	Leila	Sharif	East Side	(206) 555-8811	
4	Kevin	Andrews	City Center	(206) 555-1990	
* (New)					

6. Move the Region field to the left of the Cell Phone field. (*Hint*: Click the field name ("Region"), then drag the selected column to the left of the Cell Phone field.)
7. Save and close the table.
8. Import the **PR F-07.accdb** database from the location where you store your Data Files, then select the Pets table.
9. Open the Pets table, then add the First Name field from the Walkers table. (*Hint*: In the new field, select Lookup & Relationship, click Next, click Table: Walkers, click Next, add the First Name field, then complete the Wizard, typing **Walker** as the field name.)
10. Close the table, saving if prompted, then modify the relationship so referential integrity is enforced.
11. Open the Pets table again, then select a walker for each pet. You can determine which walker goes with which pet.
12. Create a query called Pets and Walkers that shows all the walkers along with the pets they walk. The query should include the walker's first name and last name and region from the Walkers table and the name of the pet and its breed from the Pets table.
13. Create a report from the Pets and Walkers query that is grouped by the last name of each walker, then by the first name of each walker, then by the region and that is sorted in alphabetical order by pet names. (*Note*: In a large database grouping based on three criteria helps organize the data into manageable sections.)
14. Apply the Theme of your choice, modify the column widths so that the report fits on one page, remove the date and time labels, then move the page number label at the bottom of the page so that it appears in the body of the report.
15. Click the Last Name label, press and hold the [Ctrl] key, select the First Name, Region, Pet Name, and Breed labels, then from the HOME tab apply Bold and 14 pt.
16. Increase the height of the box containing "15" at the bottom of the report so that the number is visible.

Access 2013

Independent Challenge 3 (continued)

17. View the report in Print Preview, click the Zoom button in the Zoom group, click Fit to Window, then compare it to FIGURE F-32.

FIGURE F-32

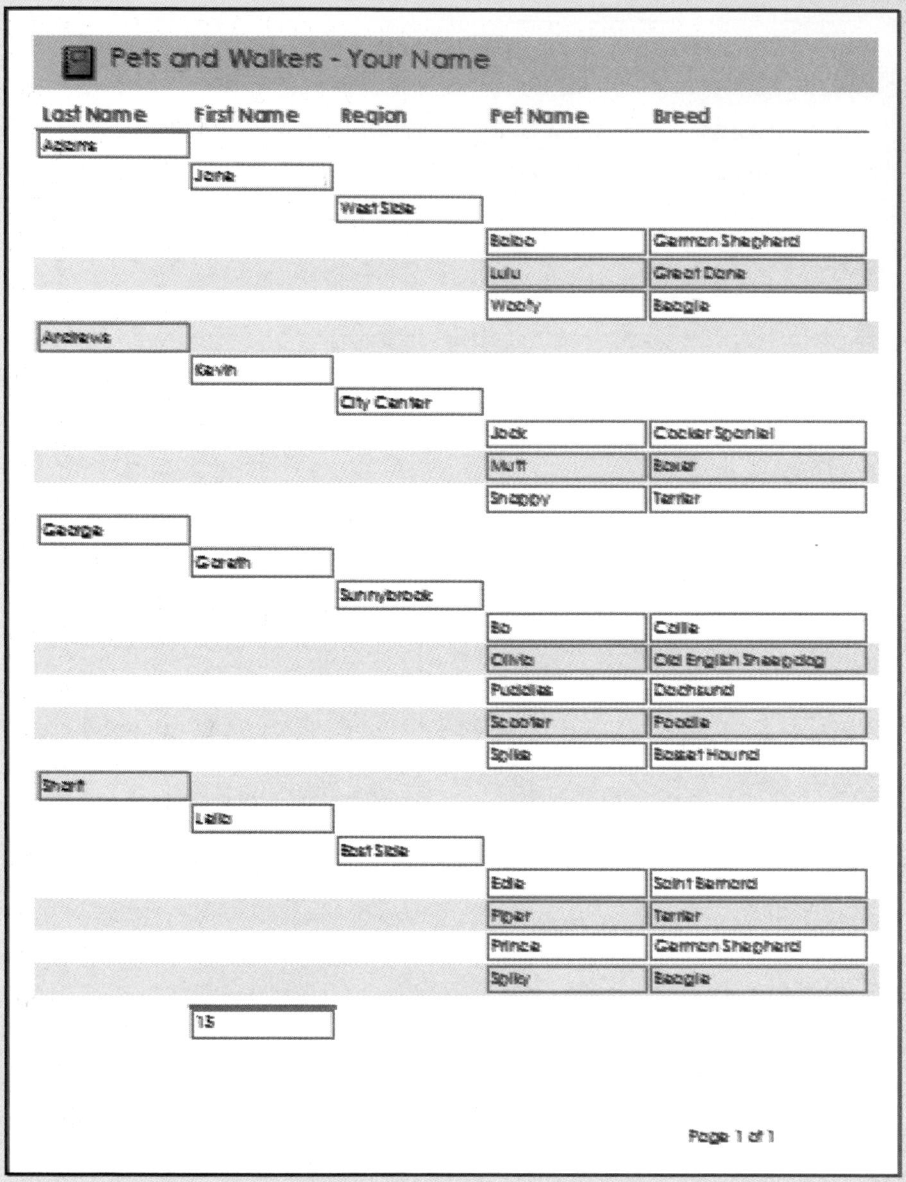

18. Include your name in the report title, submit a copy to your instructor, then close the database.

Independent Challenge 4

You've decided that you would like to investigate the possibility of studying in a foreign country for a summer, an academic term, or even a full year. From the hundreds of programs offered, you need to select one that suits your academic interests and is located in a country to which you want to travel. To help you choose the best program, you will search the Web for information about programs for studying abroad, and then you will create an Access database that contains data related to at least three programs.

1. Start Access, then create a database called **PR F-Study Abroad Programs** and save it to the location where you save the files for this book.

Independent Challenge 4 (continued)

2. In Design view, enter field names and select data types as shown in FIGURE F-33. Note that the data type for the Description field is Long Text. You select this data type so that you can enter several lines of text into the table. You do not select the Currency data type for Cost because you want to be able to enter "N/A" when you are not able to find cost information. The data type for the Web Address field is Hyperlink. When you copy the address of a Web page into this field it will be formatted as a hyperlink that you can click and follow to open the related Web page.

FIGURE F-33

Field Name	Data Type	
Study Programs		
Program ID	AutoNumber	
Field of Study	Short Text	
Country	Short Text	
Location	Short Text	
Description	Long Text	
Cost	Short Text	
Web Address	Hyperlink	

3. Save the table with the name **Study Programs**.

4. Open your Web browser and conduct a search for study abroad programs. Use keywords such as **study abroad**, **international study**, and **overseas study**. To narrow your search further, include the field of study and location that interests you. For example, you could search for "archaeology programs in Mexico." You could also explore study abroad Web sites such as www.studyabroad.com.

5. Identify a field of study and two or three countries that interest you. For example, you could decide to investigate art history study programs in Italy, France, and Spain, or natural history programs in Peru, Bolivia, and Ecuador.

6. Explore some of the Web sites you've found to gather information about three programs that you think look interesting. As you explore the sites, copy and paste relevant information to the Study Programs table in the Study Abroad Programs database. Note that you can copy and then edit a paragraph of text into the Description field because you chose the Long Text data type, which allows you to enter unlimited text. You will need to follow several links to find the information required for each program. In some cases, you will not find all the information; for example, you may not be able to find cost information. You can enter N/A where applicable in the table.

7. For the Web Address field, enter the Web page address of the page that contains most of the information you've gathered about a particular program. To copy a Web address, click the Address box in your browser to select the entire Web address, press [Ctrl][C], return to Access, click the appropriate cell in the Web Address field, and then press [Ctrl][V]. The Web site address appears as a hyperlink because you selected the Hyperlink data type for the field.

8. When you have gathered information about at least three programs, create a report called **Study Programs** with the title **Study Programs - Your Name**. Apply the Theme of your choice, select the Landscape page layout, and modify column widths as needed.

9. Delete the date and time, move the page number into the body of the report, and increase the size of the text box containing "3" (the number of Study Abroad programs listed) so the number is visible.

10. Add an image to the header area using a photograph of your choice. (*Hint*: Click the green picture icon in the header area, click Insert Image in the Controls group on the REPORT LAYOUT TOOLS DESIGN tab, then select an appropriate image file. You can find images by searching online. Check copyright restrictions before you save a picture from the Web. Make sure you modify the Size Mode to Stretch.)

11. Submit a copy of the report to your instructor, then close the Study Abroad Programs database.

Visual Workshop

Start Access, create a database called **PR F-Employee Travel Expenses**, create an Employees table and a Trips table. Use FIGURE F-34 and FIGURE F-35 to set up the table and then use FIGURE F-36 to create the report named **Employee Travel Expenses Report**. In the Trips table, create a lookup field called Employee that uses the Last name of the Employees table, then in the Relationships window, reinforce the referential integrity between the two tables. Create a query from the Trips table that includes a field called Total Expenses that multiplies the Daily Rate by the Days. Use the correct formula syntax. Create the report from the query, format the report as shown in FIGURE F-36 and insert the data file **PR F-08.jpg** as a logo in the header area. Submit the report to your instructor, then close the database.

FIGURE F-34

	ID	First Name	Last Name	Click to Add
⊞	1	Josh	Marlin	
⊞	2	Jason	Anderson	
⊞	3	Olivia	Gretz	
⊞	4	Tony	Renfrew	
⊞	5	Julio	Gomez	
*	(New)			

FIGURE F-35

Trip ID	Destination	Trip Departure	Days	Daily Rate	Employee	Click to Add
1	Paris	Friday, July 22, 2016	5	$300.00	Marlin	
2	Hong Kong	Tuesday, July 26, 2016	10	$300.00	Anderson	
3	Tokyo	Friday, July 29, 2016	10	$400.00	Gretz	
4	New York	Tuesday, August 9, 2016	12	$500.00	Marlin	
5	Mumbai	Friday, August 12, 2016	10	$250.00	Renfrew	
6	London	Friday, September 2, 2016	8	$400.00	Marlin	
7	Berlin	Friday, September 16, 2016	12	$300.00	Gomez	
8	Stockholm	Friday, September 30, 2016	10	$400.00	Gretz	
*	(New)					

The Trips table has six fields

Trip Departure field
(use the Date/Time data type and the Long Date format)

Days field
(use the Number data type)

Daily Rate field
(use the Currency data type)

FIGURE F-36

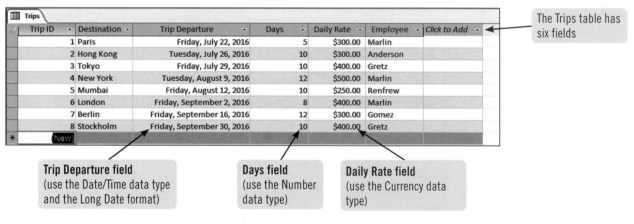

To create this report, do the following:
- Group the records by Employee and sort them by Destination
- Sum the Total Expenses and format these values with Currency
- Remove the Sum control under Daily Rate
- Delete the date and time from the header, and move the page number information into the body of the report

Integration Projects II

Projects

In this unit you will create the following:

Festival Package

Import an Access table into a database • Select an input mask • Import an Excel worksheet into an Access database • Create an Access table • Use the Lookup Wizard to link tables • Enforce Referential Integrity • Create multi-table queries • Export a query to Excel • Insert a PivotTable • Edit Field Settings in a PivotTable • Create a PivotChart • Filter and format a PivotChart • Merge an Access table with a Word document • Add merge fields to a Word document • Match merge fields in Word • Run a merge (*Skills also practiced in Independent Challenge 1*)

Multipage Report

Create an Access table • Enter categories in the Lookup Wizard • Prepare an Excel worksheet for appending to an Access table • Append an Excel worksheet to an Access table • Insert a rotated WordArt object in a header in Word • Insert text from file into a Word document • Apply styles in Word • Create queries in Access • Export a query to Word as an .rtf file • Copy cells and a chart from Excel to Word (*Skills also practiced in Independent Challenge 2*)

Collection Catalogue

Copy a Word table to Access • Create a query in Access • Merge an Access table in Word to create labels • Set up labels in Word • Insert merge codes in Word • Export an Access table to Excel • Run a custom sort in Excel • Create a Subtotals list in Excel • Create a doughnut chart in Excel (*Skills also practiced in Independent Challenge 3*)

Team Project

Files You Will Need

PR G-01.accdb	PR G-05.docx
PR G-02.xlsx	PR G-06.xlsx
PR G-03.docx	PR G-07.docx
PR G-04.xlsx	PR G-08.docx

Package for Southwest Jazz Festival

The Southwest Jazz Festival is a 3-day festival featuring performances by ten bands at three venues. You use tools in Access, Word, and Excel to coordinate festival information. For this project, you need to **Import Data into Access**, **Edit and Link Tables**, **Analyze Data in Excel** and then **Create the Confirmation Letter**.

Import Data into Access

In the past, data for the Southwest Jazz Festival was contained in both an Access database and an Excel workbook. The data was not coordinated. You create a new Festival database, then import a table from an existing database and data from an Excel workbook.

STEPS

1. **Start Access, click** Blank desktop database, **type** PR G-Jazz Festival Database, **click the** Browse button , **navigate to the location where you save the files for this book, click** OK, **then click** Create

2. **Click the** EXTERNAL DATA **tab, click** Access **in the Import & Link group, click** Browse, **navigate to the location where you store files for this book, double-click** PR G-01.accdb, **then click** OK

   You need to select the table containing the Band List.

3. **Click** Band List **in the list of tables, click** OK, **then click** Close

4. **Double-click** Band List **in the list of Access objects to open it, click the** HOME **tab, then click the** View **button to switch to Design view**

5. **Click** Short Text **next to the Phone field, click the empty cell to the right of** Input Mask **as shown in** FIGURE G-1, **click the** ⋯ **to the far right of the Input Mask text box, click** Open **if prompted, then verify that** Phone Number **is selected in the Input Mask Wizard dialog box**

   You create an input mask that automatically puts phone numbers into the format used in most of North America.

6. **Click** Finish, **click the** View **button to switch to Datasheet view, click** Yes **to save the table, then enter Records 9 and 10 and adjust column widths as shown in** FIGURE G-2

7. **Close the table, saving when prompted, click the** EXTERNAL DATA **tab, click** Excel **in the Import & Link group, click** Browse, **navigate to the location where you store your files for this book, double-click** PR G-02.xlsx, **click** Open **if prompted, then click** OK

8. **Click** Next **to accept column headings as field names, click** Next, **click the "Choose my own primary key." option button, verify that** ID **appears in the list box, click** Next, **click** Finish, **then click** Close

9. **Open the Performances table, widen columns to view the field names, then close and save the table**

   The Performances table contains the date and time of each of the ten performances scheduled for the festival.

FIGURE G-1: Setting an Input Mask

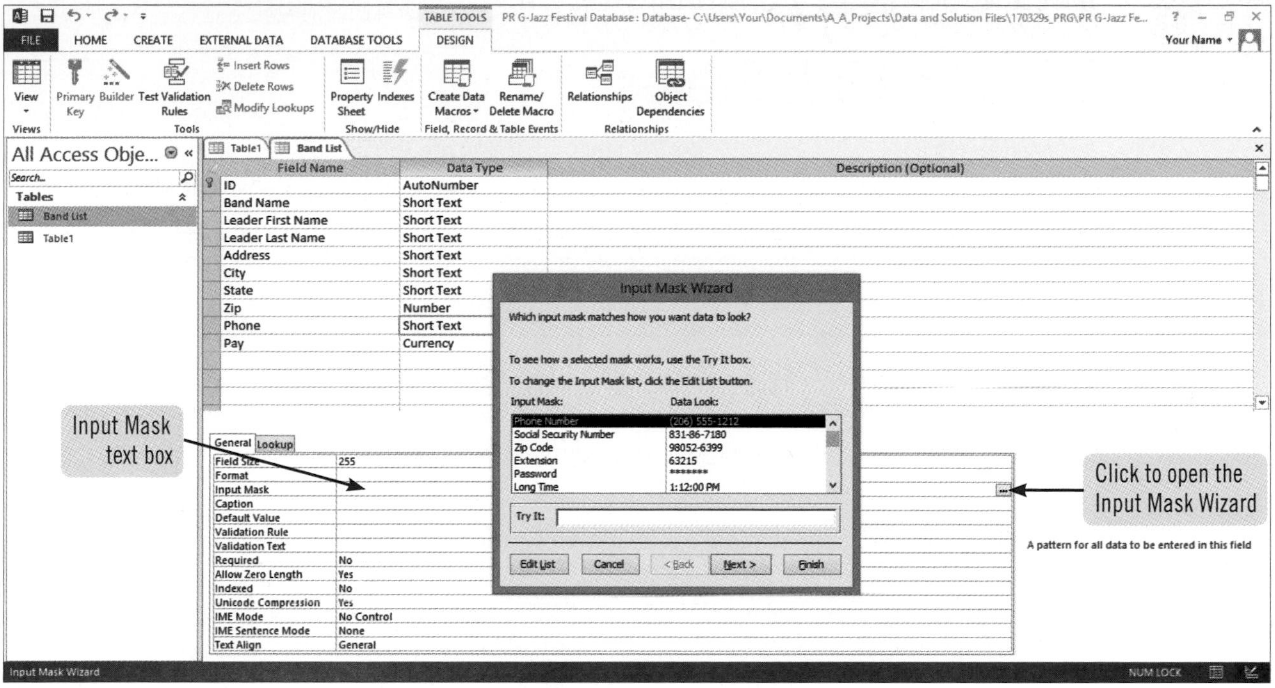

Input Mask text box

Click to open the Input Mask Wizard

A pattern for all data to be entered in this field

FIGURE G-2: Records 9 and 10 for the Band List table

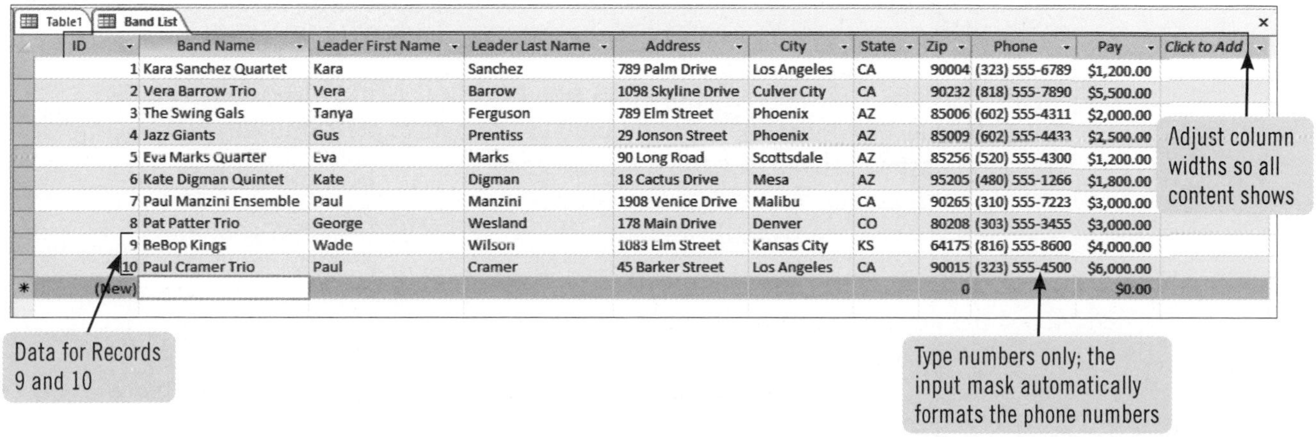

ID	Band Name	Leader First Name	Leader Last Name	Address	City	State	Zip	Phone	Pay	Click to Add
1	Kara Sanchez Quartet	Kara	Sanchez	789 Palm Drive	Los Angeles	CA	90004	(323) 555-6789	$1,200.00	
2	Vera Barrow Trio	Vera	Barrow	1098 Skyline Drive	Culver City	CA	90232	(818) 555-7890	$5,500.00	
3	The Swing Gals	Tanya	Ferguson	789 Elm Street	Phoenix	AZ	85006	(602) 555-4311	$2,000.00	
4	Jazz Giants	Gus	Prentiss	29 Jonson Street	Phoenix	AZ	85009	(602) 555-4433	$2,500.00	
5	Eva Marks Quarter	Eva	Marks	90 Long Road	Scottsdale	AZ	85256	(520) 555-4300	$1,200.00	
6	Kate Digman Quintet	Kate	Digman	18 Cactus Drive	Mesa	AZ	95205	(480) 555-1266	$1,800.00	
7	Paul Manzini Ensemble	Paul	Manzini	1908 Venice Drive	Malibu	CA	90265	(310) 555-7223	$3,000.00	
8	Pat Patter Trio	George	Wesland	178 Main Drive	Denver	CO	80208	(303) 555-3455	$3,000.00	
9	BeBop Kings	Wade	Wilson	1083 Elm Street	Kansas City	KS	64175	(816) 555-8600	$4,000.00	
10	Paul Cramer Trio	Paul	Cramer	45 Barker Street	Los Angeles	CA	90015	(323) 555-4500	$6,000.00	
*	(New)						0		$0.00	

Adjust column widths so all content shows

Data for Records 9 and 10

Type numbers only; the input mask automatically formats the phone numbers

Festival Package (continued)

Edit and Link Tables

You need to create a new table—the Venues table—that lists the three venues for festival performances. Then you use the Lookup Wizard to link the Venues table to the Performances table and add the name of each band performing to the Performances table. Your goal is to develop a table that lists each performance time and date, the performance venue, and the band that will be performing.

STEPS

1. Click the CREATE tab, click Table, switch to Design view, type Venues as the table name, click OK, enter field names as shown in FIGURE G-3, then close and save the table

2. Open the Venues table, add data and adjust column widths as shown in FIGURE G-4, close and save the table, then close Table 1

3. Open the Performances table in Design view, click the blank cell below Performance Time, type Venue, click the Data Type list arrow, click Lookup Wizard, click Open if prompted, then click Next to accept that the values for the lookup field will come from an existing table

4. Click Table: Venues, click Next, click Venue Name, click the Select Single Field button ⟩ , click Next, click Next, click Finish, then click Yes

5. Click the blank cell below Venue, type Band Name, open the Lookup Wizard and select the Band List table, select the Band Name field, then complete the wizard with all the defaults and save the table

HINT
Save time by typing the first letter or two of the Venue Name and Band Name to enter the data.

6. Switch to Datasheet view, then allocate venues and bands to performance times and dates as shown in FIGURE G-5 and widen columns as needed

7. Close and save the table when prompted, click the DATABASE TOOLS tab, then click Relationships

   When you added the Band List and Venues tables to the Performances table in the Lookup Wizard, you created relationships between the three tables. One band can have many performances and one Venue can host many performances. In this database, each band performs only once. However, the bands perform in three different venues.

8. Double-click the line between the Band List and Performances table, click the Enforce Referential Integrity check box, click OK, then enforce referential integrity between the Performances and Venues tables

9. Close the Relationships window, saving if prompted

10. Open the Band List table, click the plus sign next to the first record (for the Kara Sanchez Quartet), note the date and time of the band's performance, click ⊟ to hide the subdatasheet, then close the Band List table

FIGURE G-3: Field names for the Venues table

Field Name	Data Type	
Venue ID	AutoNumber	
Venue Name	Short Text	
Venue Location	Short Text	

FIGURE G-4: Data for the Venues table

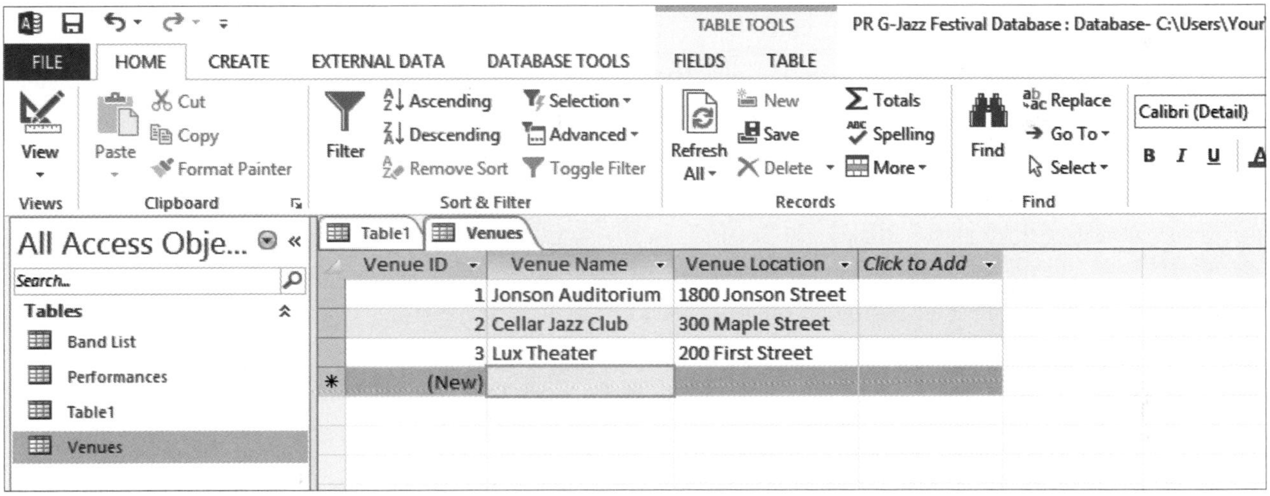

Venue ID	Venue Name	Venue Location	Click to Add
1	Jonson Auditorium	1800 Jonson Street	
2	Cellar Jazz Club	300 Maple Street	
3	Lux Theater	200 First Street	
(New)			

FIGURE G-5: Adding Venue Names and Bands to the Performances table

ID	Performance Date	Performance Time	Venue	Band Name	Click to Add
1	10/15/2016	2:00:00 PM	Jonson Auditorium	Kara Sanchez Quartet	
2	10/15/2016	2:00:00 PM	Cellar Jazz Club	Jazz Giants	
3	10/15/2016	8:00:00 PM	Lux Theater	Eva Marks Quarter	
4	10/15/2016	8:00:00 PM	Cellar Jazz Club	Kate Digman Quintet	
5	10/16/2016	2:00:00 PM	Jonson Auditorium	Paul Cramer Trio	
6	10/16/2016	8:00:00 PM	Cellar Jazz Club	BeBop Kings	
7	10/16/2016	8:00:00 PM	Lux Theater	Vera Barrow Trio	
8	10/16/2016	8:00:00 PM	Jonson Auditorium	The Swing Gals	
9	10/17/2016	2:00:00 PM	Jonson Auditorium	Pat Patter Trio	
10	10/17/2016	8:00:00 PM	Cellar Jazz Club	Paul Manzini Ensemble	

Analyze Data in Excel

You create a query that contains data you want to analyze in Excel. You then create a PivotTable and a PivotChart in Excel that shows the total fees paid to bands in each of the three festival venues.

STEPS

1. **Click the CREATE tab, click Query Wizard in the Queries group, click OK to accept the Simple Query Wizard, add the Band Name and Pay fields from the Band List table, click the Tables/Queries list arrow, click Table: Venues, add Venue Name, click Next, click Next, then click Finish**

2. **Close the Band List Query, click Band List Query in the list of All Access objects, click the EXTERNAL DATA tab, click Excel in the Export group, click Browse, navigate to the location where you store your files, name the file PR G-Jazz Festival Analysis, then click Save**

3. **Click the "Export data with formatting and layout." check box, click the "Open the destination file after the export operation is complete." check box, click OK, click the flashing Access button on the task bar, click Close, then switch back to Excel**
   The query table opens in Excel.

4. **Select the range A1:C11, click the INSERT tab, click PivotTable in the Tables group, click OK to open a new worksheet, then click the Pay and Venue Name check boxes in the PivotTable Fields pane as shown in FIGURE G-6**
   The PivotTable shows the total pay for bands in each of the three festival venues.

5. **Click cell B4, click Field Settings in the Active Field group, click Number Format, click Currency, click OK, then click OK**
   The values are shown in Currency format.

6. **Click the PivotChart button in the Tools group, click Pie, click OK, click the Band Name check box in the PivotChart Fields pane, click the Venue Name list arrow in the chart, click the Select All check box, click the Jonson Auditorium check box as shown in FIGURE G-7, then click OK**
   The PivotTable and PivotChart now summarize the pay only for the four bands performing in the Jonson Auditorium.

7. **Click the PIVOTCHART TOOLS DESIGN tab, click Add Chart Element, point to Data Labels, click More Chart Label Options, then click the Category Name check box in the Format Data Labels pane**
   With Category Name selected, both the name of the category "Jonson Auditorium" and the individual band names appear in the chart which makes the chart look very crowded.

8. **Click the Category Name check box to deselect it, click the Value From Cells check box, select the range A5:A8, click OK, then scroll to and click the Outside End check box in the Format Data Labels pane**

9. **Close all open task panes, size and position the chart so it extends from cell D4 to M22, click Total in the pie chart and type Jonson Auditorium Bands, press [Enter], click Add Chart Element, point to Legend, then click None**
   The PivotTable and PivotChart appear as shown in FIGURE G-8.

10. **Save and close the workbook**

FIGURE G-6: PivotTable fields

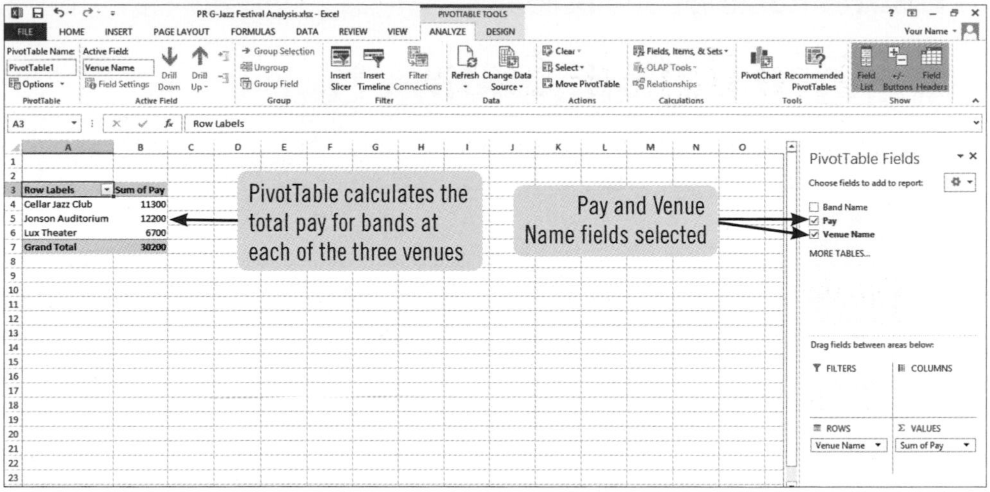

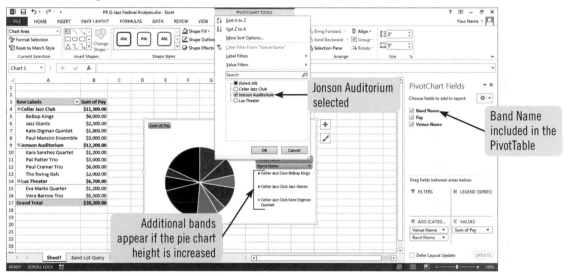

PivotTable calculates the total pay for bands at each of the three venues
Pay and Venue Name fields selected
Row Labels
Sum of Pay
Cellar Jazz Club 11300
Jonson Auditorium 12200
Lux Theater 6700
Grand Total 30200
PivotTable Fields

FIGURE G-7: Filtering a PivotChart

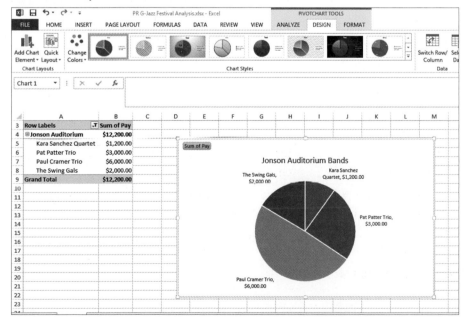

Jonson Auditorium selected
Band Name included in the PivotTable
Additional bands appear if the pie chart height is increased
PivotChart Fields

FIGURE G-8: Completed PivotChart

Row Labels
Sum of Pay
Jonson Auditorium $12,200.00
Kara Sanchez Quartet $1,200.00
Pat Patter Trio $3,000.00
Paul Cramer Trio $6,000.00
The Swing Gals $2,000.00
Grand Total $12,200.00
Jonson Auditorium Bands
The Swing Gals, $2,000.00
Kara Sanchez Quartet, $1,200.00
Pat Patter Trio, $3,000.00
Paul Cramer Trio, $6,000.00

Festival Package (continued)

Create the Confirmation Letter

In Word, you create the letter to confirm each band's performance date, time, and pay, then you merge the letter with the Jazz Festival database to produce individually addressed letters.

STEPS

HINT
Text in square brackets is placeholder text to indicate where you will insert the merge fields.

1. Start Word, open PR G-03.docx from the location where you store your Data Files, save the document as PR G-Jazz Festival Letter, then close the document and exit Word

2. In Access, use the Query Wizard to create a query table called Band Confirmation with all fields from the Band List table *except* the ID and Phone fields, the Performance Date and Performance Time fields from the Performances table, and the Venue Name field from the Venues table

TROUBLE
If you receive a warning that the database is open in exclusive mode, click OK, close the database, open it again, enable content if prompted, then repeat Step 3.

3. Close the query, click Band Confirmation in the list of All Access Objects, click the EXTERNAL DATA tab, click the Word Merge button, click Open if prompted, then click OK

4. Navigate to and click PR G-Jazz Festival Letter.docx, click Open, click the flashing Word button on the task bar if Word does not open automatically, maximize the Word window, close the Mail Merge task pane, replace Current Date in the letter with the current date, select [Address], then click Address Block on the MAILINGS tab

   As shown in the preview, only the street address, city, state, and zip appear in the address block because Word looks for First Name and Last Name fields. However, the database contains Leader First Name and Leader Last Name fields. You need to match fields.

5. Click Match Fields, click the list arrow for First Name, select Leader First Name as shown in FIGURE G-9, match Last Name to Leader Last Name, match Company to Band Name, then click OK

   The preview shows the first and last name of the leader, the name of the band, and the address.

HINT
Press the [Spacebar] where needed to insert a blank link between an inserted field name and the following word.

6. Click OK, delete [Address], select [Greeting], click Greeting Line in the Write & Insert Fields group, click the list arrow next to Joshua Randall Jr., scroll to and click Joshua, click OK, delete [Greeting], select [Band Name] in the first paragraph, click the Insert Merge Field list arrow in the Write & Insert Fields group, then click Band_Name

7. Repeat Step 6 to add the field names shown in FIGURE G-10

QUICK TIP
Adjust line spacing as needed.

8. Enter your name in the closing, click the Preview Results button in the Preview Results group, select the four lines of the address for Kara Sanchez, click the PAGE LAYOUT tab, select 10 pt in the After box in the Paragraph group, type 0, press [Enter], press [→] to dese-lect the text, press [Enter], then compare the address and salutation text to FIGURE G-11

   At the end of paragraph 2, notice that 1200 does not appear in Currency format. The formatting is not included in the merge. You can add it manually.

9. Click the MAILINGS tab, click the Preview Results button, type a $ to the left of the Pay field, click Finish & Merge in the Finish group, click Edit Individual Letters, type 1 in the From box, type 2 in the To box, then click OK

MORE PRACTICE
For more practice with the skills presented in this project, complete Independent Challenge 1.

10. Save the merged letters as PR G-Jazz Festival Merged Letters, save the PR G-Jazz Festival Letter document, submit all files to your instructor, then close all files and exit all programs

FIGURE G-9: Match Fields dialog box

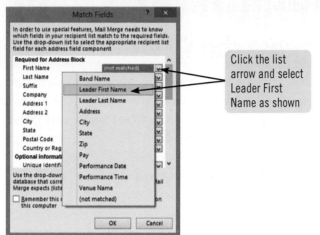

Click the list arrow and select Leader First Name as shown

FIGURE G-10: Field names inserted in the letter

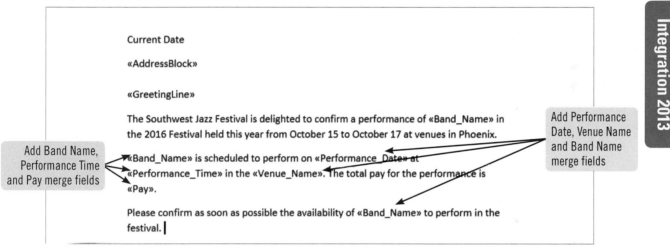

Current Date

«AddressBlock»

«GreetingLine»

The Southwest Jazz Festival is delighted to confirm a performance of «Band_Name» in the 2016 Festival held this year from October 15 to October 17 at venues in Phoenix.

«Band_Name» is scheduled to perform on «Performance_Date» at «Performance_Time» in the «Venue_Name». The total pay for the performance is «Pay».

Please confirm as soon as possible the availability of «Band_Name» to perform in the festival.

Add Band Name, Performance Time and Pay merge fields

Add Performance Date, Venue Name and Band Name merge fields

FIGURE G-11: Field names inserted in the letter

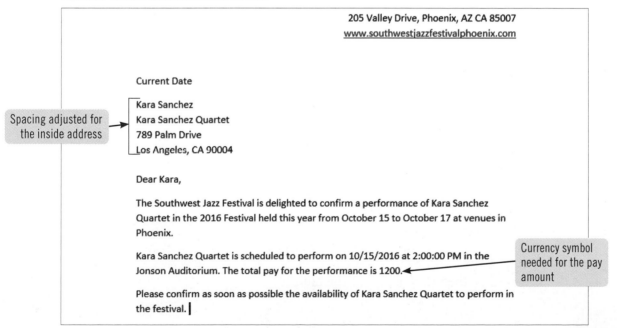

205 Valley Drive, Phoenix, AZ CA 85007
www.southwestjazzfestivalphoenix.com

Current Date

Kara Sanchez
Kara Sanchez Quartet
789 Palm Drive
Los Angeles, CA 90004

Dear Kara,

The Southwest Jazz Festival is delighted to confirm a performance of Kara Sanchez Quartet in the 2016 Festival held this year from October 15 to October 17 at venues in Phoenix.

Kara Sanchez Quartet is scheduled to perform on 10/15/2016 at 2:00:00 PM in the Jonson Auditorium. The total pay for the performance is 1200.

Please confirm as soon as possible the availability of Kara Sanchez Quartet to perform in the festival.

Spacing adjusted for the inside address

Currency symbol needed for the pay amount

Report for Silver Moon Teas

Silver Moon Teas is a small business in Victoria, BC, that sells specialty loose leaf teas from all over the world. The company has researched an opportunity to partner with Deep Bay Inn, a local boutique hotel, to feature their teas in the guest rooms and restaurant. A draft of a report describing the partnership has already been written. To complete the report, you need to **Import an Excel Workbook**, **Create the Report in Word**, and then **Add Excel and Access Objects**. The three pages of the completed report are shown in FIGURE G-18 on page 179.

Import an Excel Workbook

You need to create an Access database containing a Product List table, add records for some of the company's products, and then import an Excel workbook that contains data about the herbal teas into the Product List table. Often companies enter data into Excel first and then export it to Access.

STEPS

1. **Start Access, then create a new database called PR G-Silver Moon Teas.accdb saved to the location where you save the files for this book**

HINT

Make sure you change the data type for Price to Currency.

2. **Click the** View button, **save the table as** Product List, **type** Product # **as the first Field Name, change the Data Type to** Number, **then enter the remaining fields as shown in** FIGURE G-12

3. **Click the** Category Data Type list arrow, **click Lookup Wizard, click Open if prompted, click the "I will type in the values that I want." option button, click Next, press [Tab], type** Green **and** Black **as the two lookup values, then click Finish**

4. **Click the** View button, **click Yes, enter the data and widen columns as shown in** FIGURE G-13, **then close and save the table if prompted**

5. **Start Excel, open the file** PR G-04.xlsx **from the location where you store your Data Files, then save the file as** PR G-Silver Moon Teas_Herbal.xlsx

   The worksheet contains three columns. Before you can import this worksheet into the Access table, you need to ensure that both the Excel worksheet and the Access table contain the exact same column headings and data types.

6. **Select** column C, **click the** right mouse button, **click Insert, type** Category **in cell C1, click cell** C2, **type** Herbal, **drag the fill handle to cell C27 to fill all the cells with the Herbal label, then adjust the column width**

7. **Save and close the workbook without exiting Excel, return to Access, click Product List in the list of All Access Objects, click the EXTERNAL DATA tab, click Excel in the Import & Link group, click the** Browse button, **navigate to the location where you save the files for this book, then double-click** PR G-Silver Moon Teas_Herbal.xlsx

8. **Click the** "Append a copy of the records to the table:" option button, **click OK, click** Open **if prompted, click** Next, **click** Finish, **then click Close**

9. **Double-click** Product List **to open it, increase the width of the Description column, scroll down so you can see the five records you originally entered in the Product List table at the bottom of the list along with some of the new records as shown in** FIGURE G-14, **then close and save the table**

FIGURE G-12: Fields for the Product List table

Field Name	Data Type	
Product #	Number	
Description	Short Text	
Category	Short Text	
Price	Currency	

Product List

FIGURE G-13: Records for the Product List table

Product List

Product #	Description	Category	Price	Click to Add
5800	Kenyan Blend	Black	$18.00	
5801	Chai	Black	$15.00	
5802	Orange Pekoe	Black	$17.00	
5803	Matcha	Green	$22.00	
5804	Japanese Sencha	Green	$14.00	
*	0		$0.00	

FIGURE G-14: Excel data imported into the Product List table

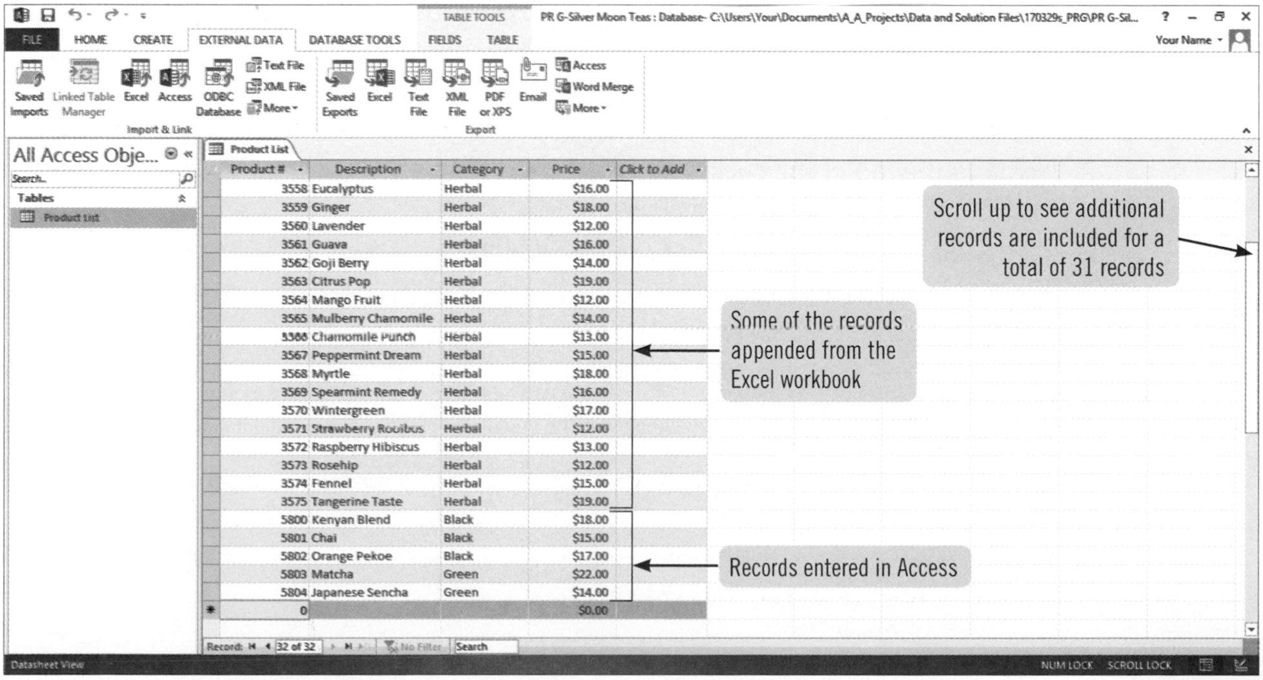

Scroll up to see additional records are included for a total of 31 records

Some of the records appended from the Excel workbook

Records entered in Access

Integration Projects II

Create the Report in Word

The report consists of three pages that will include objects copied from Excel and Access. First, you need to set up the document in Word and then you need to insert the text. You will insert the Excel and Access objects in the next lesson.

STEPS

HINT
Click the Show/Hide button ¶ in the Paragraph group on the HOME tab to show paragraph marks.

1. **Start Word and create a blank document, click the** PAGE LAYOUT **tab, click the** Margins **button in the Page Setup group, click** Custom Margins, **change the Left margin to** 2, **click** OK, **click the** DESIGN **tab, click the** Themes **button, select the** Ion **theme, then save the document as** PR G-Silver Moon Teas Partnership Report.docx **to the location where you save the files for this book**

2. **Click the** INSERT **tab, click the** Header **button in the Header & Footer group, click** Blank, **click the** INSERT **tab, click the** WordArt **button in the Text group, select the** Fill - Green, Accent 4, Soft Bevel **style (1st row, last column), then replace** [Type here] **with** Partnership Report

3. **Select** Partnership Report, **click the** HOME **tab and increase the font size to** 48 pt, **center the text if it is not centered, click the launcher** ⊡ **in the Font group, click the** Advanced **tab, click the** Spacing **list arrow, click** Expanded, **select the contents of the** By **text box, type** 5, **press** [Tab], **compare the dialog box to** FIGURE G-15, **then click** OK

HINT
If the Alignment guides are not visible, click the PAGE LAYOUT tab, click the Align list arrow, then click Use Alignment Guides.

4. **Click the** DRAWING TOOLS FORMAT **tab, click** Text Direction **in the Text group, click** Rotate all text 270°, **then switch to One Page view and use the alignment guides to position the WordArt object as shown in** FIGURE G-16

5. **Click the** HEADER & FOOTER TOOLS DESIGN **tab, click the** Go to Footer **button in the Navigation group, increase the zoom to 100%, type your name at the left margin, press** [Tab] **twice, click the** Page Number **button in the Header & Footer group, point to** Current Position, **then click** Plain Number

6. **Click the** Close Header and Footer **button in the Close group, click the** INSERT **tab, click the** Object list arrow **in the Text group, click** Text from File, **navigate to the location where you store your Data Files, then double-click** PR G-05.docx

   The text required for the report is inserted into the document.

7. **Scroll to the top of the document, select** INTRODUCTION, **click the** HOME **tab, then click** Heading 1 **in the Styles gallery**

8. **Format all the headings in the document that are formatted in uppercase letters with the** Heading 1 **style, then format all the headings in the document that are formatted in title case with the** Heading 2 **style**

   FIGURE G-17 shows some of the formatted headings.

9. **Save the document**

FIGURE G-15: Setting character spacing

FIGURE G-16: Completed WordArt object in One Page view

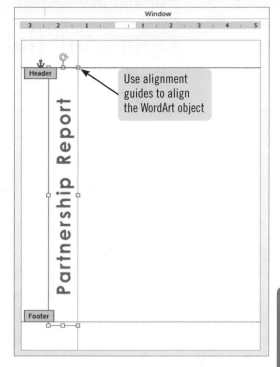

Enter "5" in the By text box

Use alignment guides to align the WordArt object

FIGURE G-17: Heading styles applied to selected text

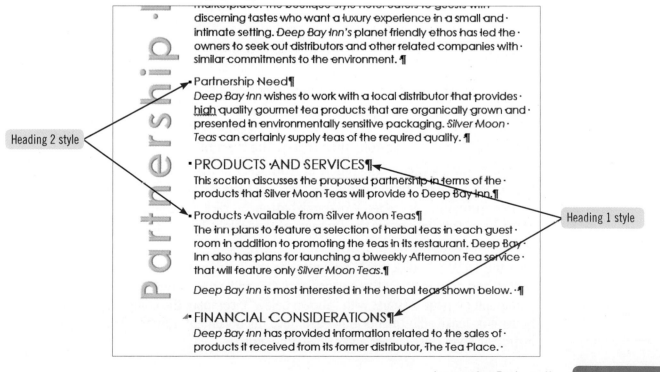

discerning tastes who want a luxury experience in a small and · intimate setting. *Deep Bay Inn's* planet friendly ethos has led the · owners to seek out distributors and other related companies with · similar commitments to the environment. ¶

Partnership Need¶
Deep Bay Inn wishes to work with a local distributor that provides · high quality gourmet tea products that are organically grown and · presented in environmentally sensitive packaging. *Silver Moon · Teas* can certainly supply teas of the required quality. ¶

PRODUCTS AND SERVICES¶
This section discusses the proposed partnership in terms of the · products that Silver Moon Teas will provide to Deep Bay Inn.¶

Products Available from Silver Moon Teas¶
The inn plans to feature a selection of herbal teas in each guest · room in addition to promoting the teas in its restaurant. Deep Bay · Inn also has plans for launching a biweekly Afternoon Tea service · that will feature only *Silver Moon Teas*.¶

Deep Bay Inn is most interested in the herbal teas shown below. ·¶

FINANCIAL CONSIDERATIONS¶
Deep Bay Inn has provided information related to the sales of · products it received from its former distributor, The Tea Place. ·

Heading 2 style

Heading 1 style

Add Excel and Access Objects to Word

To produce the three pages of the completed proposal shown in **FIGURE G-18**, you need to insert spreadsheet data, create a query table in Access and publish it in Word, and then copy a chart from Excel.

STEPS

1. Switch to Access, click the CREATE tab, click the Query Wizard button in the Queries group, click OK, move all the records in the Product List table to the Selected Fields list box, click Next, click Next, then click Finish

2. Switch to Design view, type Herbal in the Criteria cell for Category, click the Run button in the Results group, then close and save the query

HINT
The .rft extension stands for Rich Text Format.

3. Click Product List Query in the list of Access Objects, click the EXTERNAL DATA tab, click the More button in the Export group, click Word, click the Browse button, navigate to the location where you save the files for this book, change the name of the file to PR G-Silver Moon Teas Query, click Save, click the "Open the destination file after the export operation is complete." check box, then click OK

   The table opens in a Word document named PR G-Silver Moon Teas Query.rtf.

4. Select the table, click the Copy button, click the VIEW tab, click the Switch Windows button in the Window group, click PR G-Silver Moon Teas Partnership Report.docx, click at the end of the second paragraph below the "Projects Available from Silver Moon Teas" heading toward the bottom of page 1 (ends with the text "teas shown below"), press [Enter], then click the Paste button on the HOME tab

5. Scroll up and add a page break to the left of the paragraph above the table, select the table, click the TABLE TOOLS DESIGN tab, click the More button ▼ in the Table Styles group, then select the Grid Table 2-Accent 5 style

6. In Excel, open the file PR G-06.xlsx, save the file as PR G-Silver Moon Teas_Revenue.xlsx, select cells A1:E12, copy them, then switch to the report in Word

7. On the second page, at the end of the second paragraph following tourist season, press [Enter], click the Paste list arrow, then click the Picture button 🖻

   You can select the Picture option when you don't need to modify the contents of the Excel file.

8. Switch to Excel, click the Projected Sales sheet tab, select cells A1:E3, click the INSERT tab, click the Insert Column Chart button in the Charts group, click the Clustered Column chart style, click the Add Chart Element button in the Chart Layouts group, point to Legend, click Bottom, then change the chart title to Projected Sales

9. Copy the chart, switch to the report in Word, click at the end of the paragraph above the "CONCLUSION" heading, press [Enter], click the Paste list arrow, click the Keep Source Formatting & Embed Workbook button 🖾, click the chart, click the CHART TOOLS FORMAT tab, select the contents of the Height box in the Size group, type 2.5, then press [Enter]

MORE PRACTICE
For more practice with the skills presented in this project, complete Independent Challenge 2.

10. Click the VIEW tab, click the Zoom button in the Zoom group, click the Many Pages button and drag to select three pages, click OK, add a page break to the left of the last paragraph on page 2 (starts with "Shown below"), compare the completed report to **FIGURE G-18**, make adjustments as needed, save the document, submit all files to your instructor, then close all files and exit all programs

Partnership Report

INTRODUCTION
Silver Moon Teas has an opportunity to partner with *Deep Bay Inn*, a boutique-style hotel that has just opened in Victoria and is interested in offering guests premium quality teas. This report describes the partnership issues in terms of three factors: Partnership Requirements, Products and Services, and [ ] Considerations.

PARTNERSHIP REQUIREMENTS
This section provides background information about [ ] and discusses how the partnership could benefit bot[ ]

Background Information
Deep Bay Inn has made steady progress in a recepti[ ] marketplace. The boutique-style hotel caters to gues[ ] discerning tastes who want a luxury experience in a s[ ] intimate setting. *Deep Bay Inn*'s planet friendly ethos[ ] owners to seek out distributors and other related com[ ] similar commitments to the environment.

Partnership Need
Deep Bay Inn wishes to work with a local distributor th[ ] high quality gourmet tea products that are organica[ ] presented in environmentally sensitive packaging. *Sil[ ] Teas* can certainly supply teas of the required quality[ ]

PRODUCTS AND SERVICES
This section discusses the proposed partnership in ter[ ] products that Silve[ ]

Products Availab[ ]
The inn plans to fe[ ] room in addition t[ ] Inn also has plans[ ] that will feature o[ ]

Partnership Report

Deep Bay Inn is most interested in the herbal teas shown below.

Product #	Description	Category	Price
3550	Licorice Candy	Herbal	$18.00
3551	Cinnamon Burst	Herbal	$15.00
3552	Red Pepper Surprise	Herbal	$12.00
3553	Lemongrass	Herbal	$17.00
3554	Coconut Spice	Herbal	$18.00
3555	Almond Apple	Herbal	$16.00
3556	Orange Peppermint	Herbal	$15.00
3557	Juniper Berry	Herbal	$14.00
3558	Eucalyptus	Herbal	$16.00
3559	Ginger	Herbal	$18.00
3560	Lavender	Herbal	$12.00
3561	Guava	Herbal	$16.00
3562	Goji Berry	Herbal	$14.00
3563	Citrus Pop	Herbal	$19.00
3564	Mango Fruit	Herbal	$12.00
3565	Mulberry Chamomile	Herbal	$14.00
3566	Chamomile Punch	Herbal	$13.00
3567	Peppermint Dream	Herbal	$15.00
3568	Myrtle	Herbal	$18.00
3569	Spearmint Remedy	Herbal	$16.00
		al	$17.00
		al	$12.00
		al	$13.00
		al	$12.00
		al	$15.00
		al	$19.00

[ ]NS
[ ]ion related to the sales of [ ]distributor, The Tea Place. [ ]*n Teas* could expect a [ ]n the sale of products to

2

Partnership Report

Shown below are projected sales of *Silver Moon Teas* to *Deep Bay Inn* over the three busiest months of the tourist season.

Silver Moon Teas				
Sales Projection				
	July	August	September	Total
Revenue				
Black and Green Teas	$3,000.00	$3,300.00	$3,630.00	$9,930.00
Herbal Teas	$5,000.00	$5,500.00	$6,050.00	$16,550.00
Total Revenue	**$8,000.00**	**$8,800.00**	**$9,680.00**	**$26,480.00**
Expenses				
Advertising	1,000.00	1,000.00	1,000.00	3,000.00
Cost of Sales: 60%	4,800.00	5,280.00	5,808.00	15,888.00
Total Expenses	**$5,800.00**	**$6,280.00**	**$6,808.00**	**$18,888.00**
Net Revenue	**$2,200.00**	**$2,520.00**	**$2,872.00**	**$7,592.00**

Projected Revenues
The chart illustrated below shows the revenues projected for each quarter in the first year of the proposed partnership with *Deep Bay Inn*.

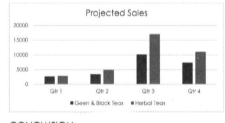

Projected Sales

CONCLUSION
Silver Moon Teas has the opportunity to increase its market share by partnering with *Deep Bay Inn*. Both companies are seriously committed to the environment and to providing their customers with a high-quality tea drinking experience.

Your Name

3

Collection Catalogue for Alpha Gallery

As the office manager of the Alpha Gallery, you decide to create a database that lists the art pieces currently being shown at the gallery, produce identification labels to attach to each piece, and create a chart showing the breakdown of paintings by price category. For this project, you need to **Create the Database and Set Up the Merge**, and then you need to **Merge the Labels and Create a Chart**.

Create the Database and Set Up the Merge

You create the database by copying a table from Word. Then, you need to create a query and merge the data in the query with identification labels you create in Word.

STEPS

1. **Create a new database called** PR G-Alpha Gallery Collection.accdb, **and save it to the location where you save the files for this book**

2. **Start Word, open** PR G-07.docx **from the location where you store your Data Files, select the table, copy it, close the document, switch to Access, click the** HOME **tab, click the** Paste list arrow, **click** Paste, **then click** Yes

3. **Switch to** Design view, **type** Art List **as the table name, click OK, change the Data Type for Cost to** Currency, **close and save the table, then click Yes in response to the warning**

4. **Click** Art List, **click the** CREATE **tab, click the** Query Wizard **button, click OK, click Open if prompted, select all the fields** except **the ID and Price Category fields, click Next, click** Next, **name the query** Identification Labels, **then click Finish**

5. **Switch to** Design view, **click the Creation Date Sort cell, click the list arrow, select** Ascending, **click the Run button in the Results group, then close and save the query**

6. **Click** Identification Labels, **click the** EXTERNAL DATA **tab, click** Word Merge **in the Export group, click Open if prompted, click the "Create a new document and then link the data to it." option button, then click OK**

7. **Click the** flashing Word button **on the task bar if Word does not open automatically, maximize the Word window, click the Labels option button in the Mail Merge task pane, click** Next: Starting document, **click** Label options, **click the Label vendors list arrow, click** Avery US Letter **if it is not the selected vendor, scroll to and select** 5163 Shipping Labels **in the Product number list as shown in** FIGURE G-19, **then click OK**
   A sheet of labels formatted as a table opens in a new Word document.

8. **Click** Next: Select recipients **in the Mail Merge task pane, click** Next: Arrange your labels, **click** More items, **click** Insert, **click** Close, **then press Enter**
   The Artist field is inserted in the first label.

9. **Click the** Insert Merge Field button **in the Write & Insert Fields group on the MAILINGS tab, double-click** Painting_Title, **then insert the remaining fields and arrange them as shown in** FIGURE G-20

10. **Save the document as** PR G-Alpha Gallery Identification Labels.docx **to the location where you save the files for this book**

FIGURE G-19: Selecting the label type

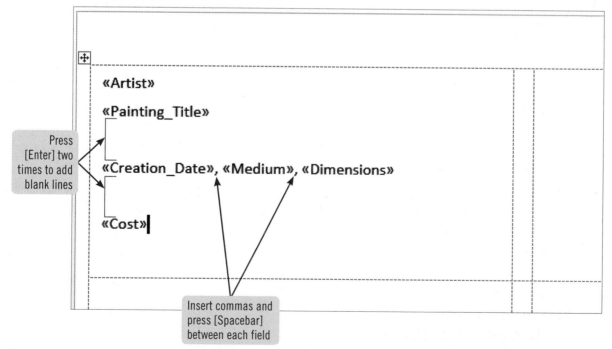

Label Options

Printer information
- ○ Continuous-feed printers
- ● Page printers Tray: CD/DVD

> Your tray setting is based on your printer, click the list arrow to change the tray setting (yours may differ)

Label information

Label vendors: Avery US Letter

> Avery US Letter vendor selected

Find updates on Office.com

Product number:
- 5155 Easy Peel Return Address Labels
- 5159 Mailing Labels
- 5160 Easy Peel Address Labels
- 5161 Easy Peel Address Labels
- 5162 Easy Peel Address Labels
- 5163 Shipping Labels

Label information

Type:	Shipping Labels
Height:	2"
Width:	4"
Page size:	8.5" × 11"

Details... New Label... Delete OK Cancel

> Label product 5163 Shipping Labels selected

FIGURE G-20: Fields for the identification labels

«Artist»

«Painting_Title»

> Press [Enter] two times to add blank lines

«Creation_Date», «Medium», «Dimensions»

«Cost»

> Insert commas and press [Spacebar] between each field

Collection Catalogue (continued)

Merge the Labels and Create a Chart

You need to format the fields and run the merge. Then, you need to analyze the Art List table in Excel so that you can create a separate chart that shows the breakdown of paintings by price category.

STEPS

1. **Format the field labels as shown in FIGURE G-21, click the Artist field, click the PAGE LAYOUT tab, change the Spacing Before to 12 pt, click Update all labels in the Mail Merge task pane, then click Next: Preview your labels in the Mail Merge task pane**

   The cost for each painting is no longer formatted in Currency style. When you merge an Access database with a Word document, you can either type the currency symbol or you can use merge field codes to apply currency formatting to number amounts.

TROUBLE
You may need to press [Fn] on your keyboard when you are asked to press a function key, such as F9. For Step 2, you might need to press [Fn][Shift][F9].

2. **Click the Cost field ("800" for the first label), press [Shift][F9] to display the merge field code, then type \# $0 as shown in FIGURE G-22**

3. **Press [F9] to turn off the display of merge field codes, click Update Labels in the Write & Insert Fields group, click Next: Complete the merge, close the Mail Merge task pane, compare the completed label sheet to FIGURE G-23, then add your name after the cost field in the last label on the page**

4. **Switch to Access, click Art List, click the Excel button in the Export group on the EXTERNAL DATA tab, click Browse, navigate to the location where you save the files for this book, change the name to PR G-Alpha Gallery Art List, click Save, click OK, then click Close**

5. **Start Excel, open PR G-Alpha Gallery Art List.xlsx, widen columns to fit content, select cells A1:H16, click the Sort & Filter button in the Editing group, click Custom Sort, click the Sort by list arrow, click Price Category, then click OK**

6. **Click the DATA tab, click Subtotal in the Outline group, click the At each change in list arrow, scroll to and click Price Category, click OK, then click cell A1 to deselect the table**

7. **Widen the Cost column, click the HOME tab, click the Find & Select button in the Editing group, click Replace, type Count, press [Tab], click Replace All, click OK, then click Close**

   You have removed the word "Count" from cells G7, G15, G19, and G20.

8. **Select cells G7:H7, press and hold [Ctrl], select cells G15:H15 and cells G19:H19, click the INSERT tab, click the Insert a Pie or Doughnut Chart button ▼ in the Charts group, click the Doughnut chart, then drag the chart below the data**

MORE PRACTICE
For more practice with the skills presented in this project, complete Independent Challenge 3.

9. **Click the Quick Layout button in the Chart Layouts group, select Layout 6, format, size, and position the doughnut chart as shown in FIGURE G-24, type your name below the chart, save the workbook, submit all files to your instructor, then close all files and exit all programs**

FIGURE G-21: Formatted fields

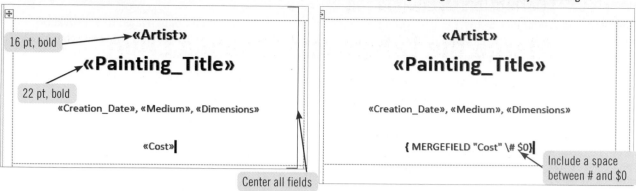

16 pt, bold → «Artist»

«Painting_Title»

22 pt, bold

«Creation_Date», «Medium», «Dimensions»

«Cost»

Center all fields

FIGURE G-22: Editing a merge field for Currency formatting

«Artist»

«Painting_Title»

«Creation_Date», «Medium», «Dimensions»

{ MERGEFIELD "Cost" \# $0}

Include a space between # and $0

FIGURE G-23: Completed label sheet

Pat Jonson	Jatinder Singh
Evening Stroll	**Horizons**
2012, Acrylic on panel, 16" x 20"	2013, Acrylic on paper, 20" x 28"
$800	$600
Juan Sanchez	Gareth Lee
Lunar Adventures	**Striations**
2013, Oil on canvas, 45" x 30"	2014, Acrylic on canvas, 56" x 72"
$1200	$6000
Takao Watanabe	Emilio Fabrizi
Into the Wild	**On the Level**

FIGURE G-24: Completed Doughnut chart

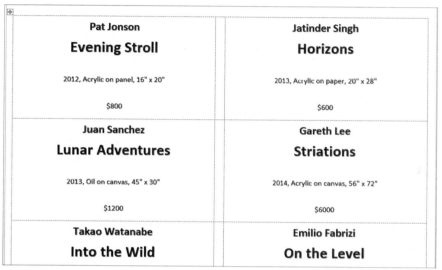

	A	B	C	D	E	F	G	H	I	J
15							Mid Range	7		
16	3	Ari Khosani	Gestures		2016 Bronze casting	24" high	7,000.00 Premium			
17	10	Gareth Lee	Striations		2014 Acrylic on canvas	56" x 72"	6,000.00 Premium			
18	14	Liz Kowalski	Daunted		2016 Oil on canvas	72" x 96"	7,000.00 Premium			
19							Premium	3		
20							Grand	15		
21										

Sales by Price Category ← Add a chart title

20%

33%

47%

- Budget
- Mid Range
- Premium

Select chart style 3

40 Your Name

Art_List

Independent Challenge 1

Create a festival database similar to the database you created for Unit G Project 1 to contain data related to a festival of your choice, such as a music festival, drama festival, film festival, and so on. Follow the steps provided to create the database, analyze the data in Excel, then merge an Access query with a form letter you create in Word.

1. Your first task is to determine the type of festival you need to create a database for. For example, you could create a database containing data about bands and performances at a folk music festival similar to the festival database you created for Project 1 or you could create a database containing information about the screenings of films at a film festival. Write the name and genre of your festival in the box:

Festival: _____

_____

2. Determine the data you need for just one aspect of the festival. For example, you could focus only on the bands playing at a music festival, the plays presented at a drama festival, or the films screened at a film festival. Limit the database to no more than three related tables. You don't need to incorporate every aspect of a festival into the database. Keep it simple for this project.

3. List the fields needed for the database. Here are some sample fields for a film festival that focuses only on the screenings of the films: Film Name, Production Company Name, Production Company Address fields (Street, City, State, Zip Code), Screening Venue, Screening Time, Film Genre, Rental Fee, and so on. Make sure that at least one of the fields contains numerical data that you can then use as the basis of an analysis in Excel. Also make sure that one of the tables contains address information that you can use to create a series of merged form letters.

4. Divide the field names into three tables and determine the relationship between the tables. For example, the fields for a film festival database could be arranged into a Films table, a Venues table, and a Screenings table as follows:

Table Name	Table Fields
Films Table	Film ID, Film Title, Film Venue, Film Category, Rental Fee, Production Company, Street Address, City, State, Zip, Phone Number
Venues Table	ID, Name, Location
Screenings Table	Screening ID, Performance Date, Performance Time, Film (to be added using a LookUp table)

5. Determine the relationship between the tables. FIGURE G-25 shows the relationships between the three sample tables based on the assumption that one venue can host many films, and one film can have many screenings.

FIGURE G-25

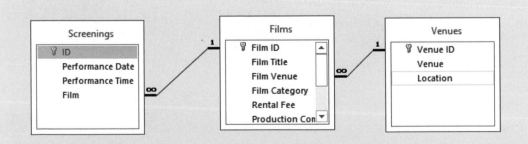

Independent Challenge 1 (continued)

6. In Excel, enter data for one of the tables. Make sure you enter the correct field names as column headings. Save the Excel workbook as **PR G-My Festival Data.xlsx**.

7. In Access, create a database called **PR G-My Festival Database.accdb**. Create the fields and data for the other two tables. Include 10 to 15 records in one table (for example, the Films table) and 3 or 4 records in the other table (for example, the Venues table). If one of the tables includes a field for Phone Number, include the Phone Number input mask.

8. Import the Excel worksheet. Make sure you create your own primary key (for example "ID").

9. Use the Lookup Wizard to create relationships between the tables. For example, you could add a Venue Name field to the Films Table, specify that the names of the venues come from the Venues table, then match venues to films. Refer to the relationships you set up in Project 1 for ideas.

10. In the Relationships window, enforce referential integrity between the related tables.

11. Create a query containing fields from at least two of the tables. Make sure one of the fields includes numerical data that you analyze in Excel.

12. Export the query to an Excel workbook that you save as **PR G-My Festival Analysis.xlsx**.

13. In Excel, create a PivotTable from the data. You determine what information you want to show. For example, the PivotTable could count the number of films being screened at each venue or summarize the rental fees paid to production companies. If the PivotTable contains dollar amounts, format the values with the Currency format. The data calculated in the PivotTable depends upon the fields you included in the Access query table. You may need to experiment to find a viable set of data to analyze.

14. In Excel, create a PivotChart from the PivotTable. Experiment with various filtering options to show specific data related to your festival. Format the chart and add an appropriate title.

15. Create a query in Access that contains the fields you want to include in a form letter. For example, you may wish to send a form letter to each production company confirming the date and time of the film screening and the rental fee to be paid. Make sure you include fields from the tables in which they originate (the "one" tables).

16. Switch to Word, set up the form letter, then save it as **PR G-My Festival Form Letter.docx** to the location where you save the files for this book. Use the form letter you created in Unit G Project 1 to help you determine the information to include.

17. Close the Word document, then in Access merge the query table with the form letter.

18. Insert fields where required and match fields where needed for the address.

19. Merge two of the letters, then save the merged letters as **PR G-My Festival Form Letter_Merged** to the location where you save the files for this book.

20. Make sure your name appears in all the files you've created, save the files, submit all files to your instructor, then close all the files and applications.

Independent Challenge 2

You work for a company called Game Time that creates imaginative computer games for teens and adults. The games sell worldwide on the Internet. You've decided to analyze the types of customers who have purchased your games in the past month in terms of occupation and country. Follow the instructions provided to create the customer list shown in **FIGURE G-26** and the report shown in **FIGURE G-27**. This document includes a table published from Access and a column chart created in Excel.

1. Start Access, create a database called **PR G-Game Time Computers.accdb**, and save it to the location where you save the files for this book.

Independent Challenge 2 (continued)

2. Create a table called **Customer List** as shown in FIGURE G-26. *Note*: The Occupation field is a lookup field (**Artist, Consultant, Lawyer, Manager, Teacher**), and the Country field is a lookup field (**Canada, Mexico, United States**).

FIGURE G-26

ID	Last Name	First Name	Occupation	Country	Product	Click to Add
1	Owen	Paul	Manager	United States	Planets	
2	Tisdale	Barry	Lawyer	United States	Jupiter Voyager	
3	Singh	Jatinder	Consultant	Canada	Grand Prix Racer	
4	Khosani	Parvin	Manager	Canada	Odyssey	
5	O'Rourke	Bridget	Teacher	United States	Music Quest	
6	Gonzales	Maria	Manager	Mexico	Pathways	
7	Rosas	Carla	Artist	Mexico	Planets	
8	Knutson	Sven	Lawyer	United States	Grand Prix Racer	
9	Mumaba	Garth	Lawyer	United States	Odyssey	
10	Wong	Doris	Teacher	United States	Jupiter Voyager	
11	Lalonde	Pierre	Manager	Canada	Music Quest	
12	Reed	Wade	Teacher	United States	Odyssey	
13	Malik	Mehdi	Teacher	Mexico	Prehistory Journey	
14	Rao	Ajala	Teacher	United States	Prehistory Journey	
15	Fuentes	Diego	Consultant	Mexico	Pathways	
(New)						

3. Export the Customer List table to an Excel workbook that you name **PR G-Game Time Analysis.xlsx** and that you save to the location where you save the files for this book. In Excel, create a pie chart that shows the breakdown of customers by occupation. You will need to sort the worksheet by occupation and create a Subtotal list to count the number of records in each occupation before you create the column chart. In the Subtotal dialog box, you'll need to select "Occupation" as the "At each change in selection" value. You will also need to remove "Count" from the worksheet so that it does not appear in the chart labels. (*Hint*: Search for Count and replace it with nothing; be careful not to replace "Country" in cell E1).

4. Format the chart so that it appears as shown in the completed report in FIGURE G-27. Use Style 12.

5. Start Word, enter only the text shown in FIGURE G-27, apply the Circuit theme, then apply the Title style to the title.

6. Save the document as **PR G-Game Time Report.docx** to the location where you save the files for this book.

7. Switch to Access, then publish the table as an .rtf file called **PR G-Game Time Customer List.rtf** to the location where you save the files for this book.

8. Delete the ID column, save the file, copy the table, switch to the PR G-Game Time Report document, then paste the table below the first paragraph of text in the Word document.

9. With the table selected, sort the table by Occupation, then click OK.

10. Apply the Grid Table 2 - Accent 1 table style, then deselect the Banded Columns check box in the Table Style Options group.

11. Switch to Excel, copy the chart, then use the Use Destination Theme and Embed Workbook paste option to paste the chart below the last paragraph in the Word document.

Independent Challenge 2 (continued)

12. Work in One Page view to adjust spacing, and resize the chart so that everything fits on page 1 of the document as shown in FIGURE G-27.

FIGURE G-27

Game Time, Inc.

Game Time, Inc., sells the majority of its computer games directly from its Web site. We have analyzed the types of customers who have purchased our computer games during one week in December 2016. The table shows the breakdown of these customers by Occupation and Country:

Last Name	First Name	Occupation	Country	Product
Rosas	Carla	Artist	Mexico	Planets
Singh	Jatinder	Consultant	Canada	Grand Prix Racer
Fuentes	Diego	Consultant	Mexico	Pathways
Tisdale	Barry	Lawyer	United States	Jupiter Voyager
Knutson	Sven	Lawyer	United States	Grand Prix Racer
Mumaba	Garth	Lawyer	United States	Odyssey
Owen	Paul	Manager	United States	Planets
Khosani	Parvin	Manager	Canada	Odyssey
Gonzales	Maria	Manager	Mexico	Pathways
Lalonde	Pierre	Manager	Canada	Music Quest
O'Rourke	Bridget	Teacher	United States	Music Quest
Wong	Doris	Teacher	United States	Jupiter Voyager
Reed	Wade	Teacher	United States	Odyssey
Malik	Mehdi	Teacher	Mexico	Prehistory Journey
Rao	Ajala	Teacher	United States	Prehistory Journey

As shown in the chart illustrated below, the majority of these are either Managers or Teachers. Game Time plans to develop a marketing strategy in consultation with contacts in the educational publishing industry to develop games of interest to teachers.

Your Name

13. Type your name in the document footer, save the document, submit all files to your instructor, then close and save all files and programs.

Independent Challenge 3

Create a database that contains information about your personal collection of CDs, records, tapes, videos, photographs, or a collection of your choice. Use the database to create labels for items in your collection. Plan and create the database as follows.

1. In Word, create a table containing headings that will differentiate the various records in your collection in terms of genre, category, or type, as appropriate. If your table lists all of your DVDs, for example, you could include fields for Title, Genre, Date, and Price. Make sure your table includes one field that contains currency amounts (for example, the "Price" field).

2. Save the Word document as **PR G-My Collection Table.docx** to the location where you save the files for this book.

3. Create a database called **PR G-My Collection Database.accdb**, and save it to the location where you save the files for this book, then copy the table from the Word document into the Access table.

4. Save the table as **Collection List**.

5. Merge the table to a new document in Word, and then follow the steps in the Mail Merge task pane to select a label, insert fields, and then format and arrange the fields. Look through the list of labels available in the Label Options dialog box to find a label appropriate for the items in your collection.

6. Complete the merge. Edit the field that contains values that should be displayed in the Currency format. (*Hint*: To change the format for a merge field, click the field name, press [Shift][F9] to show the merge field code, type \# $0, click the field name again, press [F9] to preview the result, then update the labels. *Note*: You can type \# $0.00 if you want the amount to show decimals as shown in **FIGURE G-28**.)

FIGURE G-28

> **«Artist»**
>
> «Title»
>
> «Music_Genre»
>
> { MERGEFIELD "Price"\# $0.00 }

7. Add your name to the last label, then save the label sheet as **PR G-My Collection Labels.docx** to the location where you save the files for this book.

8. Switch back to Access and export the table to Excel as a workbook called **PR G-My Collection List.xlsx**, and save it to the location where you save the files for this book.

9. Open the workbook in Excel, sort one of the fields (for example, the category field) in ascending order, apply a Subtotals list that calculates the total number of items in each category, replace "Count" with nothing, then create a chart, such as a pie chart or a doughnut chart, that shows the breakdown of items by category. Apply a chart layout, add a title to the chart, then type your name below the chart. (*Hint*: Search for [space]Count so that Excel does not also remove the "count" in "Country.")

10. Submit all files to your instructor, save and close all open files, then exit all programs.

Independent challenge 4 - Team Project

To further explore how you can integrate Access, Excel, and Word to meet a wide range of business needs, you will work with two other people to complete a team project. The subject of the team project is the development and marketing of a festival or similar multi-day event of your choice. The festival should involve workshops or performances, multiple venues, and be related to an activity of interest to the team. For example, you could develop files for a writers' festival or any festival of interest to your group. Follow the guidelines provided to create the files required for the team project. When you have completed the project, the team will submit a document containing summary information about the project, as well as the Access, Excel, and Word files related to the project.

▶ Project Setup

1. As a team, work together to complete the following tasks.
   - Share e-mail addresses among all three team members.
   - Set up a time (either via e-mail, an online chat session, Internet Messaging, or face to face) when you will get together to choose your topic and assign roles.
   - At your meeting, complete the table below with information about your team and the festival for which you are creating databases, workbooks, and documents. Note that organizing a festival in "real life" is a huge undertaking. For this project, focus only on a few events related to the festival (for example, just the performances or just the book signings).

Team Name (last names of the team members or another name that describes the project.
Team Members 1.   2. 3.
Festival name
Selected Festival events (for example, book signings, readings, workshops, etc., depending upon the theme).
Festival expense and revenue sources (expenses include payments to presenters and venues, and revenue sources include ticket sales, festival passes, donors, etc.)
Festival database tables: list all the fields needed, then work as a team to organize them into tables and determine relationships. One person will be responsible for developing the data for the database, but the entire team needs to collaborate on the types of data needed.
Team Roles: indicate who is responsible for each of the following sets of files (one set per team member). Note that the festival database will be created by one team member and then made available to the other two members to use in the creation of their files. Coordination between team members is key. Festival Database: Festival Analysis and Merges: Festival Report: Name of team folder where all team files will be saved:

Independent Challenge 4 - Team Project (continued)

> ### File Development

Individually, complete the tasks listed below for the file set you are responsible for. Note that for this project, all team members will need to work closely on planning the Access database to ensure it contains the tables and data needed to create the various components of the project. One person will then enter data for the database (see the description of the Festival Database). *Note*: All files for the Team Project will be saved to the location where you save files for this book. It is recommended that you create one team folder (as noted in the previous table) and all team members save to the same team folder. It is best if you can use a shared drive for storing your files.

Festival Database

Refer to the Festival Database you created for Project 1. For this project, you need to develop the database to include sufficient data to help your team members develop their files.

1. Create a new Access database, then save it as **PR G-Team Project_Festival Database** to the team folder created in the location where you save files for this book.

2. Divide fields into logical tables, then create the table structures for at least three tables (and no more than five tables). Keep the database structure simple. At this point, don't worry about populating the table with data. Ensure you are very clear about the overall purpose of the database. Following is an example of a database containing tables for a writer's festival that can be used to develop the other team files. Use this example and the projects you completed in this unit as your guide.

Table Name and Description	Sample Fields	Application(s)
Authors: List of authors who will read their work at the festival	Author ID, Author First Name, Author Last Name, Reading Fee, Book Name, Street Address, City, State, ZIP or Postal Code, Phone Number, Email Address	• Use fields in a query merged with the welcome letter. • Use fields in a query exported to the festival report.
Venues: List of venues used in the festival (up to four)	Venue ID, Venue Name, Venue Location, Venue Rental	• Use fields in a query exported to Excel and analyzed with a PivotTable; for example, total cost of venue rentals by reading.
Readings: List of dates and times for festival readings	Reading ID, Reading Date, Reading Time	• Link to the Venues table and the Authors table. • Use fields in queries exported to the Word report and the Excel analysis. • Use fields in the Welcome letter.

3. Add up to two additional tables as needed, depending on the wishes of the team. For example, you may want to add a table containing a list of volunteers who will work at the festival. This table could be linked to the Venues table—one venue can have several volunteers and be included in the Festival report. Make sure that you can create a relationship between at least two tables.

Independent Challenge 4 - Team Project (continued)

4. Create one of the tables in Excel. Make sure the Excel worksheet is formatted with fields starting in cell A1. Include up to 20 records in the Excel file. Save the file as **PR G-Team Project_Festival Data.xlsx**, then import the data into the PR G-Team Project_Festival Database.

5. Ensure the database includes the following components:
   a. An input mask is created for a phone number field or another field.
   b. At least one lookup field linked to a table so that a relationship is created between two tables.
   c. At least two tables are linked and referential integrity is enforced between linked tables.

6. Populate the database with data appropriate for the festival events you have chosen. Make the data as realistic as possible. For example, include the correct ZIP Codes and area codes for cities. You can make up names and street addresses. At least one of the tables should contain up to 15 records. Other tables can contain fewer records.

7. Create up to four queries in consultation with other team members containing the fields required for other components of the project. Remember to include fields from the tables in which they originally appeared (not in the linked tables) in a query.

8. Create a table named with your team name, then insert your name as the first record.

9. In the Excel workbook, enter your name in a cell below the data you exported to Access.

10. Submit all files to your instructor along with the files created by your team members.

Festival Letter and Analysis

This set of files includes an Excel workbook containing data about some aspect of the festival's financial data, and three Word documents:

- Letter containing merge fields from a query table in the PR G-Team Project_Festival Database
  (*Note*: You will need to use the Access database created by your teammate.)
- Document containing up to four merged letters
- Label sheet containing merge fields from the PR G-Team Project_Festival Database and merged to show the data

Use Unit G Project 1 and Project 3 as your models to create the files as follows:

1. From the Access database created by your teammate, export a query table to an Excel workbook saved as **PR G-Team Project_Festival Analysis.xlsx**.

2. From the data exported to Excel create a PivotTable in a new worksheet. You determine what information you want the PivotTable to show. For example, the PivotTable could add all the revenue generated from each of the venues or calculate the total fees paid to authors at a writers' festival according to the venue in which they deliver their reading. Experiment with different ways of calculating data.

3. Format any dollar amounts with the Currency format.

4. In Excel, create a PivotChart from the PivotTable and use filtering to show specific data related to the festival. Format the chart with data labels where needed and add an appropriate title.

5. Add your name to the worksheet containing the PivotTable and PivotChart.

6. Make sure the Access database contains the fields needed for two merges—one for a form letter and one for a sheet of address labels. Make sure the query includes fields from the tables in which they originate (the "one" tables).

Independent Challenge 4 - Team Project (continued)

7. In Word, write a form letter suitable for mailing to the names and addresses in the query table. The form letter could welcome participants to the festival and provide them with information about the festival or provide information for donors or confirm performance times. The content of the form letter depends upon the data included in the database and the project content established in your team meeting.

8. Include your name in the closing.

9. Save the letter as **PR G-Project_Festival Letter.docx**, close the Word document, then in Access merge the query table with the form letter.

10. Insert fields where required and match fields where needed for the address.

11. Merge four of the letters, then save the merged letters as **PR G-Project Festival Letter_Merged.docx**.

12. Merge the Access query with a sheet of labels, then save the label sheet as **PR G-Project Festival Labels.docx**.

13. Insert your name at the end of the last label on the sheet.

14. Submit all files to your instructor along with the files created by your team members.

Festival Report

This set of files includes a multipage report (up to three pages) in Word that describes the festival and includes objects from Access and Excel. Use Unit G Project 1 and Project 2 as your model to create the files as follows:

1. Create a Word document, then use WordArt to create an attractive header. Note that you can choose to rotate the WordArt object as you did for Project 2, or you can show the WordArt object behind text and lightly shaded.

2. Save the document as **PR G-Team Project_Festival Report**.

3. In another Word document, enter text that describes the festival. You don't need to worry about formatting, although you could work in Outline view to develop the report structure. Your report should consist of at least two sections describing the report and include text to introduce objects you'll insert from Access and Excel. For example, the report might include an Access table showing all the performers and the venues they will be performing in and an Excel chart summarizing festival revenue and expenses.

4. Save the document as **PR G-Team Project_Festival Report Text.docx**.

5. In the Word report, insert the festival text file, then format the headings and subheadings with styles.

6. From the PR G-Team Project_Festival Database, export a query to a Word file that you save as **PR G-Festival Query.rtf**. Copy the table into the Word report and format it with a table style.

Independent Challenge 4 - Team Project (continued)

7. In Excel, enter and format data related to the revenue and expenses of the festival. Save the workbook as **PR G-Festival Report Data.xlsx**. Limit the categories so the worksheet contains approximately 10 to 15 rows. Copy the cells containing the revenue and expenses data to an appropriate location in the Word report. Make sure the formatting of the copied Excel cells is intact.

8. In Excel, create a pie chart showing some aspect of the data, then copy the pie chart into an appropriate area of the Word report.

9. Format the Word report so that it extends across two to three pages and flows logically.

10. Include your name in the footer of the report and on all the other files you created.

11. Submit all files to your instructor along with the files created by your team members.

▶ Project Summary

As a team, complete the project summary as follows:

1. Open **PR G-08.docx** from the location where you save your Data Files, then save it to your **PR G-Team Project_Summary**.

2. Read the directions in the document, then ensure that each team member enters his or her name in one of the table cells along with a short description of the skills used and the challenges faced while creating his or her set of files.

3. Save the document, then submit all files to your instructor.

Visual Workshop

Start Word, create the table shown in **FIGURE G-29**, then save the file as **PR G-Garden Sage Products.docx** to the location where you save the files. Start Access, create a database called **PR G-Garden Sage Database.accdb**, save it to the location where you save the files for this book, copy the table from the Word document to a new table in the Access database, then save the table as **Neighborhood Sales**. Add the **Design Services** field name and data as shown in **FIGURE G-30**, then select the Currency Data Type for the three fields as shown in **FIGURE G-30**. Export the table to an Excel file called **PR G-Garden Sage Analysis.xlsx**, save it to the location where you save the files for this book, then create and format a column chart in Excel as shown in **FIGURE G-31**. Apply Style 13. Enter your name below the chart, save the Excel worksheet, submit all files to your instructor, then close all files and exit all programs.

FIGURE G-29

Neighborhood	Landscape Services	Garden Products
Arbutus	4000	3000
South Eaglecliff	3000	2000
Blue Water	5000	1000
Windsor Bay	2000	4000

FIGURE G-30

ID	Neighborhood	Landscape Services	Garden Products	Design Services	Click to Add
1	Arbutus	$4,000.00	$3,000.00	$1,000.00	
2	South Eaglecliff	$3,000.00	$2,000.00	$500.00	
3	Blue Water	$5,000.00	$1,000.00	$2,000.00	
4	Windsor Bay	$2,000.00	$4,000.00	$3,000.00	
(New)		$0.00	$0.00	$0.00	

FIGURE G-31

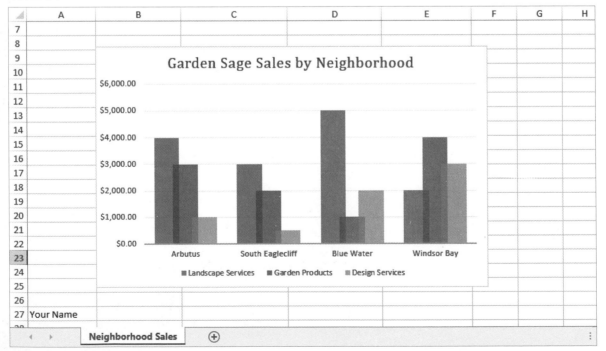

PowerPoint Projects

Projects

In this unit you will create the following:

Training Presentation

Create a presentation in Outline View • Check spelling • Select a theme and variant • Apply color and font schemes • Work with the Selection pane • Edit objects on the Slide Master • Add a footer and slide number • Insert an online picture • Adjust picture color • Create a SmartArt graphic • Apply transitions • Animate a SmartArt graphic • Print handouts (*Skills also practiced in Independent Challenge 1*)

Poster

Draw shapes and insert text • Adjust height and width of objects • Insert a table • Apply a table style • Create a custom color scheme • Add a WordArt object • Apply Text Effects • Insert a picture • Remove the background from a picture • Copy and rotate graphics • Export a presentation to a PDF file (*Skills also practiced in Independent Challenge 2*)

Animated Presentation

Insert a picture as a slide background • Crop pictures to shapes • Layer objects • Animate objects • Modify animation timings • Preview animations • Change the order of animations • Use the Animation Painter • Apply slide transitions • Insert an audio clip • Loop a presentation (*Skills also practiced in Independent Challenge 3*)

Team Project

Files You Will Need

PR H-01.jpg	PR H-06.jpg
PR H-02.pptx	PR H-07.jpg
PR H-03.jpg	PR H-08.jpg
PR H-04.mp3	PR H-09.jpg
PR H-05.docx	

Training Presentation on Oral Presentation Skills

You have been asked to teach your coworkers how to give an oral presentation. To help emphasize your points, you will accompany your lecture with an on-screen presentation that you create in PowerPoint. For this project, you need to **Create the Presentation Outline**, **Customize a Theme**, **Modify Individual Slides**, and **Edit and Show the Presentation**. The completed presentation is shown in Backstage view in FIGURE H-11 on page 203.

Create the Presentation Outline

You need to enter the information you plan to display on the slides in the Oral Presentation Skills presentation.

STEPS

1. **Start PowerPoint, click** Blank Presentation, **click the** VIEW tab, **then click the** Outline View button **in the Presentation Views group**
   In Outline view, you can enter slide titles and bulleted items in the Outline pane and then organize them just as you would do when creating an outline in Word.

2. **Click to the right of the slide icon in the Outline pane, type** Oral Presentation Pointers, **then press** [Enter]

3. **Press** [Tab] **to position the insertion point to type subtext on Slide 1, type your name, then save the presentation as** PR H-Oral Presentation Pointers **to the location where you save the files for this book**
   Slide 1 of the presentation appears as shown in FIGURE H-1. Notice how the text appears in the Outline pane and in the Slide pane.

4. **Click the** HOME tab, **click the** New Slide button **in the Slides group to start a new slide, type** Overview, **then press** [Enter]
   When you press [Enter] after typing a title, you start a new slide.

5. **Press** [Tab], **then type** Choose Your Topic
   When you press [Tab] after creating a new slide, you return to the previous slide (in this case, Slide 2). The text you typed appears as the first bulleted item on the slide titled "Overview."

6. **Press** [Enter], **type** Create Your Outline, **press** [Enter], **type** Prepare Your Slides, **press** [Enter], **type** Deliver Your Presentation, **then press** [Enter]
   When you press [Enter] after typing bulleted text, a new bullet appears.

7. **Click the** Decrease List Level button ⇤ **in the Paragraph group to start a new slide, type** Step 1: Choose Your Topic, **press** [Enter], **press** [Tab], **type** Identify a purpose, **then press** [Enter]

8. **Enter the text for Slides 3–7 as shown in** FIGURE H-2, **adding new slides as needed**
   Remember to press [Tab] to move the insertion point to the right. You can press [Shift][Tab] to move the insertion point to the left. You can also click the Decrease List Level button or the Increase List Level button to change the outline level for the current line.

9. **Click the** REVIEW tab, **click the** Spelling button **in the Proofing group, make any corrections required, press** [Ctrl][Home] **to move to the title slide, click the** VIEW tab, **click the** Normal button **in the Presentation Views group, then save the presentation**

FIGURE H-1: Title slide

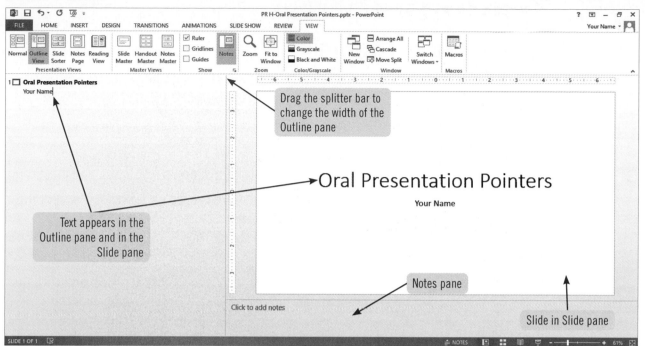

FIGURE H-2: Outline for Oral Presentation Pointers

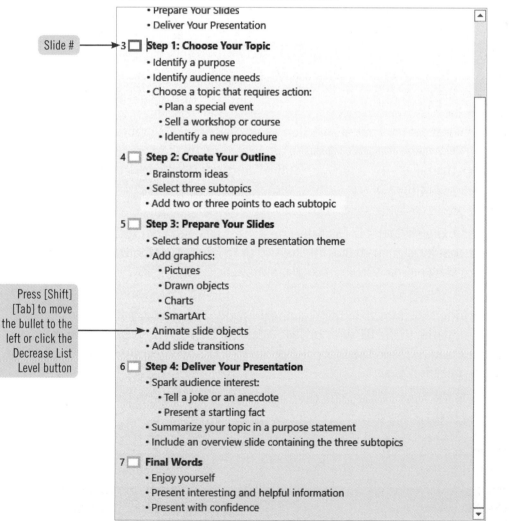

Customize a Theme

You can customize a theme by selecting a variant, changing the color and font schemes and then working in Slide Master view to apply new formats to specific parts of each slide.

STEPS

1. Click the DESIGN tab, click the More button ⏷ in the Themes group, click the Ion Boardroom theme as shown in FIGURE H-3 then click the blue variant in the Variants group

2. Click the More button ⏷ in the Variants group, point to Colors, click Blue II, click the More button ⏷, point to Fonts, then scroll to and click Century Schoolbook

   You can create hundreds of interesting presentation designs just by mixing and matching the various themes with new color schemes and font schemes

3. Click the VIEW tab, click Slide Master in the Master Views group, scroll up and click the top Slide Master in the Thumbnails pane, click a white area of the slide, click the DRAWING TOOLS FORMAT tab, then click Selection Pane in the Arrange group

   The Selection pane shows every object contained on the slide. From the Selection pane, you can select just the blue shape behind the slide title text and then modify it. The blue shape behind the Title Placeholder is Rectangle 25 in Group 8. For some objects, you need to use trial and error to determine which item in the Selection pane goes with which object.

4. Click Rectangle 25 in the Selection pane, click the Shape Fill list arrow in the Shape Styles group, then click Teal, Accent 6, Lighter 80% as shown in FIGURE H-4

5. Click Rectangle 21 in the Selection pane (the rectangle behind the slide # placeholder is selected), click the Shape Fill list arrow, then click Teal, Accent 6, Darker 50%

6. Click Title Placeholder 1 in the Selection pane, click the HOME tab, click the Font Color list arrow ▲ ⏷, click Teal, Accent 6, Darker 50%, click Text Placeholder 2 in the Selection pane, click the Bullets list arrow ☰ ⏷ in the Paragraph group, click Bullets and Numbering, click the Color list arrow, click Teal, Accent 6, Darker 25%, then click OK

   All the changes are made on every slide in the presentation.

7. Click Footer Placeholder 4 in the Selection pane, press and hold the [CTRL] key, click Date Placeholder 3, then change the font color to Teal, Accent 6, Darker 50%

   By selecting shapes in the Selection pane and then modifying them, you create a custom design for your presentation.

8. Click the Title Slide Master in the Thumbnails pane, click Rectangle 7 in the Selection pane, change the shape fill color to Teal, Accent 6, Lighter 60%, change the shape fill color of Rectangle 9 and the font color of Subtitle 2 to Teal, Accent 6, Darker 50%, then close the Selection pane

9. Click the SLIDE MASTER tab, click the Close Master View button, click the INSERT tab, click Header & Footer, then make selections as shown in FIGURE H-5

10. Click Apply to All, then save the presentation

FIGURE H-3: Selecting a Variant

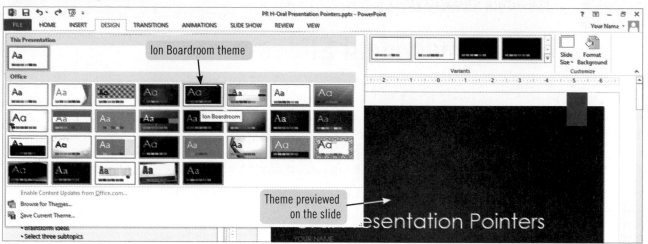

FIGURE H-4: Modifying the Slide Master using the Selection pane

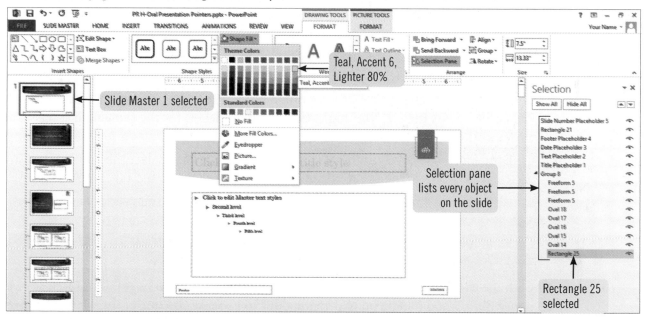

FIGURE H-5: Options selected in the Header and Footer dialog box

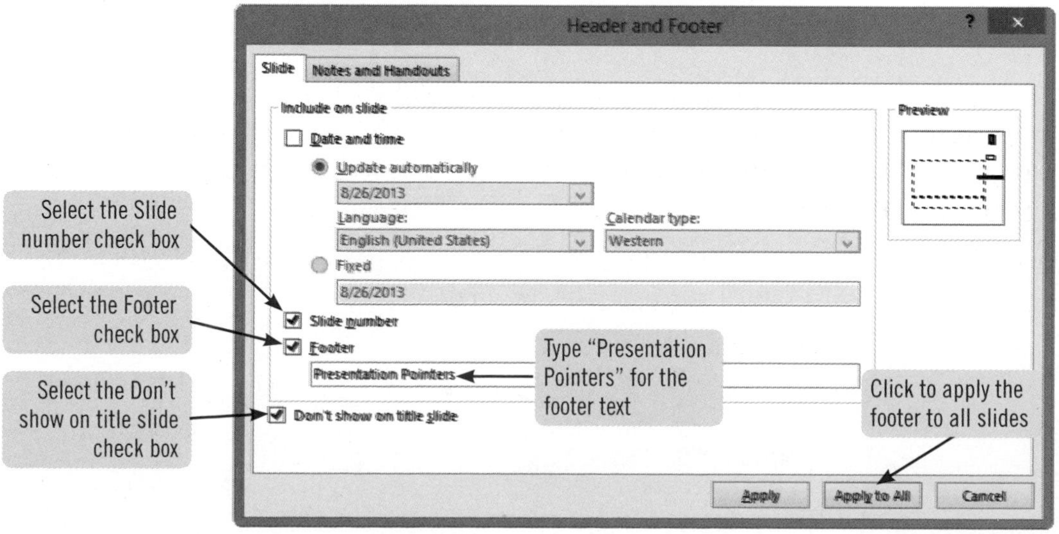

Modify Individual Slides

You need to add a clip art picture on Slide 2, and then create a SmartArt graphic on a new slide.

TROUBLE
You need to be connected to the Internet to find online clip art.

1. Click the Next Slide button ⬇ on the vertical scroll bar to display Slide 2, click the Online Pictures button in the Images group, click in the Office.com Clip Art text box, type checkmark, press [Enter], click the brown and yellow check mark picture (see FIGURE H-6), then click Insert

HINT
Drag the corner handles to decrease the size of the clip art picture.

2. Click Color in the Adjust group, click Teal, Accent color 6 Light (bottom-right selection), then use the mouse and the alignment guide to size and position the clip art picture as shown in FIGURE H-6

3. Click the Next Slide button ⬇ until Slide 6 appears (contains "Step 4: Deliver Your Presentation"), click the New Slide button in the Slides group, click the Title placeholder, then type Four-Step Process

4. Click the Insert a SmartArt Graphic button in the body placeholder, click Cycle in the left pane, click Basic Radial (third row, third from left), then click OK

TROUBLE
Use ⬇ to move to each level; if you press [Enter] and insert a new circle, click the Undo button ↩ on the Quick Access toolbar.

5. Click Text Pane in the Create Graphic group if the text pane is not open, type Great Presenting, press the [⬇], type Topic, then enter the labels for the remaining three circles as shown in FIGURE H-7

6. Click the More button ⬇ in the SmartArt Styles group, then select the Subtle Effect in the top row

7. Click the Change Colors button in the SmartArt Styles group, then click Colorful - Accent Colors (the first choice in the Colorful group)

8. Click the border surrounding the SmartArt graphic, click the HOME tab, then click the Bold button B in the Font group

9. Click the circle containing the Great Presenting text, press and hold [Shift], drag the upper-right sizing handle up and to the right to increase the size of the circle as shown in FIGURE H-8, click away from the SmartArt graphic, then save the presentation

FIGURE H-6: Using alignment guides to position the clip art picture

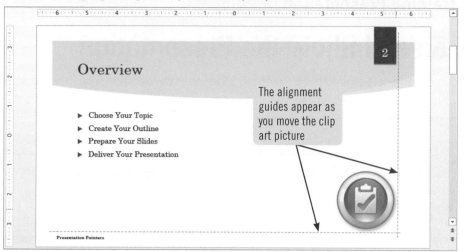

FIGURE H-7: Text typed in the SmartArt graphic

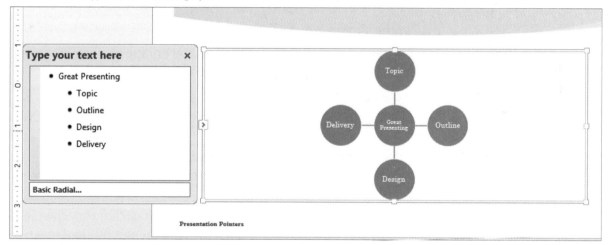

FIGURE H-8: Completed SmartArt graphic

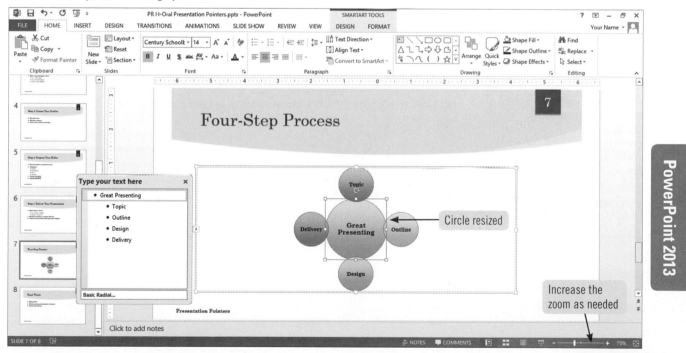

Edit and Show the Presentation

You need to select an animation scheme in Slide Sorter view, and then apply a custom animation scheme to the SmartArt graphic. Finally, you run the presentation in Slide Show view, and then print a copy of the presentation as a sheet of handouts with all eight slides on one page.

STEPS

TROUBLE
Use the slide number in the upper-right corner to find Slide 7.

1. **Click the** VIEW **tab, click** Slide Sorter **in the Presentation Views group, verify that** Slide 7 **is selected, click the** Fit to Window button **in the Zoom group, then drag Slide 7 to the left of Slide 3 as shown in** FIGURE H-9

2. **Click the** TRANSITIONS **tab, click the** More button ⬇ **in the Transition to This Slide group, click** Split **in the top row, click the** Effect Options button, **then click** Vertical In **as shown in** FIGURE H-10

   The animation effect previews on the selected slide.

3. **Click** Apply to All **in the Timing group**

4. **Verify that** Slide 3 **is still selected (it contains the SmartArt graphic), then click the** Normal button 🔲 **on the status bar at the bottom of the screen**

5. **Click the** SmartArt graphic **to select it (be careful not to select any one circle), click the** ANIMATIONS **tab, click the** More button ⬇ **in the Animation group, then click** Wheel **in the Entrance section**

6. **Click the** Effect Options button **in the Animation group, then click** One by One

   The animation effect is previewed on the slide. As you can see, each circle appears in turn, starting from the Great Presenting circle.

7. **Press** [Ctrl][Home] **to move to the first slide in the presentation, click the** Slide Show button 🖵 **on the status bar, then press** [Spacebar] **or click the** left mouse button **to move through the presentation**

   The animation scheme works nicely, and the custom animation effect on the SmartArt graphic adds interest.

8. **Click the** FILE **tab, click** Print, **click the** Full Page Slides list arrow, **then click** 9 Slides Horizontal **in the Handouts area**

   All eight slides in the presentation will print on one page as shown in FIGURE H-11.

MORE PRACTICE
For more practice with the skills presented in this project, complete Independent Challenge 1.

9. **Click the** Print button **if you wish to print the presentation; otherwise, exit Backstage view, save the presentation, submit a copy to your instructor, then close the presentation**

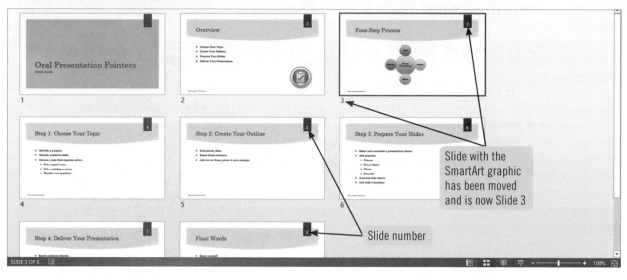

Slide with the SmartArt graphic has been moved and is now Slide 3

Slide number

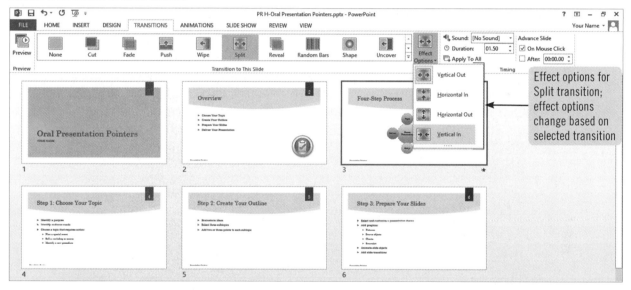

Effect options for Split transition; effect options change based on selected transition

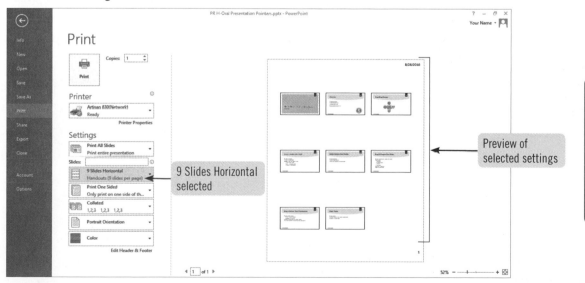

Preview of selected settings

9 Slides Horizontal selected

PowerPoint 2013

Poster for Cedar Trails Park

You are in charge of creating a poster to advertise monthly information meetings held from April through June at Cedar Trails Park. The poster will be displayed on bulletin boards in community areas and saved as a PDF (Portable Document Format) file. To create the poster, you need to **Insert Text Objects**, **Create a Table**, and then **Add Graphics and Create the PDF**. The completed poster is shown in FIGURE H-20 on page 209.

Insert Text Objects

You need to start a new presentation, draw a shape, and then enter and format text.

STEPS

1. Create a blank presentation in PowerPoint, click Layout in the Slides group, click Blank, then save the presentation as PR H-Cedar Trails Park Poster to the location where you save the files for this book

2. Click the INSERT tab, click Shapes in the Illustrations group, click Rounded Rectangle in the Rectangles section (second from the left), draw a box approximately 8" wide anywhere on the screen, then type Information Meeting
   You do not need to worry about sizing the rectangle shape exactly at this point.

3. Select the text, click the HOME tab, increase the font size to 32 pt, then apply Bold

   HINT
   You do not need to worry about positioning the text box exactly at this point.

4. Click the DRAWING TOOLS FORMAT tab, select the contents of the Height text box in the Size group, type 1, press [Enter], select the contents of the Width text box, type 9, press [Enter], then click an edge of the rectangle object and drag to position it as shown in FIGURE H-12

5. Click away from the text box, click the INSERT tab, click Text Box in the Text group, click below the rounded rectangle, type Location, press [Enter], then type the address text shown in FIGURE H-13

   HINT
   You select the border so that any changes you make will be applied to all the text in the box.

6. Select the word Location, change the font size to 20 pt and apply bold, select the two address lines, click the text box border, then click the Center button ≡ in the Paragraph group to center all the text

7. Click at the end of the address line, press [Enter] two times, type 2016 Meeting Times, then format the text with bold and 24 pt

8. Add another text box near the bottom of the slide containing the text For more information, please call Your Name at (604) 555-3488

   HINT
   You will align the boxes precisely in the next lesson.

9. Drag the two text boxes to the positions shown in FIGURE H-14, then save the presentation

FIGURE H-12: Rounded rectangle object sized and positioned

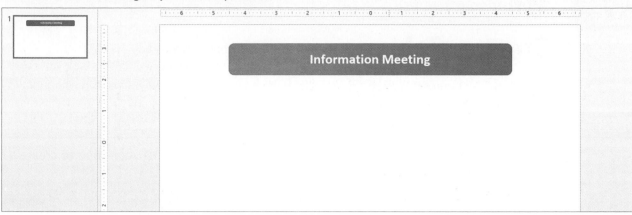

FIGURE H-13: Address text

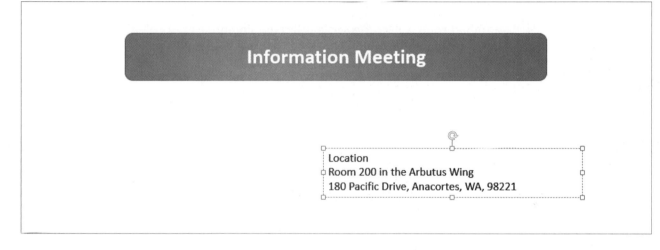

FIGURE H-14: Completed text objects positioned on the page

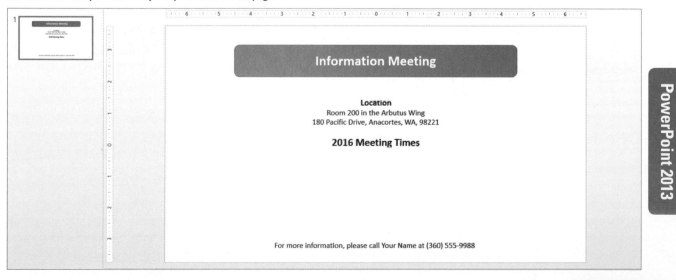

PowerPoint 2013

Create a Table

The poster includes a table that lists the meeting times for the months of April, May, and June. You need to create and then modify the table.

STEPS

1. Click the INSERT tab, click the Table button in the Tables group, then drag to create a table consisting of two columns and four rows

2. Click the More button ⊽ in the Table Styles group, select the Light Style 2 - Accent 6 table style (in the green column), then click the Banded Columns check box in the Table Style Options group to select it

3. Move the pointer over the top border to show the ⬚⃰, click and drag to position the table below "2016 Meeting Times", click the first cell, then type the text for the table as shown in FIGURE H-15

4. Select the two cells in the top row, click the HOME tab, click the Center button ☰ in the Paragraph group, select the three cells containing dates in column 1, apply bold, then deselect the cells

TROUBLE

If the border won't autofit when you double-click, drag the column divider to change the column width, then double-click the column divider again.

5. Move the pointer over the column divider between columns 1 and 2 to show +‖+, double-click to autofit the text in column 1, deselect the table, move the pointer over the right border of column 2 to show +‖+, then double-click to autofit the text in column 2

6. Click the table border, click the TABLE TOOLS LAYOUT tab, select the contents of the Table Row Height text box in the Cell Size group, type .5, click the Center Vertically button ▤ in the Alignment group, then as shown in FIGURE H-16, position the table below "2016 Meeting Times"

7. Double-click the rounded rectangle, click the More button ⊽ in the Shape Styles group, select Intense Effect - Green, Accent 6, then click away from the shape to deselect it

8. Click the DESIGN tab, click the More button ⊽ in the Variants group, point to Colors, click Customize Colors, then type Poster for the theme name

9. Click the Accent 6 (green) color box list arrow, click More Colors, enter values for Red, Green, and Blue as shown in FIGURE H-17, click OK, click Save, then save the presentation

   The Poster color scheme is saved and available for use in other presentations. You can create your own color scheme from any of the existing color schemes.

FIGURE H-15: Table text

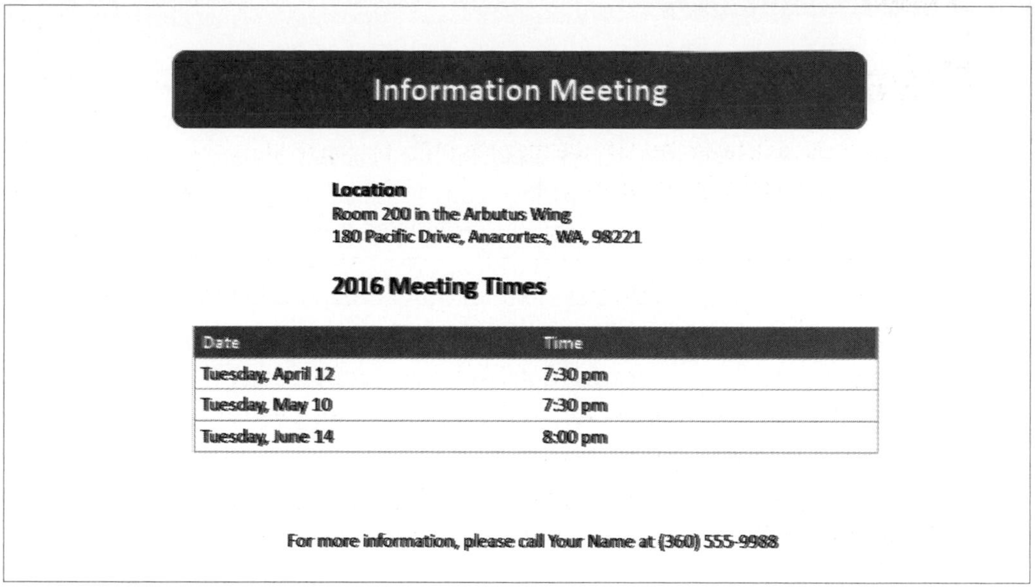
Information Meeting
Location
Room 200 in the Arbutus Wing
180 Pacific Drive, Anacortes, WA, 98221
2016 Meeting Times
Date
Time
Tuesday, April 12
7:30 pm
Tuesday, May 10
7:30 pm
Tuesday, June 14
8:00 pm
For more information, please call Your Name at (360) 555-9988

FIGURE H-16: Table sized and positioned

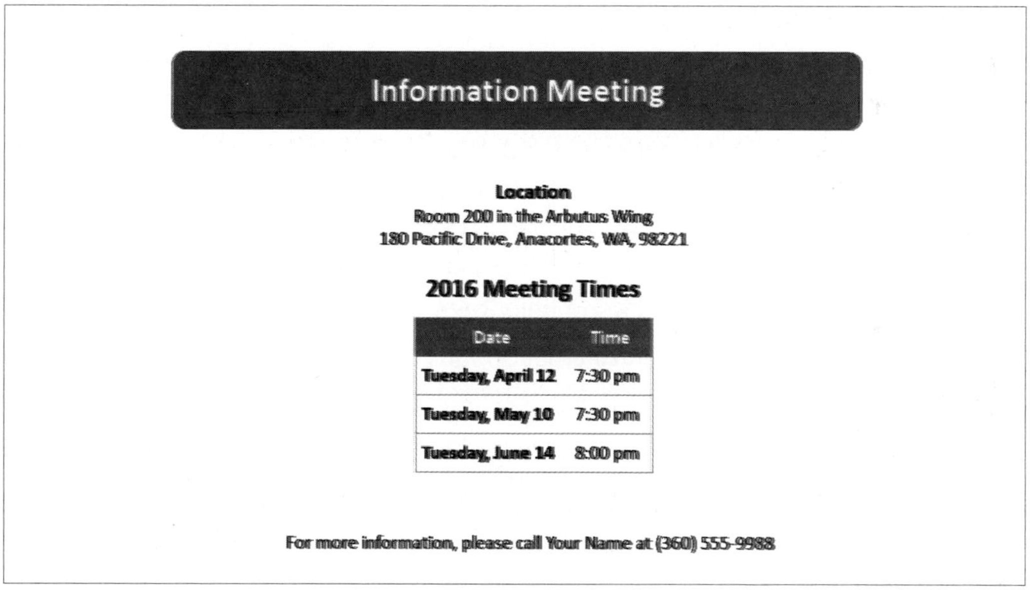
Information Meeting
Location
Room 200 in the Arbutus Wing
180 Pacific Drive, Anacortes, WA, 98221
2016 Meeting Times
Date
Time
Tuesday, April 12
7:30 pm
Tuesday, May 10
7:30 pm
Tuesday, June 14
8:00 pm
For more information, please call Your Name at (360) 555-9988

FIGURE H-17: Creating a custom color

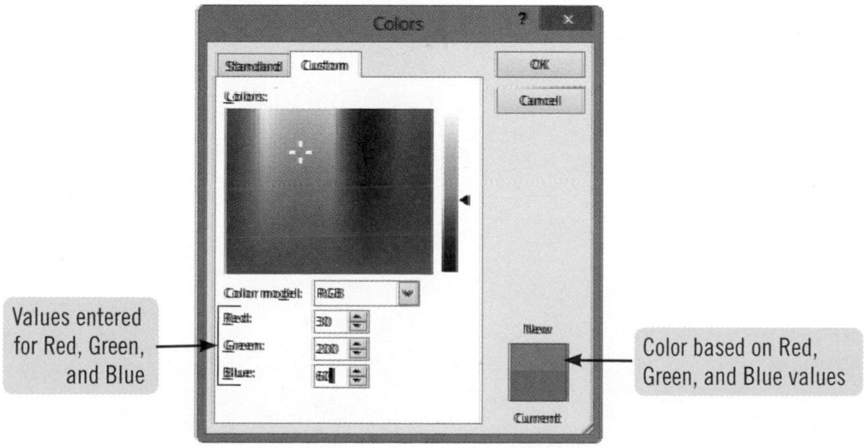
Colors
Standard
Custom
OK
Cancel
Colors:
Color model:
RGB
Red:
30
Green:
200
Blue:
60
New
Current
Values entered for Red, Green, and Blue
Color based on Red, Green, and Blue values

PowerPoint 2013

Poster (continued)

Add Graphics and Create the PDF

You need to create a WordArt object using the text *Cedar Trails Park*, insert a picture, remove its background, size and rotate the image, then copy the image and use each image as a border for the poster so the completed poster appears as shown in **FIGURE H-20**. Finally, you save the poster as a PDF file.

STEPS

1. Click the INSERT tab, click the WordArt button in the Text group, click Fill - Gold, Accent 4, Soft Bevel (first row, gold selection), type Cedar Trails Park, then drag the WordArt object below the table (don't worry about precise positioning at this point)

2. Select the text, click the HOME tab, reduce the font size to 40 pt, click the DRAWING TOOLS FORMAT tab, click the Text Effects button in the WordArt Styles group, point to Bevel, click 3-D Options, then modify the settings in the 3-D Format section of the Format Shape pane as shown in FIGURE H-18

3. Close the Format Shape pane, then use the mouse and the alignment guides to position all the objects as shown in FIGURE H-19

   You use the alignment guides to precisely align objects with relation to each other.

4. Click the INSERT tab, click Pictures in the Images group, navigate to the location where you store your Data Files, then double-click PR H-01.jpg

5. Click Remove Background in the Adjust group, click Keep Changes, click Color in the Adjust group, then click Green, Accent color 6 Light option (bottom row)

6. Click the launcher 🖼 in the Size group to open the Format Picture pane, click the Lock Aspect ratio check box to deselect it, enter 4 in the Height box, enter 11 in the Width box, enter 275 in the Rotation box, then close the Format Picture pane

7. Move the graphic so that it appears along the left side of the slide as shown in the completed poster in FIGURE H-20, click the HOME tab, click the Copy button, then click the Paste button

8. Drag the copied graphic toward the right edge of the slide, click the PICTURE TOOLS FORMAT tab, click the Rotate button in the Arrange group, click Flip Horizontal, then position the graphic as shown in FIGURE H-20

9. Save the presentation, click the FILE tab, click Export, click the Create PDF/XPS button, click Publish, submit the two files to your instructor, then close the files

FIGURE H-18: **3-D Format options**

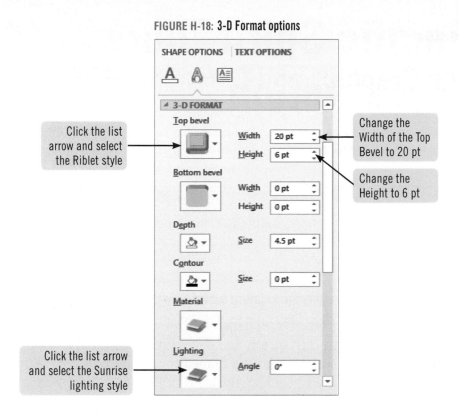

Click the list arrow and select the Riblet style

Change the Width of the Top Bevel to 20 pt

Change the Height to 6 pt

Click the list arrow and select the Sunrise lighting style

FIGURE H-19: **Using alignment guides to position objects**

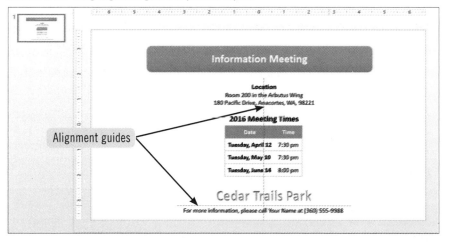

Alignment guides

FIGURE H-20: **Completed poster**

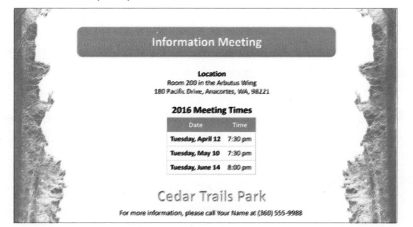

Pacific Spirit Tours Presentation

You create an animated presentation to include on the company's Web site. You need to **Animate Objects** and **Format the Slide Show**.

Animate Objects

You open a presentation, adjust the formatting, modify and animate pictures, then edit an online clip art picture.

STEPS

1. Open PR H-02.pptx from the location where you store files for this book, save it as PR H-Pacific Spirit Tours, then type your name on the title slide

2. Click the DESIGN tab, click Format Background in the Customize group, click the Picture or texture fill option button, click File in the Format Background pane, navigate to the location where you store your files, double-click PR H-03.jpg, then close the task pane

   You can make a presentation very dramatic by using photographs as slide backgrounds. In the current presentation, every slide background is now a photograph.

3. Go to Slide 2, double-click the bridge picture, click the Crop list arrow in the Size group, point to Crop to Shape, click Octagon, then drag the picture to position it in the middle of the slide

4. Click the ANIMATIONS tab, click Add Animation, click Shape in the Entrance Effects section, click Effect Options, click Diamond, then modify the options in the Timing group as shown in FIGURE H-21

5. Double-click the picture behind the bridge picture, click the Bring Forward button in the Arrange Group, crop the picture to the shape of an oval, then drag it over the bridge picture as shown in FIGURE H-22

6. Click the ANIMATIONS tab, apply the Grow & Turn animation, set the Timing to After Previous with a delay of .5, then click Preview in the Preview group to view the animation

7. Go to Slide 7, click the oval containing Amazing Guides, apply the Wheel animation effect to the currently selected oval, press and hold the [Ctrl] key, click each of the three remaining ovals, then apply the Wheel animation effect

8. Click Animation Pane in the Advanced Animation group, press and hold the [CTRL] key, click each of the four animations, change the Start to After Previous, then change the Delay to .5 seconds

9. Click away from the selected animations to deselect them, then select each animation individually and use the up and down arrows in the Animation pane to set the order of the animations as shown in FIGURE H-23

10. Save the presentation

FIGURE H-21: Timing options

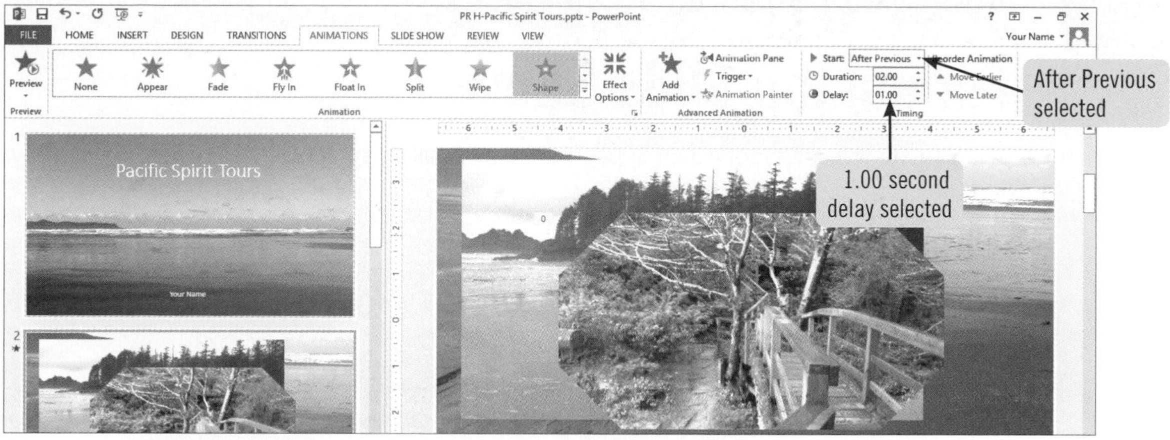

FIGURE H-22: Oval picture positioned over octagonal picture

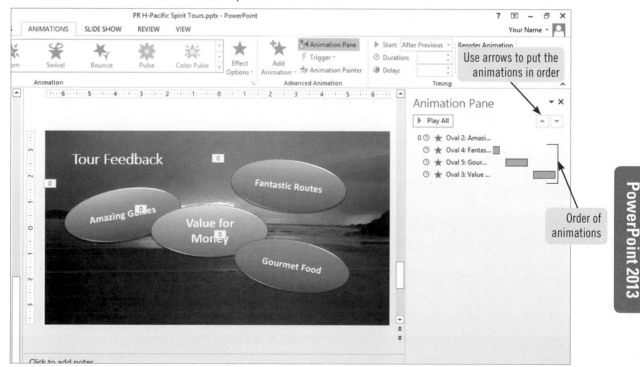

FIGURE H-23: Animation order set in the Animation pane

PowerPoint 2013

Format the Slide Show

You animate bulleted items, then apply transitions to all the slides in the presentation. Finally, you add and modify a sound file and play the presentation.

STEPS

1. Go to Slide 3, click any bulleted item, apply the Fly In Animation with the From Left effect, an After Previous start, and a delay of .5

2. Click a bulleted item again, double-click Animation Painter, click the Next Slide button, click any bulleted item on Slide 4, watch the animation, apply the animation to the bulleted items on Slides 5 and 6, then click Animation Painter to turn it off

3. Close the Animation pane, switch to Slide Sorter view, press [CTRL][A] to select all the slides, click the TRANSITIONS tab, apply the Wipe transition, click the On Mouse Click check box to deselect it, then set the After duration to 4.00 seconds

4. Click away from the slides to deselect them, click only Slide 7, apply the Curtains transition effect (in the Exciting section), apply the Origami transition effect to Slide 8 only, then scroll up to see all slides

   The presentation appears in Slide Sorter view as shown in FIGURE H-24.

5. Return to Normal view, go to Slide 1, click the INSERT tab, click Audio in the Media group, click Audio on My PC, navigate to the location where you store your files, then double-click PR H-04.mp3

6. Refer to FIGURE H-25: click the Play Across Slides check box in the Audio Options group to select it, click the Start list arrow, select Automatically, then drag the speaker icon to the lower right corner of the slide

7. Click the Slide Show button 🖥 on the task bar to view the entire presentation, then press Esc when the presentation is complete

   You can further tweak your presentation by modifying slide timings, changing animation effects, and adding different transitions effects until you are satisfied that the presentation conveys your message dynamically. You can also loop the presentation.

8. Click Slide 1, click the SLIDE SHOW tab, click Set Up Slide Show, click the Loop continuously until 'Esc' check box, then click OK

9. View the presentation and verify it loops, press the [Esc] key, save the presentation, submit a copy to your instructor, then close the presentation

FIGURE H-24: Presentation in Slide Sorter view

FIGURE H-25: Playback options for an audio clip

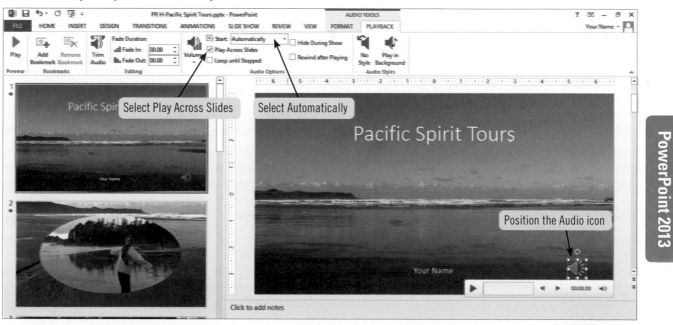

PowerPoint 2013

Independent Challenge 1

Create a six-slide presentation that you could use to help teach a specific concept or task. For example, your presentation could offer tips for taking effective vacation photographs, planning an event such as a wedding, or even enjoying the major sites in your hometown. Follow the steps provided to create the presentation in PowerPoint.

1. Your first task is to determine the subject of your presentation. Think about an activity or task that you know well and that you can present in short, easy-to-understand steps. To get started, write the words "How to", followed by a verb and then the activity. For example, your presentation subject could be "How to Set up a Blog" or "How to Plan a Hiking Trip". In the box below, write the subject of your presentation:

Presentation Subject: _____

_____

2. You need to determine three main topics related to the subject of your presentation. Each of these topics should cover a specific activity related to your subject. For example, the three topics for a presentation titled "How to Find a Job" could be: 1. Personal Profile, 2. Employment Sources, and 3. Interview Techniques. You should present each of these topics on separate slides along with three or four bulleted points that describe each topic. Write the three topics of your presentation in the box below:

Topic 1: _____

Topic 2: _____

Topic 3: _____

3. Start PowerPoint and create an outline of your presentation. Save the presentation as **PR H-My How-To Presentation** to the location where you save the files for this book. Here's a suggested format for the outline:

Slide #	Slide Title	Text
1	Presentation Subject	Title: Presentation Topic; Subtitle: Your Name
2	Overview	List the three topics that you will cover in your presentation
3	Topic 1	List three or four bulleted points related to topic 1
4	Topic 2	List three or four bulleted points related to topic 2
5	Topic 3	List three or four bulleted points related to topic 3
6	Conclusion	Create a "motivational" slide to summarize your presentation

4. Apply the presentation theme of your choice, then customize it by selecting a new color scheme and font scheme.

5. Switch to Slide Master view, click any object and show the Selection pane, then select and modify the appearance of at least three objects on the slides, including text in the placeholders. You may decide, for example, to change the font size and style of the text in the Master Title Style placeholder and fill a graphic object with a different color. Experiment until you are pleased that the custom theme provides good support for the content of your presentation. Exit Slide Master view.

6. Add a picture to at least one slide using the Online Pictures feature to access the Office.com Insert Picture window. Size and position the picture attractively on the slide and apply a color correction of your choice.

7. Insert an appropriate SmartArt graphic on one slide. Insert a new slide if necessary. Modify the SmartArt graphic attractively by applying a new style and color scheme.

8. When you are satisfied with the appearance of your slides, switch to Slide Sorter view, then add a transition effect to all the slides in the presentation.

9. In Normal view, add an animation effect to the SmartArt graphic, then edit the effect so that the various components that make up the graphic appear one by one.

Independent Challenge 1 (continued)

10. Switch to Slide Show view and run the presentation.
11. If you are able to print, print a copy of the presentation as handouts with six slides to a page. Save the presentation, submit a copy to your instructor, then close the presentation.

Independent Challenge 2

Create a poster that announces some kind of event, such as a concert series, sports tournament, or club meeting.

1. Determine the type of event you will announce. Think of your own interests. If you are involved in sports, you could create a poster to advertise an upcoming game or tournament. If you belong to a club, you could create a poster to advertise a special event such as a fund-raising bake sale or craft fair.
2. Think of an interesting title for your event. For example, a poster that announces a run to raise funds for the local food bank could be called "Run to End Hunger," while a poster that advertises a summer festival could be called "Under the Sun Celebration."
3. Determine the details that readers of your poster will need to know in order to participate in the event that you plan to advertise. You need to specify where the event will be held, when it will be held (date and time), and what activities will occur at the event. List yourself as the person readers should contact for more information.
4. On a blank piece of paper, create a rough draft of your poster. Determine where you will place the various blocks of text and one or two photographs or clip art images.
5. Create the poster on a blank PowerPoint slide. Create a custom color scheme called **Poster**. You can base the color scheme on any of the existing color schemes. Change at least one of the accent colors.
6. Include a table on your poster. Format the table attractively with one of the table styles.
7. Include at least one photograph from which you have removed the background and applied one or more effects such as an artistic effect, a color correction, or a color effect. Use the modified photograph as a design element in your poster.
8. Include a WordArt object to which you have applied and modified special effects such as a bevel or reflection. Experiment with the many ways in which you can modify the WordArt object.
9. Save the presentation as **PR H-My Poster** to the location where you save the files for this book, then save the presentation as a PDF file to the same location.
10. Submit a copy of both files to your instructor, then close the presentation.

Independent Challenge 3

Create an animated presentation designed to be looped continuously to showcase a subject of your choice.

1. Refer to Project 3 for ideas. You could develop a presentation to advertise the products offered by a new company or to celebrate an event such as a class party or festival. Choose your topic based on photographs you have available. For example, if you have several good photographs of your pet, you can create an animated presentation that features information about your pet. In the box, write the subject of your presentation:

Presentation Subject: _____

2. Determine three main topics you will cover in the animated presentation. For example, three topics for a presentation on a vacation destination could be "Accommodation," "Activities," and "Food." Write your topics in the box:

Topic 1: _____

Topic 2: _____

Topic 3: _____

3. Start PowerPoint and create an outline of your presentation. Save the presentation as **PR H-My Animated Presentation** to the location where you save the files for this book. Use the same format suggested for Unit H Independent Challenge 1 to organize your presentation subject and its three main topics.

4. Select a color scheme for your presentation, then on each slide include an appropriate photograph as the background. (*Note:* If the file sizes of your photographs are very large, click any individual photograph in the presentation, show the PICTURE TOOLS FORMAT tab, click Compress Pictures in the Adjust group, select the Screen (150 ppi) option, deselect the Apply only to this picture check box, then click OK. You should perform this step after you have inserted all the photographs required for your presentation.)

5. In Slide Master view, modify the font colors to match most of the photographs. Note that you may need to modify individual slides, depending on the photograph used as a background. A light photograph requires dark text and a dark photograph requires light text.

6. On one or more of the slides in the presentation, insert two or three additional photographs, crop and overlap them, then apply animation effects. Your goal is to include a slide where two or three pictures appear sequentially.

7. On one slide, draw and format a selection of objects to contain key phrases. Animate each of the objects to create an attractive sequence.

8. Animate the bulleted items on a slide containing bulleted text. Use the Animation Painter to apply the same animation settings to each slide containing bulleted text.

9. Check all animations to ensure that the After Previous start option is applied (in the Timing group on the ANIMATIONS tab). The final presentation should be able to run without mouse clicks.

10. In Slide Sorter view, apply one transition effect to the entire presentation and modify timing options. Preview the presentation frequently and adjust timings on individual slides as needed.

11. In Slide Sorter view, apply two additional transition effects to two other slides. Experiment with some of the Exciting transition effects.

12. On Slide 1, insert an audio file if you have one available. You can also insert an online audio file if you do not have your own file. Set the playback settings so the audio file plays automatically across all slides.

13. Set up the slide show to loop continuously, then preview the slide show and make adjustments as needed.

14. Be sure your name is on the presentation, such as on the Title slide as a subtitle, save the presentation, submit a copy to your instructor, then close the presentation.

Independent Challenge 4 - Team Project

To further explore how you can develop a wide range of presentations with PowerPoint 2013, you will work with two other people to complete a team project. The subject of the team project is promotion of a small business or organization of your choice. Follow the guidelines provided to create the three presentations required for the team project. When you have completed the project, the team will submit a document containing information about the project, as well as three files related to the project: a training presentation, a poster, and an animated presentation.

Project Setup

1. As a team, work together to complete the following tasks.
   - Share e-mail addresses among all three team members.
   - Set up a time (either via e-mail, an online chat session, Internet Messaging, or face to face) when you will get together to choose your topic and assign roles.
   - At your meeting, complete the table below with information about your team and the business you are creating presentations for.

Team Name (last names of the team members or another name that describes the project; for example, "Jones-Cho-Knorr" or "Evergreen Kayaking Tours").
Team Members 1. 2. 3.
Business type (for example, coffee shop, tour company, retail store, etc.)
Business products or services (for example, catering services, floral design, Web site design, children's toys, etc.)
Training topic (for example, staff training, customer orientation, product workshop, etc.)
Company event for a poster (for example, information meeting, special event, store opening, etc.)
Subject for an animated presentation (for example, product promotion, company overview, etc.)
Team Roles: indicate who is responsible for each of the following three files (one file per team member) Company Training Presentation: Company Poster: Company Animated Presentation:

Independent Challenge 4 - Team Project (continued)

▶ Presentation Development

Individually, complete the tasks listed below for the file you are responsible for. You need to develop appropriate content, and format the file attractively. Include the team name on all presentations.

Company Training Presentation

This presentation includes from six to eight slides containing training content on a subject relevant to the company. Create the presentation as follows:

1. Create a new PowerPoint presentation and save it as **PR H-Team Project_Company Training Presentation** to the location where you save files for this book. Include your name and your team name on the title slide.
2. In Outline view, organize the content of the presentation. Make sure you include an overview slide and three main topics. Enter the text for each slide in Outline view.
3. Customize a theme for the presentation by selecting a theme and a variant, then selecting a color scheme and a font scheme.
4. In Slide Master view, modify three objects including shapes and content placeholders. Use the Selection pane to help you select objects and experiment until you are satisfied that the customized theme is attractive and easy to read and reflects your company's brand.
5. Insert at least one online picture and adjust its color settings.
6. Insert and format an appropriate SmartArt graphic. Make sure you include appropriate text and apply a SmartArt style and color scheme.
7. Apply a transition effect to every slide in the presentation.
8. Apply a one-by-one animation effect to the SmartArt graphic.
9. Set up the presentation to print as handouts. You choose the number of slides per page.
10. Save the presentation and submit it to your instructor along with the other presentations created by your team members.

Company Poster

This presentation contains a poster that communicates information about a special event or other purpose related to the company. Create the presentation as follows:

1. Sketch the poster on a piece of paper to determine how best to organize the text boxes and other graphic objects.
2. Create a new PowerPoint presentation and save it as **PR H-Team Project_Company Poster** to the location where you save files for this book. Include your name and your team name in a text box at the bottom of the poster.
3. Create a custom color scheme called **Team Poster** based on any color scheme. Change at least one accent color.
4. Include a table that you've formatted with one of the table styles.
5. Include at least one photograph from which you have removed the background and applied one or more effects such as an artistic effect, a color correction, or a color effect. Use the modified photograph as a design element in the poster. The modified photograph should enhance the appearance of the poster.
6. Include a WordArt object to which you have applied and modified special effects such as a bevel or reflection.
7. Save the poster, save the poster again as a PDF file called **PR H-Company Poster.pdf**, then submit both files to your instructor along with the other presentations created by your team members.

Independent Challenge 4 - Team Project (continued)

Company Animated Presentation

This presentation consists of six to eight slides containing photographs and other graphic objects that are animated and looped to create a continuous presentation. The presentation could be used at a kiosk to advertise the company or saved as a video file and posted online. The content of the presentation relates to some aspect of your team's company. Use Unit H Project 3 as a guide for completing the animated presentation as follows:

1. Create a new PowerPoint presentation and save it as **PR H-Team Project_Company Animated Presentation** to the location where you save files for this book. Include your name and your team name on the title slide.
2. In Outline view, enter the text for the presentation and determine where you will insert graphics. Limit the amount of text included on each slide.
3. Include a different photograph as the background on each slide. (*Note*: If the file sizes of your photographs are very large, click any individual photograph in the presentation, show the PICTURE TOOLS FORMAT tab, click Compress Pictures in the Adjust group, select the Screen (150 ppi) option, deselect the Apply only to this picture check box, then click OK. You should perform this step after you have inserted all the photographs required for your presentation.)
4. Modify font colors to match photographs. (*Note*: You can also choose to increase the transparency of a photograph inserted as a slide background so that text shows up more clearly.)
5. On one or more of the slides in the presentation, insert two or three additional photographs, crop and overlap them, then apply animation effects.
6. On one slide, draw and format a selection of objects to contain key phrases. Animate each of the objects to create an attractive sequence.
7. Animate the bulleted items on a slide containing bulleted text. Use the Animation Painter to apply the same animation settings to each slide containing bulleted text.
8. Check all animations to ensure that the After Previous start option is applied (in the Timing group on the ANIMATIONS tab). The final presentation should be able to run without mouse clicks.
9. In Slide Sorter view, apply one transition effect to the entire presentation and modify timing options. Apply two additional transition effects to two slides. Preview the presentation frequently and adjust timings on individual slides as needed.
10. On Slide 1, insert an audio file if you have one. You can also insert an online audio file. Set the playback settings so the audio file plays automatically across all slides.
11. Set up the slide show to loop continuously, then preview the slide show and make adjustments as needed.
12. Save the presentation and submit it to your instructor along with the other presentations created by your team members.

▶ Project Summary

As a team, complete the project summary as follows:

1. Open PR H-05.docx from the location where you save your Data Files, then save it as **PR H-Team Project Summary** to the location where you save your files for this book.
2. Read the directions in the document, then ensure that each team member enters his or her name in one of the tables along with a short description of the skills used and the challenges faced while creating the PowerPoint presentations.
3. Save the document, then submit all files to your instructor.

Visual Workshop

As part of a presentation on tourism in Normandy, France, that you are giving to a local community group, you need to create the two slides shown in **FIGURES H-26** and **H-27**. Apply the Paper color scheme, enter the title and subtitle text on Slide 1, then insert **PR H-06.jpg** as the slide background. Position and format the text placeholders and align text as shown. Apply the Gradient Fill – Lavender, Accent 4, Outline – Accent 4 WordArt style to the title. For Slide 2 of the presentation, change the background to Gradient, change the layout to Blank, then create the picture SmartArt graphic shown in **FIGURE H-27**. Select the Bending Picture Captions List SmartArt and use the data files **PR H-07.jpg**, **PR H-08.jpg** and **PR-09.jpg**. Select the Cartoon SmartArt style and the first option in the Colorful color schemes. Save the presentation as **PR H-Normandy Presentation** to the location where you save the files for this book, submit the file to your instructor, then close the presentation.

FIGURE H-26

FIGURE H-27

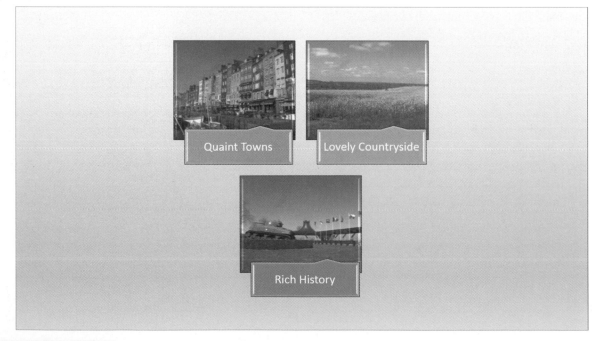

Integration Projects III

Projects

In this unit you will create the following:

Status Report

Insert a PowerPoint slide into Word as an object • Add a gradient fill to a slide background • Apply heading styles • Generate a Table of Contents • View database table relationships • Export an Access table to Word • Apply table styles • Create a two-table query • Group data in a query • Export an Access table to Excel • Create a PivotTable and PivotChart • Insert a table in PowerPoint • Copy slides to Word • Create and format a report in Access • Add an Access report to Word (*Skills also practiced in Independent Challenge 1*)

Welcome Presentation

Create an Access table in Design view • Use the Lookup Wizard • Create a query • Sort fields in a query • Copy an Access query and paste it as a link into Excel • Create a PivotTable and PivotChart • Add a picture to the Slide Master in PowerPoint • Crop a picture • Paste linked charts and data in PowerPoint • Create a screenshot • Update links from Access to Excel to PowerPoint • Break links (*Skills also practiced in Independent Challenge 2*)

Event Presentation

Adapt an Excel template • Adjust picture color • Save a graphic as a picture in PowerPoint • Add a picture as a slide background • Copy Word text to PowerPoint • Format Excel charts in PowerPoint • Set the transparent color on a graphic (*Skills also practiced in Independent Challenge 3*)

Team Project

Files You Will Need

PR I-01.docx	PR I-05.jpg
PR I-02.accdb	PR I-06.jpg
PR I-03.pptx	PR I-07.docx
PR I-04.docx	

Status Report for Unity Fitness

Unity Fitness offers a range of fitness classes, including Yoga, Pilates, Nia, and aerobics. You've been asked to present a status report to a group of potential investors. For this project, you need to **Format the Report in Word**, **Compile Source Materials**, **Add Excel and PowerPoint Objects**, and **Add a Report from Access**. The completed report is shown in **FIGURE I-10** on page 229.

Format the Report in Word

You open and format a document containing the text for the report and placeholders for objects you will import from Excel, Access, and PowerPoint.

1. Start Word, open the file PR I-01.docx from the location where you store your Data Files, save the file as PR I-Unity Fitness Report, scroll the report to become familiar with its contents, then turn on paragraph marks

2. Press [Ctrl][Home], press [Ctrl][Enter] to insert a page break, press [Ctrl][Home] again, press [Enter], press the [↑], click the INSERT tab, click Object in the Text group, scroll the list of object types, click Microsoft PowerPoint Slide, then click OK

3. Click the title placeholder, type Unity Fitness and enhance it with bold, click the subtitle placeholder, type Six Month Status Report, press [Enter], type your name, then click a blank area of the slide, making sure no placeholders are selected

4. Click the DESIGN tab, click Format Background in the Customize group, click the Gradient Fill option button, then modify the gradient fill as shown in FIGURE I-1

5. Close the Format Background pane, then click below the slide to return to Word

6. Scroll to the next page, select Introduction, click the HOME tab, click Heading 1 in the Styles gallery, then apply the Heading 1 style to the remaining document headings

HINT
The remaining document headings are Fitness Classes, Revenue Increase, Special Events, and Summary. All the headings are formatted with the Heading 1 style.

7. Scroll up to page 1, click to the left of the page break below the PowerPoint slide, click the REFERENCES tab, click Table of Contents in the Table of Contents group, click Automatic Table 1, then scroll up to view the table of contents

8. Apply the Savon theme to the document and change the zoom to 80%, then save the document

   The first page of the report appears as shown in FIGURE I-2

9. Start Access, open PR I-02.accdb from the location where you store your Data Files, then save the database as PR I-Unity Fitness.accdb

TROUBLE
To save a database with a new name, click the FILE tab, click Save As, click the Save As button, type the new filename, then click Save. Click Enable Editing or Enable Content if prompted.

10. Click the DATABASE TOOLS tab, click Relationships, refer to FIGURE I-3 to read the descriptions of the relationships between the four tables in the database, then close the Relationships window

    The database contains four related tables listing fitness classes, members, instructors, and registrations. In the next lessons, you compile source materials for the report from the Access database, and from Excel and PowerPoint.

FIGURE I-1: Applying a gradient fill to a slide background

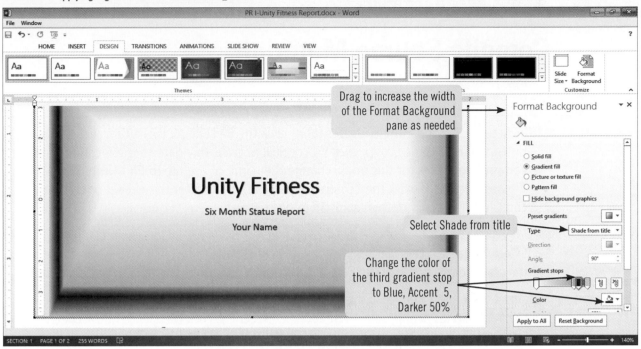

FIGURE I-2: Formatted slide and document contents on page 1

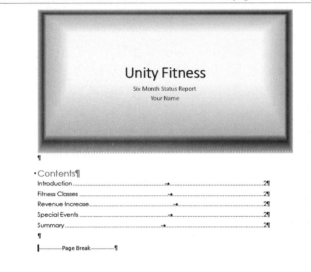

FIGURE I-3: Relationships between tables in the Access database

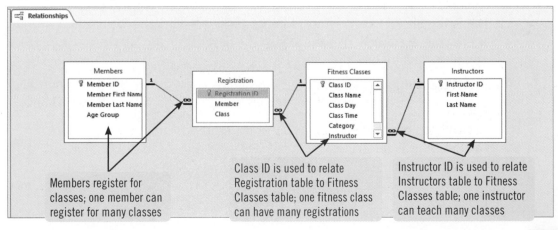

Integration 2013

Compile Source Materials

You publish an Access table in Word, then create a query to analyze in Excel.

STEPS

1. In Access, click the Fitness Classes table, click the EXTERNAL DATA tab, click the More button in the Export group, click Word, click Browse, navigate to the location where you save your files for this book, change the name of the file to PR I-Unity Fitness Classes, click Save, click the "Open the destination file after the export operation is complete." check box, then click OK

   The table is exported to Word as a document saved in Rich Text Format (.rtf).

TROUBLE
Do not be concerned that the table extends beyond the right margin; you will fix this in Step 4.

2. Select the table, press [Ctrl][C] to copy it, switch to the report in Word, scroll to and select the placeholder text [Fitness Classes] on page 2, then press [Ctrl][V] to paste the table

3. Select the table again, click the TABLE TOOLS DESIGN tab, click the More button ▼ in the Table Styles group, select List Table 2 - Accent 2, click the Header Row check box to select it, then click the Banded Rows check box to deselect it

HINT
You can also use the AutoFit Contents command in the Cell Size group on the TABLE TOOLS LAYOUT tab.

4. Double-click any column divider to autofit the table contents, deselect the table, add a blank line below the table, then increase the zoom to 120%

   The table appears in the Word document as shown in **FIGURE I-4**.

5. Switch to Access, click Close, verify that Fitness Classes under the Tables heading in the list of Access objects is selected, click the CREATE tab, click Query Wizard in the Queries group, click OK, click Open if prompted, then click the Select All Fields button >>

6. Click the Tables/Queries list arrow, click Table: Registration, add the Registration ID field, click Next, click Next, enter Fitness Class Registrations as the title, click the "Modify the query design." option button, then click Finish

7. Click the Totals button in the Show/Hide group, click Group By in the Registration ID column, click the list arrow, click Count as shown in FIGURE I-5, click the Run button in the Results group to run the query, then close and save the query

   You can see at a glance how many members took each of the fifteen fitness classes.

8. Click Fitness Class Registrations in the list of Access objects, click the EXTERNAL DATA tab, click Excel in the Export group, click Browse, then navigate to the location where you save your files for this book

9. Name the file PR I-Unity Fitness Classes, click Save, click the Export data with formatting and layout check box, click the "Open the destination file after the export operation is complete." check box, then click OK

10. Select the range D2:D16, click the Custom list arrow in the Number group, click Time, complete the Excel worksheet as shown in FIGURE I-6, then save the workbook

FIGURE I-4: Formatted table in Word

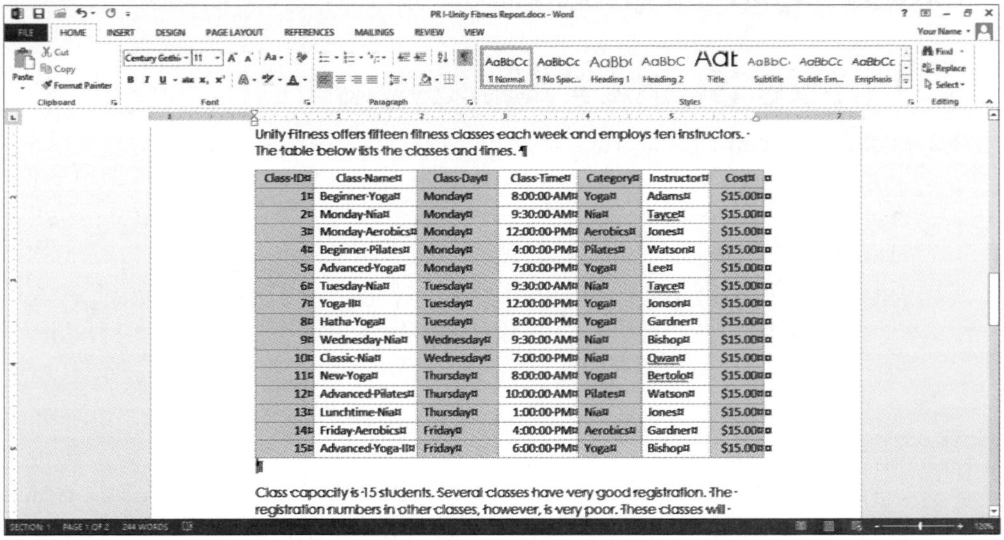

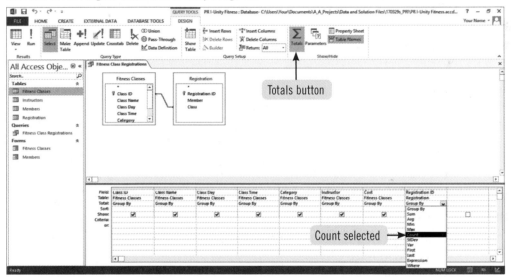

FIGURE I-5: Selecting the Count Total in Query Design view

FIGURE I-6: Completing the Excel worksheet

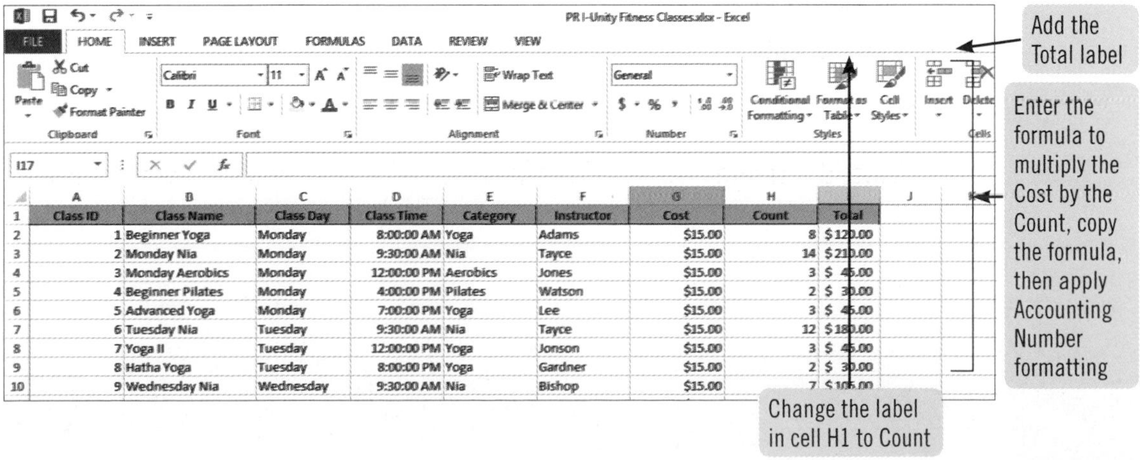

Add Excel and PowerPoint Objects

You create a PivotTable and pie chart and copy the chart to Word. You then copy two PowerPoint slides into the Word report.

1. Select cells B2:B16, press and hold [Ctrl], select cells I2:I16, click the INSERT tab, click the Insert Bar Chart button ▤▾, then click the first option under 2-D Bar

   The chart contains too many bars to be read easily. You create a Pivot Table and PivotChart instead.

2. Delete the chart, click anywhere in the table, click the INSERT tab, click PivotTable in the Tables group, then click OK

3. Select the Category check box in the PivotTable Fields pane, click the Total check box, click cell B4 in the PivotTable, click Field Settings in the Active Field group, click Number Format, click Currency, click OK, then click OK

4. Click the PivotChart button in the Tools group, then create and format the pie chart as shown in FIGURE I-7

5. With the pie chart selected, press [Ctrl][C], switch to the report in Word, select the placeholder text [Class Revenue by Category] but not the paragraph mark, then press [Ctrl][V]

6. Scroll to and delete [PowerPoint Slides] (but not the paragraph mark), click the INSERT tab, click Table, drag to create a one row, two-column table as shown in FIGURE I-8, then verify that the insertion point appears in the left cell

7. Start PowerPoint, open PR I-03.pptx from the location where you store your Data Files, click the Slide Sorter button ▦ on the status bar, verify that the title slide is selected, press [Ctrl][C], switch to the Word report, press [Ctrl][V], press [→] to move to the right cell, switch to PowerPoint, click slide 3 (Basic Principles), press [Ctrl][C], switch to the Word report, then press [Ctrl][V]

8. Double-click the slide you just copied, select the contents of the Width text box in the Size group (contains 6"), type 2.8, press [Enter], click the Picture Border list arrow in the Picture Styles group, point to Weight, select 1½ pt, then change the width and border weight for the slide in the left cell

9. Select the entire table, click the TABLE TOOLS DESIGN tab, click the Borders list arrow in the Borders group, click No Border, then deselect the table

   The two slides appear side by side as shown in FIGURE I-9.

10. Save the Word document

FIGURE I-7: Completed PivotChart

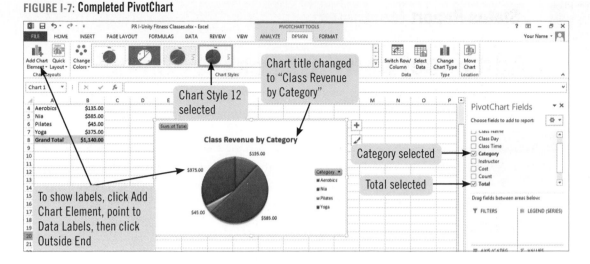

FIGURE I-8: Creating a table

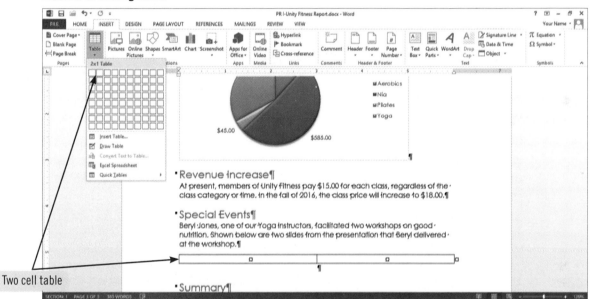

FIGURE I-9: Completed PowerPoint slides in Word

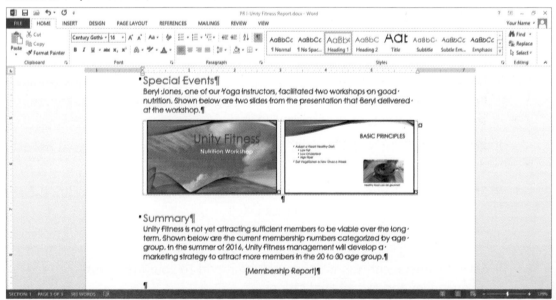

Add a Report from Access

You create a report from the Members table, then publish the report in Word and format it attractively. Finally, you update the table of contents in Word and print a copy of the report.

STEPS

1. **Switch to Access, click** Close**, click** Members **in the list of tables (not the form), click the** CREATE **tab, click** Query Wizard**, click** OK**, add only the** Age Group **field from the Members table, then click** Finish

2. **Click the** HOME **tab, click the** View button**, click the** Age Group sort cell**, click the** list arrow**, click** Ascending**, run the query, then return to Design view**

3. **Double-click** Age Group **in the Members table list to add a second Age Group field to the grid, click the** Totals button **in the Show/Hide group, click** Group By **for the second Age Group, click the** list arrow**, click** Count**, then run the query**
   The number of members in each age group is shown.

4. **Close and save the query, click** Members Query**, click the** CREATE **tab, click** Report **in the Reports group, click the** text box **in the header containing the date, press** [Delete]**, then delete the** time**,** Page 1 of**, the** 4 **that appears as a total, and the** gray line

5. **Close and when prompted save the report as** Members Report**, click** Members Report **under Reports, click the** EXTERNAL DATA **tab, click the** More button **in the Export group, click** Word**, click the** Browse button **and navigate to the location where you store the files for this book, change the filename to** PR I-Unity Fitness Members**, click** Save**, click the** "Open the destination file after the export operation is complete." **check box, then click** OK **and click** Open **if prompted**
   When the report is published in Word all the formatting applied to the report in Access is removed.

HINT
By default, Word enters a number of columns equal to the maximum number of tab characters in any one line of text.

6. **Select and delete** Members Query**, select the five rows of text, click the** INSERT **tab, click the** Table button **in the Tables group, click** Convert Text to Table**, then click** OK **to accept the number of columns entered (3)**
   The first column in the table is blank. Note that you convert data into a table so that you can quickly apply formatting.

7. **Click in** Column 1**, click the** TABLE TOOLS LAYOUT **tab, click the** Delete button**, click** Delete Columns**, select the table, press** [Ctrl][C]**, switch to the report in Word, select the text** [Membership Report] **at the end of the report, paste the table, apply the** List Table 2 - Accent 2 **table style, change the text in the top right cell to** Members**, then autofit the contents to the columns**

8. **Refer to** FIGURE I-10**: scroll through the document and add page breaks as needed so your document matches**

9. **Scroll to page 1, right-click the** table of contents**, click** Update Field**, click the** Update entire table option button**, then click** OK
   Note: If the Class Revenue chart appears in the Table of Contents, go to the chart in the document, select it and apply the Normal style, then update the table of contents.

MORE PRACTICE
For more practice with the skills presented in this project, complete Independent Challenge 1.

10. **Save the document, submit a copy of the report to your instructor, then save and close all open files and exit all applications**

FIGURE I-10: Completed report

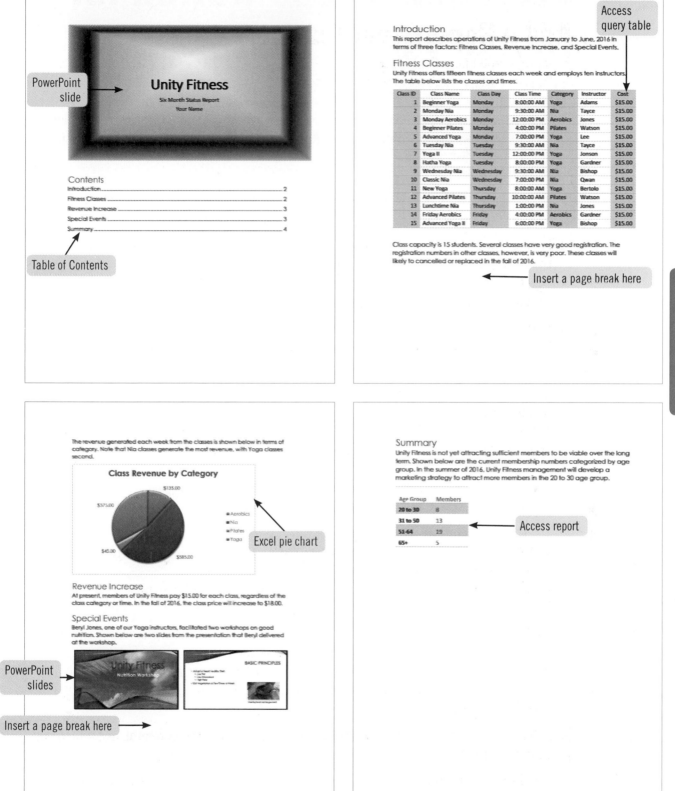

Welcome Presentation for Goose Point Estates

You work for the Sales Manager of Goose Point Estates, a new real estate development on an island north of Seattle. You need to prepare a presentation to welcome investors and provide them with important information about the development. For this project, you need to **Create a Database**, **Create a Chart**, **Create the Presentation**, and **Update the Presentation**. The completed presentation appears in FIGURE I-21 on page 237.

Create a Database

You need to enter the data in an Access table and then copy the Access table to Excel and paste it as a link.

1. Start Access, then create an Access database called PR I-Goose Point Estates and saved to the location where you save the files for this book

2. Switch to Design view, save the table as Home Designs, then enter the fields and data types shown in FIGURE I-11

3. Click the Data Type list arrow for Style, click Lookup Wizard, click Open if prompted, click the "I will type in the values that I want." option button, click Next, press [Tab], enter the values shown in FIGURE I-12, then click Finish

4. Create a lookup field for Location containing the values Ocean View, Forest View, and Mountain View

> **TIP**
> Save time by typing the first letter of the entries for the Style and Location fields.

5. Switch to Datasheet view (save the table), enter the records for the table as shown in FIGURE I-13, then close the table

6. Click the CREATE tab, click the Query Wizard button in the Queries group, click OK, add all the fields from the Home Designs table, name the query Design Breakdown, then show the query in Design view

7. Sort the Style and Cost fields in Ascending order, click the Run button in the Results group, close and save the query, click Design Breakdown in the list of All Access objects, then click the Copy button in the Clipboard group

8. Start a new workbook in Excel, click cell A1, click the Paste list arrow in the Clipboard group, then click the Paste Link button 🔗

   The Currency format applied to the values in the Cost column is removed when you copy a table from Access and paste it into Excel as a link.

9. Adjust column widths so all the data is visible, then save the workbook as PR I-Goose Point Estates Data to the location where you save the files for this book

FIGURE I-11: Fields for the Home Designs table

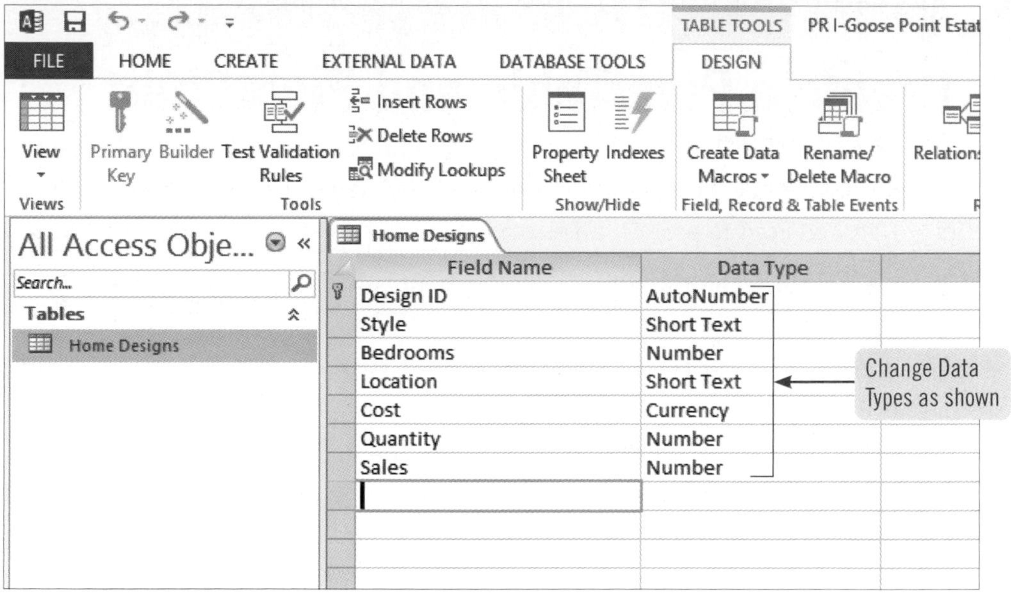

FIGURE I-12: Values for the lookup field

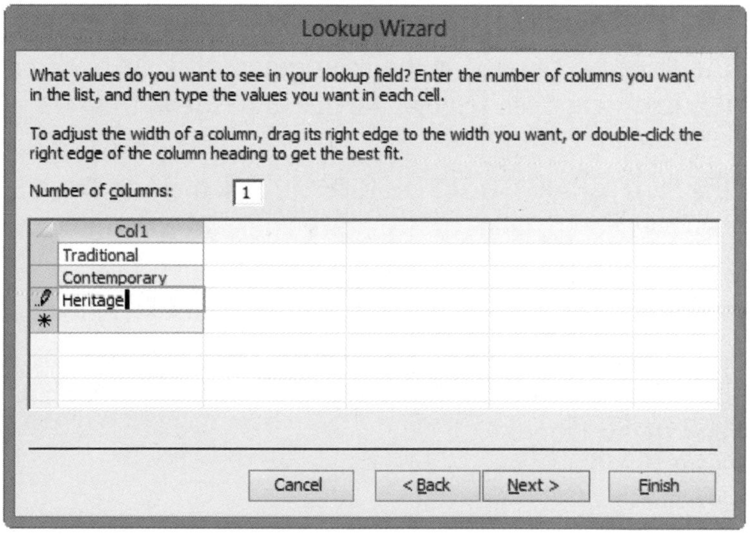

FIGURE I-13: Data for the Home Designs table

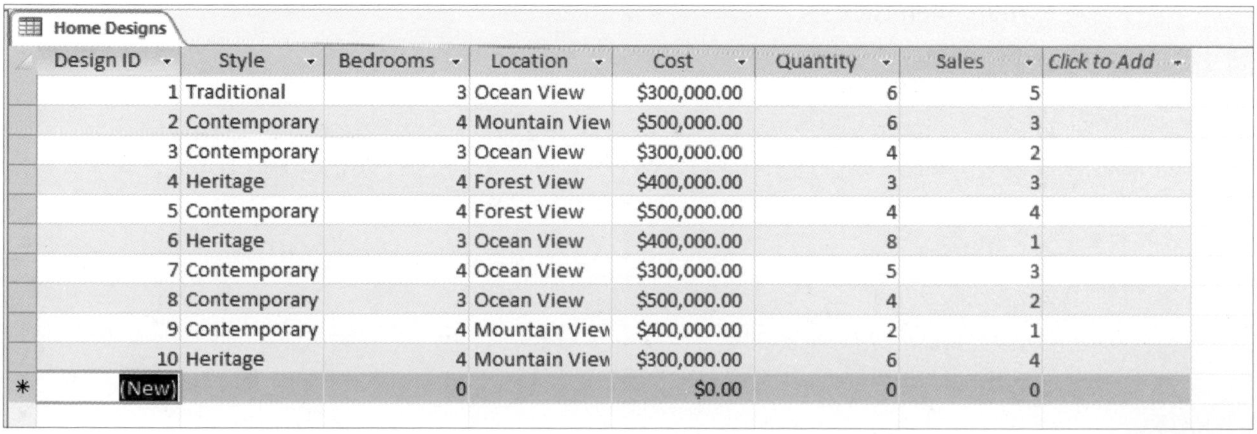

Design ID	Style	Bedrooms	Location	Cost	Quantity	Sales	Click to Add
1	Traditional	3	Ocean View	$300,000.00	6	5	
2	Contemporary	4	Mountain View	$500,000.00	6	3	
3	Contemporary	3	Ocean View	$300,000.00	4	2	
4	Heritage	4	Forest View	$400,000.00	3	3	
5	Contemporary	4	Forest View	$500,000.00	4	4	
6	Heritage	3	Ocean View	$400,000.00	8	1	
7	Contemporary	4	Ocean View	$300,000.00	5	3	
8	Contemporary	3	Ocean View	$500,000.00	4	2	
9	Contemporary	4	Mountain View	$400,000.00	2	1	
10	Heritage	4	Mountain View	$300,000.00	6	4	
* (New)		0		$0.00	0	0	

Create a PivotTable and PivotChart

You need to create a PivotTable and PivotChart to display data about the development. In a later lesson, you will copy the chart and paste it as a link on a slide in the PowerPoint presentation.

STEPS

1. In Excel, click cell H1, type Total Worth, press [Enter], type =E2*F2, press [Enter], then copy the formula in cell H2 through cell H11

2. Click cell I1, type Total Sales, press [Enter], type =E2*G2, press [Enter], then copy the formula in cell I2 through cell I11

3. Format cells E2:E11 and cells H2:I12 with the Accounting Number Format style and adjust column widths as needed

4. Click any cell in the table, click the INSERT tab, click PivotTable in the Tables group, click OK, then name the Sheet1 tab Designs and the Sheet2 tab Analysis

5. Click the PivotTable, select the Style and Total Sales check boxes in the PivotTable Fields pane, click any value in the PivotTable, click Field Settings in the Active Field group on the PIVOTTABLE TOOLS ANALYZE tab, then change the number format to Currency

6. Click the PivotChart button in the Tools group, click OK to accept the Clustered Column chart type, then remove the title and legend from the chart as shown in **FIGURE I-14**

7. Click the PIVOTCHART TOOLS DESIGN tab, click the Add Chart Element button in the Chart Layouts group, point to Axes, click Primary Vertical to remove the values in the vertical axis, then remove the labels in the horizontal axis

8. Click the Add Chart Element button, point to Data Labels, then click Data Callout

9. Resize the chart so that it extends from cell D3 to L20, click the PIVOTCHART TOOLS ANALYZE tab, click Field Buttons in the Show/Hide group to hide the field buttons, then save the workbook

   The completed chart appears as shown in **FIGURE I-15**.

FIGURE I-14: PivotChart with the title and legend removed

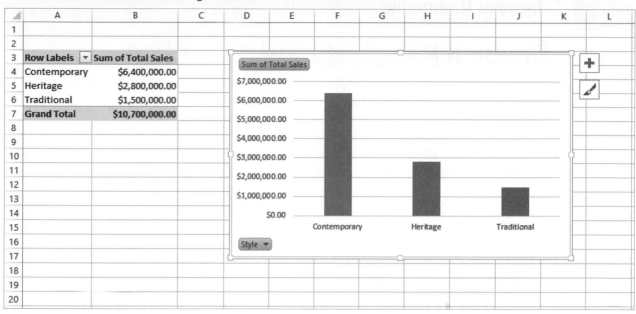

FIGURE I-15: Completed PivotChart

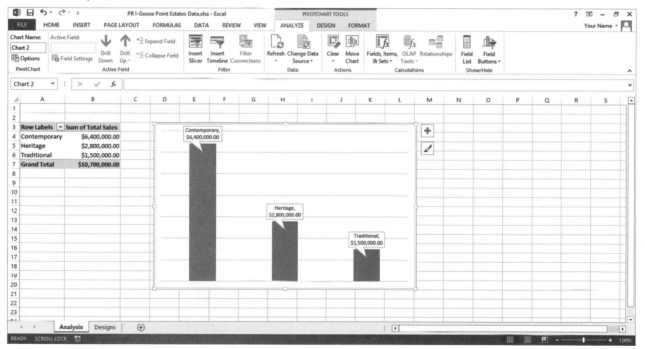

Create the Presentation

The text for the PowerPoint presentation is already stored in a Word document. You need to import the Word text into a new presentation and then modify the presentation design so that a picture appears on every slide in the presentation except the title slide.

STEPS

1. Start a blank presentation in PowerPoint, click the New Slide list arrow in the Slides group, click Slides from Outline, navigate to the location where you store your Data Files, select PR I-04.docx, click Insert, then save the presentation as PR I-Goose Point Estates Orientation to the location where you save the files for this book

2. Click Slide 1, press [Delete], click Layout in the Slides group, click Title Slide, click to the right of Buyer Orientation on the slide, press [Enter], then type your name

3. Click the DESIGN tab, apply the Retrospect presentation theme and the Green variant, switch to Slide Sorter view, click the HOME tab, press [Ctrl][A] to select all the slides in the presentation, then click Reset in the Slides group

   When you insert an outline from Word into a PowerPoint presentation and then change the theme of the presentation, you need to reset all of the slides so that they use the formats of the new theme.

4. Click the VIEW tab, click Slide Master in the Master Views group, then click the slide next to 1 in the task pane (you need to scroll up)

5. Click the INSERT tab, click Pictures in the Images group, navigate to the location where you store your Data Files, double-click PR I-05.jpg, click the Crop button in the Size group, then drag the crop handles to crop the picture to the geese as shown in FIGURE I-16

6. Click away from the picture to set the crop, click the picture again, select the contents of the Width text box in the Size group, type 13.3, press [Enter], drag the picture down so its bottom edge is even with the bottom edge of the slide, click the Send Backward list arrow in the Arrange group, then click Send to Back

7. Adjust the picture so that it appears as shown in FIGURE I-17, click the SLIDE MASTER tab, click the Close Master View button in the Close group, then return to Normal view

8. Move to Slide 4 in the presentation, switch to Excel, click the border of the column chart, press [Ctrl][C], switch to PowerPoint, click the Paste list arrow, then click the Use Destination Theme & Link Data button 📋

9. Click the Increase Font Size button A⁺ in the Font group until the font size in the data callouts is increased to 12 point, apply bold, then click the Shape Outline button to add a border line

10. Position the chart as shown in FIGURE I-18, then save the presentation

FIGURE I-16: Cropping a picture

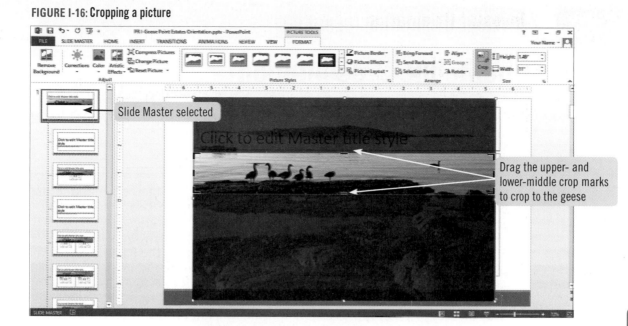

Slide Master selected

Drag the upper- and lower-middle crop marks to crop to the geese

FIGURE I-17: Positioning the picture in the Slide Master

FIGURE I-18: Column chart modified and positioned

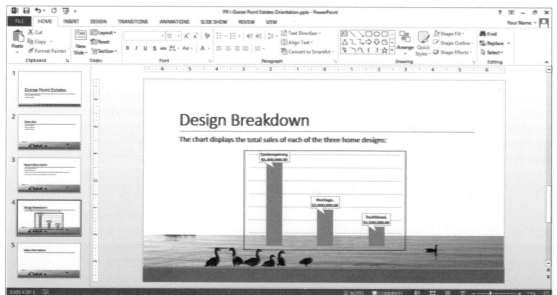

Update the Presentation

You summarize data in the Excel worksheet, copy it, and paste it as a link on Slide 5. Then, you change data in the Access database and update the links in Excel and PowerPoint. Finally, you break all the links so that you can easily move the files to different locations.

STEPS

1. Switch to Excel, click the Designs sheet tab, click cell D14, then enter and format the labels and formulas shown in FIGURE I-19

2. Select cells D14:E17, press [Ctrl][C], switch to PowerPoint, go to Slide 5, click the Paste list arrow in the Clipboard group, click Paste Special, click the Paste link option button, then click OK

3. Apply the Title Only slide layout, size and position the object as shown in FIGURE I-20, then if necessary, adjust the width of the Slides pane containing the slide thumbnails so that all five slides are visible

4. Switch to a new document in Word, click the INSERT tab, click Screenshot in the Illustrations group, click the window containing the PowerPoint presentation, then save the document as PR I-Goose Point Estates Low Sale Prices

5. Switch to Access, open the Home Designs table, increase the price of the homes in records 6 and 10 to $700,000, then close the table

6. Switch to Excel, verify that the total in cells E17 is $12,600,000, click the Analysis sheet tab, then click the PIVOTTABLE TOOLS ANALYZE tab, then click Refresh in the Data group

7. Switch to PowerPoint, verify that the value for Total Sales has been updated to $12,600,000, go to Slide 4, then verify that the Heritage column is now $4,700,000

8. Click the Slide Sorter button ⊞ on the status bar, click the first slide, then compare the completed presentation to FIGURE I-21

9. Click the FILE tab, click Edit Links to Files (lower-right corner in Backstage view), click the top link, click Break Link, click the new top link, click Break Link, click Close, then exit Backstage view

10. Switch to Excel, click the FILE tab, click Edit Links to Files, click Break Link, click Break Links, click Close, exit Backstage view, save all files and submit them to your instructor, then close all files

---

Maintaining Links

If you choose to maintain the links between files, you need to keep the files all together in the same location to avoid receiving error messages when you open the files and re-establish the links. To re-establish links, you should start with the program that does not contain links and then open the remaining files in the order in which they are linked. For this presentation, you would open the Access database first, followed by the Excel workbook, and finally the PowerPoint presentation if you had maintained the links in each of the files.

FIGURE I-19: Total Quantity and Sales values

D	E	F
Number of Homes	48	
Total Worth	$ 18,500,000.00	
Number of Sales	28	
Total Sales	$ 10,700,000.00	

=SUM(F2:F11)
=SUM(H2:H11)
=SUM(G2:G11)
=SUM(I2:I11)

FIGURE I-20: Excel object sized and positioned

Sales Information

Number of Homes	48
Total Worth	$ 18,500,000.00
Number of Sales	28
Total Sales	$ 10,700,000.00

FIGURE I-21: Completed presentation in Slide Sorter view

Goose Point Estates
BUYER ORIENTATION
YOUR NAME

1

Overview
Resort Description
Design Breakdown
Sales Information

2

Resort Description
50+ fully serviced acres
Potential for 60 lots
Largest zoned and serviced development site currently available for sale in the area
Lots have an ocean view, a mountain view, or a forest view

3

Design Breakdown
The chart displays the total sales of each of the three house designs.

4

Sales Information

Number of Homes	48
Total Worth	$ 23,300,000.00
Number of Sales	28
Total Sales	$ 12,600,000.00

5

Event Presentation

You work for a local bookstore and are in charge of organizing book launches. A few days after the launch of a new author's novel, your manager asks you to develop a presentation to describe the event, particularly in terms of its financial success. For this project, you use Excel, Word, and PowerPoint to develop the presentation. First you **Edit the Event Budget** and then you **Create the Presentation**. The completed presentation appears in **FIGURE I-27** on page 241.

Edit the Event Budget

You download one of Excel's budget templates, then enter data related to the book launch.

STEPS

1. **Start Excel, click in the** Search for online templates text box, **type** Event budget, **press [Enter], click the** Event budget **that appears as shown in** FIGURE I-22, **click** Create, **then save the workbook as** PR I-Book Launch Budget **to the location where you save files for this book**

   The template opens in Excel. The template contains three worksheets. The DASHBOARD worksheet summarizes the budget and includes charts, and the INCOME and EXPENSES worksheets contain data for the Estimated and Actual expenses and income.

2. **Change the title to** Event Budget for Book Launch of "The Painted City", **click the** EXPENSES **sheet tab, enter the** Estimated **and** Actual **expenses shown with shading in** FIGURE I-23 **and leave any unshaded values, then verify that the Estimated and Actual amounts match those same values in** FIGURE I-23

   When you use a template, you can enter different categories and you can delete rows that are not relevant to your project. For this project, you enter new data and leave blank the categories that do not require data. Note that the shading is just to help you enter the correct values. You will not see shading in your worksheet.

3. **Click the** INCOME **sheet tab, select rows 13 to 25, click the** Delete **button in the Cells group, then note the** #REF! **entries in cells F5 and G5**

   When you delete rows in a template, some formulas can be affected.

HINT
The value in cell F5 should be $1,936.00 and the value in cell G5 should be $1,831.00.

4. **Click cell** F5, **enter the formula to add the Admissions Estimated total to the Sale of items Estimated total, then enter the formula to find the Actual Total in cell** G5

5. **Enter the shaded values and delete any unused data as shown in** FIGURE I-24, **then verify that the Estimated and Actual values match**

6. **Click the** DASHBOARD **sheet tab, scroll to view the data included, then save the workbook**

   You'll use some of this data in your presentation.

7. **Start a new presentation in PowerPoint, type** Book Launch, **for, and** "The Painted City" **as the slide title on three separate lines, enter your name in the Subtitle area, then save the presentation as** PR I-Book Launch Presentation **to the location where you save the files for this book**

8. **Click the** INSERT **tab, click the** Pictures **button in the Images group, navigate to the location where you store your Data Files, then double-click** PR I-06.jpg

9. **Click the** Color **button in the Adjust group, click the** Washout **option in the top row of the Recolor section, right-click the** picture, **click** Save as Picture, **navigate to the location where you save the files for this book, type** PR I-Book Launch Picture **as the filename, delete the picture, then save the presentation**

   You'll use the picture for the presentation background in the next lesson.

FIGURE I-22: Selecting the Event Budget Template

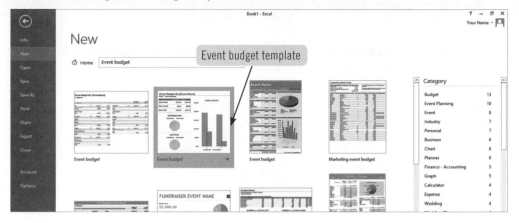

FIGURE I-23: New values for the Expenses sheet

	A	B	C	D	E	F	G	H	I
4						TOTAL EXPENSES	Estimated	Actual	
5							$1,600.00	$1,975.00	
6									
7		Site	Estimated	Actual		Refreshments	Estimated	Actual	
8		Room and hall fees	$500.00	$300.00		Food	$150.00	$400.00	
9		Site staff				Drinks	$300.00	$500.00	
10		Equipment				Linens			
11		Tables and chairs	$100.00	$100.00		Staff and gratuities			
12		Total	$600.00	$400.00		Total	$450.00	$900.00	
13									
14									
15		Decorations	Estimated	Actual		Program	Estimated		
16		Flowers	$200.00	$300.00		Performers			
17		Candles				Speakers			
18		Lighting				Travel			
19		Balloons	$50.00	$75.00		Hotel			
20		Paper supplies				Other			
21		Total	$250.00	$375.00		Total	$0.00	$0.00	
22									
23									
24		Publicity	Estimated	Actual		Prizes	Estimated	Actual	
25		Graphics work	$200.00	$200.00		Ribbons/Plaques/Trophies			
26		Photocopying/Printing	$100.00	$100.00		Gifts			
27		Postage				Total	$0.00	$0.00	
28		Total	$300.00	$300.00					
29									

Match the Estimated and Actual Expenses values

DASHBOARD | EXPENSES | INCOME

READY   SCROLL LOCK

FIGURE I-24 New values for the Income sheet

	A	B	C	D	E	F	G	H
1								
2		Event Budge		nch of "The Painted City"				
3		Income						
4					TOTAL INCOME	Estimated	Actual	
5						$2,250.00	$5,000.00	
6		Admissions						
7		Estimated	Actual			Estimated	Actual	
8		100	125	Adults @	$10.00	$1,000.00	$1,250.00	
9								
10								
11		Total				$1,000.00	$1,250.00	
12								
13								
14		Sale of items						
15		Estimated	Actual			Estimated	Actual	
16		100	300	books @ $	12.50	$1,250.00	$3,750.00	
17				Items @		$0.00	$0.00	
18				Items @		$0.00	$0.00	
19				Items @		$0.00	$0.00	
20		Total				$1,250.00	$3,750.00	
21								
22								
23								
24								

Modify your Admissions area to match

Match the Estimated and Actual Income values

Change "items" to "books"

Format with Accounting Number style

DASHBOARD | EXPENSES | INCOME

READY   CIRCULAR REFERENCES

Integration 2013

Create the Presentation

You need to complete the presentation with data copied from Excel and Word.

STEPS

1. In PowerPoint, click the DESIGN tab, click the Format Background button in the Customize group, click the Picture or texture fill option button, click the File button in the Format Background pane, navigate to the location where you store your files, double-click PR I-Book Launch Picture.jpg, click Apply to All, then close the Format Background pane

2. Click the More button in the Variants group, point to Colors, then scroll to and click Slipstream

3. Select the presentation title, click the DRAWING TOOLS FORMAT tab, apply the Gradient Fill - Orange, Accent 1, Reflection WordArt style and bold from the HOME tab, click the VIEW tab, click Outline View, then enter the outline as shown in FIGURE I-25

4. Open a new blank document in Word, enter text as shown in FIGURE I-26, then save the document as PR I-Book Launch Details to the location where you save the files for this book

5. Select and copy the text, switch to PowerPoint, view Slide 3, apply the Title Only slide layout, paste the text, increase the font size of the text to 40 pt, click the DRAWING TOOLS FORMAT tab, apply the Intense Effect - Blue, Accent 1 shape style, then size and position the object on the slide as shown in the completed presentation in FIGURE I-27

6. Go to Slide 4, apply the Title Only slide layout, switch to Excel, press and hold the [Ctrl] key, click the Estimated chart on the DASHBOARD sheet tab, scroll to and click the Actual chart, copy both charts, switch to PowerPoint, then paste the charts

HINT
To remove the Horizontal axis, click the CHART TOOLS DESIGN tab, click Add Chart Element, point to Axes, then click Primary Horizontal.

7. Refer to FIGURE I-27: move and resize the two charts, then apply Chart Style 3 to both charts

8. Copy the Total Profit chart from Excel, go to PowerPoint, paste it on Slide 5, change the layout to Title Only, then size and position the chart, remove the Horizontal axis and apply Chart Style 4 as shown in FIGURE I-27

HINT
The balloon picture you insert will include a white background.

9. On Slide 6, apply the Blank slide layout, insert a WordArt object using the same style you used for the presentation title, add the text An Unqualified Success!, insert the balloon picture shown in FIGURE I-27 (search for balloons, parties, photographs in Online Pictures), click Color in the Adjust group, click Set Transparent Color, click a white area of the picture, then size and position the WordArt object and the picture as shown in FIGURE I-27

MORE PRACTICE
For more practice with the skills presented in this project, complete Independent Challenge 3.

10. View the presentation in Slide Sorter view, compare it to FIGURE I-27, adjust object positions as needed, save the presentation and submit a copy to your instructor, then save and close all open files

FIGURE I-25: Presentation outline

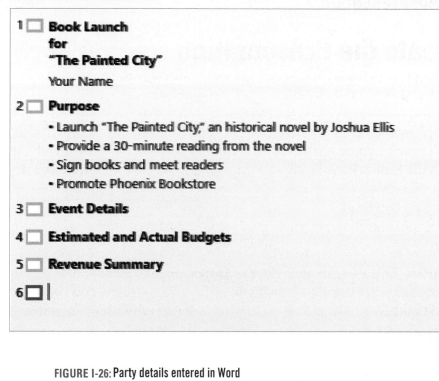

FIGURE I-26: Party details entered in Word

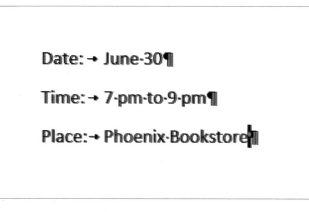

FIGURE I-27: Completed presentation in Slide Sorter view

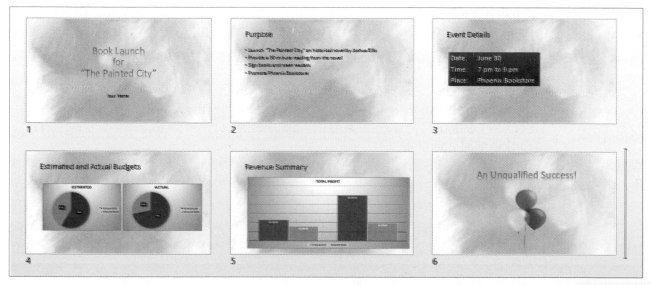

Independent Challenge 1

Create a multiple-page report in Word that includes objects from Excel, PowerPoint, and Access. Base the report on a business-oriented subject. For example, you could write a status report that describes activities over the past six months related to a company or organization of your choice, or you could write a report that proposes a change to a specific policy, such as the employee dress code or the establishment of an employee recognition program. Follow the steps provided to create the report in Word and then to include objects from the other applications.

1. Determine the name of your company or organization and the type of activities it has engaged in over the past six months. For example, you could call your organization Pacific Coast Film Society and describe activities such as screenings, lectures, and film exchanges. Write the name and a brief description of the activities in the box below:

    Company Name: _____

    Description of Activities: _____

2. Start Word, then type text for the report. Include placeholders for objects that you will insert from other applications. Your report should include space for a chart from Excel, a table from Access, a slide or two from PowerPoint, and a report from Access. You also need to include a table of contents.

3. Include your name and the page number in a footer, then save the report as **PR I-My Integrated Report.docx** to the location where you save the files for this book.

4. Apply the theme of your choice, format headings with heading styles, then generate a table of contents above the first page of the report text.

5. Create a PowerPoint slide as an embedded object somewhere in the report. You can choose to include the slide as your title page or insert it in another location. Enter appropriate text, then apply and modify a gradient fill to the slide background.

6. Start Access, create a database called **PR I-My Integrated Report Database.accdb** and save it to the location where you save the files for this book.

7. In Access create two related tables containing data relevant to your report. Refer to the database you worked with in Unit I Project 1 for ideas. You need to publish one of the tables in Word, export a query to Excel, and publish a report in Word. In one of the tables include data that can be grouped, summarized, or calculated. For example, you could create a table listing the results of a customer survey. Categories such as "Age," "Nationality," and "Rating" can be included. You can then export the table to Excel and create a PivotTable and PivotChart that counts values in a particular category.

8. Publish one of the tables in Word, copy the table, then format the table in your Word report with a table style. You don't need to save the exported .rtf file.

9. In Access, create a query containing data appropriate to your report. Make sure the query includes values that you can analyze in Excel.

10. Export the query to Excel, then use it as the basis for a PivotTable and PivotChart that summarizes some aspect of the data. For example, a PivotTable could add all the sales in each sales category or count all the members in each age group.

11. Format the values in the PivotTable appropriately, then create a PivotChart.

12. Copy the PivotChart to an appropriate area in the Word report.

13. Create a short presentation in PowerPoint containing at least two slides that you will copy to the Word report. Format the slides attractively in PowerPoint, then copy two slides to a table in Word. Reduce the size of the slide objects, enclose the slide objects with a border line and remove the table border. Save the presentation as **PR I-My Integrated Presentation**.

14. In Access, create a report, then export the report to Word in a file called **PR I-My Integrated Access Report.rtf**.

15. Remove the report title, the date and the time at the top of the page and the page number at the bottom of the page, convert the text to a table, remove any blank columns and rows and adjust the location of the data where needed, then copy the table to an appropriate location in the report.

Independent Challenge 1 (continued)

16. Format the table with a table style.
17. Update the table of contents, save the report, submit a copy to your instructor, then save and close all open documents and applications.

Independent Challenge 2

Create an on-screen presentation of six to eight slides that highlights sales information and recommends marketing strategies for a company or organization of your choice. For example, you could create a presentation for the continuing education department of a local college that presents the revenues from the last 10 courses offered and recommends a marketing plan for the courses that generated the most revenue. Follow the steps provided to create a table in Access, charts in Excel, an outline for the presentation in Word, and the presentation in PowerPoint. Data in the Access table should be linked to the Excel worksheet and to the Excel objects that are copied into PowerPoint.

1. Determine the name of your company or organization and the type of products or services that it sells. For example, you could call your company My Food Store and describe it as an online grocer that delivers organic fruits and vegetables and health food products to households in the Los Angeles area. Write the name and a brief description of your company in the box below:

Company Name: _____

Description: _____

2. Start Access, create a database called **PR I-My Sales Presentation Database.accdb** and save it to the location where you save the files for this book, then create a table consisting of at least four fields and 10 records. Call the table **Sales**. Include fields in the table that you can use in charts. For example, a table for the My Food Store presentation could include the following fields: Product, Category (e.g., Fruit, Vegetable, Dairy), Number of Sales, and Sale Price. Include at least one Lookup field in your table.
3. Create a query called **My Sales Query** that sorts the data by category. Copy the query and paste it as a link into a new workbook in Excel. Apply number formats (for example, Currency formatting) where needed.
4. Calculate total sales, then save the workbook as **PR I-My Sales Presentation Data.xlsx** to the location where you save the files for this book.
5. Create a PivotTable to summarize the data copied from Access. For example, you can calculate the total sales by product category. Format any dollar amounts in the PivotTable with the Accounting Number format.
6. Create a PivotChart. For example, you could create a pie chart that shows the breakdown of product sales by category. Format the chart attractively so it is easy to read and understand.
7. In Excel, name the two sheet tabs.
8. Switch to Word, create an outline for the presentation, then save the document as **PR I-My Sales Presentation Outline.docx** to the location where you save the files for this book.
9. Add additional topics to your outline, if you wish. Remember to format all the headings with the Heading 1 style and all the bulleted items with the Heading 2 style. If you work in Outline view, the text is automatically formatted with the appropriate headings.
10. Save the outline in Word, then close Word.
11. Create a new presentation in PowerPoint, then create slides from the Word outline. Save the presentation in PowerPoint as **PR I-My Sales Presentation.pptx** to the location where you save the files for this book.
12. Remove the blank slide, then apply the presentation design of your choice. Apply the Title Slide layout to the title slide, then in Slide Sorter view, select all the slides and reset the layout.
13. Switch to Slide Master view, then add a photograph or a clip art image to the slide master so the image appears on every slide in the presentation except the title slide.

Independent Challenge 2 (continued)

14. In Normal view, paste the chart from Excel as a link using the Use Destination Theme & Link Data paste option to the appropriate slides. Modify the chart as needed so that it is easy to read.

15. Start a new document in Word, then take a screenshot of the slide containing the chart copied from Excel. Save the Word document as **PR I-My Sales Presentation Original Data** to the location where you save the files for this book.

16. Change some of the values in the Access table, then verify that the chart updates in Excel and PowerPoint. Remember to refresh the data in the PivotTable. (*Note*: If the data is not updated immediately in either or both applications, click the FILE tab, click Edit Links to Files, select each link in turn, then click Update Now or Update Values, depending on the application.)

17. Break the links between the Excel workbook and the Access database, then break the links between the PowerPoint presentation and the Excel workbook.

18. Save the presentation and submit a copy to your instructor, then save and close all open files.

Independent Challenge 3

Create a presentation that summarizes a special event, entertainment, or party of your choice. Refer to Unit I Project 3 for ideas. For this project, you use Word, Excel, and PowerPoint only.

1. Create an outline in PowerPoint that includes slide titles with the following information:
   a. Type of party or event
   b. Purpose of the party or event
   c. Location, time, and cost
   d. Chart showing Estimated and Actual Income and Expenses
   e. Motivational closing slide

2. Save the presentation as **PR I-My Event Presentation.pptx** to the location where you save the files for this book.

3. Format the presentation attractively. Insert a picture and adjust the coloring so text will appear clearly when the picture appears as a background, then save the picture as a .jpg file called **PR I-My Event Presentation Picture** to the location where you save the files for this book.

4. Modify the background of the presentation so that the picture will appear as the background on every slide in the presentation.

5. Enter the event details in Word, save the document as **PR I-My Event Details.docx** to the location where you save the files for this book, copy and paste the text into PowerPoint, then format the text to make it clear and easy to read. For example, you will need to increase the font size, and then you may want to format the text box with one of the preset shape styles. Change the color scheme for the presentation if you wish.

6. In Excel, select one of the Event budget templates and modify it for your event. You can select the Event budget you used in Project 3 or you can select a new budget template. Change the title of the worksheet to match your event. Enter both Estimated and Actual expenses where needed. In the Income sheet, delete rows you don't need and modify formulas as needed. Save the workbook as **PR I-My Event Budget.xlsx** to the location where you save the files for this book.

7. Copy one or more charts from the budget to appropriate slides in your presentation. Depending on the template you chose, you may have more than one chart to copy. Format all charts so they are easy to read.

8. Include a graphic and WordArt object on the final slide in the presentation.

9. Save the presentation and submit a copy to your instructor, then save and close all open files.

Independent Challenge 4 - Team Project

To further explore how you can integrate Access, Excel, Word, and PowerPoint to meet a wide range of business needs, you will work with two other people to complete a team project. The subject of the team project is the development and marketing of a non-profit organization of your choice. The organization should include members and/or volunteers and activities such as workshops and programs, product sales, fundraising events, etc. For example, you could develop files for a community recycling depot, an arts organization, or a charity. Follow the guidelines provided to create the files required for the team project. When you have completed the project, the team will submit a document containing project summary information about the project, as well as the Access, Excel, Word, and PowerPoint files.

▶ Project Setup

1. As a team, work together to complete the following tasks:
   - Share e-mail addresses among all three team members.
   - Set up a time (either via e-mail, an online chat session, Internet Messaging, or face to face) when you will get together to choose your topic and assign roles.
   - At your meeting, complete the table below with information about your team and the organization for which you are creating databases, workbooks, documents, and presentations. Note that managing a nonprofit organization–or any organization–in "real life" is a huge and complex undertaking. For this project, focus only on a few aspects of the organization such as volunteer coordination or the planning of a special event.

Team Name (last names of the team members or another name that describes the project.
Team Members 1. 2. 3.
Organization name
Selected Organization activities (for example, membership drive, fund-raising events, product sales, etc.)
Expense and revenue sources (expenses include payments for marketing materials, Web sites, products, salaries, etc., and revenue sources include membership dues, donations, grants, etc.)
Database tables: list all the fields needed, then work as a team to organize them into tables and determine relationships. One person will be responsible for developing the data for the database, but the entire team needs to collaborate on the types of data needed.
Team Roles: Indicate who is responsible for each of the following sets of files (one set per team member). Note that the organization database will be created by one team member and then made available to the other two members to use in the creation of their files. Coordination between team members is key. Organization Database: Organization Status Report: Organization Presentation: Name of team folder where all the team files will be saved:

Independent Challenge 4 - Team Project (continued)

⇒ File Development

Individually, complete the tasks listed below for the file set you are responsible for. Note that for this project, all team members will need to work closely on planning the Access database to ensure it contains the tables and data needed to create the various components of the project. One person will then enter data for the database (see the description of the Organization Database below). *Note:* All files for the Team Project will be saved to the location where you save files for this book. It is recommended that you create one team folder (as noted in the previous table) and all team members save to the same team folder. It is best if you can use a shared drive for storing your files.

Organization Database

Refer to the Database you worked with for Project 1. This database contains four related tables listing members of a fitness facility and the fitness classes available. Study the tables and relationships and adapt them for your organization. For this project, you need to develop the database to include sufficient data to help your team members develop their files.

1. Create a new Access database, then save it as **PR I-Team Project_Organization Database** to the team folder created in the location where you save files for this book.
2. Divide fields into logical tables, then create the table structures for at least three tables (and no more than five tables). Keep the database structure simple. At this point, don't worry about populating the table with data. Ensure you are very clear about the overall purpose of the database.
3. Add up to two additional tables as needed, depending on the wishes of the team.
4. Ensure the database includes the following components:
   a. At least one lookup field is linked to a table.
   b. Referential integrity is enforced between linked tables.
5. Populate the database with data appropriate for the organization. Make the data as realistic as possible. For example, include the correct ZIP Codes and area codes for cities. You can make up names and street addresses. At least one of the tables (for example, the Members table) should contain up to 25 records. Other tables can contain fewer records.
6. Create at least two queries in consultation with other team members that contain the fields required for other components of the project. Remember to include fields from the tables in which they originally appeared (not in the linked tables) in a query.
7. Create a table named with your team name, then insert your name as the first record.
8. Post the completed database in the team shared folder and notify your other team members that the database is ready for them to use.
9. Submit the database file to your instructor along with the files created by your team members.

Organization Status Report

This set of files includes an Excel workbook containing a table exported from Access, a PivotTable and PivotChart, a Word document containing the text of the report, and an embedded PowerPoint slide. Use Unit I Project 1 as your model to create the files as follows:

1. From the Access database created by your teammate, export a query table to an Excel workbook saved as **PR I-Team Project_Organization Status Report Data.xlsx**.
2. From the data exported to Excel create a PivotTable in a new worksheet. You determine what information you want the PivotTable to show. Experiment with different ways of calculating data.
3. Format any dollar amounts with the Currency format.
4. Create a PivotChart from the PivotTable. Format the chart with data labels where needed and add an appropriate title.
5. Add your name and your team name to the worksheet containing the PivotTable and PivotChart.
6. Create a Word document, apply the theme and color scheme determined by your team, then save the document as **PR I-Team Project_Organization Status Report.docx**.

Independent Challenge 4 - Team Project (continued)

7. Insert a PowerPoint slide on the title page. The slide should include the name of the organization, your name, and your team name. Format the slide background attractively with a gradient fill you have modified. Change the color scheme in PowerPoint to match the theme and color scheme selected for the Word document.

8. Write text for the report that summarizes some aspect of your organization. Format headings with heading styles and include a table of contents below the PowerPoint slide title.

9. Insert placeholders for the following objects:
   a. An Excel PivotChart containing data exported from an Access table
   b. An Access table

10. Copy the PivotChart from Excel and paste it into the Word document.

11. Export one of the tables from Access to Word, copy the table from the .rtf file (you don't need to save the .rtf file), then paste it in an appropriate location in the Word report. Format the table with a table style.

12. Submit all files to your instructor along with the files created by your team members.

Organization Presentation

This set of files includes a PowerPoint presentation that describes the organization for prospective members or donors and includes objects from Access and Excel. The PowerPoint presentation is based on a Word outline, containing the headings and subheadings that become the presentation slides. Use Unit I Project 2 and Project 3 as your model to create the files as follows:

1. Create an outline for the presentation in Word with headings for six to eight slides in PowerPoint. Remember that a Level 1 heading will be a slide title in PowerPoint, and a Level 2 heading will be a bulleted item. Include your name and the team name in the document footer, then save the document as **PR I-Organization Presentation Outline.docx**.

2. In PowerPoint, import the Word outline, delete the blank slide, apply the Title layout to the title slide, then reset the layout for all the slides in the presentation. Include your name and the team name on the title slide, then save the presentation as **PR I-Organization Presentation.pptx**.

3. On the main Slide Master insert a picture that will appear on every slide in the presentation except the title slide. Modify the picture in some way (for example, cropping, color adjustment, etc.), then position it on the slide. Exit Slide Master.

4. From Access, copy a query table and paste it as a link into a new Excel workbook. Save the workbook as **PR I-Organization Presentation Data.xlsx**.

5. In Excel, make calculations from the data as needed, then create a PivotTable and PivotChart suitable for the presentation. Include your name and your team name on the PivotTable worksheet.

6. Name the two sheet tabs in the workbook.

7. Copy the PivotChart to an appropriate slide in the PowerPoint presentation and paste it using the Use Destination Theme & Link Data paste option.

8. From Word, take a screenshot of the slide containing the PivotChart, then save the document as **PR I-Team Project_Organization Presentation Original Values.docx**.

9. In Access, change some of the data in the table linked to Excel, then verify that the data updates in Excel and PowerPoint.

10. Break all links in Excel and PowerPoint.

11. Submit all files to your instructor along with the files created by your team members.

▶ Project Summary

1. Open **PR I-07.docx** from the location where you save your Data Files, then save it to your **PR I-Team Project_Summary**.

2. Read the directions in the document, then ensure that each team member enters his or her name in one of the table cells along with a short description of the skills used and the challenges faced while creating his or her set of files.

3. Save the document, then submit all files to your instructor.

Visual Workshop

You've been asked to create a presentation on cultural tours of Europe. One of the slides in the presentation will be a pie chart that shows the breakdown of participants by tour category. Create the Tours table, as shown in **FIGURE I-28**, in an Access database called **PR I-Cultural Tours.accdb** and saved to the location where you save the files for this book. Create a query called **Tours Query** that sorts the records in ascending order by Theme. Copy the query table and paste it as a link into a new Excel workbook. Reapply Currency formatting. Calculate the total revenue for each tour (Participants*Price), then create a PivotTable that calculates the total revenue by theme. Format values with the Currency format. Create a PivotChart pie chart that shows the percent of total revenue generated by each tour theme. (*Note*: At this point, your values will differ from **FIGURE I-29**.) Copy the pie chart and paste it as a link using the Use Destination Theme and Link Data paste option in a new PowerPoint slide formatted with the Title Only layout. Add a title to the slide and format the slide and pie chart as shown in **FIGURE I-29**. (*Note*: The Wisp theme with the blue variant is applied. You also need to increase the font sizes of the data labels to 16 pt and apply bold.) Create a document in Word, take a screen clipping that includes only the slide, apply a border to the screen clipping in Word, then save the Word document as **PR I-Cultural Tours Original Tour Totals.docx** to the location where you store the files for this book. Switch to Access, then change the number of participants in both the Ancient Rome and Magical Greece tours to **25** and close the table. Verify that the pie chart is updated in Excel (refresh the PivotTable data), save the Excel workbook as **PR I-Cultural Tours Data.xlsx** to the location where you save the files for this book, verify that the slide is updated in PowerPoint, add your name to the slide footer, then save the PowerPoint presentation as **PR I-Cultural Tours Presentation.pptx** to the same location. Break the links to all the files, add your name to the presentation footer, save the presentation and submit the file to your instructor, then save all open files and exit all applications.

FIGURE I-28

Tour ID	Tour	Theme	Country	Participants	Price	Click to Add
1	Ancient Rome	History	Italy	10	$2,500.00	
2	Magical Greece	History	Greece	12	$2,800.00	
3	Spanish Modern Art	Art	Spain	10	$2,500.00	
4	Dutch Masters	Art	Netherlands	15	$3,200.00	
5	Medieval Majesty	History	Italy	18	$3,500.00	
6	Basque Country	Culinary	Spain	15	$2,500.00	
7	French Taste	Culinary	France	20	$4,000.00	
8	Vienna Waltz	Music	Austria	15	$3,800.00	
9	Rhine Journey	Music	Germany	18	$4,000.00	
10	Taste of Italy	Culinary	Italy	15	$4,200.00	
* (New)					$0.00	

FIGURE I-29

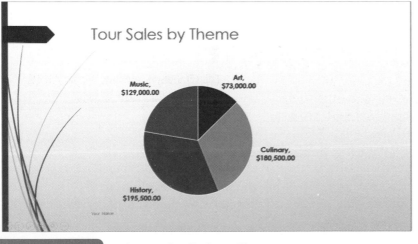

Index